CLINICAL SUPERVISION
Special Methods for the Supervision of Teachers

ROBERT GOLDHAMMER

Holt, Rinehart and Winston, Inc.

New York   Chicago   San Francisco
Atlanta   Dallas   Montreal   Toronto   London   Sydney

*I dedicate this book
to two dear friends
whose searching minds
and values on learning
excite and inspire me.*
LE ROY PATRICK and LEWIS SCHWARTZ

Library of Congress Catalog Card Number: 79-81177
ISBN 0-03-077545-0
Printed in the United States of America
123456 038 9876543

Foreword

Anyone who has served in an American classroom, or who has ventured to influence what happens therein, will appreciate that all too few are the resources by and through which teachers are helped to grow. Though we live in a time when much professional energy and substantial funds are being invested in the enterprise of staff development, with commensurate effort in the development and application of theories of supervision, it remains that too little is known and done about supervisory practices that in fact contribute to the strengthening of those who work with children. One reflection of this is the relative dearth of a significant literature on which viable teacher-supervision models can be based. Another is the paucity of clinical training programs within which the would-be supervisor can acquire and sharpen the tools with which he works. The appearance of a volume which both broadens and deepens the literature, and at the same time equips the practitioner with a potent operational model, is therefore a propitious and noteworthy event.

In these pages, Dr. Goldhammer has described and exemplified a clinical approach to supervision for which in his own mind the most productive analogues are certain forms of teaching and of ego counseling. The five-stage sequence on which his prototypical model is based, and around which he has designed his material, is one he first encountered in the 1962 Harvard-Lexington Summer Program, where Morris L. Cogan and others were engaged in the exciting but demanding task of building a new training mechanism for principals, supervisors, and teachers in leadership positions.

In the Harvard-Newton Summer Program, on which the Harvard-Lexington program was partially modeled, Cogan and his colleagues had for six or seven years previously been engaged in the development of this model, whose ingredients included the intensive and systematic analysis of teaching episodes. Whereas Harvard-Newton was designed for inexperienced trainees in the opening months of a master's degree program, Harvard-Lexington served experienced teachers and administrators who were, among other motives, eager for a supervised introduction to the then relatively new world of cooperative teaching. In the six-week program, each trainee spent approximately one third of his time in curriculum planning, another third in teaching (thus implementing the planned curriculum), and yet another third in an "observation cycle" during which the teaching of fellow trainees was observed, analyzed, and discussed in a supervisory conference. It is the latter cycle, which Goldhammer helped to refine and extend as a faculty member in the 1963 Harvard-Lexington program and also during his five years on the faculty at the University of Pittsburgh, which forms the backbone of this book.

As one who shared in the development of the Harvard-Newton and Harvard-Lexington programs and who, in addition, served as one of Dr. Goldhammer's teachers in both of his degree programs at Harvard, I confess to an extraordinary and personal interest in this volume. The material is close to my own heart and experience, and I have almost unlimited confidence that, if taken seriously, Goldhammer's recommendations could literally transform the quality and effectiveness of supervisory practice in American schools. The book has a definite prospect of becoming a landmark in its field, and not only are its ideas fresh and powerful, but the Goldhammer style is almost guaranteed to catch the profession's attention and perhaps increase its adrenalin count.

The author's own preface serves as a good introduction, and I urge that the reader turn to it before tackling Chapter I. To share a professional secret, there were moments during the prepublication stage when the fate of this high-intensity introductory discussion was in question. In some ways it is a separate treatise on the problems of American education. However, as Goldhammer points out, his purpose in the chapter is primarily to dramatize the need for the model of supervision to which the book then turns and through which one hopes to eliminate the horrors which now exist. This it does well, and I am pleased that it is being included.

This book should be of great interest both to supervisors and to teachers. It seems safe to predict that no supervisor will be quite satisfied with his own practices by the time he has read these pages, and few teachers will be unaffected by the values which permeate this work and the highly personal interpretation that Goldhammer gives both to teaching and to the role interactions which take place during supervision. Undoubtedly, some will find his language and his examples rather strong; but in the end, few will dispute that Goldhammer is a professional's professional, an author who really cares about things that matter.

With great sadness, I must report that Robert Goldhammer's life came to a sudden and tragic end in April, 1968. Fortunately, this book, in final draft, was virtually completed by the time of his illness, and it was therefore necessary for me to make only a few minor changes and additions to the material he left. That he will not be with us to pursue the ideas and practices in which he and others have invested so heavily, and that he will miss the exciting arguments and the profound discussions that his book will surely stimulate, are sad and lamentable facts. However, few men even in a full lifetime make so great a contribution to their fellows as Dr. Goldhammer has made to us in these powerful pages. American education receives this work at a time when bold and stirring ideas are not unwelcome, and we may at least hope that the Goldhammer plea for radically improved supervisory services will meet with an enthusiastic response.

ROBERT H. ANDERSON
Professor of Education
Harvard University

Cambridge, Massachusetts

Preface

Supervisor education has never occupied an important place in America's colleges and graduate schools of education, nor has supervision of instruction ever emerged as a systematic professional discipline. From time to time, serious literature has been produced on the subject and, especially in recent years, this field has attracted the interest of some researchers. Nonetheless, by comparison to teaching, administration, and, more recently, school counseling, useful literature on supervision is disappointingly sparse. Its authors and students have constituted an energetic, but dismayingly small, minority in the educational community.

In the schools, supervision has fared even less well than in the universities. Despite some efforts by professional writers to free it from its watchdog origins, supervision remains a bugaboo for many teachers, an experience to be avoided at all costs. In common practice, supervision is still encumbered by threatening administrative sanctions: rating, promotion, tenure, salary increases, and, for the student teacher, grades. These are all interwoven with supervisory intentions and methods and relationships. Besides the inherent risks of having one's professional behavior examined, the supervisee must generally mobilize himself against a dozen extrinsic dangers associated with the supervisor's presence. Because it generally counts for so much, supervision often counts for nothing. Too often, its principal misfortune is that in addition to failing to improve conditions of learning for the children, supervision fails equally to enhance the teacher's dignity or, for that matter, the supervisor's. Too often, the supervisory relationship is mutually thwarting.

This malady, I suspect, is not simply to be understood as guilt by association, that is, as a result of supervision's adulteration by external issues. The problem is, more seriously, an internal one: that in the absence of some cogent framework of educational values and of powerful theoretical systems, operational models, extensive bodies of case material to consult, rigorous programs of professional training, and a broad literature of empirical research, supervision has neither a fundamental substantive content nor a consciously determined and universally recognized process—both its stuff and its methods tend to be random, residual, frequently archaic, and eclectic in the worst sense.

Even today, supervision is often wasted on superficialities. When it is not, its focus is generally aimed at technical improvement. Such supervision might be more commonly useful, were it not for three handicaps which it tends to incorporate. The first is that even when supervision is intended to heighten teachers' technical proficiencies, the very techniques that their supervisors advocate, culled largely from their own prior experiences as teachers, as students in educational methods courses, and from the manuals of national curriculums, are likely to be educationally invalid. Such is the state of instructional methods even presently, that very few certainties exist about whether specific, technical patterns of teaching behavior are sound or unsound— whether, plain and simple, they are likely to result in useful payoff without producing undesirable side effects. A second, almost universal deficiency among supervisors, is their inability to deal with the emotional ramifications of teaching, of learning to become a teacher, and of being supervised. They often lack either the incentive to deal with such problems, techniques for dealing with them effectively, or both. And little wonder: they have not, as a rule, been trained in such things. A third problem is that supervisors often fail, in their own supervision, to exemplify the principles of good teaching that they profess, and even an unconscious sense of double standards tends to be demoralizing for almost anyone except, perhaps, an avowed cynic.

For all of this, there is nevertheless a growing optimism among educators for supervision's future. My own commitment to the education of supervisors began to take shape in the Harvard-Lexington Summer Program of 1962, where I had the good fortune to discover "clinical supervision"[1] which, at that time, was becoming developed

---

[1] Although the term "clinical supervision" is intended to carry generic meaning, it has also been adopted as the name of the specific model to be developed in this writing. A preliminary definition can be found at the beginning of Chapter II.

largely by the efforts of Professor Morris L. Cogan, who directed an institute for supervisors in that setting. Since then, I have been involved in many such institutes, some of them lasting for an entire year, and have become increasingly aware of stirrings in supervision which have begun in schools of education throughout the country. In the public schools, particularly at the elementary level, team teaching has suddenly opened new vistas for supervision. Opportunities for teachers to be observed and to observe one another's work are dramatically more abundant than ever before in the schools' history, and interest in problems of analyzing teaching behavior and in the development of feedback techniques is unprecedentedly high. There is currently a corresponding surge of activity among writers in the field, and an increasing number of doctoral students of education are undertaking dissertations investigating a wide range of problems in supervision. Experienced supervisors are benefiting by expanded support of in-service training, and prospective supervisors are finding it less difficult to obtain some measure of preservice training, although such opportunities at both levels have only begun to materialize. Universities offering degree programs in clinically oriented educational supervision still represent an exception.

My desire to write this book has arisen partly from unhappiness with the past and partly from excitement for the future. It is intended to contribute momentum to the development of clinical supervision as a professional practice, to constitute one of its genetic elements. It aims, doubly, to project detailed images of supervision and methodological models by which to make them intelligible, on the one hand, and to prepare for further theoretical advancement and for the creation of extensive case materials and of training films, on the other. In one sense, this is naturalistic writing. It attempts to portray the denizens of supervision and to describe some salient characteristics of their professional interactions. In another sense, it aims to present some tentative propositions for theory and method, whose acceptance, as far as I am concerned, is less consequential, for the moment, than the professional inquiries they are intended to provoke.

Clinical supervision is begun, but not nearly completed. Its final forms will differ substantially from its present ones, and I would be gratified for this writing to guide its transfiguration. One of my immediate aims is to proclaim certain values and to assert various ideas: to own them, to feel responsible for them, and to write, in effect, toward periods and exclamation points. Another, more significant goal, however, is for this volume to culminate in questions. It *must* do so to be consistent with the discipline's existing level of maturity, its adolescence. What the moment requires is generation of problems and issues for research and development, rather than findings, although the time for hard research, I think, is near at hand. Our most fundamental question is of what, in its ultimate forms, one might soundly expect to achieve by clinical supervision and of what its inherent limitations are: logically, ethically, psychologically, and technically, both in general terms and in relation to the specific contingencies that arise from moment to moment, from person to person, and from setting to setting in supervision.

In the first chapter, I have offered some personal perceptions and impressions of the schools, a *weltanschauung* intended to provide reasons for the existence of clinical supervision as I conceptualize it. The writing in this section is intentionally kaleidoscopic, shifting randomly from this to that in much the same fashion, I propose, as classroom experiences are likely to for the children in them. In certain respects, the picture I have tried to create is neither balanced nor just. To some readers, it may seem distorted; to some, offensive; for some, it may ring true, and for others it may seem excessively emotional. It is not as important to me for this chapter to satisfy the scholarly traditions of historical writing, which it certainly fails to do, as it is to report experiences that have been true, at least some of the time, for me and for children, students, teachers, and supervisors whom I have known.

If better things exist that I overlook or fail to credit, then so do the misfortunes that I talk about. And that *they* exist is all that matters for their citation to be warranted. I have tried to create a phenomenological frame of reference in this chapter, a composite framework of troublesome experiences which this child and that one are likely to have sometime or other during their schooling. I have tried to capture some of the ironies that exist in school life, more by reflection than by writing deliberately intended to create ironies. My major reason for describing this chapter in this manner presently is to make the point that its intent, its flavor, its license, its form, and its emotion are substantially different from those qualities of the succeeding chapters.

From the second chapter onward, I have presented some ideas and descriptions, rationales, and methods for a supervision whose existence I think would be useful, both in the crazyquilt world I have described and in saner scholastic environments. I am committed to the hypothesis that whereas clinical supervision is most likely to succeed in the most educationally favorable environments, it is also more likely to be potent in momentarily bad schools than other supervisory approaches that we know about. It is crucial to stress "hypothesis," for clinical supervision is no present panacea; nor may it ever become one. If anything, this book should articulate more problems than it can solve. Supervision requires meaty and manageable problems, for the time being, perhaps more than anything else. At the same time, however, this writing would fail if it did not offer ideas, possibilities, and suggestions that are incorporable into present practice and study. I have not avoided making suggestions that may be helpful to supervisors and to teachers right away. But in no sense is this volume intended as an operational manual, a kit with all parts included, for building the complete supervisor.

The book is designed around a simple structure. First, a prototype of a sequence of clinical supervision is described, in which five stages of supervision are named: Preobservation, Observation, Analysis and Strategy, Conference, and Post-conference Analysis. Next, the principal rationales and purposes for each of the five stages are formulated. Third, the major bulk of this writing describes methods that clinical supervisors generally employ at each stage. In this section, such methods are presented in relatively idealized forms, as they would exist, in effect, if they were problem-free. In the following chapter, I have set out—this time with as much historical integrity as I could muster—the things that go wrong in actual practice: the dilemmas, the mistakes, the confusions, and other blunders of clinical supervision that have occurred as we attempted to implement the basic model. The final chapter is for taking stock of where the profession is presently, of the directions in which it should develop, and of the pitfalls it should avoid, at least momentarily.

This material is written from a bias and within a framework of values that begin in counseling psychology. To what may prove to be the psychologist's chagrin and the educator's skepticism, however, it moves past counseling and past teaching, at least as teaching is conventionally defined, to envision what must ultimately become a new ethic, new methodologies, and new training strategies for the practice of educational supervision.

I am indebted to Morris L. Cogan for the basic ideas from which clinical supervision emerged and for the years of collaboration in which he and George Bradley Seager helped to develop my thinking in this area. I am immeasurably grateful to the devoted friends who have generously assisted me by their responses to this manuscript, most particularly to Robert D. Marshall, William F. Murphy, Samuel N. Francis, and Sally Madaras. Special thanks are due to John A. Guthrie, without whose sympathetic support I could never have completed this writing. I deeply appreciate the patience with which Florie, Anne, and Elizabeth Goldhammer have endured my labor. My most profound thanks go to the wonderful people who, although they are called my students, are principally responsible for my daily learning; especially to Ann Marshall and Jeremiah Horgan.

R. G.

Pittsburgh, Pennsylvania

Contents

I
A Context for Supervision

The models of supervision to be developed in this book have been motivated, primarily, by contemporary views of weaknesses that commonly exist in educational practice. Their goals and techniques have been conceptualized with real schools in mind and have originated, for the most part, in response to observations of what tends to be wrong in today's curriculums and methods of instruction. While the establishment of "clinical supervision" is not seen as a cure-all for scholastic ills, its proponents maintain that, at least, such supervision addresses a wider spectrum of significant problems than have generally been attended by supervisors in the past. We believe that its potentialities for remedying instructional weaknesses are greater than those of other supervisory approaches that have been employed in education.

This chapter does not deal with supervision explicitly. It is intended to set the stage by generating images of what school can be like, particularly in the children's experience. It is intended to provide a starting place, a baseline, a psychological frame of reference, a picture of the difficulty we are in, a context of problems in which urgency exists for useful forms of professional supervision to be initiated. At the conclusion of this book, after clinical supervision has been presented,

1

we will return to examine the implications carried for its practice by the problems to be defined presently, and we will consider the question of what hope may exist for this discipline to become a major element in scholastic reconstruction.

DOWN THE DOWN STAIRCASE

Let us begin with the premise that a human personality tends to take on the psychological characteristics of its environment. This is no more than to say that if I am forced to exist in an environment filled with insanity, in time my own behavior will begin to incorporate the insanities that have surrounded me. If, as one suspects, this premise is valid, then some urgent questions follow for the school, for if we wish the youngsters to emerge from formal education as bright and as healthy as can be, then we must ask whether the schools themselves tend to be basically sane and intelligent places. Our premise implies that if, in truth, the school becomes a stupid or crazy environment, it will tend to create stupid and crazy learners by the time it has held them captive for twelve or more years. By such terms, incidentally, I mean to describe the dysfunctional behavior—stupidity and craziness— that we all sport in some degree, rather than florid psychopathology. I am thinking, by and large, of people like us.

I ask of my experiences whether, in fact, they include evidence that the schools have their demented aspects. I ask such a question lovingly, for I am deeply committed to the school's success and identify myself very closely with its existence. Having both survived and, in certain respects, prospered from my scholastic education, I have no doubts that the educational establishment has provided something of value in my life. It has been partly responsible, however, for making me as I am; and although I would not readily exchange identities with many other people, I am sometimes painfully aware of how my own intellectual condition is shot through with inadequacies that I also attribute, in some part, to the twenty years in which I was "student" and to the twelve years in which, by one denomination or another, I have been professionally involved in education. Taken together, both these periods represent the frame of reference upon which I am about to draw.

Although my response to this question is offered partly with tongue in cheek, it is also, basically, an honest response, one accompanied by genuine feelings. I can think of many places to begin: the curriculum, the instructional methods, the social and moral and esthetic values that the school perpetrates, its rules and rituals, and various sacred categories of teaching practice, such as *discipline, motivation, lesson planning, pupil evaluation,* and *professionalism.* Since it doesn't seem to matter, and keeping in mind that we are deliberately setting out to unearth some of the school's deficiencies—its virtues are momentarily irrelevant—let us, at random, begin by examining the curriculum.

CURRICULUMS

Imagine a unit of study, somewhere in the primary grades, on "The Family." And imagine, if you will, the stories in the reader and in the materials assembled by the librarian, and the character of classroom dialogue in this context. Even if you are not presently employed in an elementary school, your childhood memories of first grade should provide appropriate images: in this regard, things have not changed very much. How is "family" generally represented in the early grades?

The houses in which families live never, as far as we are told, include toilets. Members of the family never scratch themselves, utter obscenities, cheat on their wives, fix traffic tickets, drink beer, play the horses, falsify their tax returns, strike one another, make love, use deodorants, gossip on the telephone, buy on credit, have ulcers, or manifest a million other signs of life that even the most culturally deprived child knows about in the most intimate detail. Indeed, one suspects that children of poverty are at least as knowledgeable about such intimacies of living as their more affluent counterparts.

Certainly, at their dinner tables, no textbook fathers talk about having outbargained that New York Jew, about the niggers who are trying to take over the neighborhood, the cops, the Birchers, the hippies, the war, and so on. On the contrary, one may safely expect the textbook family to be disembodied, apolitical, generally without a specific ethnic identity or religious affiliation, free of social prejudice, innocent of grief, economically secure, vocationally stable, antiseptic and law-abiding straight down the middle. It occupies a universe from which disaffection, divorce, cynicism, loneliness, neurosis, bastardy, atheism, tension, self-doubt, wrecked cars, and cockroaches are inevitably absent.

Unless he is downright dull, it is almost impossible to imagine that at some level of experience the child is not aware of the thundering disparity between the real world and the school's priggish, distorted, emasculated representations of that world. It seems reasonable to suspect that the child's knowledge almost certainly includes the realization that, in plain language, the curriculum is phony, at least in relation to the example we have considered.

A little later, I will discuss "incidental learning," but, for the moment, let's consider one example of that phenomenon. One wonders whether, from such teaching—about the phony family—the child is not

likely to learn that the teacher (the text, the curriculum) is putting him
on, that the school is attempting to perpetrate a hoax, and that, consequently, the teacher, who is a liar, and the school, which promulgates
the lie, are not to be trusted: in addition to or instead of the established
stereotypes that the teacher *intended* him to learn. In other words, one
wonders if the cumulative effects of such blatant unauthenticity in the
curriculum can help but teach the pupil that the school is strikingly
distinct from the real world and, in practice, teach him to become
alienated either from academic involvement, from reality, or in some
measure from both.

Perhaps the greatest misfortune is that, more often than not, the
child's own perceptions, rather than the school's representations, become suspect. Given his infantile dependencies for protection, it can be
safer, in certain respects, to doubt *his* own hold on things than to doubt
the school's institutional integrity. That precious capacity to see the
emperor's nudity succumbs early in his scholastic experience. Like sex
and digestion and God, and like politics, questions of curricular authenticity are strictly taboo, strictly *verboten*. Ironically, some of his teachers try at certain isolated moments to teach the learner "critical thinking" in the advanced grades and ridicule him, then, for his gullibility
and sluggishness.

Several other problems of curriculum are worth noting. My students keep telling me that they recall episodes of their own elementary
and secondary school experience in which the curriculum, by which
they mean the subject matter content, did not have utility for them,
seemed difficult to relate to, and was generally "unmeaningful." Although I am not completely certain of what they mean, my own
experience tends to confirm the general feeling of curricular lacunae, of
periods of emptiness in which I cannot, for the life of me, remember
what I was being taught. As I think about myself, observe current
classroom teaching, and talk to other people about their memories of
school, an image forms of having sat endlessly through classes in which
the stuff seemed somehow remote, somehow unessential, and somehow
unrelated to my own personal necessities, to the vivid immediacies of
my moment-to-moment existence. "Remoteness" is quite the word to
describe my relationship to the stuff, or perhaps more accurately, its
relationship to me.

This recollection leads me to the question of whether my own
experience was idiosyncratic—what people tell me suggests that it was
not—and to the second question of what factors might commonly
operate to make the curriculum seem remote from the learners. Here
are some tentative hypotheses that occur to me.

Already, we have the notion of *phoniness* as one quality of the
curriculum that is likely to make it seem inconsistent with the learners'
phenomenal experiences of reality. *Temporal remoteness* represents a

second possibility. Should the curriculum comprise studies of ancient pasts or distant futures, it is likely to seem vacant of existential meaning. Left by itself, ancient Rome simply does not turn me on. I could not care less about its succession of emperors unless, by one means or another, their existence and their sequence carried some meaning and vitality in the sensible framework of my own existence. As a young student, I am unlikely to work very hard to develop such touchpoints between ancient times and the world I know or feel I need to know. Why should I? And, caring too little to take the pains myself, it is unlikely that the teacher can lead me easily to it unless he threatens, bribes, or seduces me, as teachers are often forced to do in common practice.

Spatial remoteness is much the same sort of condition. "Our Friends in Ecuador" are at an awful competitive disadvantage to my friends (and enemies) on the block. What's in it for me to mess my mind with facts about Ecuador? What incentives exist for that expenditure of energy? How will that help me to be what I need to be, to be more than I am, to be less afraid, or to feel more viable in the universe through which *I* must move? Alabama primaries, Canadian Mounties, even gang wars in Brooklyn, and *de facto* segregation in New Rochelle have, as far as I can see, little to do with my problems of being a kid between 219th Street and Gun Hill Road in the Bronx. Things that are too far away are likely to seem too far away.

I am *not* suggesting that all the curriculum should be is what is happening right this minute between 219th Street and Gun Hill Road. I am proposing, however, that if the content is way before or after the learner or some place very distant from him, it automatically follows that it could easily seem remote and unessential. Rather than worry about solutions for the moment, let's, instead, expand this inventory of factors that might logically or psychologically operate against the student's investment in the curriculum or promote his alienation from it.

Putting myself in the pupil's place, I suspect that *cultural remoteness* might turn me away from the subject matter. Although I am entertained by the fairy-tale quality of other people in other places—fantasies can be fun—their entertainment value is short-lived. Having to make it, as I must, in my ghetto, I have little patience or appetite for prolonged study of your suburb, or vice versa. If the curriculum is written in your jive (linguistic remoteness), and if I don't dig your jive, or if your curriculum portrays a kind of living for which I dare not cherish hope or which I have strong reasons to hate or to fear, then you and I are irrevocably out of touch. The mystique of samurai is so impossible to understand that I cannot understand it. And I lack reasons to.

Because of its *level of abstraction* or complexity, the curriculum can seem remote from me. An unvisualizable algebra, an infinite celestial universe, a statistical genetics, a free counterpoint, an algorithm of division, a categorical imperative, a biconditional case, an Aristotelian diversity, a Shavian subtlety, a moral paradox, a Meno's rule, a past pluperfect, a "predicate nominative with the copulative verb 'to be,' " an epistemological paradigm, or a commutative principle may be simply and terribly inaccessible to me, either because it is too hard or because it seems too easy. To be asked to comprehend the incomprehensible or to bore me with an endless quibble will, in either case, repel me from the curriculum which, perforce, will seem hopeless or useless.

Another possibility is that at any given moment the curricular content will be *emotionally too hot* for me to handle. Although this possibility may seem bizarre in some ways, we might, at least, consider it briefly. We have all, by now, developed some awareness of Freudian symbolism. By this time, we all know what dreams "mean." The idea here is that besides having meaning at its face value, the content of the curriculum or the processes involved in dealing with the content can carry unconscious symbolic meaning for the learner, a set of meanings that are neither apparent on the face of the material nor of which the learner is explicitly aware but by which he can *feel* threatened.

Consider one esoteric example. If, at this moment in my psychosexual development, the greatest portion of my psychic energy is being channeled toward the resolution of an Oedipal dilemma and if my "castration anxiety" is particularly virulent or my ego is particularly weakened or, for some reason, I have become fixed in the horrors of castration fantasies, I might consequently mobilize myself against objects and operations in the surrounding environment that are symbolically tantamount to the feared castration. For example, I might manifest a disability in the mathematical processes of division, subtraction, and in work with fractions because of their common symbolic characteristic of representing loss of parts, destruction of wholes, fractionation, and so on. Should my mathematical disablement actually arise from such unconscious sources, I might very well prove refractory to special tutoring directed at mathematical operations. Instead, my "learning problem" might really require psychotherapy or, more likely, a sufficiently long vacation from mathematics for appropriate movement to occur through developmental time. In any event, under such circumstances, my need to protect myself from threatening stimuli might force me to become temporarily alienated from the substantive curriculum.

In more homely terms, the curriculum abounds in materials and topics that seem, for all the world, to be emotionally innocuous but which, for the individual learner, may carry strong emotional baggage. By use of mnemonic devices, potentially neutral material is often encumbered with powerful and irrelevant associations, at least some of which are likely to force the learner's emotional retreat. In a kindergarten lesson on writing numbers, the teacher pointed out that zero looks like a face (Marcia's face is disfigured by a large birthmark), two looks like a turkey (Alice left home screaming that morning because Papa had threatened to slaughter her pet turkey for the Thanksgiving meal), and four looks like a flag (Joe's father has just been jailed for burning his draft card). The story for the day was about Miranda and Johann and their wicked stepparents (after being divorced, Arnold's mother is about to remarry; a new sibling is imminent in Charles' family). Are there psychologically significant relationships among these variables?

Let us consider some additional possibilities. For one thing, curriculums are often invented by authors who are a thousand miles away from the schoolrooms in which they are used. Certain curriculums are national institutions. Their creators, one may safely assume, do not know the children or their teachers or the special problems in their lives. And if a principal reason for the curriculum seeming remote to the learner is that it is not very accommodative or responsive to the learner—as any preordained, written *in absentia* curriculum is likely to be—then the individual student's prognosis in such a curriculum grows dim. Another alarming fact that is generally true of curriculums, whether composed at a distance, beforehand, or *in praesenti*, is that the knowledge they incorporate is organized into arbitrary sequences and categories that may have no relationship at all to natural sequences of human learning or natural processes of human cognition. If one is to trust the discoveries of contemporary epistemologists, then the traditional convention of teaching mathematics, for example, in the sequence: naming numbers, counting, addition, subtraction, multiplication, division, fractions, decimals, and so forth, is nonsense. "Modern mathematics" notwithstanding, this instructional rite of passage remains deeply entrenched in mathematical instruction.

Because he has not been trained to, the schoolman tends to know little (and, sometimes, to care less) about the logical organization and structure of bodies of knowledge. He is equally ignorant, as a rule and for the same reason, of psychological organization and sequences of learning. Knowing neither the knowledge nor the learner, his attempts to bring the two together are not likely to be very efficient. If the curriculum has seemingly little correspondence to natural sequences of mental development, it also tends, particularly in the elementary grades, to infantilize the learner by forcing his attendance upon puerilities, superficialities, and insipid stereotypes to which his teachers generally refer as "grade-level material" and which have been deduced, in turn, by authors of curriculum, from a context of what they conceptualize as "age-typical behaviors." Despite their pretensions, most primary-grade curriculums provide, in effect, a regimen of little ideas for little people and very thoroughly preclude possibilities for the children to experience and be delighted by mastery of intellectually substantial problems.

The mysteries of carrying, borrowing, and multiplicands stand in place of noneuclidean geometries, propositional algebra, and set theory as intellectual grist. The curriculum reflects very little of our existing information—which is itself very little—on what people might be able to learn if they were to prosecute spontaneous lines of inquiry, of what people can be conditioned to learn—Skinner makes hawks of doves—or of how the stuff to be learned could be organized in a manner that might give the learner a decent chance and a feeling of productive activity. "Our Helper the Mailman" is one mighty peculiar derivative from the social sciences.

If curricular organization of knowledge is generally arbitrary, then the selection of curricular content is equally arbitrary—May the lord protect my house from *Silas Marner!*—and what is absent from the curriculum is also arbitrary. Its omissions are, perhaps, the curriculum's most horrifying aspect. Is it possible to believe that besides a whole lot of slaves, tap dancers, ball players, Booker T. Washington, and George Washington Carver, a legion of other Negroes has been ungloriously responsible for the political, technological, scientific, and humanistic culture that one generally supposes to have originated without them? Is it conceivable that some direct relationship exists between the "soaring incidence" of sociopathic behavior, unsuccessful marriage, vocational dissatisfaction, and emotional collapse in our culture, and the absence from the curriculum of any systematic treatment of love, intimacy, sex, feeling, fantasy, death, law, work, or real life? Or between the fact of my loneliness and the mystery of myself to me and the unmitigated absence of "me" as an object for explicit study in the curriculum?

It is difficult to imagine how educational priorities that elevate penmanship to a realm of moral significance could ever have come into existence—you had better believe how much humility my left-handedness in a right-handed school cost me—while "me," through which all of my knowledge of the universe and of the dreams inside me is filtered and composed, was never a worthy enough subject to justify even a single course in human behavior during twelve years of public education, nor any opportunities for helpful counseling, nor any deliberate scholastic effort to teach me skills of self-examination. It is difficult not to attribute at least some portion of my agony of self-ignorance, my uncertainty of who I am and how worthy, how powerful, how limited, how good, and how bad I am to the schools who had a hold on me for such a long time and who, in this context of knowledge, deprived me and betrayed me so completely.

Another kind of curricular omission is represented by the schoolman's failure, generally, to conceptualize the school's internal social system as a dimension of the curriculum. While to define curriculum as "life" may be extravagant, it is not so unmanageable to conceptualize experiences that can be *planned and regulated by the schools* as their curriculum. Indeed, recent newspaper articles reporting the expulsion of pupils because of their long haircuts testify that, at least in certain limited respects, school people have begun to catch on to this idea, albeit in unconstructive applications. It is tragically ironic that in many instances the very same administrator who worries about the social ramifications of coiffure, supports the establishment's whim to perpetuate *de facto* racial segregation in city schools, not realizing, apparently, that under such conditions *all* of the schools are likely to be bigot factories.

My final indictment of the curriculum, for the time being, relates to the priority it has attached to assimilation of substantive information by the learner. It is truly a content curriculum, a curriculum in which nothing is more holy or more rewarded than answers. In its most barbaric extreme, the New York State Regents' Examination for high school students and its effects upon curricular priorities illustrate the disaster to which I am referring.

One can imagine that several hundred years ago it might have made some sense, especially for the "gifted learner"—this means someone who can remember a great deal—for education to aim at the acquisition of information as its principal goal. There wasn't, after all, a great deal of knowledge extant several hundred years ago, certainly not by comparison to current knowledge. To compare the parameters of knowledge in both times must lead one to wonder whether it is reasonable to hope for more than pale ghosts of Michelangelo in this world or to be surprised by the notion that renaissance man required the renaissance world for his existence, or by the fact that dilettantism and "underachievement" are hallmarks of contemporary culture.

We hear constantly about the present proliferation of knowledge and about the rate at which the proliferation is changing. Our situation seems to be one in which it is impossible to know everything; the disciplines themselves are so abundant and diverse (cybernetics, general semantics, exobiology) that it is impossible even to acquire a reasonably thorough sampling of all fields of knowledge; the limited sectors of knowledge that we call "specialties" comprehend so much information that most men cannot hope even to master a single specialty; and even if I were to learn all the knowledge subsumed by some narrow specialty, such as neurosurgery or psychological statistics, by the time I had done so, much of the knowledge I had learned would be obsolete; and much of the remainder would be obsolescent.

It may be disturbing to see how limited a concept of knowledge I have employed in this argument. In effect, "knowledge" has been conceptualized simply as "information," and "knowing" has been made to seem like a simple and static condition, that of having assimilated bodies of information. I have not projected this image because I like it, but only because it seems implicitly—sometimes explicitly—to be the conceptualization that motivates content curriculums as we commonly know them. If the image is barren and hopeless and makes very little psychological sense, that is unfortunate. The point I mean to make is that even with this simplest of simpleminded definitions, even with a definition that excises entire dimensions of knowing and that disregards all features of knowledge except for its factual substance, even if these definitions were *valid,* the content curriculum, its rationales and objectives would be futile. If there is too much to know, too much to sample, too much to enable most men to master specialties, and too much, too fast, in any event, to keep up with, then a curriculum whose chief aim is to transmit information and whose highest priority is upon answers is worse than an ostrich with its head in the sand: it is an ostrich in quicksand.

It is not only an untenable, unfeasible curriculum; but even if the learner approximated its goals and learned a great deal of information indeed, there is little reason to suspect, consequently, that he would be intellectually viable in this generation. To have employed richer definitions of knowledge and of knowing, presently, would simply have underscored the point. Requirements of "intellectual viability" remain to be described, and I will turn to them a bit later. For now, I offer the observation that even though curricular priorities have begun to shift and even though some authors of curriculum have found more solid footing, in classroom practice, generally, the premium upon answers and, particularly, upon short, simple, factual answers can hardly be overstated. If answers are prized generally, then the best answers of all are predetermined answers—predetermined by the teacher, the text, or the examination.

Let me summarize these problems. My experiences as pupil, teacher, and listener to other people's comments attest to the observations that the curriculum is frequently unauthentic (both objectively and in the pupils' frames of reference), remote in one manner or another, arbitrarily selected, arbitrarily organized, inconsistent with natural learning, vacant of systematic study by the learner of himself, composed *in absentia*, preordained, unresponsive to the learners' individual requirements—goals are generally uniform: the same outcomes for everybody—heavily invested in substantive content, and principally directed toward the learners' acquisition of correct and authoritative answers, infantilizing, and as likely to stunt intellectual capacities as to enhance them.

I have advanced a great many stereotypes and sweeping generalizations and have not troubled to assemble documentary proof in this writing. Neither have I troubled to acknowledge the existence of good curricular inventions: of curriculums that can be acquitted of these charges. I have not provided a balanced picture. I have not talked about what is good because my intent has been to direct us toward what is bad. Unfortunately, the coexistence of occasional strengths in the curriculum does not begin to offset its weaknesses, and I believe, in any case, and will try to demonstrate that compensations and corrections for what is bad are sometimes possible to achieve through supervision and generally impossible to achieve by other means, including the invention of new curriculums.

Even when teachers get hold of relatively good curriculums, they often ruin them. From what I observe in the schools, it would seem that "professional growth" resulting from in-service curriculum workshops is often represented by the substitution of new stupidities for old ones. Observers of teaching will know what I mean if they can recall or imagine a situation in which, using the language of "regrouping in base ten," the teacher leads the pupils dutifully through a lesson in "borrowing," a mechanistic, procedural mapping of what to cross out at what moment in the minuend in order to make believe certain things about the subtrahend, to determine, in the end, what's the difference. The methodological question to be examined is, except for a new and often cumbersome terminology, *what's the difference?*

TEACHING PATTERNS AND "INCIDENTAL LEARNING," MOTIVATION, AND DISCIPLINE

Having done with curriculum, let's stay, for a time, with problems of teaching, remembering that our goal is to illustrate a context of scholastic bedlam in which a professional discipline of clinical supervision can be developed. Perhaps the most salient feature of most of the teaching that goes on, from nursery school to the graduate seminar, is its absence of reasons: of explicit rationales and of reasons generally from the pupils' frames of reference. The following excerpts should make my meaning clear because they are so familiar:

Open your books to page seventy.
Do rows A through F for tonight's homework.
Will each of you in Sally's row put one example on the board?
Today, we will begin *Hamlet.*
Pay attention; this is important.

There is probably no limit to the number of instances in which what the teacher asks, what the teacher assigns, and what the pupils must do are unassociated with any explicit *raisons d'être.* The pupil's is not to reason why, but rather to do what he is told. For every pupil to demand reasons for every order might result in anarchy. For every pupil to do what he is told unquestioningly, slavishly, can result in death: his own or other people's. Tom Lehrer sings:

> "Once the rockets are up
> Who cares where they come down?
> That's not my department,"
> Says Wernher von Braun.[1]

To make the point clear, it is time now to consider two concepts parenthetically: "incidental learning," to which I have already referred, and "motivation," a shibboleth of modern teaching. By "incidental learning," I mean to name a classroom phenomenon: that in addition to the learning outcomes sought deliberately by the teacher, the pupils, individually and collectively, learn a great spectrum of things that the teacher did not intend them to learn, generally without the teacher's awareness that they have been learned, and as a direct result of the teacher's behavior and of the pupils' tendencies toward learning in certain categories. Experience suggests that, for the most part, such unintended or incidental learnings concern the teacher himself, the pupil's relationship to the teacher, the pupil's relationship to the school, and the pupil's relationship to learning. Incidental learning can potentiate intended learning, can be irrelevant to the intended learning, or can be at direct cross purposes to it. Even when incidental learning is irrelevant, there is little evidence about the actual relative distribution of incidental learnings in each of these categories, but I suspect that probability favors the latter two and I know that the last subset is not an empty one by any means. Let us consider the following patterns of teaching and speculate on what incidental learnings they might logically foster:

1. TEACHER: What do you think we're going to do today?
   TEACHER: I'm thinking of a word. Can anyone tell me what the word is? It begins with "E."
   TEACHER: You'd better pay attention because this question is just likely to come up on the test.
   As a pupil in this class, I might learn: "My job is to guess what the teacher has in mind and then to give him what he wants."

2. Whenever a pupil gives a response, the teacher repeats his response verbatim.
   I learn: "There is no point in listening to anyone in here besides the teacher because he will say everything eventually."

---

[1] From "Wernher von Braun," recorded by Tom Lehrer on Reprise Records RS6179, "That Was the Year That Was." Copyright © 1965 by Tom Lehrer. Reprinted by permission.

3. TEACHER: America was discovered by . . . ?
TEACHER: Three and what are seven?
TEACHER: In a molecule of water, there are two atoms of hydrogen and one atom of oxygen. True or false?
TEACHER: Was Socrates a real person?
I learn to give short answers.

4. Whenever a pupil gives a response, the teacher paraphrases or otherwise elaborates the response.
I learn: "I can never really win in here. No matter how hard I try or how successfully I frame a response, the teacher will always be able to do it better."

5. The teacher responds to almost every pupil's recitation with a stereotyped, "OK, very good."
I learn, "Anything goes."

6. The teacher gives reading assignments to be done at home, but never refers to the material in class or on examinations.
I learn not to do the assignments.

7. The teacher often asks "poll-taking" questions, for example, "*How many* of you read this chapter? *How many* of you understand this?" and then remonstrates, "I don't see very many hands!"
I learn to raise my hand.

8. The teacher often has one pupil state a question, another pupil state the answer, a third pupil tell how the problem was solved, and a fourth pupil put the question and the answer on the board.
I am likely not to learn a complete process of framing questions, developing strategies for their solution, and figuring out their answers. Instead, I learn unconnected parts of the sequence which may never become properly integrated.

9. In situations where the teacher is recording pupils' successful responses on the board, he does so in precisely the language used by the pupil.
I learn, "This is a place in which my ideas count for something."

Whether or not such incidental learnings will actually result from the patterns of teaching described is an empirical question for which, obviously, I cannot offer a conclusive answer. Neither can I assert that in response to any given pattern of teaching behavior, the incidental learnings will be the same for everybody or for any individual from one time to the next. And finally, although my examples make it seem that way, there is little reason to suspect that patterns of teaching behavior will always exist in one-to-one correspondence with simple incidental learnings. On the contrary, multiple learnings, complex learnings, ambiguous and mutually conflicting learnings can, theoretically, derive from the same stimuli in any number of combinations and hues of reinforcement.

Even if these examples were not totally convincing, I should maintain, nevertheless, that the general phenomenon is authentic. My reasoning incorporates certain assumptions that are empirically demonstrable: I have, for example, assumed that human behavior is patterned and that teaching behavior, being subsumed by general behavior, is also patterned. Of the various characteristics associated with behavioral patterning, its repetitive aspect is all that concerns us in this connection.

The notion is simply that certain components of teaching behavior tend to be repeated again and again, that the teacher's unique identity can be defined largely by his peculiar set of patterns, that many teaching patterns are common rather than idiosyncratic, and that, especially in their cumulative effects, such patterns of teaching give rise to incidental learnings which tend to be reinforced again and again by the same teacher, and, if my observations are accurate, often from teacher to teacher. It is important to understand, in relation to the examples above, that if the teaching behaviors represented occurred only once, they would not have much consequence for the learner one way or another. Their potency lies in their repetition and in the cumulative effects, five hours each day, 180 days each academic year, of their existence.

If there is difficulty believing that human behavior is patterned or imagining what behavioral repetitions might look like, consider the case of the man whose pattern of courtship is first, to find a desirable woman; second, to excite her affection; third, to consummate their romance in some act of unequivocal possession; and fourth, knowing for certain that he's got her, promptly to lose interest and move on to other territory to repeat the same process all over again. Or consider the man whose capacity for alienating people at first contact seems uncanny but of whom people generally agree, "He's OK once you get to know him." Or consider the supervisee who consistently begins conferences by derogating his teaching in every possible manner and thereby, having prepared himself for all eventualities, not only precludes criticism from his supervisor but, in fact, elicits expressions of sympathy that had never occurred to the supervisor to offer beforehand.

My supervisory forays into the classroom have taught me that certain patterns of teaching are extremely common and that their commonality, as I will argue later, is generally explicable. This time, I will describe some patterns that I have encountered repeatedly—the fact that I tend to see certain phenomena over and over again may reflect something about my own patterns—and ask the reader to imagine what incidental learnings they might logically promote. I will share some of my own guesses later in the book.

> All directions are given by the teacher.
>
> All questions originate from the teacher.
>
> All evaluations are performed by the teacher.
>
> The pace of instruction and all sequences of instruction are determined by the teacher.
>
> An "I" pattern exists; the teacher's questions and directions are generally enunciated in the first person: "I want you to open your books. Will you take out your workbooks for me? Do you remember what I said about that yesterday? I want you to read for me now. I have a sore throat, and you're not helping it any!"
>
> A "multiple questioning" pattern exists: [Without any pauses.] "Do you know what holiday we celebrate next week—who knows something about Independence Day—do you know what we celebrate on the Fourth of July—when was the Declaration of Independence written?"
>
> Ninety percent or more of the words spoken during any given lesson are spoken by the teacher.
>
> The teacher calls only on children who have raised their hands.
>
> The teacher asserts that he will not call on people who call out, out of turn, but he often does.
>
> The teacher uses school work as an instrument of punishment:
>
> *a.* Pupils who have committed a disturbance are required to copy the "W" pages from the dictionary for homework.
>
> *b.* Having observed that Tony is staring through the window in a trance-like state, the teacher asks, "And what emotion was associated with the Dorian mode—Tony?!"
>
> The teacher insists that pupils stand whenever they say anything.
>
> The teacher takes the entire class to the bathroom at the same time every day.
>
> The teacher assigns extra work, that is, more of the same thing, to children who finish their assignments quickly.
>
> A reward pattern: When a pupil has finished reciting, the teacher generally responds, "Yes, but . . ."
>
> Another reward pattern: "William, you have done so well in arithmetic today that you may wash the boards and empty the basket."
>
> The teacher gives gold stars.
>
> The teacher corrects papers, figures attendance, and so on, while, at the teacher's direction, a pupil is reciting.
>
> Sarcasm: "I see you have four pencils on your desk, Timmy.

Have you four hands? No? Then put away the extra pencils,
Timmy."

Ritual questions: "Would you like to open your books to page
ten now?"

Gratuitous questions: "What am I holding in my hand [when
the teacher is holding a board eraser in his hand]?"

A tendency to make pupils' responses correct:

a. "What Arnold was really thinking was that . . ."

b. "You really meant to say, 'divide,' didn't you?"

A tendency to make one pupil responsible for describing
another pupil's thinking: "Johnny, what did Fred really mean to
say? Billy, how did Joshua get that answer?"

Habitual use of diminuitive adjectives: "Barbara has a little
something she brought to show us. Greg, what was your little
idea?"

The teacher seizes every opportunity to teach, under almost any
circumstances. For example, grammatical corrections are pressed
while a pupil is telling about some experience.

Whenever, while he is writing, a pupil asks the teacher how to
spell a word, he is told, "Look it up in the dictionary."

After quizzes have been collected, scored, and returned, the
teacher asks each pupil, in turn, to call out his score in order for it
to be recorded in the gradebook.

I should be very surprised if many of the patterns illustrated
above seem unfamiliar. If we ask ourselves, "As a pupil, what might I
learn from the habitual repetition of any of these patterns of teaching
behavior?" we begin to develop a panorama of side effects, most of
them undesirable, that can be described appropriately as incidental
learnings.

When a pattern of teaching behavior promotes incidental learnings
that distract pupils from the intended object of study or when a pattern
tends to teach the children self-perceptions, perceptions of the school,
or perceptions of learning that lead to self-deprecation, distrust, cynicism, or feelings of unsafety or confusion, then, I should say, a negative
pattern exists. If, on the other hand, teaching behavior gives rise to
incidental learnings that heighten the learners' sense of worthiness and
engagement in useful activity, then a positive pattern exists. In many
cases teaching patterns could validly be assigned a $\pm$ value. That is to
say, in some instances a specific teaching pattern generates both positive and negative effects in relation to different members of the group
or in relation to specific individuals at different times. I have not
intentionally included positive patterns among the examples offered. In
my judgment, some of them are inescapably "minus" while others, but

only a few, might be thought to incorporate strengths and weaknesses simultaneously.

Before turning to the problem of an absence of reasons from teaching, I have some thoughts to express about motivation. The concept or, rather, the word "motivation" is part of teaching's unfortunate legacy from psychology—"unfortunate" because that legacy seems mostly to contain piecemeal extrapolations from psychology rather than cogent adaptations of whole theories, a jumble of unrelated bits and pieces. From what I am able to observe, motivation, in the teacher's frame of reference, generally means to get the pupils to do what he wants them to do. It is conceptualized as a manipulation whose components are likely to include some form of bribery or seduction. It is construed as a separate act, or set of acts, that occurs at the beginning of a lesson and which involves the use of "motivational techniques" (or "devices"). Lesson plans often include a section called "motivation," where the noun heads a list of things that the teacher intends to do to make the children motivated. This section of the plan often follows a section called "goals" or "objectives." Goals are generally expressed in terms of cognitive or affective outcomes which, being *invisible*, make it impossible for the teacher to know whether he has gotten the payoff he wanted at the start.

Although some teachers still persist in "motivating" the children by telling them that the material about to be taught is important for a test, that it is necessary to review, or that it will help them to understand something that the teacher believes is important for them to understand, and whereas some teachers continue to use competition as a motivating gambit ("Let's see who'll get more right, the boys or the girls."), most of the teachers I see, nowadays, "develop motivation" by directing the pupils' attention to something about which they are likely, in the teacher's judgment, to be enthusiastic. This tactic derives from the generally accepted principle that the children will learn the stuff better if it is related to their prior experience, and the corollary that if academic material can be associated with some pleasurable prior experience, its pleasure will be transferred to the subject matter.

In practice, it usually works something like this. The teacher wants the pupils to read a story in which Mary Anne has a birthday party. The objectives of the lesson might be "to develop powers of recall; to expand esthetic sensitivity; to recognize words that describe," or more similarly useful (and invisible) educational outcomes. The teacher begins:

> TEACHER: How many of you boys and girls are having a birthday this month?
> [If that question doesn't elicit much response, the teacher may

shrewdly substitute the question, "How many of you will have a
birthday sometime this year?" which is more likely to evoke
responses from the children who are listening.]

[Several hands are raised.]

TEACHER: Oh my! Can somebody tell us what you do at your
birthday party? Tommy?

[Tommy, incidentally, is not one of the pupils who raised a hand
in the first place.]

TOMMY: Well, we have cake and Pepsi and ice cream—

SALLY: And favors and candy—

TEACHER: One at a time, Sally. We can't hear if everybody
speaks at once.

TOMMY: And we play games of "pin the tail on the donkey."

TEACHER: Oh my! What kind of *cake* do you have?

[At which point the children excitedly tell about many flavors,
sizes, and ingredients of cakes they have known or have dreamed
about (yellow cakes with white icing and pink and green roses;
white cakes with layers of bananas and whipped cream; sponge
cakes soaked in brandy), in increasingly *aqueous* exclamations.
After this has gone on for some time, the teacher says:]

TEACHER: Well, that's wonderful! I hope some of you invite me
to your next birthday party because I like cake too. Now, today we
are going to read about Mary Anne's birthday party. You read to
find out what kind of cake Mary Anne had and about what
surprised all the children about Mary Anne's cake. When you
have finished reading this story, answer the questions on page nine
of your workbook. Any questions?

BILLY: Should we read the whole story or just one page?

TEACHER: Read the entire story. When you have finished the
first page, go on to the next. Read all of the pages until you have
finished the story.

Thus begins the "activities" phase of the lesson. Presumably, the
pupils have been successfully inducted into their reading by means of a
motivation which has provided an experiential framework for the task.
The only problem seems to be that many of the children are apparently
listless and agitated and find it difficult to settle down to work. By the
end of the hour, most pupils have not even begun to do the workbook
exercises.

What should we suppose the trouble is?

Could it be that rather than feeling motivated to read, the children
feel motivated to *eat?*

Might we suppose that if, as my literature professor, you asked me
to recall nights in which I frolicked on the beach with naked Polynesian
beauties, nights of erotic pleasure along the Ginza, private cruises I
have taken on the Aegean with my crew of Cretan peasant girls—that

if you asked me to recall these experiences in their most vivid detail—
that you would have motivated me to perform an analytical reading of
Boccaccio's tales? Do you really believe that you would have motivated
me to *read* anything?

If you do, you are badly mistaken, and if, under such circumstances, you happened to be a beauty yourself, your best strategy
(listed under "activities") would be to run very fast in the opposite
direction unless you, too, were "motivated."

There seems little question that talk of cakes and parades and
circuses and pet monkeys is likely, in at least some sense of the term, to
be motivating—certainly stimulating—for the children. An unfortunately large proportion of the "motivations" I observe, however, although they are stimulating, and often, overstimulating, do not seem to
hit the mark at all. Instead, they tend to excite various hungers in the
pupils which are simply not about to be gratified by literature or by
other vicarious representations. In short, "motivations" of this kind are
self-defeating, for not only do they fail to motivate appropriately, but
they create monumental distractions from the required work.

Having witnessed so many instances of misconceived motivation,
incorrectly applied principles of learning, applications of invalid educational principles, instructional practices that are no less senseless because they utilize modern terminology than the ineffectual practices
which modern methodology was supposed to supplant—rote learning in
base six is no less barbaric than rote learning in base ten—and an
endless parade of teaching patterns such as those I have cited, I reach
the conclusion that teachers often have very little sense of the effects
their own behavior is likely to have upon the pupils' learning. It is sad
enough to recognize that sometimes even the teacher's planned behavior, for example, the "motivation," is ill conceived, being based upon
invalid assumptions of psychological cause and effect. If anything, it is
worse to discover that the greatest portion of the teacher's behavior is
unplanned, *ad hoc*, unexamined, unknown, and unrelated by the teacher to the possibility of its having significant positive or negative consequences for the children. Least of all is the teacher likely to be aware
of how the pupils' behavior tends to reinforce his own behavioral
patterns and, especially in the context of "discipline," he is often blind
to how his own behavior reinforces precisely the patterns of pupil
behavior that he wants to extinguish.

If we stop to think about it, we are certain to recognize that even
though some teachers complain bitterly about unruly classes, and generally attribute disciplinary difficulties to conditions that inhere in the
learners, the fact is often that, the learners' predispositions notwithstanding, their misbehavior can be directly related to conditions that
the teacher has unthinkingly created.

Consider the following examples:

1. Teacher A, who is a ruthless disciplinarian, insists that the

pupils cannot be trusted, that it is suicide to leave the room or to turn one's back on them for a minute. It has not occurred to him, however, that a part of the problem is that his very ruthlessness, his smothering control, has, at best, taught the children to behave themselves while he is with them. Because they are afraid, they will generally maintain some degree of order while he is in the room. In effect, they have learned to be regulated. They have *not* learned to be self-regulating because the teacher has not taught them how nor given them chances to rehearse whatever skills are required for effective self-regulation. Moreover, the rigid controls he imposes upon their movement are often so neurologically impossible for the children to endure that they simply must break out into releasing activity when opportunities arise, and are sometimes forced to, even in the teacher's presence, despite inevitable punishment. Ironically, such discipline, rather than heightening the pupils' capacities for autonomous self-control, self-defeatingly increases their dependency upon external control.

2. Teacher B, because his teaching is so egocentric, so thoroughly laced with self-reference, for example, "You have made me very unhappy today. I want to be proud of you. I want you to do good work. I want our class to win the essay contest," has effectively armed his pupils with lethal ammunition against him. Analogously, think of the young mother who, when her toddler seems off his feed, begins to exhort, "Please eat your yumyum for Mummy; Mummy will love you if you eat your yumyum; Mummy wants Bubby to be big and strong." If I were the brat, having learned, as one does, to feel murderous from time to time toward members of one's family, I would promptly develop a most convenient predisposition toward fasting. While eating or not eating had no special significance for me before, I have now learned, "By not eating, I can get a terrific rise out of the old lady," and poor Mama has inadvertently armed me with that knowledge.

Living as closely together as they do, tensions are bound to arise between teachers and pupils, and means for expressing anger must be learned. It follows that the teacher who insists on the pupils' good behavior for the sake of his own comfort and pleasure—or on their academic achievement or any other form of achievement for that purpose—can blame no one but himself for the ensuing and wonderfully effective punishments he receives from the children. I am only likely to constitute a feeding problem if I have been taught that I can get some mileage from such behavior.

3. Teacher C is constantly bewildered by the unpredictability of his students' behavior. Sometimes they are little angels, and at other times they are uncanny troublemakers; and there is no knowing how they will be functioning from one hour to the next. An impartial observer is able to note that every so often an audible drone arises from the students. Keeping their expressions innocent and their lips very still, some individual sets up a nasal "hmmmmmm" which is soon

taken up by his classmates. Intrigued by this phenomenon, the observer tries to discover whether these vibrant interludes have any correspondence to some other variable(s) operating in the classroom. Unsurprisingly, he winds up with a graph on which humming is plotted against the existence of clearly defined tasks.

During the time when various pupils were reporting visits to their homes by a federal census-taker and the things that they said to fool him, there is no humming. During the moments required for the teacher to tell them which pages to read in the social studies book and for them to get their materials organized, the humming is audible. Once the pupils have begun to read, the room is temporarily silent. As some of the children discover that the text is dull or incomprehensible and turn away from it, and as others finish the assignment, a marvelous crescendo of rumbling fills the hall. Knowing he is beaten, the teacher pretends to be deaf. By the end of the morning, the observer's graphs tell a story: when the pupils were busy at something (even though they might not have had good reasons of their own for doing the work), they were quiet and behaved well. When the pupils had nothing to do, they hummed and behaved badly. Confronted by this evidence, the teacher was politely amazed. Deep down, he still believed that the pupils were simply capricious in their behavior. But rationality triumphed sufficiently for him to give the observer's hypothesis some credence and to endeavor, the next day, *to keep all of the pupils busy all of the time.* Because he was relatively untutored in logistics, his attempt was not wholly successful, although it was clear to everyone that an unusual degree of busywork had been imposed. On this day, the children sat studiously at their desks, eyes focused on their workbooks, expressions of intense concentration on their faces. There was no humming whatsoever. They tapped their feet.

4. Teacher D unconsciously persecutes several children and is heard to remark that a strong tendency toward scapegoating exists among his pupils. If, by his own unpremeditated acts, the teacher creates conditions that foster poor discipline, it is also forlornly true that his own undisciplined and unanalyzed behavior sometimes interferes with the pupils' productive thinking and sometimes makes such thinking impossible. His wise and thoughtfully conceived strategies are frequently eclipsed or canceled by the incidental learnings he promotes.

RITUALISM AND THE ABSENCE OF REASONS

Let us turn, now, to the problem of "reasons." I have tried to develop testimony for my contention that explicit reasons for doing what one must are rarely present in classroom teaching, and the concept of incidental learning as a basis for estimating the conse-

quences of that fact. It is almost never true that the pupils determine
what they are to learn or rationales for learning what they choose. It is
extremely rare to hear a teacher pose the question, "Having done the
work we have done, what do you suppose it would be useful to do
next?" and then, "What reasons can you offer for your proposals?"
Think of the difficulties that might follow: the students are likely to
choose a topic about which the teacher has no authoritative knowledge,
to raise questions for which he has no answers. Not all of the pupils
may want to do the same thing. Problems might be proposed that are
supposed to be treated at some other, more advanced grade level: "I'm
sorry, Butchy. This is fourth grade and that's a fifth-grade question."
Appropriate "resource materials" might not be immediately available.
The students might answer, "Nothing!" Having not been asked to
enunciate reasons previously, the pupils might want to but be unable to
do so fluently.

If teaching in which the pupils decide *what* to study and the
reasons for studying is difficult and risky, the risk is somewhat less
when the teacher determines what is to be studied but waits until the
children have formulated reasons before beginning the work. "Having
studied sea life, we will now turn to life along the shore. What good
reasons can you imagine for doing that?" In this situation, the student is
stuck with the topic whether it seems reasonable to him or not, but at
least some time has been provided for him to find reasons and to
sample his classmates'. Rather than jumping headlong into "Creatures
of the Shore" simply because the bell rang, he can maintain at least
some illusion of autonomy or dignity by being able to tell himself and
other people why he is performing the tasks at hand in more hopeful
terms than "because it's the next chapter in the book."

Next lowest, in this hierarchy of reasoned beginnings, is the practice in which the teacher decides what is to be studied next, the
relevant justifications, and has the decency to let the kids in on *his*
reasons: "We will now read *Oklahoma* because it represents an important turning point in musical theater." At least there is a "because,"
but, of course, the students may not feel as persuaded by his reason as
the teacher does—or, even worse, they may be persuaded simply
because it is *his* reason—and some of them may not have been paying
close attention when he offered it.

As we recall from our own experiences, the most unreasonable
and arbitrary way to begin a unit of study is also the most prevalent:
"We will now study the life cycle of the European wrasse. Open your
books to Chapter 80."

In all but the first of these approaches, there is some chance that
even if the student proceeds, having possession of explicit reasons, his
reasons will be logical or academic but not personal. As a student, I
could see perfectly well why it might make sense to study simple

machines before trying to understand complex ones. But I might, in any event, simply not give a hang, at least for the time being. I might be satisfied to stop at the concept that my teacher is a wedge, having learned that "the wedge is the simplest tool known to mankind."

Given a chance, as in the first case, to generate my own curriculum based upon my own cogent reasons, I might still do so without having invested much libido in the process. But at least I will have been given a chance to avoid precipitous decisions; a chance to wait until some feeling of conviction arises in me before I must commit myself; a chance to withhold my commitment until, having examined myself and the surrounding possibilities quite closely, I have developed some explicit understanding of how it might serve my best interests to do anything in particular—in short, of what's in it for me.

Unless I am very unusual and have strong capacities for bucking the system, my teacher will have to help me to function in this framework of personal reference. He will have to teach me to be able to trust it, and he will have to teach me new ways of understanding the environment in reference to my personal requirements. I will have to learn how to determine what I need and then how to formulate suitable problems. To judge a problem's suitability and wieldiness, I will need to know certain things about my own intellectual behavior, my own mental powers and limitations, and I will have to be able to understand the environment in relevant terms, in relation to which environmental factors *are* relevant to my problem and, among them, which represent obstacles to my inquiry and which represent potential resources. In other words, knowing pertinent information about myself, I will have to be able to assess reality in relation to whether or not it will permit me to get something that I care about.

Having framed the problem, I will have to learn how to develop strategies for solving it, how to implement my strategies operationally, and how to know when I am done. If I am really lucky, my teacher will be bright and unhurried enough and will care enough about *me* to help me through a retrospective examination of my intuitions and reasons; an assessment, in that connection, of where to go next; and an analysis of the appropriateness and efficiency of my behavior, vis à vis my prior intentions. He will try to facilitate pragmatic learning about my own cognitive behavior as well as of techniques, for example, for avoiding construction of parallel fifths in a figured bass exercise. In the end, I should be more of myself instead of simply being filled with more useless nonsense.

In either event, that is, either if my reasons are relatively superficial and unspecific or if they have been carefully and systematically composed, *my* intuitions and *my* reasons will have counted for something; my initiative in the process will probably make me feel more invested in it than I would under orders; and, win or lose, I will at least have been chasing something that mattered to me, so that if at any point in the process someone were to ask, "Why are you doing this?" I would not have to feel like a fool or a lackey by answering, "I don't know" or "Because I was told to."

But experience suggests that none of these good things are likely to happen regularly or intentionally. Still, as the student, I am not likely to be very lucky in this regard. My teacher, first of all, will almost certainly not have been very well educated in this professional orientation. He will, typically, see himself as the person who knows and who is supposed to know, and me, as a person (or person-to-be) who does not know and who must, perhaps in spite of himself, be made to know. For one must know things, especially the school's things, in order to be a GOOD CITIZEN, and it is the teacher's job to TRANSMIT THE CULTURE to me so that my MAXIMUM POTENTIALITIES can be fulfilled so that I can take my PLACE IN SOCIETY just as he has.

Any interested observer can confirm that many teachers view themselves as occupying a position somewhere directly between the learner and the knowledge. Their principal function, as it seems, is to mediate the knowledge for the learner: to transmit it, to program it, to interpret it, to simplify it, that is, to "teach" it. Only the rare teacher regularly steps aside to let the pupil come to grips directly with knowledge rather than with his representations of it. And from this view and this behavior certain serious consequences follow.

First of all, it follows that the teacher must have mastery over the substantive content for which he is responsible. If his job is to teach the stuff, then, certainly, he must know his stuff. Our earlier observations on contemporary knowledge suggest, however, how virtually impossible it is for the teacher to be such a master. If the teacher were really a master of some discipline, in all probability he would not be a teacher. By the values of our culture, he would be worth too much. If the teacher cannot be, or is unlikely to be, a master of broad or special knowledge, then of what does his mastery consist? Perforce, it consists of mastery over the material to be taught at the level at which it is taught. The third-grade teacher, consequently, if he is any kind of master at all, is bound to be a master of third-grade knowledge; the seventh-grade teacher knows secondary school science; the tenth-grade civics teacher knows tenth-grade civics but not, necessarily, grownup political science, sociology, economics, or law.

If what the teacher has mastered is the curriculum to be taught, then what has he mastered indeed? Our observations on the curriculum suggest that, in large measure, he has mastered various caricatures of knowledge, make-believe disciplines consisting of fictitious and distorted facts, conscienceless omissions, archaic puritanical values, and other intellectual junk.

The teacher is clearly in a bind. On the one hand, he must maintain an authoritative posture. He must seem to be a repository of knowledge. That is why lecturing represents the safest form of instruction. If, as the teacher, I have decided in advance exactly what I am going to say, and if I have precluded all possibilities that my students will distract me or will ask questions that I cannot answer, my position is as secure as it can be. On the other hand, however, if what my knowledge comprehends, for the most part, is incomplete, unauthentic, and distorted; if, in other words, my expertise is in essentially superficial knowledge, then, while I may not dare risk exposure, I may neither maintain a position of authority because to do so betrays my students. I become a pretender, a posturer, or a propagandist, but in no worthy or legitimate sense am I a teacher.

One finds, too often, that this dilemma is "resolved" by holding on, very tightly to an authoritative demeanor and, less often, by teachers who are relatively unafraid, by casting themselves as students of knowledge and accepting the vulnerabilities of that position. If, in fact, teachers are more often *poseurs* than scholars, then it is certainly a fact that the students, the parents, the administration, the teacher educators, the curriculums, the professional organizations, and the general expectations of the culture reinforce the condition of "knowing" and do not tend to reinforce anything less than that. For the teacher to be perceived as an avid learner is not only insufficient but is, additionally, likely to prove threatening to other teachers who think of themselves as a consummate intelligentsia. All's right with the world when the teacher knows his stuff. If he seems not to know his stuff, then everyone, particularly the students, feels scared.

In order to fulfill his authoritative role (and to play it safe), the teacher must generally conspire to move the pupils through the content rapidly (if the students are in a hurry because they have to get the stuff done, then there is no time for their questions); in large groups (if there are too many students, then lecturing is the most efficient method, and uniform, rather than individualized, goals are mandatory); in accordance with directions, questions, sequences of study, and evaluation criteria that he has formulated (who else?); and in a manner in which the child is expected or compelled to take it for granted that reasons exist somewhere for him to be doing what he is doing, even though he might not be bright enough to recognize them. Above all, explicit reasons must be avoided. There is no time for them, no reason for them, no value in them and, indeed, the question of "reasons"— particularly of "reasons why"—threatens to undermine the system's very foundations. The professional fabric could be torn by them.

In any event, teaching has found successful substitutes for reasons. They are generally called "rationales" and they can be found in the opening section of almost any teacher's manual. From time to time, educators are obsessed about them in two-day workshops and at professional conventions. By and large, educational rationales are used to justify rather than to generate professional practices; they are almost always composed retroactively in order to rationalize curricular and methodological inventions and, among professional ranks, are often grouped together under denominations intended to seem esoteric and dignified as, for example, "learning theory."

Authoritative teaching and the content curriculum, to which it is handmaiden, result in certain advantages to the scholastic status quo, namely, the reduction of students to a condition of docility, dependency, and ignorance; that is, a condition in which they are nonthreatening. In such a system, the teacher is invariably king of the mountain; because the subject matter, the questions, the answers, the books, and the tests are his, and because the students are really in class by his sufferance, the teacher exists in a universe that is almost perfectly free, internally, from competition or attack. Teacher training institutions in the common tradition might, more honestly, advertise programs in how to get away with being a teacher than programs in elementary education, special education, early childhood education, and the like.

If the LIFE OF A DEMOCRACY depends upon an ENLIGHTENED CITIZENRY, it is also true that the teacher's power demands constant vigilance to protect it. He must be quick to extinguish expressions of nonconformity because the pupils are likely to learn incidentally that if the school is too weak to suppress peculiar haircuts or dress styles, it might also be too weak to ward off deviational ideas or original questions. Taking the church as their model, it would seem, schoolmen know that ritualism is one of the institution's most powerful means for insuring conformity and obeisance, both of which are required for institutional stability and duration. One might isolate, as the school's crowning achievement, its almost absolute success in making so many people accept so much on faith, the parents and teachers no less than the learners. Collectively, the rituals of school life combine to form a penumbral mystique. The school's mystique is largely what makes it such a peculiar place: so distinct from a world in which sensible causes and effects are so relatively easy to discern. Consider these examples of common scholastic rituals. As *a student*:

I must do certain assignments in ink, others in pencil.
I must regularly participate in various patriotic litanies, for
example " . . . for Richard stands, one naked individual . . ."
I must stand whenever I recite, even though neither visibility
nor audibility is a relevant factor.
I must raise my hand.
When bells ring, I must stop what I am doing and what I am
thinking and go to other places.

I must add, subtract, and multiply from right to left but must divide from left to right.

I must follow lines and arrows painted on the floors when going through the halls, even when I am the only student in the hall.

I must go up certain stairs and down others.

I must participate in ceremonies, for example, the annual maypole dance and planting a tree on Arbor Day (both fertility rites).

I must memorize poems.

I must bring notes from home if I need anything or want anything that is different from what the others generally need.

I must wear a tie to assemblies and must attend assemblies regularly, even though they are hateful and boring.

I must do homework.

I must do homework that no one ever examines, for reasons I do not comprehend.

I must copy information from encyclopedias for reports, instead of reading such information directly from the encyclopedia.

Although I have nothing to do during large chunks of class time, I am not allowed to do my homework during that time.

I must prove my points by citing evidence (that is, by quoting authorities), even though the teacher never does.

I must relieve my thirst and my bladder when everyone else does, at certain specified times.

I must spend years practicing handwriting, even though I can type.

I must study what I am told to study, whether or not that represents something I would like to study.

I must participate in air raid drills that everyone knows are absolutely worthless.

I must cover my books, and I am not allowed to write in them.

I must endure sarcasm, punishments and humiliations from the teacher but must never reciprocate in kind.

I must always be ready to account for my behavior to the teacher, but am not allowed to ask the teacher to account for his behavior.

I must often express myself in terms the teacher prefers rather than in terms that come more naturally to me, that could serve just as well, and that I prefer.

I am not allowed to smoke in the building even though the teachers smoke in the building.

I am required to participate in various forms of school and class government (DEMOCRACY), but everyone recognizes that the only decisions that will stand are those approved by the teacher.

I must prepare seasonal decorations for the classroom.

If I am young enough, at Easter time my teacher makes me

(and the others) put on a foolish, flowered, paper bonnet that I
(we) have made and parade through all of the other classrooms
while the older children laugh at me (us).

I may not talk during lunch.

I may not talk on the bus.

I may not talk in the halls.

I may not talk on the playground.

I may not talk in class.

I may not talk in the lavatory.

I may not talk when anyone else is talking.

I may not talk when no one else is talking.

I may not wear my shirt out.

I may not talk in gym.

I may not talk in the locker room.

I may not talk in the auditorium.

I may not chew gum.

I may not pass notes.

I may not sit next to my friend.

Periodically, I am asked to write down whom I like best among
my classmates, but nothing ever happens as a result.

I must regularly read aloud from reading books.

I must participate in classroom games, for example, in spelling
bees.

I must study for tests.

I must be examined.

I must be graded.

I must be punctual and must not be absent.

If I finish my work before the others do, I am rewarded by
having to do more work.

If I am bad, I must do extra work for punishment.

If I displease the teacher in some manner, I must remain in
school for extra time as punishment.

If I do something well (in the teacher's terms), I am likely not
to hear about it or to be rewarded by some entirely unrelated
device.

If I do something badly (in the teacher's terms), I am likely to
hear about it and to be punished in some entirely unrelated
manner.

The teacher asks if there are any questions but goes on before I
have time to think of any questions.

Sometimes I am encouraged to ask questions, but at other times
I am punished for asking questions.

Sometimes the teacher praises me when I report someone else's
misbehavior.

Sometimes the teacher accuses me of being a tattletale when I report someone else's misbehavior.

I am taught to value freedom, but have little opportunity to experience it.

I am arbitrarily assigned readings about democracy.

I am evaluated in cryptic symbols like "A's" and "85's" and am thought rude if I ask what they mean.

I am supposed to learn that "mankind are brothers," but I attend an urban school in which all the other pupils and the teachers and the principal are white like me.

My point is that Ritualism is a *sine qua non* of the school and explicitly or not, everyone expects it to be. As a pupil, most of what I do there—most of the rules, the questions, the assignments, the cere-monies, the practices, the observances, the methods, the evaluations, the logistics, the grouping, the grading, the sequences, the pacing, the timing, and just about everything else—is mysterious to me. For the most part, I do not know why I do what I do; no one seems to care if I know; people rarely bother to explain such things to me; and my questions are generally resented or precipitantly dismissed. I must not ask, "Why should I?" or "So what?" As an educator, I am alarmed by the probability that having spent twelve or sixteen or nineteen years of my life in such irrationality, I will have become pretty cuckoo in the process, as inmates of concentration camps sometimes do as a result of the insane existence imposed upon them. In a moment I will explain my view of our dementia, but first here are two anecdotes for your entertainment. The first is true, the second apocryphal; both are tragic.

1. The particular catechism that I was taught for doing subtraction went, "Three and what are eight? Three and five are eight." Being in the Bronx, the language of my classmates and teachers had heavy New York inflections and was often hard to understand, even for us native New Yorkers. I don't know about the others, but what I learned was that a certain word must be spoken when one does subtraction. One comes upon the example; one says the word; and then one records the answer. I learned to perform the rite: "Three enwah eight? Three and five are eight. Put down the five." "Schmiggy" would have done just as well for me as "enwah."

2. TEACHER: [Producing a large mercury barometer.] Johnny, your science test consists of just one question. If you can answer this question correctly, you will pass science, and I will be able to promote you to seventh grade. The question is, How would you use this barometer to measure the height of the Empire State Building?

JOHNNY: [After a moment's thought.] I would take the barometer to the roof of the Empire State Building and would have a friend with a stopwatch stand on the sidewalk beneath me. At a given signal, I would drop the barometer; he would hit the stopwatch; and he would stop the watch the instant the barometer struck the ground. Because I know how fast freely falling bodies travel, I could calculate the height of the building from the recorded time.

TEACHER: [Showing some exasperation.] That's not the right answer, Johnny. Please concentrate because this is important. How could you use this *barometer* to measure the height of the Empire State Building?

JOHNNY: [After several moments' thought.] I know. I would take this barometer to the roof of the Empire State Building. I would then lower it slowly over the side on the end of a rope. When it touched the ground, I would mark the rope, reel it back in, and then measure the amount of rope that had been used.

TEACHER: I'm warning you! You are wrong again and I don't like your tone at all. Now stop trying to tease me. This is absolutely your last chance to tell me how to use this barometer—*barometer,* Johnny, to measure the height.

JOHNNY: [After a full, tortured minute of concentration, a look of peace lights his face.] Now I know! I would take the barometer to the basement of the Empire State Building. I would find the janitor. And I would say to him, "Mister—you tell me how high this damn building is, and I'll give you a barometer!"

Other aspects of the school are strange and puzzling. The teachers expect me (the child) to become something good for which they give me almost no practice and no reinforcement while they've got me. They make various wild assumptions, for example, that mathematics will DISCIPLINE MY MIND, that for me to analyze beautiful objects will enhance my capacity for experiencing beauty, that for me to study rules of honesty will make me honest, that for me to be controlled will build my self-control, and that for me to be told about freedom will make me free. They champion an indirect approach and hope that learning about geometrical equalities will teach me, implicitly, about human equalities; that THE SCIENTIFIC METHOD will make my mind logical; and they believe that my acquisition of a foreign language involves a precise recapitulation of the mental processes by which I learned my first language.

In the new school, I am placed in HOMOGENEOUS GROUPS whose homogeneity is *invisible to me*—except that I read with the other Bluebirds—and *worthless to them* because it is, first of all, determined in reference to such a small number of variables that my idiosyncracies are never overshadowed and, last of all, because those variables are fictions that have so little to do with me. How foolish it is to suppose that my achievement test score in arithmetic tells anything of consequence about the character of the mathematical operations I perform!

I am placed in large groups and small groups and grades or nongrades—except that everyone in the nongraded school knows what grade he is really in—and I am instructed by teaching teams (in my frame of reference this generally seems like nothing different from old-fashioned departmentalization), in study carrels, and through the media of closed-circuit television and teaching machines which, generally, offer me the same awful curriculums that Teacher used to but even less responsively than Teacher did. In certain experimental situations I am taught inductively or "nondirectively," which means that instead of telling me the answer, the teacher teases me with various cues until I can guess his answer, or he tells me, "Figure it out for yourself."

Perhaps I attend a *really* modern school that offers guidance services. If so, the benefit provided is that if my sullen withdrawal, my chronic absenteeism or my ACTING-OUT, ATTENTION-GETTING BEHAVIOR begins to affect the teacher's equanimity, he can REFER me to the counselor and, by that action, both satisfy his conscience, that is, his sense of responsibility to me, and wash his hands of me at the same time. The counselor, whose service deprives me of one study hall each week (no loss), seems compelled to reassure me that it is really OK to masturbate.

I suspect that part of the blame for the pupils' being "had" so badly by the schools can be attributed to two tendencies that commonly operate together among schoolmen. The first is their commitment to orthodoxies. The second is their habit of elevating single, isolated concepts to the status of "principles," which then become slogans. I suspect that schoolmen are no different from other people in this respect or in most other respects. The trouble is that when schoolmen, in their professional capacities, behave as stupidly as other people do, the consequences of their behavior have special significance, namely, in the education of students. Perhaps this is the sense in which the teacher TRANSMITS THE CULTURE.

An example of the tendency to seize isolated concepts for defense of professional practices is represented by the fact that invariably, in the graduate courses I teach on curriculum and supervision, some student (who is a teacher) will ask, "But isn't it true that by age three the human personality is pretty much as it will always be and that, for that reason, the school is neither as harmful nor as helpful a place as you make it out to be?"

Bless Papa Freud for his emancipation of the human spirit from

Victorian repression and for having given us all so much to laugh
about. But curse him for the concept of psychic determinism and the
sins it has been used to justify by educators. Just as poor Einstein gave
us the bomb, poor Freud gave us the finished three-year-old, which
proves how foolish wisdom can be. Such distortions demonstrate, in any
event, how foolish educators can be.

Their commitment to orthodoxies—again, this is not exclusively
the educators' problem—is well documented by the metaphorical pen-
dulum that is known to thrash back and forth through educational
theory. The most familiar contemporary example of how an orthodoxy
was formed and of the chaos it produced exists in the educators'
adoption of John Dewey's thinking and of the travesties of PROGRES-
SIVE EDUCATION that followed. The pattern is for a fervent commitment to a body of theory to arise, for simple elements of the theory
(that seem to make some sense) to be isolated, and for practices to be
innovated around such elements which inevitably bear no sensible
relationship to the parent theory. To popularize and to cheapen the
products of seminal minds is an old story indeed:

   Dewey, as we have seen, was sold out by the *educators*.

   Freud was a giant, but the extravagant devotion by some *Freudi-
ans* to psychoanalysis borders on fetishism.

   Carl Rogers brought genius and optimism to counseling psychology, but orthodox *Rogerians* are often misguided gamesters.

   Marx revolutionized social theory, but *Marxists* are generally beyond
the fringe.

And, of course,

   Christ was divine . . .

   Let's look at "evaluation."

EVALUATION AND TESTING

Perhaps the strangest of all school rites are those associated with
testing and evaluating the pupils. Reason suggests that the most sensible way in which a teacher can begin to plan for the next sequence of
instruction is by referring to what was accomplished and what failed to
be accomplished in the present sequence. In more simple terms, in
order to decide rationally what to teach tomorrow, it would be convenient to know what the pupils have learned by today. As a teacher, I
should also know other, more complex things about how my pupils
learn, but let's deal with a comparatively simple problem at present.

In practice, there is commonly little or no attempt made to use
today's level of accomplishment as a basis for planning tomorrow's
work. Incidentally, it is also true that, by and large, teachers do not
bother to develop logical transitions from one unit of study to the next,
especially across subject areas. When they do, it is generally in refer-

ence to some contrived theme as, for example, "Technological De-velopment," rather than in connection to personal principles of inte-gration, such as the pupils' varied individual reasons and their con-scious needs. A related phenomenon is that teachers tend to go ahead and teach whether they are prepared to do so or not. For reasons that are entirely mysterious to me, teachers apparently believe that it would be unprofessional or somehow damaging to let the children read comic books or just talk to one another for a few hours, but that it is not so bad to instruct them even when, for perfectly legitimate reasons, the teacher was simply unable to plan the instruction. There is a funny duplicity: it's OK for the teacher to teach even when he is not ready to teach, but it is not all right for the pupils to learn what they will by themselves. In any event, the teacher's plans are generally a ritual affair consisting of brief, cryptic notes written in small boxes for the benefit of the principal, should he happen to drop in.

Returning to the point, one must ask why, when today's level of achievement seems like such a sensible point of departure for tomor-row's study, this relationship is so frequently absent from the teaching strategy. I have several hunches and some pertinent observations. One hunch is that many teachers tend to conceptualize forward motion in reference to the content curriculum rather than in relation to the students. By this reasoning, the time to move on to *H* is when we have finished covering *G*, and what the pupils are like makes hardly any difference at all. "My job is to cover the material and their job is to keep up." A more compelling hunch is that even though they fool themselves some of the time, teachers are aware of how lacking they are in evaluation strategies, techniques, and constructs. What is the actual situation like?

1. "Evaluation = tests" is a popular professional notion.
2. "Tests" generally means formal achievement tests, chapter tests, unit tests, and other standardized examinations. The more highly regimented and ritualistic the instrument is, the more of a test it is:
"When I say 'Begin,' pick up your pencils and open your test booklet to page two. Fold your booklet so that only one page at a time shows. . . ."
Machine-scored tests are the best tests (they are bound to be impartial), and, for the rest, homemade tests are called "quizzes," which are something different.
3. Formal tests are administered at the end of things rather than while things are going on. This practice is especially peculiar because it is clearly impossible to use such tests (supposing that they do actually test something significant) for planning the pupils' future work if the work in question has already been brought to a close.

4. Quizzes are sometimes invented by the teacher and sometimes provided by the publishers. They are generally administered during a unit of work rather than after it has been terminated. Most of the time they consist of questions invented by the teacher; they are scored by a point system invented by the teacher; and the scores are translated into letter grades by some arbitrary system devised by the teacher.

5. On some tests, PARTIAL CREDIT is given for partially correct answers as, for example, when the substantive response is very sophisticated but spelled incorrectly (photosinthisis).

6. Some tests are CLOSED BOOK, that is, tests of memory; some are OPEN BOOK BUT NO NOTES; some are ANYTHING GOES EXCEPT TALKING WITH YOUR NEIGHBOR; some are to be done in class; some are TAKE-HOME EXAMINATIONS; some are timed; others are not timed; some are accompanied by PRETESTS which provide some opportunity for rehearsal; some are self-corrected; some are corrected by other students; some are teacher-, reader-, or machine-corrected; some are SHORT ANSWER OBJECTIVE or MULTIPLE CHOICE (*E*: None of the above); some are ESSAY EXAMINATIONS; some are DIAGNOSTIC TESTS, while others are REVIEW TESTS; some tests are given for disciplinary purposes:

"All right! If that's how you're going to behave, clear your desks; we're going to have a spelling test."

And many tests, perhaps a majority of them, are discarded after a period of time without ever having been scored at all.

7. Equally varied are the practices of reporting test results back to the students. Numerical scores are very popular, although letter grades still offer stiff competition in the field. The two most prevalent practices, especially in connection to quizzes, are either (*a*) for papers to be returned with checks, crosses, and letter grades added in red pencil, or (*b*) with incorrect items marked wrong and some number of points subtracted from a total number of points (usually ten or one hundred) to derive a numerical score, also indicated in red pencil.

Sometimes, but not often, the students are shown how well they did in relation to their fellow students. The most common technique is to ask:

"How many got one wrong, raise your hands? (Pause.) How many got two wrong? Three? Four? Ten? More than ten?" so that each student can see just where he stands. Almost universally, the emphasis is placed on how many wrong instead of how many right. In any event, "right or wrong" is of paramount importance, not "how," which is so much more difficult to think about.

One ingenious practice is for the teacher to distribute ungraded tests to the pupils so that no one gets his own paper. Either the teacher or selected pupils then recite the correct answers, and the tests are pupil-scored accordingly. Grades are called out so that the teacher can record them. Papers are returned to their owners, and sometimes an opportunity is given for the pupils to clarify items they still do not understand or to complain about their neighbors' scoring (the accuracy of which depends on whether the specific neighbor in question is friend or foe). What is ingenious about this practice is that, simultaneously, it gets the job done; it consumes an entire period; it provides a chance for each pupil to see whether his answers agree with everyone else's; and, best of all, it spares Teacher the trouble of having to examine the pupils' work directly.

One interesting side effect is that because the same people tend generally to do well or to fail, the former group of children are able to learn time and again how smart they are while children in the latter group are deservingly humiliated to punish their ignorance. While the dumb kids have simply to adjust to the realities of being stupid, the smart kids are sometimes confused because they no longer seem so smart when they transfer to other schools or go on to other teachers. This phenomenon, of a FAST LEARNER doing poorly on examinations, is variously referred to as a LEARNING PLATEAU, UNDERACHIEVEMENT, or TEST-PHOBIA, depending upon the time and place. Although SLOW LEARNERS occasionally surprise everyone by doing well on tests, it is generally known that such occurrences are flukes. But it doesn't really matter anyway because, even though they may make individual progress, SLOW LEARNERS do not perform as well as FAST LEARNERS, which is what really counts. Fortunately, they tend to compensate for their academic disabilities by demonstrating athletic prowess and having neat appearances. HARD-CORE SLOW LEARNERS don't even do that.

If these observations seem confused and bizarre, that is because I am frankly confused by what I see going on every day in the name of TESTING and PUPIL-EVALUATION. It is truly a Thurber carnival, but with the dogs missing. We should not bother, here, with a discourse on "Tests and Measurements" because abundant information about problems of validity, reliability, sampling, halo effects, and skewing can be found in the appropriate literature. But, short of a gratuitous lecture, I feel that I must provide some representation of problems in this area because of how consequential they are in the *students' lives.* I am only interested in the question of evaluation as it exists or is likely to exist in the students' experience because I suspect that this is the context of school experience in which, especially, most of them are driven to despair.

What seems worst of all is how little apparent correspondence there must be, in the child's frame of reference, between what he knows and what he can and cannot do, and the tests he is given and the grades he receives. Even more stunning is to see that, although, as a student, how well I do on tests is likely to have some effect on how much the teacher *likes* me, there is usually no palpable relationship between my test performance and the work I am assigned subsequently. After the test is over, no matter what, the teacher continues to have everybody do the same thing at the same time, either the entire class or the subgroup to which I belong.

Sometimes there is a discernible relationship between my test results and my subsequent assignments: if I have done very, very poorly, the teacher makes me do a great deal more of the same thing to teach me how to do it. The trouble, however, is that, being unable to do it in the first place, I am still disabled; and the assignment tends to demoralize me. If I have done very, very well, I am again required to do a great deal more of the same thing, this time because the teacher has to freeze my level of performance until the others catch up to me. It is no trouble for me to do more of the same thing (Rows *B* through *W*), but it does get terribly boring. As you might guess, the strategy Teacher uses to get the rest of the pupils to catch up to me is to have them do a great deal more of the same thing until they have learned it. What generally interrupts this sequence of INDIVIDUALIZED INSTRUCTION—"individualized," in that the reasons for the successful, the average, and the unsuccessful testees to do a great deal more of the same thing are different in each case—is that the teacher feels he has run out of time and must get on to the next unit of work. *"Ready or not, here I come!"*

It is also forlornly true that if I feel I have not learned anything, the test simply serves to remind me of that and to make me feel even less adequate. [The PROGRAMED TEXT tells me: Go back to Page 1, Stupid; do not collect two hundred dollars.] If I feel that I *have* learned something, however, and have even enjoyed doing the work in question, it is particularly frustrating to discover that for one reason or another the test questions do not correspond very well to what I know but manage to skirt my knowledge and to fasten on details that I have not troubled to remember. Although sometimes I protest, "Unfair! Unfair!" and accuse the teacher of playing dirty pool ("That question was just to trick you"), I am more inclined, after many such experiences, to conclude that I was mistaken in my own assessment of the situation and that I did not really learn the important material. After all, that's what the tests show. As time goes by I deliberately restrain the frivolous abandon with which I formerly allowed myself to enjoy learning certain things that seemed useful to me, then concentrate on calculating what is most certain to appear on future tests, and then on guessing responses that are more likely to succeed.

Never, in my entire school career, am I likely to be made privy to the secrets of what A's and F's mean or of how they are determined. All that I know is that A's are very important and that, somehow or other, I must manage to get them. While bribery is unlikely to work, cheating can become a fine art and a welcome test of my ingenuity.

Since homogenization is such common practice these days, I am likely to attend a school that assigns pupils to levels, groups, tracks, tracts, or placements—these are all euphemisms for "prisons"—and if I should be placed in a middle or slow track (on the basis of DIAGNOS-TIC TESTING), special difficulties will follow. What happens is that, although, by some miracle, I may achieve substantial progress in relation to the level at which I was performing a year ago, that progress will not be reflected by A's on my report card. It can't be, because A's are reserved for pupils in the fast track. How could the principal ever account to the parents for the fact that children in slow tracks made A's? Everyone knows that it is unfair to give me an A that does not reflect the same level of objective excellence as the A assigned to my brighter counterpart, because in the outside world of colleges and employment agencies those A's would look the same and that would be an injustice. So, no matter how hard I try and no matter how successfully I advance myself, my individual progress cannot be rewarded by good grades as long as any serious disparity exists between my work and that of the faster kids. Since they generally have better teachers, better classmates, and different curriculums, it is difficult to imagine how the gap can ever be closed. Now, whereas I must concede that I am not COLLEGE BOUND (I can't be because I am not in an ADVANCED PLACEMENT GROUP), A's are nevertheless important to me. They are important because every time I bring home a report card filled with D's, I get whipped. Although myths of homogenization are being exploded, the practice is likely to continue for many years: among other things, it's a dandy way to resegregate Negro children after they have been bussed in.

Whether I am slow or fast, it is almost inevitable that I will get to feel about tests the way I feel about visits to the dentist. But, being incapable of evaluating my own work, just as I am incapable of repairing my own teeth, I will become progressively more dependent upon the tests and the grades which are so loathsome to me but which are my keys to the future. If ever I should take my destiny into my own hands and reject the tests and the grades and refuse to be degraded by guessing and cheating and worrying and second-guessing and trying to understand what is incomprehensible, the school would throw me out. For while it has means for containing my slowness and my failures, it cannot tolerate any such show of independence: the pupil's dependency upon the school and his reduction to that dependency by its mysteries are crucial, or at least have been historically, to the school's existence.

If these conditions, which bring me to my knees, are not a reflection of some wicked conspiracy against me, they are surely expressions of what the teachers do not know about testing and evaluation and of consequences that result when, in a condition of ignorance, they do what they do anyhow. What are some common mistakes?

1. Because of the synonymy they tend to imagine between evaluation and formal testing, teachers fail generally to be sensitive to feedback constituted by the pupils' behavior from one moment to the next. If he chose to think of it that way, the teacher could deduce diagnostic meaning from the million recitations, responses, questions, and spontaneous utterances the pupils make which generate a truer and fuller representation of their intellectual condition than the tests are likely to. But, in fact, the largest part of pupils' behavior is wasted diagnostically, partly because the teacher does not think of its diagnostic potentialities, partly because he does not know a great deal about inferring cognitive behavior from overt behavior, partly because he lacks observational skills, and partly because the teacher does not trouble to record behavioral minutiae which occur randomly and in such profusion. Indeed, he does not know how to because neither his preservice training nor his current supervision (if he has any) have taught him techniques of systematic observation, of recording and organizing observational data, or of interpreting such data. It is additionally true that in many instances the teacher's instructional style ties him up in didactic information-giving more than he needs to be, with the result that he is too busy to record data. Situations in which the pupils might generate useful data are minimized because opportunities for them to be active are forfeited to Teacher's own activity.

2. The level of diagnosis at which tests are employed is usually very superficial. They provide rather gross indications of what substantive questions the pupil can and cannot answer and sometimes disclose that the pupil's inability to answer stems from a more basic inability to perform certain logical or computational operations upon which the correct answers depend. Stuck with a collection of minimal cues, rather than supplied with a diagnostic basis of any consequence, the teacher is frequently unable to proceed directly from the test information to appropriate "treatment" strategies. In other words, showing whatever it shows, the test does not generally provide clear indications of what to do next. To discover simply that a pupil does not know something he is supposed to know often does not lead anywhere in particular except to a renewed effort to teach him the stuff all over again. But since the

original teaching seems not to have taken, the likelihood that it will be effective a second or third time around is not very great. Indeed, it is hard to know whether what is being tested are competencies that reside in the learner or instructional techniques that have been used by the teacher.

When testing has been completed, the teacher still lacks a *differential diagnosis* of the pupils' mental activity and an intelligible evaluation of his own teaching behavior. And a whole spectrum of other variables is unaccounted for by the common test: motivational factors; attitudes toward the test, the subject, and the teacher; emotional interference deriving from unrelated problems; physical factors; and so on. Demonstrating as little as it does, one wonders whether the test is worth the effort in most cases.

3. Human beings tend to invent facts when facts are incomplete and to organize existing facts by fictions when "truer" organizational principles are not at hand. Tests commonly fail to reveal mental processes, and techniques for the deliberate elicitation of such processes are often not incorporated by the teacher's diagnostic repertoire. It follows from these conditions that, much of the time, teachers project their own mental processes upon the pupils. Working deductively from the students' incorrect answers, the teachers attribute errors of reasoning to them that they (the teachers) would have made had they produced the same incorrect answers. The teacher mistakenly supposes that his knowledge of the steps involved for solving some set of algorithms necessarily corresponds to the actual steps taken by individual students attempting their solution. An unfortunate consequence of this error is that Teacher becomes caught up in a set of diagnostic fictions that have little, if any, relevance to the learner's predicament. He tries to correct ostensible errors in reasoning by teaching that is gratuitous and only likely to confuse the pupil.

Such misevaluation penalizes the pupil doubly: having misconceptualized the problem initially or having employed erroneous strategies for its solution, he is likely to be thrown further adrift by remedial efforts based upon misconceptions of his difficulty. Although one might concede that by this practice the teacher at least provides what, for the pupil, is a novel perspective on the problem from which correct understanding may follow, this approach is nevertheless indirect and, for that reason, apt to be weaker than one departing from the pupil's own framework of understanding.

It is also true, incidentally, that besides failing to reflect pupils' reasoning processes, tests often do not even begin to indicate the *modes* of thought pupils have used in their problem solving. For example, in mathematics the examiner is not likely to discover whether a child's attack upon a problem incorporated an imagery of signs and words or of seemingly irrelevant haptic, auditory, or wordless visual symbols, or whether his reasoning proceeded by small increments of logic or by large intuitive leaps, by means of conventional tests. While it is perfectly possible that, being fluent only in his own modes of thought, the teacher could not readily comprehend different mental processes and that, even if he understood them, specific treatment strategies would not necessarily be indicated, it is nevertheless noteworthy that failing to touch upon the quality of thought at all, the common test does nothing to help teachers or pupils to gain insights of this kind. This outcome is particularly unfortunate for teachers, because learning impasses are often more likely to be overcome when remedial efforts are aimed at the learner than when they are focused directly at the content.

4. It occasionally appears that teachers are motivated to administer tests by their own desires for reinforcement rather than by any special diagnostic concern. The trouble here is that if students do poorly, the affront thereby constituted to the teacher is more likely to alienate him from them than to bring him rushing to their assistance. And, if they do well, although the teacher may feel rewarded—it is easy to forget that the test may just have been too simple—he is nevertheless unable to know precisely which elements of his behavior were responsible. Global reinforcement, that is, reinforcement of his total behavior, precludes differentiated reinforcement of only his technical strengths.

5. As soon as he becomes embroiled in the arithmetic of test scores, either of standardized or of homemade tests, Teacher may easily become mesmerized by the illusory objectivity of quantification. Only the rare teacher escapes the tendency to reify all those lovely numbers; to believe that they actually stand for something real. In addition to being seduced by his statistics, the teacher is often haphazard, sloppy, and mistaken in the way he handles his numbers. The points that he assigns arbitrarily to items on a test and the "weights" he distributes in that manner may positively obscure the pupils' actual knowledge by creating all sorts of unidentifiable quantitative artifacts. The fiction becomes compounded when he arbitrarily converts scores into letter grades. Perhaps it is just as well that teachers don't often use their tests as a basis for future planning. If they did, given the distortions that can result from their statistical caprice, they would probably stress elements of the curriculum that had no correspondence to what the pupils needed because their numbers told them to.

6. One example of the inequities that can result from all of this is of how the individual IQ test, which has certain virtues as tests go, has been employed to suppress various groups of students. Subverted in some cases by the school's ignorance or malevolence, this holy of holies represents the source of all power, the seat of all mystery: "You don't have to take my word for it, Mrs. Washington. *The tests show* that little Booker can't learn."

7. Besides inventing examinations in which, although they are each worth five points, individual questions are of varied complexity and difficulty for the students, instructors lurch drunkenly from PRE-TEST to POST-TEST, from QUIZ to UNIT TEST, and from one test to an "equivalent" MAKEUP TEST, when such tests, being equally whimsical in their construction, have either no substantive or cognitive continuity or uniformity and consequently generate LONGITUDINAL PROFILES of the students' learning that are positively invalid. My point is that the felony is compounded: a sequence of individually bad tests is used as the basis for determining (rationalizing) a final, composite grade.

8. The last phenomenon we should identify in this context is that one cause of the stereotypy, globalness, and subjectivity that characterize teachers' evaluations so generally, and one reason that their evaluations of their own effectiveness as instructors are so wanting in precision, is that teachers mistakenly believe that they can see things that are invisible. When Teacher says that he has *seen* that the pupils were bored, enthusiastic, depressed, confused, motivated, interested, or antagonistic, or when he reports having *seen* that the pupils developed the understandings, appreciations, attitudes, and sensitivities for which he aimed, I see behavior that shows a manifest capacity for self-deception. Is it pedantic to insist that inasmuch as these conditions cannot be seen directly but can only be inferred from visible behavior, and that because, whenever inferences are made, they can be drawn incorrectly, a distinction between observable behavioral data and the interpretations we attach to them may be crucial for the teacher to maintain? "Nit-picking," one might say.

But surprisingly, in repeated trials, we have discovered that teachers' intuitive evaluations of lessons they have taught, "That stunk!" or "That was great"; their descriptions of how well certain children achieved the lesson's goals, and the "perceptual" evidence they cite in this connection, are frequently inconsistent with pupils' self-reports and their appraisals of the lesson. Of course, the pupils don't always see straight either. But, in any event, such inconsistencies occur often enough for red flags to be raised justifiably against metaperceptions, that is, against the kind of statement that says, "I can see that they are bored with history," when it is truly impossible to *see* any such thing.

Clinical literature abounds in examples of perceptual distortions created, in effect, by the patient's tendencies to see what he wants to see or to see what he especially does not want to see, and one's own experience confirms the phenomenon. For every meliorist you know, I can find someone who sees the Devil's work everywhere.

I use the word "crucial" to describe distinctions between perceptions and inferences because of one major implication for professional practice: if I tend to believe what I "see," I will probably let it go at that, will not inquire further, and, if I have not seen right, will consequently plan my future behavior on the basis of false assumptions. If, on the other hand, I maintain some skepticism toward my perceptions, particularly those that seem most compelling ("The students hate me"), at least some of the time I can discover the truth before it is too late and adjust my behavior accordingly. Many of the teachers who perceived my interest over the years were duped: I learned early, in school, how to look interested. What incidental learnings do you think might result should the pupil discern that Teacher frequently proceeds from false premises concerning his own condition; that, for example, when Teacher tells him, "This will be easy; that will be hard; I can see you understand this," and the like, he is wrong?

I will never forget Dick Gregory's poignant anecdote relating to the occasion on which his homework assignment was rejected for being sloppy. As he reports it, the reason for his messy paper was that the previous night was a cold one, no heat was provided in his apartment building, and he consequently did his homework under the covers in a bed shared by several children in the family, including a younger sibling who urinated on Gregory's homework. Or his remark to the effect that when teachers deny their pupils' poverty by protesting that they always seem to have plenty of candy, they miss the point that candy represents the children's entire diet. My point is that, in the social context as well as in academic contexts, teachers sometimes "see" things that are not there to be seen.

One might go on at length speculating about what consequences follow from these problems for the pupils, in terms of their experiences of the school and of themselves. It is probably enough to recognize the likelihood, however, that in one form or another, each pupil will learn how little his own real, true, and precious identity is acknowledged by the school. Sad to reflect, one can hardly imagine how, being cut down so often by invalid, unnecessary, and ill-used examinations—*important* examinations—the pupil's identity can seem precious for very long. In the face of such massive opposition, what chance has one but to capitulate?

I suspect that bright children who test well probably forfeit no less than children who test badly, although there may be different pains in each case. My principal point is that rather than to help me, the pupil, to know what I am, the tests positively interfere with my acquisition of such knowledge much of the time; instead of helping me to accept myself, the tests and the practices that surround them tend to diminish me or, at least, to make me feel diminished. If I am not aware of the predicaments that the school's evaluations create for me, more the pity, for what I don't know can hurt me and, under such circumstances, already has.

I have repeatedly stressed the school's role in reducing pupils to a dependent state, largely through ritualistic practices, and its overriding mystique, and I have pointed particularly to the offensive aspects of testing in this connection. I should stipulate one qualification before bringing this diatribe to an end—that, in itself, childhood dependency is completely natural, that prolonged dependency is quintessentially human and constitutes a basis and a requirement for the advanced development of human intellect, and that under proper conditions the care and feeding of dependent children by the school might be generally productive. If what the child brings to the problem of learning is his dependency, what the school might bring to his dependency is a set of responses that are conducive to productive learning. But the school frequently doesn't.

What one observes suggests that the school values the pupils' dependencies and fosters their continued dependency in its own insidious ways, *not* to enhance their learning by appropriate responsive behavior, but rather to insure their complacency by keeping them infantile (no less the university). For dependency to result in productive learning or in learning that is fun, it must be accompanied by trust. If the child's trust is not inspired, he will tend not to be receptive or inquisitive; that is, he will do his darndest to be self-sufficient and independent because, lacking trust, all his dependency is likely to get him is punishment. If the school sustains dependency, what it betrays is the pupils' trust. One example of this fairly simpleminded formulation is represented by the premature self-sufficiency of slum children, by their characteristic mistrust of the school, and by their characteristic failure to learn very much that's worthwhile from it. How the school regularly betrays such children is a very open secret. In the most unfortunate situations:

> The slum child can't trust the school to protect him, because it doesn't—neither from the violence that surrounds him nor from its own violence. In fact, he needs protection from it.
> The slum child can't trust the school to provide love or sympathy or kindness. Many of his teachers don't like him, resent having to teach him, think of him as some kind of obscenity, and consistently reject his overtures (if he makes any) and punish him.
> The slum child can't trust the school to treat him fairly. Oversized groups make group punishment necessary; some pupils must be made into examples; sheer force of numbers forces the teacher to struggle for simple survival; and since he (the teacher) is often dealt with unfairly, it seems only reasonable to pass that on to the pupils who are the cause of it all.

The slum child can't trust the school to be honest with him. He is constantly lied to by teachers, by curriculums that are false, and by tests that are fictitious.

The slum child can't trust the school to give him useful information or to help him get along. The information it provides is not useful, and no one seems to care whether he gets along.

The slum child can't trust the school to help him to understand things better. The teacher would rather he did not understand many things.

The slum child can't trust the school to listen to him, to hear him, because nobody in the school cares to hear or has time to listen or can understand the way he talks anyhow.

If you were to point out that things are not always like this, I would have to concede the point. I would, however, have to point out, in turn, that things are frequently like this and that sometimes one fails to notice even though it is like this right under one's nose.

The treachery involved is that while the school contrives to foster the children's dependency, having gotten them that way or having kept them that way, it rarely keeps its half of the bargain by being decent to them. And this way of life is so dismally self-defeating because, having been invited to trust the school and having, subsequently, been kicked in the teeth, the pupil is unlikely to keep loving the school *ad infinitum*, no matter how stupid or masochistic he is. Again, although the accoutrements may differ, the suburban schoolchild's trust is just as badly abused and his ultimate disenchantment almost as inevitable. Even when the school does not treat me or my parents like dumb niggers—I know of one Negro parent who used exactly these words to describe his treatment by a principal and teachers, and I have witnessed many instances of the kind of behavior to which he was referring—at best it treats me like a fool and expects me to keep coming back for more. I have deliberately used anthropomorphic references to the school to keep the fact clearly in focus, that the school is its people; it has human as well as corporate identities.

OUR SCHOLASTIC LEGACY

Here is a partial accounting of the ways in which we are incomplete, less than sane, partly crazy. These are my impressions of what we have inherited largely from our schooling, of what outcomes our incidental learnings have produced, and of what it has cost us to have lived so much in an environment without reasons. Whether the schools are irrational because people tend to be or whether people are driven berserk by the schools is moot and, in certain respects, irrelevant. Both conditions are true, but the second one provides a professional focus for us.

We accept an absence of reasons as a normal condition, particularly in scholastic situations. We very rarely ask why, and generally do not expect to be told why, we should do what we are told to do.

As students, we are docile. We almost never say no. We wait for lines of inquiry and tasks to be initiated by someone else and almost never initiate deliberate learning for ourselves.

We are easily intimidated by institutional authority and let ourselves be abused by it. For example, having paid exorbitant tuition fees to attend class, we settle for second-rate ideas enunciated by second-rate lecturers; we study material that seems intellectually and pragmatically useless to us; we study for examinations that we fear and that often appear to have little relevance to the material we have studied (which was not worth much in any event); and we accept grades that are determined by such examinations and which materially affect our future, in each case because we are "required" to.

We have strong dependencies, particularly upon authority. We generally think of research as an activity performed by looking up other people's ideas in the library. Our papers are filled with quotations and plagiarisms of what authors have said, as though publication necessarily implied wisdom. We are so impressed by "erudition" and so poorly equipped to ferret out the author's underlying assumptions, let alone to attack them, so unable to detect lapses in logical reasoning and so generally incompetent to evaluate research designs or to distinguish data from inferences about them, that our loyalties become fickle: we tend to agree with the author we are reading at the moment. We feel threatened by conflicting opinions and intellectual differences and cling tenaciously to the hope that the differences we encounter are "semantic" rather than real and that, barring real differences, all conflicts can be reconciled somehow. Having little toleration for theory, because it is "too abstract"—by which we mean too impractical—we look to the literature for answers and hardly ever attempt to formulate cogent answers of our own. Indeed, we lack the skills for doing so.

One result (or cause?) of our dependency is that we exhibit little confidence in, or affection for, ourselves or for other students like us. While we are apt to take copious notes on what the authority says, we are most unlikely to note ideas expressed by our fellow students and certainly do not expect anyone to bother noting our ideas on those infrequent occasions when we express them. Time and again we complain about the seminar, reject inductive or dialectical treatment of problems, beg for lectures (in order to hear the real truth), and complain that since they are as ignorant as we are, there is no point in discussing problematical issues with our peers.

We are generally bound by conventions of social behavior and find it difficult, if not impossible, to function according to technical, professional, logical, scholarly, or critical conventions when to do so would be entirely appropriate and might be crucial. For example, disagreement and disputation seem like hostile acts rather than like tools of inquiry to us. Intellectual aggressiveness, the capacity to cut across irrelevancies and digressions and specious reasoning by identifying them, seems impolite. With few exceptions, we manifest the scared-bunny syndrome in graduate seminars: you be good to me and I'll be good to you. We do not hesitate to complain outside of school about the opinionated, bullheaded, long-winded members of the group. But we do nothing to counteract behaviors by other students or by the instructor that interfere with our own learning, interrupt our own progress, and cheapen the quality of what goes on, at propitious moments during class.

Indirectiveness is an associated difficulty. We are so cluttered with scholastic pedantry that a straightforward approach is often the last one that occurs to us. Instead of talking patiently with a child to find out how he feels about school, what worries him, what he likes, what he wants, and the like, we are inclined to show him inkblots and to interpret his apperceptions to gain such information. Instead of asking the child—helping the child—to explain at what step his ability to handle multiplication of fractions breaks down, we test him with a series of problems and then attempt to infer, from his answers, features of his underlying cognitive behavior. Unfortunately, the inadequate mental processes that we attribute to him in this manner frequently do not correspond to his actual cognitive behavior. While indirect testing, projective or otherwise, is sometimes required, and while good reasons may exist in some instances to begin by indirect testing without alerting the child to what we really have in mind, it is ridiculous to employ indirect methods generally. If we want to know, let's ask him; and then let's help him to tell us.

Our thinking tends to be single-tracked rather than pluralistic. Single answers, single models, and single strategies are much more attractive to us than multiple answers, multiple models, and the like. Once having performed an interpretation or having reached a conclusion, we show great reluctance to formulate or to consider other possibilities and virtually never have the intellectual adroitness to conceptualize opposite conclusions. If someone else troubles to demonstrate opposite possibilities for us, it seems that he has engaged in some form of intellectual legerdemain, that he must really be thinking arbitrarily, and that, in any case, his reasoning processes are mysterious and somehow awesome. Interpretive hypotheses become ruts.

We cheat, having been taught to do so by the school's priorities. For the success of our reality testing in this respect, we are to be congratulated.

We tend to distrust and to disparage people who are different from us. We may be bigots.

We depend heavily on other people's evaluations of our behavior. Lacking strong incentives for self-evaluation and being unequipped with skills for systematic self-examination, we are largely at the mercy of other people's perceptions which, in most cases, are based upon minimal or distorted data and refer to evaluation criteria that are inappropriate or ambiguous, even to the people who employ them. When the world is friendly, we are happy; when it is hostile, we are depressed. Even a fisheye from the bus driver is unsettling.

In connection to our abhorrence of theory and anti-intellectualism, we have strong vocational orientations and tend to be activists. It seems a waste of time to investigate anything that does not have immediate payoff in our work, that is, that does not make the next day's vocational activity simpler. And, particularly if we teach, we care very little about examining the problems of our profession and want, simply, to be shown the "right way to do it." We repeatedly institute curricular and methodological and administrative novelties, for example, team teaching, teaching machines, homogeneous grouping, and modern math, as though newness necessarily implied improvement. Because we act in advance of reasons, we generally botch up new operational modes by incorporating old mistakes and stupidities in them. We engage in expedient practices rather than in examined practice. In general, we tend to make major decisions on the basis of minimal data and analysis.

Those of us who are bright often feel worthless, whereas those of us who are stupid tend to have exaggerated impressions of our worth.

We lack fluency. Our language lacks precision and we often use words incorrectly.

We listen very poorly and often engage in parallel soliloquies when we think that we are engaging in discussion.

We find it extremely difficult to enter unknown bodies of knowledge (which we are disinclined to do in any event), largely because we do not know how to frame efficient and manageable entry questions.

What we do is often inconsistent with our descriptions of what should be done.

We distinguish work from fun and tend to feel punished by work. We use work as a means of penance.

We are superstitious and engage in many ritualistic behaviors and beliefs, for example, "He's due for a hit."

Like cultural primitives, we tend to attribute complex phenomena to magical causes, for example, "All this rainfall is the result of nuclear testing," and "I can tell a lot about a man by the way he writes his name."

In connection to ritualism, we ordinarily expect tasks to be defined as rites rather than rationally, for example, we ask, "How long should this paper be?" and "Do I have to use footnotes?"

Our respect and allegiances are often determined by custom rather than by reason: we treat professors with deference because they are professors, and old people with courtesy because they are old, apparently not recognizing that an old, simpleminded, autocratic professor is unworthy of our consideration, his age and rank notwithstanding. It is partly our fault that he occupies a position in which we must endure him.

Our techniques for logical reasoning and for logical analysis are sparse.

We are frequently afraid.

Our means for expressing love and hostility are grossly inadequate, as are our means for dealing with expressions of love and hostility by other people, although we are generally more successful in coping with their anger than with their affection.

We are often bored.

We require considerable structure in order to operate comfortably but frequently complain that we are enslaved by other people's structures (for example, the teacher by the curriculum) and have too little freedom. In this connection, we tend to construe autonomy as license.

We believe that hard work is virtuous.

We find it difficult to concentrate.

We feel that some things are best not to know.

Our sexual adjustments often leave much to be desired.

We feel guilty about many of our thoughts and about things we imagine.

We anthropomorphize animals; sometimes, plants and machines.

We prefer vicarious experience to direct experience and pay little heed to the meanings of direct experience. Being selective, our perceptions are sometimes more influenced by our prejudices than by the objects they record.

Our behavior is sometimes self-defeating in that, by our own acts, we make it difficult or impossible to have the things that we want most.

Although we like to think about ourselves as moral, ethical and professional people, our behavior is often governed by three principles: "live and let live," "keep your nose clean," and "don't rock the boat," which, although they are thoroughly established among many teachers, result in mutual protectiveness and passivity that no one, perhaps, except teachers could regard as "professional" behavior. For example, we tend to believe that to bring a colleague's incompetency to the attention of the school administration would be unprofessional behavior.

It makes us fearful to have our work observed.

We cannot readily admit to ourselves that we dislike certain children because we feel that that is a bad thing for an adult to do.

What we tend to want most from life is to be treated gently by it.

We prefer being soothed by art to becoming engaged in it. Music provides background for our fantasies.

We clamor for freedom of choice but feel threatened by having to make choices.

This, too, must end somewhere.

My comments have focused primarily on our intellectual deficits, the limits of our knowledge, the sparseness of our reasoning skills, the dullness of our critical faculties, the recalcitrancy of our biases, the impoverishment of our incentives to learn, and the helplessness with which we confront unknown knowledge. I have worried about the archaic dependencies we manifest upon authority for initiation of intellectual tasks and lines of productive inquiry. I have worried, particularly, about our self-ignorance, our uncertainties, and our paucity of methods for systematic self-examination. I am troubled by what seems to be the common absence of intellectual autonomy and the common prevalence of docility and anti-intellectualism among us. I am troubled and often puzzled by my students' vocationalism, by their hunger for simple and concrete answers, by their intolerance of abstract reasoning and theory. I am frightened by our conformity and by the forms our nonconformity takes. I am saddened by our emotional constriction, our waste and disregard for the experiences we have, and our hesitancies to reach for new, rich, direct experience.

If my tone sounds cynical to you, perhaps it arises from my alarm at the millionfold cynicism of educators, particularly of the teachers who retreat progressively further behind their desks day by day and who, for all practical purposes, have given up. And appreciate how difficult it is for me to trust my observations when what I observe is so abundantly bad: supervisors who are martinets; curriculums to choke on; teachers who do not like children or teaching; who, in some instances, are bigots and innocents and stupids; and who, moment by moment, kill off what was intellectually alive in the students by humiliating them, ignoring them, deceiving them, infantilizing them, depriving them of direct access to information and knowledge, forcing upon them priorities on learning what is mundane and arbitrary; filling them so full of extrinsic goals that unique, personal incentives atrophy; making them the same and mediocre; and failing to accept, acknowledge, reward, or strengthen their individual motives and competencies and integrity. I wonder why there is often so little dignity in the school experience for either the pupils or their teachers and why such dignity that exists is often superficially defined in terms of neatness and obedience and punctuality.

I don't have to be persuaded that there are good teachers; that there are beautiful teachers; and that, heaven knows, there are some good schools. I know that and believe it and could take you there. And if you are such a teacher, you should not be offended by what I have written. I don't believe that you should worry, either, that this writing is damaging because it will turn readers against the schools or will undermine many teachers' already tenuous morale. One part of my purpose has been to make vague discontent articulate so that we can begin to formulate articulate designs for change. Deficiencies are never fun to contemplate, and my punishment in this process is no less vivid than yours. I am willing to accept the discomfort—yours and mine—if that will help us to get a firmer grip on better things and can provide some impetus for moving toward them. I can easily rejoice in the existence of good teachers and good schools, but not so easily in an educational system that makes them so rare.

As I have remarked, the condition of knowing and the criterion of seeming to know are deeply pervasive in school culture, no less at the graduate school of education than in the elementary grades. And that seems such a shame when, instead of sustaining our pretensions, our energies could be spent so much more beneficially in developing skills of inquiry and analysis; when instead of feeling required to demonstrate mastery of the right answers, educators could justify their professional existence by other means, in other terms, and according to eminently more rational and humane values.

Being unable to demonstrate positively that our tissue-paper intellects, our self-defeating modes of existence, and our various other fragilities are attributable to the schools that educated us, I can accept, without much difficulty, the proposition that they have certainly had a hand in it and, as a working hypothesis, that modifications in the schools for the better would affect modifications in our lives for the better. I am not convinced that because the pupils do not protest as a rule and, if you ask them, are likely to say that everything is all right in school, that that's how things really are. First of all, they are not asked such questions commonly enough. Second, their reasons for giving false answers might be considerably more realistic and rational than reasons for answering truly: flatteries are not as likely to provoke retribution as complaints. If I don't trust the teacher's sincerity or my parents' ability to protect me from the school, I'd be foolish to buy myself trouble by mean-mouthing the school. Third, experience suggests that when pupils are occasionally asked how they feel about what is done to them, even if retributions do not result, appropriate changes do not result either. What is the point, one wonders, of providing feedback to the instructor on the last day of class? Whatever I say can be of no earthly good to me because the class is over. And I do not find it reassuring when the instructor makes it a special point to tell me that he will solicit feedback only after the grades are in: he protesteth too much. So much for reasons to doubt and reasons to lie.

A worse problem exists when the pupils are simply not aware of how badly off they are, and this, I suspect, is an almost universal predicament. As a child, I felt wrong for writing with my left hand. It never occurred to me to doubt the school's position. Strictness, boredom, punishments, gold stars, and all the rest, is how things are; and knowing nothing different, I assume that is how they should be. I am brainwashed. I also tend to be loyal to those teachers who terrify me the most; "reaction formation" is a pupil's best friend.

One element of this outlook should be examined before we move on to the constructive work. I have taken a biased view of intellectual fitness, and you may ask whether that is a fair view. Should everyone function autonomously? Should everyone be self-analytical? Should all people be mentally aggressive; moving toward inquiry and knowledge by their own initiative; active rather than complacent; rational when their situations require rationality; curious; happy to deal in hypothetical cases, with abstract problems, and with theoretical propositions? Is this how plumbers should be?

As for this question, I suggest that although the plumber's fitness will not necessarily show the same face as the scholar's, and while the five-year-old's brilliance will be something different from the fifty-year-old's, nevertheless, some common elements give connection and continuity among plumbers and scholars and children and adults. And I, for one, am willing to settle for an image of fit plumbers and unfit plumbers, where the critical differences are represented by some of the factors we have reviewed. Having no better alternative premise nor any more specific premise, I must start with what I've got. Although some may object, I accept that my plumber and I are more the same than we are different in the problems of living we confront and that his viability and mine are composed, essentially, of the same sort of stuff. I cannot see that to be encumbered by a "slave psychology" is any more fitting for one or the other of us, and I cannot see that our freedom requires different internal capacities. I *do* know that we both went to the same school.

For better or for worse, that school, and others like it, represent the context in which constructive supervision must occur, if it is to occur at all. In the next few chapters, I will offer descriptions of a supervision by means of which we hope to rectify some of the misfortunes noted above and to create a professional way of life intended to reduce the likelihood that they will continue to arise so innumerably. Although the commentaries I have offered will be echoed in specific examples of teaching and of supervision in the succeeding sections, their substance should recede in our minds as we begin, now, to consider clinical supervision. In the final chapter, I will try to bring both things together, namely, supervision and the troubled schools, in order to appraise education's future in light of the possibilities we will have examined.

II

A Model of Clinical Supervision

A NOTE ON TERMINOLOGY

One problem that those of us involved in the development of clinical supervision have faced all along is that the word "clinical" poses difficulties for many people and seems to carry all sorts of connotations that are either irrelevant or opposed to our intended meaning. "Clinical" tends to carry suggestions of pathology: clinical medicine and clinical psychology are often among the images evoked by the term. Although it is true that we speak of supervisory "treatment," and although at certain times in the past we have thought about providing "cures," I like to believe that these have simply been handy metaphors and that, essentially, clinical supervision is not an analogue of medical treatment or hospital psychiatry and does not presuppose pathological conditions at all. If anything, models of certain forms of teaching and of ego counseling are the most productive analogues to employ at this stage of our thinking.

Accompanying connotations of disease, "clinical" has also suggested to some minds the notion of manipulation, Machiavellian or otherwise: "Go in there and strip to the waist." Again, although we may be manipulative at times in supervision and may seem to be manipulating at times when we are not, such instances are coincidental and generally reflect our personal frailties and technical errors rather than our explicit or deliberate intentions. Whether we tend to deceive ourselves in this regard is a question that should be kept in mind throughout this reading.

If the reader will conceptualize "clinical" in the following manner, then we will be thinking about it in the same way. First of all, I mean to convey an image of face-to-face relationships between supervisors and teachers. History provides the principal reason for this emphasis, namely, that in many situations presently and during various periods in its development, supervision has been conducted as supervision from a distance, as, for example, supervision of curriculum development or of instructional policies framed by committees of teachers. "Clinical" supervision is meant to imply supervision up close. Later on I will refer to variations of the basic model that include group supervision, that is, supervision of individual teachers by groups of supervisors, groups of teachers by groups of supervisors, and groups of teachers by an individual supervisor, but in every case the notion of face-to-face contact will be fundamental.

The term should also denote supervision of actual professional practice, of actual practitional behavior. What the teacher *does* is central in clinical supervision, of which one hallmark is that the supervisor is an observer in the classroom and that the observational data he collects represent the principal foci of subsequent analyses. A condition of intimacy is implied by this description and will be examined later on.

Given close observation, detailed observational data, face-to-face interaction between the supervisor and teacher, and an intensity of focus that binds the two together in an intimate professional relationship, the meaning of "clinical" is pretty well filled out. An image of idiographic analysis of behavioral data and a tendency to develop categories of analysis *after* teaching has been observed, rather than beforehand, completes the picture.

I am sorry to have to attach such a weight of meaning to one word, but I frankly lack the ingenuity to find a more acceptable, economical way to communicate these ideas. One saving fact is that in order to move forward, it will not be necessary to keep such an elaborate definition in mind. It would be enough simply to avoid those other connotations of "clinical" that have nothing to do with our thinking, our practice, or with the ideas to be set out forthwith.

A FRAMEWORK OF VALUES FOR SUPERVISION

Our ideas and practice of clinical supervision arise from a framework of values in connection to which the discipline acquires its purposes and its rationales. We value the educational priorities that are mainly attributed, nowadays, to such authors as Joseph Schwab, Glen Heathers, and Jerome Bruner and which find expression in the work of dozens of other authors and critics of contemporary public education.

Most prominently of all, we cherish the notion of individual human autonomy: for people generally and, in our specific frame of reference, for teachers and their supervisors, particularly. We are driven by images of teaching that enhance the learners' self-sufficiency and freedom to act; of supervision that facilitates such teaching and aims for a parallel condition in the teacher's own existence; and, finally, of a supervision in which the supervisor's own capacities for autonomous functioning are heightened by the very practice in which he himself engages.

We value learning that focuses upon its own processes and structures as well as upon external objects. We value inquiry and analysis and examination and evaluation, especially when such activities of the mind are self-initiated and self-regulated. We believe that any supervision intended to facilitate such outcomes must be inherently humane, conceptually tough, grounded in intellectual humility, and based upon a determination to discover more about reality and to construct behaviors that are rationally related to such discoveries.

The supervision we envisage is intended to increase teachers' incentives and skills for self-supervision and for supervising their professional colleagues. It is additionally intended to become progressively more useful as teachers become increasingly capable of employing it creatively. We imagine, in other words, a supervision that becomes more and more productive as the teacher achieves higher and higher levels of technical and professional sophistication, most notably the ability to reach out for the special provisions that clinical supervision incorporates potentially. Our minds struggle for images of a supervision whose principal effect is to expand the sense of gratification experienced by students and teachers and supervisors, gratification in being and gratification in the work they do.

In its present stage of development, the clinical supervision that our minds can formulate and which we practice does not completely fulfill the ideology that occupies our imaginations. Day by day we know, better, what it is, in life and in professional life, that we're after. And, by small increments, we are getting to know, better, how to get what we're after. The following model of clinical supervision and the writing that surrounds it are mainly an expression of our trials. They show more of what we are trying for than of what we can assuredly do, although, to the degree that we can do anything at all, our existing proficiencies are also described.

In the way we teach children and supervise teachers and prepare clinical supervisors, we want, in each case, to be supportive and empathic; to perfect technical behaviors and the concepts from which they are generated; to increase the efficiencies and pleasures of learning and of becoming; to treat one another decently and responsibly and with affection; to engage with one another in productive and rewarding encounters; and to move toward our own destinies and toward one another's, honestly.

In practice we cannot always behave as we would like to behave or accomplish the ideals we cherish. Ironically, at moments when we feel that the stakes are highest and, consequently, when we want most to achieve our desired effects, we trip upon our individual frailties and wind up with other, less desirable outcomes. We are, nonetheless, committed to success and plea for our efforts to be tolerated.

If technical improvement stands as an important objective for clinical supervision, and if the results of improved teaching and supervisory technique should constitute a betterment of everyone's condition, then the means we employ toward that end must incorporate a profound measure of human compassion and patience and a great sense of one's own behavior and of its impact upon others. The outcomes we prize are very difficult to achieve and shall be permanently elusive if our feeling of urgency impels us toward immoderate behavior which, by its failure to be compassionate, becomes self-defeating.

The aims of clinical supervision will be realized when, largely by virtue of its own existence, everyone inside the school will know better why he is there, will want to be there, and, inside that place, will feel a strong and beautiful awareness of his own, individual identity and a community of spirit and of enterprise with those beside him. These are the values that motivate our work and give rise to our ambitions. While we cannot, obviously, make promises that are as large as our dreams, we can proclaim those dreams and let ourselves be guided by them.

THE STRUCTURAL MODEL, ITS RATIONALES AND PURPOSES

The basic model consists of five stages to which I will refer collectively as the "sequence of supervision." A collection of such sequences will be called the "cycle of supervision." My plan for the remainder of this volume is *first*, to describe the general purposes and rationales of each of the five stages; *second*, to present methodological techniques employed at each stage; *third*, to examine certain problems that often arise at each stage in practice; and finally, to examine some aspects of our past and of our future. Taking the model's structure as the organizing principle of this writing, I will identify its major underlying premises and the system of values from which it has grown, step by step as the presentation progresses.

THE FIVE STAGES

The prototype of a sequence of clinical supervision consists of the five stages:

STAGE 1: Preobservation conference
STAGE 2: Observation
STAGE 3: Analysis and strategy
STAGE 4: Supervision conference
STAGE 5: Post-conference analysis (nicknamed the "post-mortem")

Let us imagine a hypothetical sequence of supervision occurring sometime after the supervisory relationship has been inaugurated. Initial sequences pose special problems and incorporate certain unique goals that we will consider later on as a special case and in relation to a spread of issues concerning "beginnings" in supervision.

STAGE 1: Rationales and Purposes of the Preobservation Conference

This stage is mainly intended to provide a mental framework for the supervisory sequence to follow. Although its functions can be viewed somewhat differently by the teacher and the supervisor, in general, in our practice, it has served the following purposes:

(*a*) REESTABLISHING COMMUNICATION; RELAXATION: I would like to avoid using the term "rapport" which is so badly overworked in both clinical and educational literature and which generally conveys mystical rather than technical meaning. Like the attorney who is smugly satisfied that even though the judge has declared, "Strike that last question and the witness's response from the record," the jury has heard the thing and is not likely to forget it, I am satisfied that by saying "rapport" and then, "forget it," I will have produced the effect I am after.

The idea here is simply that it can be useful for Teacher and Supervisor to talk together sometime in the sequence before the supervision conference, if only to renew their habits of communication, their familiarity with one another's intellectual style and expressive rhythms, for both of two reasons: (1) in some measure, to eliminate problems of reestablishing mutual adjustments from the supervision conference (at which the stakes are sometimes rather high), and (2) to reduce anticipatory anxieties as both parties prepare to join again in important collaboration. In homely terms, we seem to find that Supervisor and Teacher can be more relaxed in the following stages of the sequence if they have been able to talk together successfully in the initial stage. This implication is not that this stage should be all fun and games nor that simple good fellowship is a sufficient cause for the preobservation conference.

(*b*) FLUENCY: Both Teacher and Supervisor require fluency in Teacher's plans for the teaching that will, presumably, be observed. The teacher's fluency is demanded for seemingly obvious reasons: the better he knows his intentions, both means and ends, the better he can implement them. The supervisor must know the teacher's intentions in order to share his framework of meaning and to understand the teacher's reasons, his premises, his doubts, his explicit professional motives, and the specific payoff he envisions.

Understanding the teacher's frame of reference is necessary for either of two purposes—for helping him to function successfully *in his own terms* or for modifying his plans according to concepts existing in the supervisor's frame of reference. In the latter case, I suspect that for Supervisor to introduce constructs of his own into Teacher's thinking, particularly if such constructs lead logically to changes in Teacher's plans and in his subsequent teaching behavior, the reasons and justifications for such changes should make sense in the teacher's *existing* conceptual framework. While the technical modifications that the supervisor proposes may be novel in the teacher's experience, his reasons for them must be communicable in language with which the teacher is already familiar.

I am making another assumption about requirements for fluency, namely, that there is generally a positive relationship between one's *explicit* knowledge of one's intentions and operational strategies and one's subsequent control over instrumental behavior. Although intuitiveness and spontaneity often appear as elements of "successful" teaching, it seems nonetheless true that beyond certain limits, predominantly intuitive approaches are more likely to wind up on the rocks than explicitly planned approaches. Retroactive analyses of teaching often reveal that loss of control or focus or efficiency was absence of *explicit* understanding of certain prior assumptions or of other elements of the teaching in question.

The principal means, in this stage, for enhancing both members' fluency, is for the teacher to present his most polished and updated version of plans whose formulation was begun during the prior sequence of supervision in this cycle. His presentation serves dual purposes: Supervisor learns just what Teacher has in mind, and Teacher is able to test and increase his own fluency by verbalizing his ideas to Supervisor.

(*c*) REHEARSAL: In a rudimentary sense, we can imagine that the simple enunciation of his plans provides Teacher with a degree of rehearsal for his teaching, at least a conceptual rehearsal. Additional opportunities exist in Stage 1 for more thorough rehearsal of instructional behavior. For example, should either member anticipate that at certain points in the lesson problems might be created by the pupils' failure to produce some specific verbal response or by some pupil's verbalization of an unanticipated response, Teacher and Supervisor might role-play those episodes of the lesson in order for Teacher to sharpen his resiliency and to heighten his readiness to refocus the inquiry or to prosecute some new line of inquiry, should the proper indications arise.

Although one might argue that under such circumstances rehearsal would be overly specific—Supervisor cannot role-play every unanticipated response. Nonetheless, experience has shown that the teacher's general capacity to cope with unexpected outcomes can be heightened by this practice and that in many instances their combined imagination, which is rooted in Teacher's and Supervisor's background of classroom experience, enables the members to predict "unanticipated" responses right on the button and to be consequently forearmed to deal with them. I suspect that this general capacity consists partly of developing an emotional tolerance for surprises and partly in knowing the general categories of distortion or misunderstanding in which pupils' spontaneous responses are likely to occur.

Analogously, as a student of flying, I have learned very specific techniques for dealing with unexpected stalls, spins, turbulence, icing, instrument failure, and the like. It is true, however, that in every emergency, every storm, and every cross-wind landing, the aircraft's behavior is unique in some respect, as are environmental variables and elements of my own psychological functioning. While I have not rehearsed every conceivable condition of flying, which would be impossible, my rehearsal of various aeronautical crises has given me the emotional fortitude and sufficient experience with *general* problems to enable me to make *specific* behavioral adaptations to cope with unexpected terrors when I must. I hope.

Another possibility for rehearsal arises from circumstances in which, although the teacher knows generally what key questions and directions he will use, he has not formulated them verbatim. If Teacher or Supervisor suspects that because of improper or ambiguous phraseology, Teacher's questions or directions may fail to achieve their intended outcomes, such key items can be rehearsed by role-play or other means and committed to more precise forms. For example, if one of Teacher's goals is to start things off by posing a question that demands a highly developed response from the pupils (because, let us suppose, Teacher has attached a high priority to pupils' verbal participation in this instance), and if he should then commence teaching by stating a complex question that is answerable by a single word or by an otherwise

meager response, his strategy would thereby be undone. Anticipating
this eventuality, Supervisor can exercise Teacher by helping him
through successive approximations of a maximally efficient question
until both are satisfied that the risks involved have been substantially
reduced. Such problems for rehearsal may arise from either Teacher's
or Supervisor's concerns and may be initiated by either member in the
preobservation conference.

(*d*) REVISIONS: Besides providing Teacher with a chance to
rehearse planned episodes of his instruction, Stage 1 creates an opportunity for last-minute revisions in the lesson plan. As you might suspect, certain spine-tingling problems are often associated with this
practice and will be examined below when we talk about problems in
the supervisory sequence.

(*e*) CONTRACT: However you might choose to think about it,
for example, as role-definition, as defining shared goals, or as agreeing
to ground rules, I am satisfied that to imagine, metaphorically, a
supervisory "contract" is an easy way to get a handle on this concept. I
mean to suggest that the preobservation conference is a time for
Teacher and Supervisor to reach *explicit* agreements about reasons for
supervision to occur in the immediate situation and about how supervision should operate.

Among other things, having established what the teacher is after
and how he thinks he feels about the whole business, the question
ought to be raised of whether observation and the rest of the sequence
should take place at all. If it makes sense and can be useful to the
teacher, in his own terms, for supervision to continue, then surely it is
worthwhile to take the trouble to say how and why and to make
deliberate decisions about what is to be done. If, on the other hand,
convincing reasons do not seem to exist for continuing the sequence,
then it is best to ascertain that fact in time to quit.

The best way I can think of to avoid ritual commitment to the
supervisory sequence, or supervision that is motivated by conflicting
purposes, is to talk the matter over beforehand and to arrive at some
contractual understanding before anything else happens. Once having
reached agreements, both members must be ready at later stages to
modify the contract if necessary and must understand that any such
modifications must be made explicitly in order to be kosher. In other
words, having decided upon certain rules, "This is what you will do,
this is what I will do, and here's why" (the contract), those rules
should not be changed in the middle of the game except by mutual
agreement and with mutual understanding.

The need for setting *a priori* contracts is indicated by two common
conditions: (1) that supervision is often enacted ritualistically—"My
job is to supervise, your job is to be supervised, today's the day, let's

get it over with"—and (2) that without explicit prior agreements (sometimes even with them), supervision is likely to operate according to social conventions, to become basically a social process, rather than to aim for specific technical and process outcomes which require behavior governed by specialized professional conventions. When it is a tea party or a wrestling match, it is not supervision.

While Stage 1 contracts are generally short-term affairs, applying principally to a specific supervisory sequence, long-range contracts affecting cycles of supervision and long-term supervisory relationships can also exist and may provide contexts for Stage 1 dialogue. What we do today should be focused on specific problems with which Teacher is attempting to cope today. Those problems, however, rather than coming from nowhere, may derive from a sequence of problems which constitute the basis and orientation of Teacher's professional development and for the supervision intended to facilitate it.

STAGE 2:   Rationales and Purposes of Observation

The supervisor observes to see what is happening so that he can talk about it with the teacher afterwards. He generally writes down what he hears and sees as comprehensively as possible. Instead of recording general descriptions, the observer should get the stuff down verbatim: everything everybody says, if that's possible, and as objective an account of nonverbal behavior as he can manage. Why?—because in the supervision to follow, the main job will be to analyze what has taken place in the teaching. Whether analysis will be centered in problems identified beforehand (in Stage 1) or will emerge freshly from the new data, it is crucially important that the data constitute as true, as accurate, and as complete a representation of what took place as possible. If the data are seriously distorted, then the analysis will be worthless because, never existing for its own sake in clinical supervision, its chief purpose is to provide a sound basis for planning future teaching. "Futurity" is one hallmark of a successful conference and, I suspect, the more explicitly it exists, the better.

Today's data are employed as a source of tomorrow's problems for supervision. To be isolated for supervisory treatment, problems should have some consequence for Teacher. But if, in effect, tomorrow's problems and plans are structured upon false representations of reality, then the whole business will have been a terrible waste and will not be likely to result in anything better than disenchantment. Even worse, if things keep up that way, Teacher's demoralization and withdrawal from the supervisory relationship could easily follow.

One reason for Supervisor to observe is that, being engaged as he is in the business of teaching, Teacher cannot usually see the same things happening as a disengaged observer can. By adding eyes, the data are increased. Another reason—this also backfires occasionally—

is to demonstrate commitment to Teacher, a serious enough commitment to justify paying such close attention to his behavior as the observer must. And, in this connection, Supervisor's work at observation gives weight to the technical balance in supervision and should serve as evidence that the relationship is not merely a social one: that social incentives are not *sufficient* in the supervisory framework.

Another rationale for Stage 2 is that by putting himself in close proximity to the teacher and the pupils at the very moments when salient problems of professional practice are being enacted, the supervisor occupies a position from which he can render real assistance to Teacher, in Teacher's terms, and according to specific observational foci (tasks) that Teacher may have defined in Stage 1. For example, if the best way that Supervisor can acquit himself is by seeming helpful, then if Teacher has asked, "Will you please keep your eye on Group One while I am working with Group Two because I haven't been able to determine whether the work I assign Group One is really enough to keep them busy," and if, subsequently, Supervisor can furnish the information Teacher has requested, we can rack one up for Supervisor and, perforce, for the good of the relationship (unless, of course, this task was a red herring intended to divert Supervisor from other things). At least possibilities for being helpful exist in such proximity that could not exist without it.

If observational data can be used for developing solutions to problems of practice, then such data can also be employed to authenticate the existence of certain problems, to make sure they are real, and as bases for articulating previously undefined problems.

Perhaps I should make it clear at this point that by "problems" I mean complex or problematical issues in teaching. Problems are not necessarily bad; they do not necessarily imply weaknesses. A problem, for example, might be how to secure some element of practice that seemed to be particularly productive; how to understand better under what circumstances it should be used; how to elevate it to a more general level in teaching. "Why do objects fall?" and "How do you blow glass?" are problems in this sense. "That jerk has some real problems" is not what I mean, although problems of that kind clearly generate problems of the former kind.

An ancillary benefit may result from observation, namely, that using his own observational techniques as a model, Supervisor can teach them to Teacher who, in turn, may employ them for his own learning when opportunities to observe other teachers arise. In a more direct manner, Teacher can learn methods of systematic observation for use in his own classroom and, in this fashion, can become more independently able to obtain broader data for self-analysis when he is not tied up counting milk money.

In the most general sense, observation should create opportunities for supervisors to help teachers to test reality, the reality of their own perceptions and judgments about their teaching. I have argued that supervision should result in heightened autonomy for Teacher and, particularly, in strengthened capacities for independent, objective, self-analysis, and that supervision which increases Teacher's dependency upon Supervisor to know whether his teaching is good or bad, that is, supervision in which Supervisor's unexamined value judgments pre-dominate, is bad supervision. But the supervisor's perceptions and evaluations, rather than counting for nothing, represent a potentially excellent source of data from which consensual validation can be obtained: given his own perceptions of what has taken place, Teacher can test "reality" by ascertaining whether Supervisor's observations (and later his value judgments) tend to confirm or to oppose his own.

STAGE 3:   Rationales and Purposes of Analysis
and Strategy

Stage 3 is intended for two general purposes: first, in *Analysis*, to make sense out of the observational data, to make them intelligible and manageable; and second, in *Strategy*, to plan the management of the supervision conference to follow, that is, what issues to treat, which data to cite, what goals to aim for, how to begin, where to end, and who should do what.

If, as I have suggested, observation is a fundamental element in clinical supervision, then analysis is its heart. Rationales for analysis can be formulated either historically or methodologically. Historically, supervision has been deeply entrenched in evaluation (rating), and supervisory evaluations have generally had only the most tenuous relationships to objective evidence. One common pattern has been for Supervisor to observe some teaching and then, if he troubled to offer any feedback at all, to render his judgments to Teacher either on the way out, later in the office, later in a written memo, or much later in a summary evaluation of Teacher's work during the year.

Supervisors' comments have often concerned superficial aspects of teaching—bulletin boards, window shades, physical posture, and the like—and have dealt with arbitrarily selected issues, often in an arbitrary and capricious manner. This is really to say that if, conventional-ly, supervisors' value judgments have been reasoned at all, they have not been reasoned out explicitly for the teacher in common practice. It is, and has been, even more rare for supervision to provide systemati-cally for teachers *to participate in developing evaluations of their own teaching.*

One problem has been that because educational values and princi-ples of educational practice are so ambiguous and uncertain, profes-

sional evaluators have almost been forced to choose issues and evaluation criteria arbitrarily. Another problem is that, by and large, supervisors have not known very much about educational theory or practice—
being untrained or poorly trained in poor ideas—and, not having been
schooled in any special discipline, have had to function idiosyncratically, according to home remedies, that is, as eclectics in the worst sense.
The supervision they have performed has generally mirrored supervision they received as teachers. They have focused upon elements of
teaching that their own supervisors treated and which, in the absence of
a professional discipline or a scientific method, are only authentic in the
sense that they exist, enduringly, in the folklore and mores of teaching.

A third problem is that since supervision has never really been
defined as a professional practice, no special conventions have been
invented to govern supervisory behavior. Being untechnical, supervisory practice has failed to generate a body of specialized technique.
Having not been confronted with problems of supervision in their own
training, it is little wonder that supervisors evaluate arbitrarily or
glibly: there are few reasons for them to do otherwise, and no *useful*
models of how else to operate have been available. Unlike the psychiatrist, for example, the supervisor has no special theory to learn, no
special competencies to master, no body of case material to study, and
no regular supervision of his own practice.

A fourth problem arising from such conditions is that teachers
generally expect supervision to be punitive, to be anchored in an
"odious system of administrative sanctions." One might guess that what
most teachers have learned best under supervision is how to second-
guess the supervisor, how to anticipate what will please him, how to
stage appropriate performances for him to observe, and how to jolly
him up for their own protection. Given the mystique that inevitably
surrounds unexplicit systems of evaluation, a secondary result is that
teachers' dependencies upon supervisory evaluation have grown very
strong, despite its fearful and threatening aspect.

From a historical perspective, consequently, a rationale for extensive analysis of empirical data in supervision is that teachers' anxieties
and mistrust of supervision, their expectations of punishment, can only
be alleviated if teachers of the future learn that supervision is (or can
be) an essentially rational practice, that its methods are those of logical
reasoning and forthright analysis, and that it incorporates neither the
sanctions nor the mysteries nor the vagaries that have made them so
helpless, so disquieted, and so dependent in the past.

The analytical component of clinical supervision is intended to
make it safer—less whimsical, less arbitrary, less superficial—than
supervision of the past. And particularly when Teacher is trained to
participate in analysis of his own teaching, based on the truest and
most comprehensive representations of that teaching that can be

created, his chances of experiencing profit from the enterprise are most favorable. Perhaps the best way that supervision can outlive its unfortunate history is by becoming something useful in the teacher's existence. Except for teachers who feel endangered by realism—we will examine this problem later—analysis of their teaching should be the most useful thing that anyone else can do in relation to it.

Methodologically, analysis exists for the sake of understanding true events in order to exercise greater control over future events. In other words, analysis of today's teaching is primarily for the sake of greater power, for a higher probability of success in tomorrow's teaching. Besides eliminating inequities from supervision, for example, hierarchical inequities and injustices arising from the imposition, by an outsider, of unexamined value judgments, analysis provides possibilities for Teacher to be vigorously engaged in examination of his work and to function autonomously, rather than dependently, in framing decisions that affect his work. The problem of having to accept someone else's word on faith is largely avoided. If, as your supervisor, I have shown you the (recognizable) evidence that has led me to certain questions or judgments about what you have done, and if I have enunciated the sequence of reasoning by which I traveled from perceptions of your teaching to inferences about it, then I have made myself sufficiently vulnerable for you to discover logical inconsistencies in my reasoning, to be able to read the data differently, to offer alternative interpretations, to provide missing data, to isolate other issues, to frame questions that may be truer or, in some way, more productive to treat—or, if it works out that way, to be persuaded by my evidence and by my reasoning and to commit yourself to work through the problems I have identified.

At the very least, my involvement in analysis of your teaching should demonstrate my degree of commitment to you—I haven't simply verbalized it; I have done actual work to show it—and should reassure you that although I may be threatening in other respects, at least I am not carefree in my attention to your professional behavior. To have matched your energy and sobriety in connection to issues that are awfully important to you should make the work I do seem at least tentatively trustworthy. In any event, analysis as a supervisory method is used in clinical supervision as a mode of learning and as a medium through which to modify teaching behavior. In a later chapter, I will illustrate some of the specific analytical techniques that clinical supervision employs.

Supervisor's next step, after having performed an analysis of the observational data, is to make decisions about how the supervision conference should be conducted. According to this model, his latitude is broad enough for the decision, "not to decide anything in particular in advance" to be tenable. Indeed, Supervisor may have decided much earlier not even to do his own analysis of the teaching but, rather, to wait until conference time and then to begin from scratch with the teacher (this technique has been named the "full analysis").

For the present, let us deal with the prototype, and let's imagine Strategy in a sequence of supervision in which no specific foci were stipulated during the preobservation conference. The principal rationale for Strategy, like that of instructional planning, is that a planned approach toward specified goals by deliberate processes is more likely to work out than a random one. Obviously, this simple formula fails if, for one reason or another, the plan is poor. In any case, it is theoretically acceptable to think of planned conferences and to suppose that if the plan is a good one it should enhance Supervisor's responsiveness to Teacher instead of retarding it and should culminate in behavior that Teacher finds useful. Even in the most nondirective branches of counseling psychology and in the most process-conscious models of instruction, treatment plans and instructional plans are acceptable. (I suspect that even the most dyed-in-the-wool existentialist "prepares" himself, somehow, for a happening.) The problem is partly to decide upon what antecedents such plans should be structured and partly to determine who exercises what degrees of initiative in formulating plans to affect the supervisee's (the client's, the pupil's) behavior.

If Strategy exists for the sake of efficiency, it is also intended for protection. It is generally safe to assume that the teacher's work is important to him and that even if his conscious motives for teaching are superficial or extrinsic (for example, teaching represents a stable source of income and provides attractive fringe benefits), observation and analysis of his behavior will, nonetheless, be important to him—if only because of its evaluative character and of the emotional implications evaluation carries for most people.[1]

Given the assumption, therefore, that the business to be transacted in the supervision conference will be emotionally important for the teacher (and, presumably, important in other terms as well), it follows that the conduct of such business ought to be considered carefully in advance. If the emotional stakes may be high, then possibilities for feeling hurt or being hurt may be high. Where possibilities for pain exist, that is, for someone else's pain to arise more or less directly from my own behavior toward him, at the very least I am responsible to exercise some deliberate control over my behavior. Even though I am unlikely to be cavalier in any case, it is not much to ask that I give some reasonable attention to my behavior beforehand. My acceptance of this requirement is not motivated only by humane and ethical considerations. I am equally motivated by pragmatism: clinical super-

---

[1] I do not mean to suggest that evaluation carries the same emotional meaning for everyone but, rather, that it tends to have emotional significance for everyone, one way or another.

vision (my professional practice) is not likely to remain viable if my clients feel damaged by it. In this context, it would seem that my self-interest, that is, my investment in supervision, functions to protect the supervisee's interests as well as my own.

Strategy is also intended to provide continuity in supervision. If it becomes important to stick to certain specific lines of inquiry throughout a cycle or over longer periods of time, if supervision has become a vehicle for "longitudinal" development of one kind or another, or if, for any other purposes, it seems important for supervision to have a fabric, a cohesiveness, a unity, then Strategy provides a natural time to pick and choose issues from the analysis for continuity's sake.

In a more general sense, if supervision is intended to result in process outcomes as well as in purely technical ones, that is, if it is intended to affect patterns of behavior and underlying psychological predispositions as well as simply to transmit substantive information, then it is more difficult to prepare for supervision than it would be otherwise. Rather than simply having to prepare one's *material*, as for a lecture, one must additionally prepare oneself for *collaboration* intended to benefit one's supervisee: both technical and process outcomes depend very much upon one another. I must prepare in several integrated dimensions; and Strategy is my time for doing so, if I conceptualize supervision in these terms.

Another rationale for Strategy, which is perhaps more a hope than a reason, is, again, that Teacher's confidence in supervision is more likely to be inspired if he perceives that Supervisor has put a great deal of work into it than if Supervisor appears to be working off the cuff. Another rationale, when it is possible for Teacher to be freed from other responsibilities in order to have time to develop his own strategies for supervision before the conference—this *possibility* should always exist, although, in actual practice, it generally does not—is to enable the teacher to compose his ideas and to assemble his wits beforehand. If Teacher is functioning well in supervision, if he is relaxed, intelligent, committed, professionally creative, and functioning autonomously, then Strategy gives him time to order his priorities and to screen issues for the conference accordingly. If, on the other hand, Teacher views supervision as a battleground, then at least he has been given the same chance as his opponent to mobilize his forces (although he is nevertheless handicapped inasmuch as it is *his* teaching that's at stake). In more realistic terms, Teacher can be protected from the disadvantages of having to deal all at once, without forethought, with problems that are already well rehearsed for the supervisor.

STAGE 4: Rationales and Purposes of the Supervision Conference

All roads lead to the conference. Whereas it is sometimes appropriate to omit earlier stages of the clinical sequence for special reasons, and whereas even on certain occasions shortages of time may preclude any supervisory contact except a conference, once a sequence has been begun it is almost never acceptable to quit that sequence before the conference. Even if it should seem that because of extraordinary circumstances the teacher was unable to perform his work or, for any reason, his anxiety rose so critically that he could not be expected to engage in an analysis, a conference of some kind, even a very abridged one, would generally be indicated. Such a conference might be used, first of all, to help Supervisor test his impressions of Teacher's condition. Additionally, it might focus upon the anxiety rather than on the teaching. Or, it might serve simply as a time to offer reassurances and to make decisions about what should happen next. Or, it might be used for planning future teaching without including systematic analysis of the observed teaching, and the like.

But in one way or another, some kind of conference is almost always preferable to no conference at all, for example, if only to signify that Teacher is important to Supervisor whether he executes his plans or not and that Supervisor is not going to abandon the relationship at moments of failure or crisis when Teacher is more likely to require support than at any other moment. Later on we will examine one principle that underlies this reasoning, namely, that supervision is most likely to succeed if Supervisor can accept the existence of problems without attaching any stigma to Teacher for having them.

Another thought, in this connection, is central in clinical supervision. Understanding that even under the most favorable conditions observation is likely to be accompanied by some feeling of stress, I propose that a minimum responsibility incumbent upon the observer is to discuss what he has observed with the teacher. My experience suggests that in many cases supervision is less punishing even when it must address very inadequate teaching than it is when Teacher is left only with his fantasies about how Supervisor feels because, having observed the teaching, Supervisor did not follow through with conversation about it. The probability of such an outcome is especially vivid when, as it commonly happens, Teacher does depend very much upon Supervisor's evaluation and has not yet learned to value self-initiated analysis or, indeed, any form of analysis in favor of prompt and positive feedback from Supervisor. In my work with supervision students in professional practicums, rule number one is, generally, "Stay out of the classroom unless you are committed to a full sequence of supervision. Your participation in a conference is what earns you your right to observe."

This idea can be expressed in yet another variation: until they meet in conference, Teacher has been highly vulnerable while Supervisor has been practically invulnerable. Again, it seems true that in any supervisory-like relationship, the supervisee experiences an inevitable handicap inasmuch as it is *his* work (rather than anyone else's, including Supervisor's) that is being examined. I suggest that whatever handicaps Teacher must endure in supervision ought not to be avoidable artifacts that result from what Supervisor does, particularly when the supervisor could have elected other alternatives.

My sense of the teacher's vulnerability can be imagined best in connection to observation: while Teacher performs nakedly, Supervisor, it seems, must only watch. While Teacher's mistakes may be apparent, Supervisor's perceptual errors and errors of interpretation are invisible. As one might guess, it is not uncommon for Teacher to "see" Supervisor's displeasure—he frowns and scowls and grimaces—when, in point of fact, Supervisor has been working assiduously to remove a morsel of bacon from between his teeth while attempting to record notes on the teaching. It is additionally true that in Preobservation, while Supervisor has nothing to lose, Teacher's sense of intention and plans for instruction can be thoroughly undermined. And, as it most often happens, by conference time Supervisor enjoys a relatively organized intellectual preparation while Teacher is still panting from his other responsibilities during the intervening period.

Teacher's first real opportunity to move from behind the eight ball occurs in conference. Now, as he becomes an active agent and must enunciate ideas, Supervisor begins to generate behavior and products that are as vulnerable in analysis as Teacher's. Especially when he begins to commit himself to judgments concerning elements of the teaching, Supervisor's constructs, his patterns of reasoning, his professional assumptions—the logical and substantive integrity of what he says—have become public and exposed and open to examination.

Perhaps the most oppressive element of conventional supervision is that Supervisor has been able to play a closed hand. To open his hand and to make himself deliberately vulnerable is one of Supervisor's principal purposes in the conference. Therein lie possibilities for justice, or at least for evening the psychological score, that could not exist otherwise. Stated positively, Stage 4 is intended to give Teacher opportunities to deal aggressively with Supervisor's analysis of his teaching and to initiate his own problems of analysis: in short, to take control of his own destiny and to make explicit decisions about his own behavior more freely and to greater advantage than he has formerly been encouraged to do.

In succinct terms, the supervision conference is additionally intended:

1. To provide a time to plan future teaching in collaboration with another professional educator. Perhaps the best measure of whether a conference has been useful, in Teacher's framework, is

whether it has left him with something concrete in hand, namely, a design for his next sequence of instruction.

2. To provide a time to redefine the supervisory contract: to decide what directions supervision should take and by what methods it should operate (or whether supervision should be temporarily terminated).

3. To provide a source of adult rewards. In common practice, teachers have few opportunities for their value to be acknowledged by other adults who have professional sophistication and who know their work, that is, Teacher's work, intimately.

4. To review the history of supervision, that is, of the problems that Supervisor and Teacher have addressed formerly and to assess progress in mastering technical (or other) competencies upon which Teacher has been working.

5. To define treatable issues in the teaching and to authenticate the existence of issues that have been sensed intuitively.

6. To offer didactic assistance to Teacher, either directly or by referral, in relation to information or theory that Teacher requires and of which Supervisor may have relatively advanced knowledge.

7. To train Teacher in techniques for self-supervision and to develop incentives for professional self-analysis.

8. To deal with an array of factors that may affect Teacher's vocational satisfaction as well as his technical competency. The question of what issues of this kind are appropriate to treat in supervision depends largely upon the participants' inclinations, the supervisor's special skills for such work, pertinent situational variables and the overriding question of how supervision can be therapeutic (small "t") without becoming Therapy (large "T").

Whether a conference begins to fulfill any of these potentialities depends partly on what has come before, partly on psychological variables that operate for or against successful work, and largely upon the manner in which Supervisor operates. As with other stages of the sequence, there are never any guarantees. Simply because clinical supervision offers a conference and even though Supervisor may conceptualize "conference" in all the right terms, conferences may nevertheless fail terribly by any reasonable criteria that one might choose. Strategies to minimize risks and to alleviate problems that commonly occur will be examined in the following sections.

STAGE 5: Rationales and Purposes of the Post-Conference Analysis ("Postmortem")
If "clinical" has morbid connotations for some people, imagine how our students tend to react when we talk to them about the "postmortem." Perhaps "premortem" would be more appropriate.

Because Stage 5 was invented in a context of group supervision in which some member(s) could analyze the supervisory behavior of some other member(s) after the supervision conference was over, it is difficult to describe Post-Conference Analysis as a solo activity. Nevertheless, we can examine the concept and talk about its rationales, leaving methodological questions for later on.

In retrospect it seems that although each of the stages reviewed so far has plural purposes and multiple rationales, each nevertheless seems also to have some essential commitment. Preobservation serves largely to set the contract; Observation takes place to capture realities of the lesson; Analysis is intended to make the data intelligible by unearthing logical relationships among them; Strategy produces an operational plan for supervision. In essence, the postmortem serves as clinical supervision's superego—its conscience.

It is the time when Supervisor's practice is examined with all of the rigor and for basically the same purposes that Teacher's professional behavior was analyzed theretofore. In both instances our principal rationale is that examined professional behavior is more likely to be useful—for everyone—than unexamined behavior; that, perhaps, the only truly worthwhile existence is an examined existence. In one sense, this can be construed as an ethical rationale: as supervisors—the same holds for teachers—we are responsible for protecting the interests of the people we serve and, given the profession's clinical character, our first line of defense for them is represented by deliberate consciousness of, and purposeful control over, what we do. According to this view, decisions affecting the conduct of our future behavior must arise, in large part, from objective analysis of our past behavior and from as fine an understanding as we can develop of what consequences it has had.

And again, the postmortem arises from pragmatic, methodological, and historical considerations. First, it represents a basis for assessing whether supervision is working productively, for ascertaining its strengths and weaknesses, and for planning to modify supervisory practices accordingly. In this context, any and all variables are appropriate to review: supervisory technique, implicit and explicit assumptions, predominating values, emotional variables, technical and process goals, and the like. Second, Supervisor can demonstrate skills of self-analysis by familiarizing Teacher with the work he does regularly in postmortem. In other words, if he chooses, for example, to have Teacher witness his verbal enactment of a postmortem in the context of some other teacher's supervision, by this technique Supervisor could turn the PM to didactic advantage in *his* supervision. Third, Teacher's awareness of Supervisor's regular practice of Post-Conference Analysis should help to offset misgivings that may exist concerning Supervisor's commitment and the historical disparity between his professional vulnerability and Teacher's.

When Supervisor operates alone, that is, in one-to-one supervision

rather than in group supervision, Post-Conference Analysis is a soli-
taire. He contrives, somehow, to collect data from earlier stages of the
sequence, possibly by tape-recording. Because, having engaged in Analysis and Strategy alone, Supervisor spoke no words during that stage,
he is forced to rely solely on whatever notes he assembled and on the
reasoning he can recall from that period of activity. By and large,
Supervisor directs his attention to behavior in the conference. He
reaches back to material from his observation notes, and so on, when
analysis of the conference requires it.

His methods are essentially the same as those employed in analysis of the teaching and will be discussed below. One of the obvious
advantages of group supervision, that is, of supervision undertaken
collaboratively by two or more supervisors, is that in such practice
certain members may be assigned responsibility for conducting the
postmortem and, from the beginning, can collect data at each stage of
the supervisory sequence for that purpose. Particularly when Supervisor
is not yet able to perform an objective, full-bodied self-analysis, the
utilization of other analysts to examine his behavior may be crucial for
his own professional growth and for the protection of Teacher's interests.

Even at the most advanced stages of his technical development, I
propose that Supervisor's practice should, itself, be supervised from
time to time. In the writing that follows, I will develop a model that
incorporates supervision of supervision as well as supervision of
teaching.

III
Methodological Techniques for the Preobservation Conference and for Observation

In certain respects, the writing in this section will be unbalanced. For one thing, my ideas on method are more highly developed in connection to Observation, Analysis, and Strategy than they are for Preobservation. For another, it is easier to speak categorically about methods pertaining to mechanical functions like data gathering and to formal analysis than it is in relation to interactional behavior, for example, in the supervision conference. Contingencies are more predictable in the former category than in the latter. A third note is that for various reasons I am attempting to keep the prototype model separate from problems that commonly arise in practice for the time being: historically, the model came first, and the problems came afterward. I think it would be "simplest" to develop a clear vision of the model before turning toward the complexities that arise from it.

STAGE 1: METHODS FOR THE PREOBSERVATION CONFERENCE

How Supervisor manages Stage 1 depends very much upon what he already knows about Teacher from their earlier work together.

Above all, it is important in preobservational activity not to do anything that is likely to unsettle Teacher before he steps into class. If there is nothing that Supervisor can do to enhance Teacher's probabilities of success—perhaps nothing needs to be done—at the very least, Supervisor should not reduce Teacher's chances.

In any given supervisory relationship, one must learn, largely by trial and error, what the individual teacher is likely to find useful, before he is observed. In some instances it seems sufficient to pay a courtesy call: to ask, simply, whether the plans discussed yesterday are still set for today's teaching; to signify, by one's appearance, "I am here, just as we planned; all systems are go."

My experience suggests that it is generally reassuring for Teacher to observe that Supervisor is actually there, when he has said, yesterday, that he would be. With or without excessive anxiety, certainties tend to be more reassuring than ambiguities. When anxiety does run high, predictability and structure often provide comfort. If I know that although we are running late, the plane I must catch will wait for the plane in which I'm flying to land and that there will be time enough to make the connection, I feel better than if I have to wonder about it. If we become very late, I am less likely to worry if the flight captain says why than if he remains mute. If Supervisor and I (the teacher) have labored over plans for today's teaching and have set certain problems, that I care about, to examine today, it is nice to know that he is actually here rather than being towed along the Long Island Expressway, and, for that reason, it is good practice for Supervisor to make himself visible to me as early as he can, if only by saying hello.

When all systems are, indeed, go, when the decisions Teacher made yesterday are still in effect and when neither he nor Supervisor feels any need to change their contract, then "hello" is often enough. Ritual commitment to a more elaborate preobservation conference would be unhelpful, if not damaging. In order to establish whether or not such a conference is required, particularly if Supervisor is ready to proceed according to prior agreements, a good question to ask is, "Is there anything we can do together right now that would be helpful?" (For reasons that should become evident in a moment, this question is preferable to, "Is there anything I can do to help you this morning?" or "How can I help you?")

If Supervisor has reason to suspect that although he feels comfortable about the way things stand, Teacher may want to do something more before the lesson, a somewhat better question might be, "What can we do right now that would be helpful?" While the first question (above) is a "yes-no" question and can be deliberately used for efficiency, that is, if Supervisor feels fairly certain that Teacher does *not* want additional preparation for the lesson, the second question is less likely to elicit a one-word response (certainly not "Yes" or "No") but, nevertheless, provides Teacher the option to say, "Nothing." If, on the other hand, Supervisor feels that additional preparation is necessary or, feeling satisfied himself, suspects that Teacher wants to do some more planning, he can either say what's on his mind straightforwardly— I consider this the best approach unless special reasons exist not to use it—or, in the second case, can ask any of a variety of more directive questions, for example, "What, exactly, is the sequence of instruction that you intend to follow?" or, "What key questions do you intend to ask?" or, "Will you give the directions before you distribute the materials or afterwards?" or, "About which sequences of the lesson, if any, are you uncertain?" or, "What are your thoughts about how this technique will operate to achieve the goals you're after?" or, "What decisions have you made concerning the unresolved issues we talked about in yesterday's planning?" In some instances, when supervision has ripened and communication has become very efficient, it is possible to begin almost anything by some simple opening like, "What gives?" or, "Ready?" or, "You dig?" depending on what idiom is current. If Teacher's response is that he does not want to do anything more at the moment and if Supervisor trusts his response or, being unable to trust it, believes that for other reasons it would be best to accept it at face value, then it is best to part company until it is time to observe the lesson.

If there is work to be done, then how Supervisor proceeds depends on what tasks must be performed. It is very important for Supervisor to be sure he understands exactly what it is that Teacher wants to do and, with such understanding, to function responsively. Or, if it is the other way around, Supervisor should take pains to insure that Teacher understands his (Supervisor's) intent and is presently capable of moving in Supervisor's directions, before diving into the work. My reasoning, in this connection, is that if Teacher sees fit to raise questions in those last precious moments before the teaching, it follows that such questions are likely to have a large measure of importance for him (unless he just talks a lot). And if that is the case, then it becomes all the more urgent for Supervisor to respond as adequately as he can to Teacher's questions rather than to his own distortions, misinterpretations, or misunderstandings of Teacher's questions. When time is short and the stakes are high, it can represent a major economy to make sure communications are straight. The same reasoning applies if Supervisor wants to broach questions of his own in those precious moments, knowing full well that to do so may undermine Teacher's equilibrium in the lesson to follow.

I have found that a good rule of thumb is to deal in Teacher's terms, that is, in Teacher's frame of reference during Stage 1 (if not all of the time) and to reserve issues arising from Supervisor's imagination for treatment during the supervision conference (Stage 4). When there is any chance that for Supervisor to introduce his own constructs would unsettle Teacher's equanimity or would confuse him, it is best that he should not do so immediately before the teaching.

If supervision is operating properly, complex decisions relating to teaching will be formulated early enough beforehand (as, the day before) for a sufficient margin of time to exist in which Teacher can assimilate his plan, rehearse it conceptually, and produce last-minute refinements. Goal setting, developing rationales for instruction, and laying out instructional methods are hardly appropriate to undertake in the final moments—better to give the pupils a period of "music appreciation." Assuming that such prior conditions have been satisfied, then what tasks are appropriate to tackle at Stage 1, and what supervisory methods are likely to succeed?

Once again, one's choice of methods should depend upon the specific tasks, and upon whatever identifiable psychological variables may be operating. For example: if Teacher's expressed problem is to be certain that the wording he intends to use in a specific set of directions is precise enough, Supervisor might, appropriately, run him through the directions in question to see how they sound to new ears. But this solution is not so simple because of the question of whether it matters, or in what ways it can matter *how*, that is, by what specific technique Supervisor performs that function. This is, in effect, a problem of supervisory priorities; a question of relationships among technical and process goals.

If, for example, supervision (in this hypothetical case) is *also* intended to increase Teacher's professional autonomy by encouraging him to initiate his own issues in supervision, by reinforcing spontaneous self-initiated inquiry when it occurs, and by creating conditions conducive to self-evaluation, then it would seem inconsistent with such goals (at least at face value) for Supervisor to begin:

> SUPERVISOR: How can I help you; what can I do for you this morning?
> TEACHER: I'm not sure that I got these directions buttoned down the way you want them.
> SUPERVISOR: All right. Supposing you run through the directions right now. I'll tell you whether they seem adequate. Go ahead.

Supervisor's emphasis upon giving help (implicitly, "My job is to help; your job is to be helped"), on doing something for Teacher; Teacher's emphasis on doing things the way Supervisor wants them done; and Supervisor's evaluative posture (implicitly, "It is for me to decide whether your performance is adequate") and directiveness (implicitly, "In this relationship, I decide what is to be done"), all seem more apt to heighten Teacher's dependency and to cast him as a passive agent than to achieve opposite effects.

I have included the qualification "at face value" to allow for the possibility that in a supervisory relationship in which Teacher *does* take major initiative and *does* function autonomously, it might not matter so much if, on isolated occasions, Supervisor moves in quite aggressively. I am unlikely to change a man who is basically self-sufficient by rendering judgments about his work or offering him advice or directions from time to time. On the contrary, if you are neither excessively dependent upon me nor afraid of me and I should say something as stupid as, "That lesson stank," it would not matter very much to you—which is as it should be—especially if you perceived evidence to the contrary. Trusting in your own perceptions and judgmental adequacy, my evaluations may represent useful data to you, but you are not, in any event, at their mercy.

In the example above, Teacher seems to betray an opposite condition when he stresses "the way you (Supervisor) want them." While we should not be excessive in "diagnosis" based on such limited excerpt, a guess that Teacher has learned to depend upon Supervisor for evaluation and looks to Supervisor for direction would seem better founded than the contrasting hypothesis. Consider a very different example:

SUPERVISOR: How do things stand?

TEACHER: It's pretty well set, but I'm still not sure that the directions will be clear to everybody.

SUPERVISOR: Would it help to run through them?

TEACHER: Yeah—I think I'm just too close to them right now to see them clearly. Let's give it a try.

[Teacher recites his direction.]

SUPERVISOR: Well?

TEACHER: Actually, that sounded OK to me.

SUPERVISOR: Yeah. You know, I was a little worried as I read these directions in your plans—they're sort of complicated—but as you said them, the pauses you made and the way you used your voice to emphasize certain things—"Be *sure* to turn off the *oxygen* first; *first* the oxygen and *then* the acetylene"—it was really very clear.

TEACHER: Ah! Yes. I was thinking so much about what words to use that I didn't really think about my voice. I think that's the solution. If I take it slow and listen to what I'm doing, that ought to take care of it.

SUPERVISOR: I think so.

This excerpt communicates a substantially different flavor. Rather than implicitly defining his own role as "helper" (which, incidentally, tends to put Supervisor one up on Teacher), Supervisor's opening question expresses considerably more confidence in Teacher. It does not suggest that he is helpless: it asks for *his* appraisal, *his* perceptions, *his* judgments: in short, for him to take things in any direction that seems useful to him. Teacher expresses an uncertainty, but one that is considerably more specific than that expressed in the first case. Instead of saying, in effect, "I'm not sure whether my plans will meet your approval," Teacher asserts that the plans satisfy his own criteria, by and large, but identifies one technical problem that remains. Supervisor's response, framed as a question, leaves room for Teacher to elect many alternatives, for example, "No, I think it would be best not to fuss with it any more," or "I think it might help me if *you* read these directions out loud so that I could get some distance from them."

Supervisor might, indeed, have simply waited for Teacher to prescribe an exercise of some sort instead of suggesting a rehearsal. However, he apparently decided, perhaps for efficiency's sake, to introduce the idea himself, tentatively, as one possible course of action. His prior experiences with Teacher may have suggested that directiveness of this magnitude would be appropriate. Teacher, in turn, provided a rationale for following Supervisor's suggestion and affirmed the suggestion himself. When he had finished reciting the directions, Supervisor passed the initiative for evaluation back to Teacher. Once Teacher committed himself, Supervisor offered consensus and, moreover, provided a reasoned rather than an arbitrary consensus. Teacher expanded Supervisor's concept by translating it into an operational strategy for the lesson. Once again, Supervisor offered consensus.

While it is clear, in this case, that Teacher did depend upon Supervisor for assistance, the quality of his dependency does not seem inconsistent with essentially autonomous behavior. Having used Supervisor as a source of reactions, Teacher made productive use of Supervisor's responses on his own initiative. Again, such sparse data do not justify very elaborate interpretations, but somehow, one does not feel that Supervisor's evaluations were prized for their own sake, as reflections of approval. Whereas this teacher may value approval by others, as most men do, at least he does not seem to be gasping for it. His conscious focus is upon mastering problems in his own technical behavior. If, in the course of events, Supervisor also loves him, so much the better, but success does not depend on it.

In my discussion of methodologies in the conference, I will talk much more fully about autonomy and dependency in supervision. Other examples having no direct relationship to problems of autonomy could have been used here equally well. In any case, the examples should serve to demonstrate the point that *how* Supervisor behaves may be at least as consequential as the substantive content and the technical focus of his remarks. Teacher learns things from both dimensions of Supervisor's behavior. At the very same moment that the two of us are talking about sociometric variables in your classroom, you may be learning about who's boss, who knows more, who decides what's best—any number of self-definitions and definitions of our relationship, the goals of our relationship, our roles in the relationship, and all kinds of other things about what is appropriate in supervision and what is proscribed—simply from the way I conduct myself. For this reason, Supervisor's decisions about how to operate in the preobservation conference are monumentally more difficult than they would be if he only had to decide what to talk about. During Stage 1, he must be conscious of and must exercise deliberate control over his interactional behavior, in addition to thinking about the issues being discussed.

In the event that reasons do not seem to exist for rehearsal or review of the teaching plan during Stage 1, it is sometimes useful to reaffirm or to redefine the goals for that sequence of supervision, that is, to address the supervisory contract rather than the teaching to be performed. Should yesterday's definitions of what Supervisor and Teacher will do in today's supervision have been especially complex, a restatement of the contract could insure that both parties understand the course to be followed. If a variety of plausible contracts were identified yesterday, and if it was decided to hold selection in abeyance until Teacher could sleep on the possibilities for awhile, then Preobservation would be the natural time for final agreements to be made.

Again, Supervisor's technical conduct is important in relation to incidental learnings likely to arise from it.

1. SUPERVISOR: Now remember what we decided: your job, for today, will be to avoid asking "multiple questions." My job will be to keep track of your questioning and to note every multiple question you ask.

2. SUPERVISOR: OK, I'll try to be especially careful to get your questions down verbatim and the children's responses to them so that we can examine the questioning patterns afterwards.

3. SUPERVISOR: Yes, it makes good sense to me to work on questioning patterns if you'd like to. I remember that the last time we focused on questioning [some months ago] you brought that pattern of rhetorical questions under control very quickly. Do you think it would be useful for me to limit my data [gathering] to those episodes of the lesson containing questioning sequences, or should I get the whole business down?

4. SUPERVISOR: Well, supposing, since we've got the problem pretty well defined at this point [having treated it through several sequences of supervision], I stop observing for awhile so that you have a chance to work on it by yourself? I think your idea about tape-recording your teaching and then analyzing the tapes for questioning patterns afterwards is a very good one, particularly because you seem so comfortable with the recorder going and the kids have apparently gotten used to it. You know where to reach

me. If you'd like me to go over any tapes with you, I'd be happy
to. In the meantime, go ahead with it, and get in touch whenever
you want to take this up again or to move on to new issues.

I suspect that if you were the teacher in each of the examples
above, your learnings, your feelings, your expectations, and your general outlook on supervision, your teaching, and yourself might differ
considerably from case to case. You might note that in every instance
the technical object of study was approximately the same, namely,
"patterns of questioning."

As I have said, it is very difficult to prescribe methodology for
preobservation and supervision conferences because of how different
they tend to be. Differing issues, different people, different situations,
differing value systems, variations in the importance and urgency of
issues to be treated, and differences among psychological variables from
one instance of supervision to another make it just about impossible to
articulate categorical techniques. However, some guiding methodological principles can be stated. In the preobservation conference:

1. Do not raise questions (offer criticisms, objections,
suggestions, and the like) that are likely to undermine Teacher's
strategy for the teaching about to be undertaken.

2. If Teacher feels unready to teach—perhaps his plans are
insufficiently formulated or, for any reason, he has serious
misgivings about the lesson—and expects failure, encourage him
not to teach the lesson in question. A simple "filler" of some sort is
likely to be less disabling for Teacher and less useless or damaging
to the pupils than a lesson that fails, if only because Teacher
expects it to.

3. Avoid introducing novelties at Stage 1. Except for small,
manageable refinements that Teacher can incorporate easily into
his plan (and only Teacher knows, ultimately, what is easy and
what isn't), new ideas, new goals, and new strategies are not likely
to be assimilable or reproducible if they are formulated directly
before teaching is to occur.

4. Deal in Teacher's terms, in his conceptual framework, rather
than in Supervisor's or in external, theoretical frames of reference.
In other words, if "operant conditioning" is not the framework in
which Teacher has conceptualized his lesson, Stage 1 should not
be the time to examine it in those terms, precisely for the reasons
enunciated in Items 1 and 3 above.

5. Avoid supervisory techniques that have proved unsettling to
Teacher in the past or might, predictably, be disquieting at the
moment. For example, if Teacher has formerly become anxious

when Supervisor employed inductive techniques to pursue some line of inquiry; or, if Teacher typically seems uncomfortable when supervision follows a pattern of interrogation; or, if Teacher tends to be upset when Supervisor uses comparison (between Teacher and other teachers or Teacher and himself) to demonstrate his point, then such techniques should be deliberately avoided in Preobservation.

6. Take special efforts to insure that communication is clear, that Teacher and Supervisor understand each other's meanings precisely.

7. Deliberately control your impulses to direct. Give Teacher every opportunity to move in his own directions, to set his own issues, to lay things out however he pleases: to the extent that he is comfortable in doing so or unless he seems to be plunging into deliberations that are likely to work against him.

8. Avoid ritual commitment to the Preobservation Conference. If strong reasons do not exist for holding it, don't—and the same for every other stage of the supervisory sequence.

9. Supervisor's planning for Stage 1 and his self-awareness as he participates in Preobservation ought to incorporate process goals as well as technical ones. That is to say that Preobservation is most likely to succeed if Supervisor is as attentive to its interactional processes as potential sources of incidental learning as he is to the business at hand. My insistence upon this principle is motivated as much by practical concerns as it is by philosophical ones. If Supervisor is indeliberate in the conduct of his behavior, then that behavior can more easily operate at direct cross-purposes to his intended outcomes. If my intention is for you to do something adequately, but I seem to treat you as though you were totally inadequate, then, in all likelihood, I am simply spinning my wheels.

There is nothing easy about functioning according to this model. In many respects, traditions of supervisory behavior and conventions of social behavior work against us: it is neither simply a case of listen-and-talk nor one of "You do what I say." What is most difficult of all for Supervisor to achieve in practice is the multidimensional functioning that we envision.

Let us imagine an ideal supervisor. All in the same counterpoint, he must formulate his ideas and statements; he must hear what Teacher is saying and must understand Teacher's intended meanings; he must read Teacher's meanings both at face value and in symbolic terms, that is, he must be able to read between the lines sufficiently to detect signs of anxiety or any stressful internal condition that is active enough to create interference with intended outcomes; he must develop responses aimed, appropriately, at both overt and disguised expressions of ideas and feelings; he must delimit his range of behavior to keep it consistent with long-range supervisory goals as well as relevant to the immediate problems of supervision; he must monitor his own feelings and impulses and motives in order to keep the work aimed at Teacher's welfare rather than at his own; and he must make examined, yet almost instantaneous decisions about what to broach and what not to, what to give, what to withhold, what to reinforce, what to set into special relief by selective emphasis, and so on.

These "musts" are certainly not offered as professional imperatives. Neither do I mean to imply that they should be accepted as doctrinal elements of a supervisory orthodoxy. Instead, they represent a distillation from supervision I have practiced and observed of techniques that seemed to work and of elements of supervision that seemed to be missing on occasions when, by one measure or another, supervision failed. The picture should become clearer in later sections of this writing where case materials and special problems in supervision are examined.

In very simple terms, I mean to make the point that time after time we have discovered that unsuccessful supervision could be explained, at least partly, by Supervisor's failure to approximate this operational model and that successful supervision has often seemed accountable in just the opposite terms. While the multidimensional concurrency I envision might be impossible for most men to master, except in moments of intense concentration and at the expense of great psychological energy, my experience confirms that deliberate and prolonged practice which, itself, is carefully supervised, can begin to make important differences in surprisingly little time. As something to approximate, I have found the model useful. To think of it as defining minimum criteria for successful supervisory behavior, on the other hand, would have driven me from supervision a long time ago.

It should probably also be pointed out that this image of highly sophisticated technical behavior is *not* predicated either by the notion that Teacher's behavior and Teacher's success or failure are determined exclusively by Supervisor's behavior, as, for example, in a simple cause-effect paradigm, nor by an expectation that teachers are generally fragile. It sometimes seems, erroneously, that clinical supervision operates from the premises that teachers have marginally stable personalities, that supervisors hold the power of life and death over them, and that should Supervisor zig instead of zag, Teacher will plummet, shrieking, into a chasm of insanity or will disintegrate to dust forthwith. Hardly. By and large we neither save souls nor condemn them.

I do conceptualize clinical supervision as a facilitating practice designed to enable teachers to rise through a developmental sequence of technical competency and professional actualization at a faster pace and in a more thorough and integrated fashion than would be likely to occur without supervision. Hopefully these words will become more substantial as we move further into this presentation. While it is completely true that we have hurt teachers from time to time or, at least, that they have felt hurt by "what we have done to them," we have not killed anyone and do not think of ourselves as holding the power to do so.

Instead, I stress degrees of self-awareness and self-control that behoove supervisors to adopt because of the simple idea that relatively random motion will not lead me to my goals (which are likely to be congruent with Teacher's goals if I am operating properly) as certainly as directed motion could. It is rather to increase efficiency than to avoid danger that I advocate this model of conduct. If, when danger does exist, this model offers special protections, so much the better. I additionally trust that examined and deliberately disciplined supervision will generate many positive side effects, to some of which I have already alluded.

Analogously, it is argued every so often in the educational literature that some kind of psychotherapeutic experience should be incorporated into the professional preparation of teachers. In most instances, this proposal is not motivated by the fear that unless he is cured, Teacher will constitute a psychological menace to the children. While teachers are not generally libidinous monsters, sad to say they tend to be not nearly as psychologically useful to their pupils as they could be. By this thinking, I can strive to make them more useful without starting, necessarily, from the premise that they are sick or from a motive to pull their claws.

The methodological principles we have examined will be amplified in the context of Stage 4, the Supervision Conference.

STAGE 2: METHODS FOR OBSERVATION

The principal purpose of Observation is to capture realities of the lesson objectively enough and comprehensively enough to enable Supervisor and Teacher to reconstruct the lesson as validly as possible afterwards, in order to analyze it. Problems of observation will be addressed explicitly in the next chapter. For the present, I will review various data-gathering techniques that we have employed and will prescribe certain methods for observation in clinical supervision.

The first rule in Observation is for Supervisor to write down what he sees, *not* (simply) how he feels about what's going on. His notes should incorporate perceptions of, rather than inferences about, the lesson; they should be record rather than commentary. If it were possible to video tape a lesson and to record every sight and sound in a manner that overrode the camerman's selective biases, then the resulting record would probably be as complete and as undistorted as possible (unless, of course, everyone were outfitted in space suits that monitored neurophysiological processes as well). Even if it were generally feasible to produce such a record, however, it seems likely that its very completeness would make it unmanageable for supervisory purposes; data processing would take too long. It takes as long to air a tape as it does to film it, even longer to edit our sections for supervision, and longer still to air selections from the tape a second time in the conference. Moreover, since teachers can generally reconstruct episodes of teaching very quickly in their imaginations with the aid of written, verbatim, observation notes, it would consequently be wasteful to recapitulate taped episodes that take as long to see as they did originally— unless, perhaps, *pacing* represented a focal supervisory problem.

Audio tapes are even less satisfactory inasmuch as children's voices often seem very much alike, and it is sometimes impossible to identify individual speakers without being able to see them. In addition, temporal problems are the same for processing sound tapes as they are in relation to kinescope films. And in most situations the quality of recording equipment available is unsatisfactory for use in groups, particularly when people move about physically or manipulate equipment.

Except in special instances in which some quality of timing or of sound or of sight evolved as a salient supervisory issue, written data have proven most useful and most wieldy to clinical supervisors. Perhaps the greatest advantage of a written record, as I have suggested, is that Teacher and Supervisor can assimilate it most rapidly and most easily; the eye can incorporate, almost instantaneously, evidence that took a relatively long time to unfold in the lesson. Best of all, one can generally flip back and forth between pages of notes more quickly than it is possible to return to sections of a tape, even when the tape deck is equipped with an accurate clocking device.

Another excellent advantage of written notes is that by drawing arrows or circling passages or rearranging pages or chopping them up with a scissors, either Supervisor or Teacher can artificially juxtapose sections of the material in order to authenticate patterns of teaching or to ascertain various effects in the teaching. For example, if at nine o'clock Teacher instructed the children not to go on to Section Two of the test until they were told to, but at nine-twenty he berated Arnold for just "sitting there stupidly and wasting time" while other pupils moved on to the next section (without having been explicitly directed to do so), then there is, perhaps, nothing quite so persuasive as pulling these two incidents together (visually) where they can be examined, literally, side by side.

Or, if Marlene insists at some point, "You said we could do it in pencil," while earlier evidence proves that Teacher said, "Ink only!" or if Teacher seems unhappy because pupils' responses were sparse or confused and his key questions can be dredged up from the material and shown to be ambiguous and inadequately structured, then everyone enjoys the advantage of knowing, at least, that they are reviewing events which actually occurred if they can *see* the whole business all in a single moment. In other words, possibilities for rearranging written data reduce the likelihood that quibbles will arise in connection to who said what, and Teacher is not forced into the position of having to accept Supervisor's word for anything. Such advantages, of course, are based on the sometimes invalid assumption that Supervisor's hand (or mind) did not slip and that he truly recorded what actually occurred. We will examine problems of this kind later.

I have sometimes found it useful to combine sound recording with my written record, but in general practice no procedure has shaken down as successfully as note taking. Every so often I do encourage teachers to tape-record their own teaching for purposes of self-examination, but under such circumstances technical problems of data processing are not as severe. Although listening still is relatively inefficient, Teacher has more time at home in the evening to fiddle with the thing than the two of us would ever be likely to have during the school day. On one memorable occasion, I was supervising an experienced teacher whose teaching had some awful weaknesses, including biting sarcasms and infantilizations that rained down upon the pupils almost incessantly. Among other things, Teacher talked very rapidly and very percussively, like the rat-a-tat of an automatic weapon. Because I had only begun to work with this woman and because our relationship was circumscribed by the few remaining weeks in a summer program, I was rather in a quandary about what issues to pursue in supervision, if any.

At one point Teacher declared that during her whole career she had never been supervised systematically, that her teaching had never once been examined in detail, and that (although to me she seemed virtually immobilized by anxiety and extremely defensive in supervision) she really wondered how her teaching might seem to impartial observers, that is, to observers not connected to her own school system. Largely, I think, because of my own cowardice, I seized the opportunity to suggest to Priscilla that she tape-record some of her own teaching, listen to the tape privately at home, and then decide whether she could find issues in the teaching that she felt might be useful to examine with me.

Early the next morning, long before the day's work was officially under way, Priscilla came to my office, red as a beet, perspiring profusely, seemingly mortified. I asked what was the matter. She replied, "I thought the machine was broken; I thought it was playing at the wrong speed; I tried to slow it down," from which point, as it developed, the two of us had plenty to talk about for the remainder of the program. The point of this anecdote is that on certain occasions electronic recording represents the method of choice in Observation, although not in most instances.

Two limiting factors must be compensated in note-taking. Most observers find it difficult to keep up with the lesson, particularly if anyone is talking a great deal or very rapidly, and they also complain about not being able to see enough of what is happening around them because their eyes remain glued to their note pads. Both of these problems tend to become less severe with practice, although for some observers and in some situations they prove insurmountable. On such occasions electronic recording is sometimes forced upon us, at least as a supplementary measure. More often, we have found that group super-vision (which incorporated group observation) can be coordinated to alleviate problems of this kind.

The following techniques have been helpful although, clearly, none of them is problem-free.

    1. Shorthand or speedwriting can be very handy if the observer is proficient. However, unless Teacher can interpret Supervisor's shorthand, this technique precludes possibilities of sharing written data with Teacher at the conference. Shorthand transcriptions also seem too mysterious and untrustworthy at times (to Teacher) to be worth their obvious advantages.

    2. By omitting vowels, employing homonyms, and using phonetic representations, I have been able to develop a method of note taking that is comprehensible to me and can be made recognizable to Teacher with very little effort. In effect, I employ an idiosyncratic speedwriting. It looks something like this:

    SPOKEN LINE: I want you to turn to page forty-four.
    TRANSCRIPTION: I wnt u 2 trn 2 pg 44.
    SPOKEN LINE: Why don't you understand this? It's so simple!
    TRANSCRIPTION: Y dnt u undrstnd ths? S'o smpl!
    SPOKEN LINE: Write in ink, rather than pencil. If you don't know the answer, do not guess. Any questions? [Pupil raises his hand.]
    TRANSCRIPTION: rite n nk, rt pncl. F u dk th ans, do nt gss. Ny q's?
    $P_1 : \psi$
    Over a period of time, I have developed certain abbreviations that I now use consistently:
    Don't know: dk
    Rather than: rt
    Question: q

Teacher: T
Pupil: P# (where # indicates an individual pupil).
Raised hand: ⍦
No response: —
Two, too, to: 2
Four, fore, for: 4
See, sea: c
You: u
Why: y

As you might guess, what generally happens at the beginning of such an experiment is that by the time Supervisor has taken his notes off someplace to review, they make absolutely no sense whatsoever to him. Practice, however, makes better if not perfect, especially when accompanied by strong desire.

I have no direct knowledge of stenotype machines. I know, simply, that they are used by court stenographers, they punch or imprint a tape with various symbols, they have small keyboards and operate silently. It might be worthwhile to investigate how much trouble it is to train supervisors and teachers to use such equipment efficiently. Once again, the great advantage of a stenotyped transcript would be its visibility and ease of manipulation. Also, the recorder need not look at his machine. In practice, many clinical supervisors fail to observe nonverbal behavior because of their "busyness" in recording verbatim material. Except by means of group observation, we have not developed technical solutions for capturing both kinds of behavior at once.

Various researchers in supervision use observation schedules, both as a means of organizing data for research and for the sake of data-gathering efficiency. While such instruments may prove valuable for compiling normative information on teaching behavior, I have not found them to be particularly useful in individual supervision. In the first place, rather than recording Teacher's behavior in detail, observation forms generally record Supervisor's interpretations of what is happening, for example, at specified time intervals Supervisor may check "Accepting Behavior" to indicate that Teacher has acknowledged some pupil's response acceptingly or sympathetically. Like standardized achievement tests which only record answers but fail to provide detailed information about the testee's cognitive behavior, such check marks cannot differentiate qualitative differences among teachers earning checks in the same categories at approximately the same frequencies. Even worse, while in certain respects achievement test scores are unambiguous—the answer is either "e, none of the above" or it is not—supervisors' check marks are not nearly so reliable. What I see as "accepting behavior" you may see as something quite different, and the child may experience in still different terms.

It is not so much that supervisors are unlikely to check their schedules uniformly—indeed, if they are all working the same setting, have been trained to use their instrument by the same director, and are all supervised together, it is easy to imagine that reliability could be achieved—but rather that in the end, because, such schedules tell more about Supervisor than about Teacher in many instances, they are unsatisfactory for clinical supervision.

A closely related problem is that observation schedules tend to force teaching behavior or, at least, observations of teaching behavior, into *a priori* categories that may not correspond meaningfully to what Teacher is actually doing. Or they may fail to capture the significance of Teacher's behavior by forcing it into a framework of prior signification that is neither very useful nor particularly valid in the immediate situation. Furthermore, when they do not record pupil behavior, the data they provide are often useless for identifying relationships between teaching and learning. Consequently, we normally eschew observation schedules in clinical supervision and enjoin our supervisors to record everything they can that is spoken in a lesson (by both Teacher and pupils) along with whatever other events they can capture, for example, boardwork, A-V techniques, and physical arrangements of persons and materials. My thought, in this regard, is that while Supervisor can select certain episodes or issues from a complete record, he is not as able to broach phenomena that he failed to record during Observation: memory distorts and details become lost; reconstructed data lack authenticity and persuasiveness.

On certain occasions Supervisor and Teacher agree beforehand that Supervisor will only collect data in relation to some specific problem or category of teaching behavior, for example, "direction-giving." When Supervisor allows himself to be bound by such an agreement, he must recognize in advance that unless he attempts to get everything down anyway, he must resist temptations to treat other issues (for which documentary data have not been collected) later in the conference. Although exceptions are sometimes necessary, I generally consider unrecorded events to be irretrievable for supervisory purposes and find, incidentally, that to have lost certain opportunities because of preclusive contracts is often just as well. If an unrecorded pattern of teaching behavior is really important enough to isolate for supervision, then it will undoubtedly be recapitulated in later teaching performances. If it is not, ten-to-one such a pattern is not nearly as salient as Supervisor suspected.

Verbatim records are preferable to descriptive records because if anything needs to be modified, it is what Teacher says or does, *not* Supervisor's descriptions of his acts. On countless occasions one sees supervisors and teachers stumped when, for example, Supervisor asserts, "You used many complex and undefined technical terms in this lesson," but for want of verbatim data he cannot recall exactly what they were. Teacher can't either. Both parties become frustrated and uncomfortable, and nothing very useful happens: Teacher mumbles, "I'll try not to do that in the future."

By and large, our observational methods incorporate the following principles and techniques:

1. Record as much of what is said and done as possible; record speeches verbatim.

2. Record comments and questions about the teaching marginally (if at all), in some manner that separates them from the raw data.

3. Descriptions of nonverbal behavior should be recorded as factually and as objectively as possible, for example, "Johnny chewed his pencil, Andrew passed notes to Sally, and Sally dropped Andrew's notes into her desk without reading them," is preferable to, "The children seemed bored."

4. The observer's physical position in the classroom ought simultaneously to be minimally distractive to the pupils and to provide him with a different vantage point from Teacher's unless, for specific reasons (for example, Teacher may want Supervisor to see the class essentially as he does himself), other arrangements have been made in advance.

5. Observation should not be undertaken unless Teacher and Supervisor share common reasons for it in advance.

6. Teacher should expect Supervisor to record written data and should understand what the character of those data will be and the reasons for which they are being collected. Observation notes should ordinarily be made accessible to the teacher upon request, especially if Teacher has free time to examine them before the supervision conference.

7. As a rule, Supervisor should not intervene in the teaching in any manner during Observation. In the event that children approach him spontaneously with questions, he should explain to them afterwards that his job is to write down what is happening in class, and the like.

8. Supervisor should only intervene by explicit prior agreement with Teacher, and in a manner seeming mutually agreeable and appropriate to both except, of course, in physical emergencies. [I once intervened unhesitatingly when I observed a child attempting to boil liquid in a sealed test tube.]

9. Every so often, Supervisor should note the time marginally in order to be able to reestablish the duration of sequential episodes

later on. Unless a clock is situated behind Teacher, Teacher ought
to understand in advance that Supervisor will consult his watch
occasionally and his reasons for doing so.

10. If the lesson's pace precludes complete, continuous
recording, it is generally better to capture specific episodes in their
entirety than to collect otherwise piecemeal and fragmentary
notes. Although, subsequently, certain episodes will be taken from
context in the conference, at least such sections of the lesson will
be relatively intact.

11. Some means should be employed to identify individual
pupils in the observation notes (for example, a coded seating
plan), especially if their names are unknown to Supervisor. It may
be important to establish later which children made specific
responses as well as what responses were forthcoming.

12. Unless Teacher has been explicitly informed that
Supervisor will not remain present for the entire lesson, it is
generally best for Supervisor to stay until the end. Unexpected
early departures can be very alarming, particularly if Teacher
feels that things are not going well or that Supervisor has missed
the lesson's culmination.

13. Diagraming the teacher's and pupil's positions in the
classroom can be useful, for example, for keeping a running tally
of verbal participation or for illustrating interactional patterns
(Teacher-to-pupil; pupil-to-pupil) should such issues become
important in supervision.

To avoid artifacts that can be created by an observer's presence in
the classroom or to alleviate doubts that such artifacts have resulted
even when no demonstrable proof exists, one-way viewing screens
(mirrors) are often advantageous for observation. Unfortunately, the
increasing popularity of such devices has created a generation of children who know all about them. The existence of such sophisticated
pupils along with that of occasional teachers for whom the problem of
never knowing whether anyone is watching or not is bedeviling, make
viewing screens something less than an observational panacea, however.

My first traumatization by one-way mirrors occurred when a naive
female counseling intern used such a device to adjust an intimate
garment before her client arrived. As it happened, at the time I was
present with a group of other interns on the opposite side of the thing,
and everyone broke up so badly that we were unable to do anything
besides adjourn to the corridor. Nonetheless, with a modicum of self-
discipline and properly fitting underwear, the viewing screen can be an
excellent tool for observers.

In addition to developing mechanical techniques and special short-cuts for recording data, the clinical supervisor must also establish infinitely more complex methods to deal with perceptual biases and distortions, with tendencies to project, and with emotional factors that create unconscious selectivity during observation. We will examine this dimension of observation under "problems."

IV
Methodological Techniques
for Analysis and Strategy

PART 1

STAGE 3: ANALYSIS AND STRATEGY

(A) Methods of Analysis

Before dealing directly with techniques and methods of analysis, it seems best to establish a conceptual framework for Stage 3 by speaking first of *patterns* and *categories* of teaching behavior and, second, by augmenting previously stated ideas concerning *a priori* categories of observation and analysis.

Let's begin with a notion that was touched on briefly in the last chapter, namely, that human behavior is patterned, that is, in certain respects it is repetitious and that, as a subset of general behavior, teaching is also patterned. And if it is true that certain elements of any teacher's behavior tend to be repeated over and over again in his teaching, that patterns of his teaching on the first day are recapitulated almost every other day, then it follows, in my reasoning, that the cumulative effects of such patterns are more likely to have consequence for the pupils' learning, for better or for worse, than occasional, isolated elements of the teaching whose existence is either not incorporated by continuing patterns or whose relationship to such patterns is not immediately apparent.

Whereas it may be that no element of an individual's behavior represents behavior of which that individual is incapable and that, in effect, every behavior reflects a unique, enduring, underlying "self," it seems true, nonetheless, that certain constellations of behavior tend to express a man's quintessential self more than others do. We know an individual principally by his salient behavioral patterns, by the manifest style that makes him peculiarly what he is. My guess is that the teacher's unique identity has special significance in both of two senses.

First, inasmuch as it is most commonly true in teaching that the learners' relationships to the content are mediated by the teacher (that is, that rather than dealing directly with content most of the time, the students deal with Teacher's representations of that content instead), the quality and character of their substantive learning is affected by Teacher's influences upon the material as it is filtered through his own sensory, cognitive, and expressive apparatus. Who the teacher is, therefore, inevitably makes differences in how and in what the pupils learn of the material because his biases, his values, his distortions, and the like infuse the stuff he teaches. Teacher becomes subtly, inextricably, and inevitably insinuated into the curriculum.

Second, it is just as necessary to suppose that who the teacher is chiefly determines (along with who the learners are) what incidental learnings will be established. Taken together, these suppositions imply that both in relation to intended curricular outcomes and to unintended learnings relating to all sorts of other things that may directly affect conditions of learning, Teacher's salient patterns of behavior count more than anything else about Teacher, for ill or for good, and that for supervision to have any palable effects upon the students' lives, it must be aimed at strengthening, extinguishing, or in some other way modifying these saliencies of the teaching performance. Besides the fact that Teacher's patterns fill the air more than anything else about him, one must appreciate how potently learnings resulting from certain stimuli can be reinforced by repetitions of those stimuli and of how important this can be either when what is learned makes particularly good sense or when what is learned is nonsense—especially important when such learning is of reasoning processes, personal and role concomitants of learning, self-definition, and of intellectual behavior generally.

In this frame of reference, clinical supervision has been committed to center around salient teaching patterns rather than unusual or relatively superficial variables in teaching. By this commitment the clinical supervisor has bought himself a great deal of trouble and probably requires strong masochistic tendencies in order to be very successful. Just as a preview, we might consider that *salient* characteristics of behavior are more likely to resist change than superficial ones; that

Teacher manifests the patterns he does because they are or they seem to be useful to him (even seemingly self-defeating behavior can be useful if what the man needs is to fail); and that of all the factors tending to rigidify Teacher's patterns, their *reinforcement by the pupils*, day after day, is not the least significant.

But let's leave the difficulties for the next section. Let us presently consider the question of how Supervisor formulates *categories* of teaching behavior in order to organize his data meaningfully. And let us imagine that, in a hypothetical instance of supervision, my contract with Teacher requires me to observe the entire lesson and to be ready to broach any issues at all that seem to exist in the teaching.

Since I have deliberately not structured my observations in advance so that, for example, I should only record data in certain predetermined categories, and since I have collected as many data as possible in order to alleviate unconscious selectivity, I must now, *ex post facto*, invent categories of some kind. I must organize the data into classes of one sort or another in order to be able to talk about them. At this juncture I have reached the point where all the pains I have taken to be objective until now (for example, my efforts to record everything) threaten to be undermined by the subjective intrusions I am about to make. Categories of behavior have no objective existence of their own; they do not exist independently in the real world; I make them up.

I operate from the premise that the categories I invent can vary along a continuum of validity: I can be altogether capricious, on the one hand, or I can try very hard to stay close to the data and to keep my inferences modest, on the other. I tell myself that there is some sensible difference between imposing categories upon the data arbitrarily and extrapolating categories from the data carefully. I tell myself that I will do the latter, suspecting all the while that my distinctions between imposition and extrapolation may be fictional, but trying, nevertheless, to follow certain rules and guidelines which will be described below, to keep adulteration minimal.

Whereas it is true that my past experience in clinical supervision has conditioned me to be alert to certain categories of teaching that, over and again, have proven to be pertinent and useful in providing contexts for supervision, for example, questioning, rewards, interaction, and direction-giving, by staying deliberately loose I am able to discover new categories from time to time which expand my conceptual repertoire and increase my analytical versatility. Every time I "detect" a pattern in the raw data, I risk distortion. And every time I force a detectable pattern to fit a category, I run the same risks. Not only may my fittings be invalid, but to have considered a pattern in relationship to some specific category (for example, a pattern of teaching in the first person, "I," into a category, "egocentrism") will probably bias my thinking about that pattern subsequently, even if I consciously decide to unglue it and to fit it in somewhere else.

The premise that directs me, in any event, is that forced and invalid fits are more likely to occur in conjunction with observational schedules, that is, with an *a priori* set of categories through which the teaching is viewed from the beginning, and less likely to occur if I fish for categories after the fact, after the history has been recorded. One critical variable for objectivity will be my ability to relax my predispositions as I observe and as I explore the data for patterns. Even though I know that I cannot escape my own biases altogether and that I cannot shed my history of experience as a supervisor, I elect, nevertheless, to run risks of prejudice and self-deception rather than to stack the odds against discovery by deliberately deciding in advance what kinds of phenomena I ought to see.

An opponent of this reasoning might argue that at least with an *a priori* schedule or with a predetermined analytical grid the supervisor can know *explicitly* about existing dangers of misrepresentation, while by our method, interpretive biases are more likely to intrude undetected. While the point is well taken in certain respects, it overlooks the chance that subjective interference will take place anyway. My hunch is that despite the way it looks, great distortions can arise in the first method partly because of the feeling one is likely to develop that one's technique, cut and dried, keeps one safe. I doubt it. Having no illusions of safety beforehand, I am stuck with the conscious weight of my frailties afterward and cannot pretend that it is all right to ignore them. The burden of systematic self-examination is built right into our practice of clinical supervision. One can dodge it but, especially in group supervision, one can rarely get away with it. One never has recourse to checks in boxes or to magic numbers as a basis for rationalization although, heaven knows, with strong enough needs for such foolishness one can always find a way.

Given the incentives and skills to do so, I suppose that the supervisor who uses observational schedules and prestructured analyses is as able or as unable to discipline himself as any other supervisor. Being unable to claim any greater virtue for my people in this regard than for other people, I suspect, in any case, that discovery of novelties in teaching and the possibility of finding connections spontaneously in analysis are inhibited by most forms of preordination. In the final analysis this may prove to be simply a matter of personal preference and personal temperament. I choose to court Serendipity.

Let us turn now to the actual work of analysis. Imagine: I (the supervisor) have just come from observation and have copious notes, verbatim quotations, times, and the like from which to develop a design for supervision. My first problem is to create a more streamlined version of what happened than the raw data themselves provide. I want, simultaneously, to condense the material to a wieldy size and to avoid introducing biases that distort what actually occurred in the lesson. I want to wind up with a representation of reality, namely, of the teaching, that is true to life and as economical as it can be—a goal that is never completely possible.

Having determined that patterns of teaching behavior, once identified by analysis, generally ought to serve as the substantive content of supervision conferences, I proceed to search the data for behavioral patterns and employ the following measures to keep me from butchering them too badly. My first concern is to insure that the regularities which I will eventually attribute to the teaching are authentic, that is, that what I call patterns will really be patterns. My first criterion is that the behavior in question must be repetitious; whatever its character, the ploy must be repeated from time to time in order to qualify as a teaching pattern. Just as two points, at least, are required to define a line, we can generally assume that some minimum number of repetitions is needed to establish a pattern.

Much of the time my job will be easy because behavioral repetitions will occur within the context of the lesson observed. Sometimes the problem of authenticating patterns becomes more difficult. For example, since their periodicity varies, patterns may occasionally comprise behaviors whose repetitions are thinly distributed. Their rarefaction may cause me not to recognize their relatedness or, believing in such things, I may be tempted to suppose that some single datum does reflect a behavioral pattern whose attenuation makes empirical documentation impossible or very impractical. In such a case, if it seems important to be able to document a pattern empirically before broaching it with the teacher, I may be forced to withhold the pattern in question until persuasive evidence can be collected over a cycle, that is, over more than one sequence of supervision.

In hierarchical order, three principles will govern my analysis. Keeping in mind that I am not simply collecting patterns as an indoor sport and that patterns selected for treatment in supervision will presumably be chosen because they represent teaching behavior that may be significantly related to the pupils' learning, my first choice (all else being equal) will be patterns whose consequences are *demonstrable in the data.* For example, if I have detected a pattern of sarcasm with which I hope to confront Teacher for the sake of establishing whether children are getting hurt and are developing unfriendly attitudes toward the school, it would be very nice indeed if the data provided several instances in which, immediately after Teacher has thrown a verbal barb, each child who had been a target rose to his feet, tears running down his face, screaming hysterically:

"I hate this stinkin' school! I hate you! I hate learning! You
have hurt me! You should fall down a sewer!"

I would merely, under such circumstances, have to present my evidence
and then rest my case. If I mean to establish causes and effects, the
sweetest data of all are those in which effects are clearly demonstrated.
In real life, unfortunately, consequences of teaching behavior must
generally be inferred because they are not directly visible. If I disciplined myself to cite only those patterns whose effects were visibly
manifest, I should often be immobilized from doing anything. Nevertheless, "visibility in the data" is my first selection criterion.

My second test of whether a pattern I have identified is likely to
be of much consequence consists of the question of whether my hypothesis can be *supported by theory*. In other words, being unable to
prove effects directly from the data, the next best possibility is to be
able to summon existing theory in support of my predictions. Let us
suppose that Teacher tends to remedy her first graders' occasional
inattentiveness by saying:

"If you don't pay attention, a big dog with pointy teeth will
come while you are sleeping and will eat up your arms and legs."

Although it might be nice, it is not really necessary for the pupils to
lapse into catatonic trances in order to develop the possibility that this
technique fails to achieve certain pedagogic ideals. Having *An Elementary Introduction to Basic Psychoanalysis for Lay Readers, Made Simple* at my fingertips, I feel sufficiently armed to raise tentative questions
about this practice during supervision. If, whenever a child offers a
response to one of Teacher's questions, Teacher turns his back toward
the child, I would probably feel, having some knowledge of operant
conditioning, that a sufficiently reasonable basis existed in theory to
raise the issue. While some theories are clearly better than others, being
more relevant or more generally accepted than others, almost any
theory is better than no theory at all.

My least acceptable alternative, albeit one that I feel I must
employ from time to time, is to isolate a pattern for examination simply
because of *hunches* I have about it. Failing to have documentary
evidence and failing to be cognizant of satisfactorily applicable theory,
I may follow my intuitions and address the pattern anyway. I must
recognize in advance, however, that if Teacher is unready to believe
me in any event, I am least likely to be persuasive on this basis; I am
most likely to be wrong (assuming that examined theories have been
more rigorously substantiated than my hunches); and I run the risk of
teaching, incidentally, that hunching one's way through supervisory
analyses represents acceptable practice which, in our framework of
clinical supervision, it emphatically does not: certainly not as a principal mode for supervision.

At this point I should describe distinctions between "patterns" and "categories" and explain their relationship to one another. Once I have unearthed patterns in the data by methods that will be described shortly, one of my means for deciding whether or not they are significant and, if so, what specific importance they carry, is to name general categories of teaching into which they may logically fit. For example, if Teacher continually asks many-pronged questions, I could think of "questioning" as the relevant category and of "multiple questioning" as one of this teacher's salient patterns in that category. While identification of patterns is represented simply by a sorting and collation of empirical data, the invention of categories and the naming of patterns by reference to them represent processes that enable me to elevate the data to a level at which they can be understood by theory.

Despite prior awareness of common categories, my explicit attendance upon categories occurs *a posteriori*. After the data are in and after their salient patterns have been identified, my thoughts turn to building a paradigm of the teaching by constructing a taxonomy to describe it. Having assembled the paradigm, I can move beyond simple descriptive classification to problems of interpretation and meaning, first, by summoning whatever theory I have available for a conceptual framework and second, by shifting to more differential analysis of the patterns in question. In more concrete terms, if I have observed a pattern of multiple questioning, I may first direct my attention to whatever I know generally about questioning as a component of teaching and, second, to problems concerning the special importance that a multiple questioning pattern may have in the immediate situation. My analytical focus may shuttle back and forth so that having jumped from a pattern to a general category, my thoughts can proceed to new questions of which I have been reminded by thinking of that category; to the detection of additional patterns to which I had not been alert previously; and from new patterns to new categories, etc.

In many instances a given pattern will be incorporable by more than one category. For example, a pattern of multiple questioning, while fitting the category "questioning" might also fit a category "centeredness," if the teacher has framed his multiple questions consistently in the first person (a pattern of egocentrism), so that the implicit reason for the pupils to address the question(s) in the first place is for Teacher's sake: "*I want* you to tell me how the elements are ordered in the periodic table; can you name the first five *for me*; can you *tell me* about their electron structures; why is hydrogen number one; *I want* you to *tell me* what is the difference between atomic weight and atomic number?" The very same pattern may have different (plural) qualities of significance depending upon the categories in which it is conceptualized, and its differing qualities may be mutually reinforcing, mutually opposing, mutually canceling, counterbalancing, or mutually irrelevant in the context of the pupils' learning and experience. The fact that a specific pattern has categorical concurrency may be significant in its own right. It often appears that complex patterns of this kind incorporate both strengths and weaknesses simultaneously, either of which could easily be eclipsed if only a single, global category were employed in analysis.

Methodologically, my first move is to peruse the data for easily identifiable patterns. By just scanning the stuff, for example, I am likely to discover that every other verbalization in the lesson was by Teacher. In this case I have identified "teacher-pupil" as the dominant interactional pattern (later, I may decide to address the category "interaction" in the conference). I may also see at a glance that Teacher heavily outweighs pupils in the ratio of talk: Teacher speaks fifty words for every student's word. It may also be easy to see that whereas twenty-five children attended class, dialogue involved only seven of them during the lesson and that, of the seven, two had the lion's share. My eyes may be struck at once by specific words that are repeated frequently, for example, Teacher: "OK, very good!" in which case I may have unearthed some kind of stereotyped response, in this case a pattern of stereotyped rewards (two categories spring to mind, namely, "rewards" and "stereotypy").

In this fashion my eyes disclose patterns. It picks out recurring elements. You will note that visual scanning may reveal teaching patterns to me even before I have paid any explicit attention to the substantive content of the data. I am aided by my capacity to form visual gestalts which give me respite from intellectual labor. It sometimes happens, however, that I am weakened by the same mechanism, when I allow visual primacy to take over and, having at least found something to talk about, I send my brain on a holiday and fail to deal with more important issues that only it could have revealed to me.

After my eyes are done with their pickings, I turn from the form of the stuff to its substance: having looked at it, I now read it. If I am sufficiently alert, there is just no telling what my reading will dig out. At this stage I am generally more productive if I can pay direct attention to what is there than if my mind goes squirreling off in its own directions as it did while my eyes were doing the work. The content analysis may reveal that from time to time Teacher imposes his own value judgments upon the pupils as, for example, when he tells them that certain problems are harder than others, certain tribes were good Indians but other tribes were bad Indians, and that Democracy is best.

I may discover that Teacher's values are communicated more implicitly by information he includes or omits from his exposition: rich people attend the opera; Russian citizens do not criticize the state; poor people are culturally deprived; or that his omissions give rise to factual distortions: all objects can be classified as living or nonliving; all points in a continuous curve will admit of a tangent; America was settled by

Europeans fleeing religious persecution; or that, plain and simple, he is communicating incorrect information: Jews never make good soldiers; the earth is flat; the moon is made of green cheese.

I may discover that Teacher makes promises which he generally keeps or does not keep. I may find that Teacher uses specialized terminology inconsistently, for example, sometimes he calls them "minus numbers," and other times he calls them "negative numbers"; sometimes they are "lines," but at other times they are "rays" or "line segments." I may find that Teacher's meanings do not always correspond with pupils' meanings, even though conversation proceeds for a time as if there were mutual understanding. For example, it may be clear from Teacher's context that he means "independence" to connote fresh, insubordinate behavior, whereas the Pupil's context independence seems a virtue, as in the Declaration of. Or, Teacher's having put the example three hundred thirty-three times three hundred thirty-three on the board, and having asked at one point, "And what do we do now with the three?" it may become clear at once that although Pupil's answer was correct, it was in reference to the wrong three and that, consequently, as Pupil's comments indicate, the rejection of his answer was confusing to him and seemed unfair.

I may discover that Teacher tends to conduct private communications publicly, for example, when he reminds Seymour that he must take his pill at eleven o'clock at the same level of audility at which he might appropriately announce, "The king is dead; long live the king!" or, in the opposite direction, makes public communications privately, as for example, by telling Lena that the harmony exercise should both begin and end with a tonic chord although that information should, logically, have been directed toward the entire class. I may discover that in the very process of teaching grammar, Teacher commits precisely the errors against which he is cautioning. It may become apparent that in connection to teaching about inductive reasoning, Teacher is exemplifying such reasoning in his own behavior.

In short, by reading the data and asking the question, "What is happening at this point?" I discover sequences of behavior, I make tentative inferences about them, I find whether the behaviors in question constitute salient patterns in the teaching, I review my inferences and test them against data and theory, I find which hunches are supportable and which are not, and, withal, I assemble a collection of patterns and, in effect, a collection of issues among which I must sort and select all over again to develop strategies for the supervision conference. Having found what I have found, as in the examples above, I now attempt consciously to reason my own value judgments on each of the patterns, partly because I have not done so (explicitly) before and partly to illuminate and confront value judgments that I made without full consciousness at earlier stages of the analysis. Knowing that I never was able to suspend my values, even while all I was doing was searching the data, and realizing that my search and my discoveries were governed, in some degree, by implicit value judgments, I must now open the whole system as well as I can. I must do whatever I can to avoid running a conference in which the only reason for addressing something and the only reason for believing that something is good or bad is because that's how I feel about it.

Perhaps the most vulnerable aspect of my approach consists of my attempts to adopt the children's frames of reference as one basis for deciding in what manner some feature of the teaching is likely or unlikely to be significant. It is very hard, largely because it seems so easy, to second-guess how specific children or groups of children will experience the teacher's behavior. All that I have working for me is the fact that I myself was once a child, plus the clinical experiences in which I have, presumably, learned something about how children operate and obtained a considerable background of classroom observation.

What makes things awfully difficult at certain moments is that I feel convinced that Teacher's behavior is engendering certain feelings and certain attitudes among the pupils, but it is likely that if I were to ask the pupils outright what they felt, their responses would not support my hypotheses. "Do you have a depreciated self-concept? Are you being taught to cheat? Have you learned that in this place your ideas count for nothing? Would you like to kill Papa and possess Mama?" *"Who, me?"*

Nevertheless, when attempting to decide whether a teaching pattern is likely to have important consequences, I generally do try to imagine that behavior as if I were a child in the class and to imagine what effects might occur as that behavior was reenacted throughout the year. Although wonderful opportunities exist, in this connection, for systematic phenomenological research, I am not aware of any that has been undertaken so far. The worst fault in this process is that my supervision is only likely to be as good as my guesses (and, later, Teacher's), my generalizations, my inferences, and my predictions; and there are never any guarantees. Later on, as I develop strategies for the conference, I will play the same game all over again, this time trying to imagine the likely effects resulting from the children's behavior, and from what will be my own behavior during the conference, in the teacher's frame of reference. Although Teacher is older and more fluent than the pupils, and certainly more accessible to me, I am sometimes still in a Russian roulette: a chamber I thought was empty turns out to be emotionally loaded for Teacher who is summarily shot from supervision with a resounding thwack. Or, wanting to skirt delicate issues, I tiptoe through supervision and discover later that I might just as well have worn cleats.

No matter, I have learned from experience that many teachers often do not really think much about how things may be experienced by their pupils or they tend to assume that events in the children's frames of reference will be very much as they see them in their own. For example, as often as not, teachers gauge progress by a measure of what material has been covered. Implicitly they assume that what has been taught has been learned. If not, then why the great thrust to cover Chapter Six by the end of the week? How often have you turned from the end of a lesson feeling it was good, simply because you felt fluent in your teaching and covered, pretty much, what you wanted to? Certainly it seems true that when teachers do think about what class was like for the pupils, their thoughts generally fasten on a very limited sector of the pupils' experience, namely, that relating directly to the content being taught. It is unusual to find a teacher who, on a regular basis, thinks explicitly about what else the children may have learned from him besides chemistry or "the scientific method."

I continue to examine teaching patterns in a hypothetical framework of pupil experience (when the data do not provide clues to their real experiences), partly to establish that practice in the teacher's own behavior, even though our specific guesses on any occasion may be quite wrong. I trust the probability that over long periods of time, Teacher's guesses will get to be better than mine because of his continuing proximity to the students and his greater familiarity with them.

Most of the time my principal criterion for evaluating patterns is the question of whether or not they helped Teacher to get what he was after. Allowing that goals must sometimes be reformulated as a lesson proceeds and taking into account that any lesson may have both long- and short-term objectives, that is, as well as general results, there may be moment-to-moment payoff as specific tactics are employed to move inquiry from one juncture to the next (which, in some degree, either work or don't work), the question can be sharpened: does the evidence suggest that this pattern helped Teacher to get what he wanted at the moment(s) it was manifested? Another question for evaluating patterns is whether, irrespective of Teacher's prior objectives, the outcomes likely to have arisen from their existence, particularly the incidental learnings, seem generally worthwhile or not.

Sometimes the very goals toward which Teacher is aiming may seem untenable or undesirable to the supervisor. Under such circumstances a double analysis can be developed: on the one hand, patterns can be evaluated vis-à-vis Teacher's intentions and, on the other, in relation to alternative goals that Supervisor may favor. Sometimes such conflicts relate to ends. Teacher feels that every student should understand the mechanics of the electoral college but Supervisor does not.

Sometimes, they simply relate to means. Teacher and Supervisor agree that the pupils should find pleasure in music but do not agree on how to transport them.

After having identified patterns in the data, visually and by analysis of the substantive content, and after having attempted to determine their significance by reference to *Teacher's goals* and to the *pupils'* demonstrated or inferred *experiences*, my final step in analysis is to discover whether the documented patterns can be arranged in some hierarchical order. Some teaching patterns will be more prominent than others. Some patterns will seem more consequential than others, if not in relation to their frequency, then because of the likelihood that they affect particularly important areas of the pupils' learning and development, for example, the degree to which they accept and value themselves. Some patterns will seem to have special importance because of their superordinate relationships to other patterns. For example, if Teacher initiates all questions and directions (category: "origins"), if Teacher performs all evaluations of the pupils' academic progress, if Teacher conducts his classes so that pupils never have opportunities for conversing with one another, and if Teacher displays a prominent "I" pattern, then "teacher-centeredness" or "egocentrism" might logically be established as the superordinate pattern in reference to which all other patterns acquire special significance. "Centeredness" may be placed at the top of the hierarchy and may be employed as the organizing principle of the analysis and, subsequently, of the supervision.

Consideration of patterns in a hierarchical arrangement may send me back to the data to see if other relevant patterns exist, if additional evidence exists to confirm or to reject hypotheses already developed, and to take another sounding on whether the hierarchical organization I have invented rings true in the natural flow of the lesson. Having selected portions of data and having rearranged them according to my view of "what goes together," that is, into arbitrary sequences, I must take special pains to insure both now and later (in the conference) that the resulting distortions are justifiable.

(B) Methods of Strategy

There are several levels at which we can conceptualize the activities of this stage. We might say, for example, that Supervisor has already begun work in this context at the moment he decides whether or not to prepare a prior strategy for the conference to follow. The decision to stop or to go on to a formal plan, is one of Strategy. Once having decided to go ahead, Supervisor engages in two forms of activity that will occupy our major interest in this section, namely, of making decisions about *what* should occur in supervision, *what* outcomes should result from supervision, and other decisions about *how* to bring about the events and achieve the results he is after. I intend, at this point, to make a twofold distinction: first, "*what*-and-*how*" is one way to distinguish the ends-means relationship or, in more scholastic language, the "goals-and-procedures" categories into which teaching plans are commonly divided. Second, Supervisor's interest, in this connection, is centered both upon the conference and upon events that will occur after the conference: in future teaching, in future cycles of supervision and, generally, in the future development of Teacher's professional behavior. In short, Strategy incorporates decisions relating to means and ends, presently and for the future.

Having analyzed his observation notes and having isolated various patterns of teaching behavior from the data, Supervisor must decide which issues to select for the conference. This means, in effect, that he must begin to set goals in relation to which he can formulate selection criteria. Supervisory goals are generally conceptualized in a multidimensional framework: in a context of issues and problems deriving from several overlapping frames of reference.

Some goals, for example, are generated by the data. Supervisor can take his leads from features of the teaching that stand out in particularly sharp relief; from patterns of teaching which, for one reason or another, attract his special attention. Catch-as-catch-can, it is almost always true that certain patterns of teaching seem to carry special significance as one analyzes observational data. Of course, the tendency to isolate specific teaching patterns may simply reflect Supervisor's perceptual or professional biases rather than any measure of their objective importance, and this is one problem that we shall have to consider later on.

Instead of beginning from the press of data, Supervisor may define goals in reference to continuing problems with which he and Teacher have been working. In other words, from a framework of already existing supervisory issues, Supervisor may select elements of data which, to the casual observer, might not seem particularly important for supervisory treatment. Indeed, should certain issues take precedence because of earlier priorities, and should it happen that no material from the current data is germane, Supervisor might deliberately elect to ignore the immediate lesson or to defer its analysis in order to stay engaged in lines of inquiry that require extension or culmination or closure. Ideally, it is best to determine that observation would be gratuitous beforehand, in time to avoid it, but in many cases one cannot be sure about such things in advance.

Another basis for determining goals might exist in Supervisor's conceptualization of some genetic sequence of problems that should represent a long-range design for supervision. He might, for example, have decided that certain categories of teaching should be examined in some logical, sequential order according to a genetic model which suggests, in effect, that development of teaching technique requires certain technical competencies to be established in order for other, dependent competencies to be establishable: in simple terms, a technical model that prescribes first things first. Neither will every such sequence be equally valid or useful nor, in all probability, is there any specific sequence that can have equal validity for all teachers. In any event, Supervisor's goals for a particular conference might be generated by a "master plan," in which case his selection of issues for treatment (and of relevant data) could appear quite different from those of another supervisor who took his leads directly from the raw data.

I have intended these examples to suggest that Supervisor's goals and his rationales for supervision may come from different places at the same time. Indeed, as we examined methods for Preobservation earlier, we saw that sometimes his goals will have been stipulated beforehand in the contract, at the beginning of a sequence of supervision. It is unnecessary to place such frameworks for goal setting in any order of value. Let us simply recognize that a plurality of contexts for defining goals exists, that the few examples given above do not represent an exhaustive collection of possibilities, and that, in common practice, multiple frames of reference can operate concurrently as Supervisor tries to decide what he is after.

It should also be emphasized that I have spoken about what *Supervisor* is after only for simplicity's sake: it would be mistaken to suppose that these examples are meant to imply that Supervisor should make such decisions unilaterally or that his rationales for goal setting should be kept secret from Teacher. On the contrary, clinical super- vision attaches very high priorities to collaborative goal setting, to the adoption of supervisory goals deriving from Teacher's own system of priorities, and to the practice of making Supervisor's goals explicit and of reaching agreement on them in instances when *his* goals set the directions for supervision. Implicitly, in other words, the press of data, reference to things that have come before in supervision, and reference to a long-range supervisory plan might each be incorporated by an even larger system of meaning, namely, by Teacher's frame of refer- ence, to the degree that Supervisor can understand it. Even though Supervisor must often review his notes, perform analyses of the teaching, and formulate strategies for supervision by himself, he should, nevertheless, function as Teacher's advocate during these stages—not, necessarily, as an advocate of what Teacher has *done*—and should take pains later on to establish whether or not he anticipated Teacher's requirements accurately.

We have raised the question of goal setting, assuming that Super- visor needs goals in order to decide which teaching patterns to select for supervisory treatment. It could equally well be argued that Supervisor needs analyzed data in order to formulate goals. I am afraid that goals are to data as chickens are to eggs and that no simple solution to the problem of which comes first is likely to be sufficient. In practice, Supervisor generally engages in a process of shifting back and forth between his observation notes and his other frames of reference as he tries to lay plans for the next step. *There is no single correct sequence for handling this task.* It is neither more correct to begin with goals nor to begin with data and, operationally, it is often impossible to make such distinctions. Indeed, one must avoid blinding oneself to either dimension of the problem or allowing oneself to adopt either approach exclusively.

As long as it doesn't matter, theoretically, where one starts, I should like to begin by discussing some general methods for selecting patterns of teaching for supervision. We may assume that Supervisor works from certain *a priori* goals, that his data, in turn, generate new goals, and that his goals have been and will continue to be formulated in a context of priorities that derives largely from Teacher's own frame of reference. Moreover, according to this model of clinical supervision, we can anticipate that Supervisor will define both *technical* goals and *process* goals. Methods for structuring such goals will be examined below.

In general, how does Supervisor select specific patterns with which to deal? In general, three principles serve as selection criteria for material to be addressed in supervision. The teaching patterns (and associated issues) discussed should be *salient, few in number*, and, as well as can be judged beforehand, *intellectually and emotionally accessible to the teacher for analysis and treatment.* Before dealing directly with specific techniques employing these criteria, I should spend a moment to describe the clinical supervisor's reasons for adopting them.

REASONS FOR SALIENCY: One set of reasons for "saliency" has already been offered above in the section on analysis. I have argued, essentially, that salient patterns will probably have the greatest effects upon the pupils' learning. A second rationale can be expressed by the proposition that even though there may sometimes be discomfort associated with treatment of prominent teaching patterns, nevertheless, Teacher's confidence in supervision, his incentives for supervision, and his rewards from supervision are likely to pale if, in his perception, supervision is merely a quibble, a string of equivocations, an obsession with superficialities. His morale, *qua* supervisee, will depreciate if supervision merely wastes his time. For supervision to be important and for it to seem important, it must deal with issues that are important, and salient features of the teaching are more likely to satisfy this condition than peripheral ones.

A third reason is that it is generally easier to establish the significance of ancillary patterns by reference to salient patterns than vice versa. That is to say, prominent patterns of teaching can more readily serve as organizing principles for the data than lesser elements. A fourth reason is that Teacher can generally recognize saliencies in his own behavior more easily than superficialities, partly because they express more of his style and partly because, by definition, more data are available to document salient patterns. Although one occasionally encounters defensive flights into superficiality or a teacher's apparent inability to recognize prominent regularities of his own behavior, such cases represent exceptions (or reflect Supervisor's failure to have predicted "treatability" accurately). Further on, we will deal with them.

REASONS FOR FEWNESS: By committing the error often enough of saturating supervision conferences with so many issues of such great significance that not even the spongiest teacher could be expected to assimilate all of them, I have learned that "few" is better than "many" in much the same sense that silence is golden. First off, the time available for any supervision conference is not infinite, although such conferences occasionally seem endless. Secondly, even in infinite time, Teacher does not have an infinite patience nor an infinite capacity for assimilating ideas or generating them, and anyhow, assimilation is only an intermediate goal at best: the real goal is to develop reasons, strategies, and techniques for working on the patterns considered, something considerably more difficult and complex than simply recognizing their existence.

REASONS FOR "TREATABILITY": I suspect that reasons for this criterion are self-evident. I might say that even after supervision has become an old shoe, Supervisor sometimes guesses wrong about the psychological accessibility of certain issues and, when he compounds his error by persevering in their treatment, generally winds up having squandered the conference. At best, it has been a waste of time. At worst, if this sort of thing happens repeatedly, Teacher may reject supervision altogether.

(C) Implementing the Three Criteria: Some Specific Methods

In the larger context of methods for strategy, one might say, recalling the "what-how" distinction made earlier, that the very decision to choose on these criteria *is* an element of method. The next methodological question is how to do so.

SALIENCY: How can Supervisor determine whether any given pattern of teaching is salient? What referents are germane? The most easily satisfied condition for saliency is probably that the pattern in question should appear frequently in the teaching. Frequency and abundance are generally simple to detect. There is always the possibility, however, that frequency alone is not a sufficient condition for establishing saliency for supervisory purposes. If it happened, for example, that every time a pupil responded, Teacher scratched his ear, nonetheless, "ear-scratching," despite its frequency, might not be worth troubling with in supervision. Unless, because the pupils had caught on to this flection's relationship to their own behavior and were deliberately attempting to condition Teacher to tear his ear off, Supervisor could establish the pattern's special significance for them, he would probably not give it any second thoughts.

Thus, it would seem that "frequency" must be joined with "significance" in order to establish *useful* definitions of saliency. One might, in fact, attribute saliency to a pattern because of the clarity of its demonstrable effects upon the students, irrespective of its frequency in the teaching. If Teacher only made Roger cry once during the lesson, but if it were easy to show that he cried because of something Teacher did to him, then, somehow, however it was that Teacher behaved might seem salient in the context of that lesson, certainly in the context of Roger's experience. In any event, frequency has been the handiest and most useful index of saliency in our practice of clinical supervision thus far.

As I suggested in our earlier discussion of analysis, some teaching patterns will seem to be highly important, even when their effects upon the children are *not* directly demonstrable. Such patterns might seem significant because of their ostensible emotional effects or, perhaps more commonly, because of their intellectual character: they might, for example, seem very appropriate or completely inappropriate to the children's actual levels of cognitive functioning. My point is that Supervisor may justifiably elect to deal with some pattern of teaching because it seems to be salient in relation to theory. Learning theory, developmental theories, and personality theories serve us most commonly in this connection. Should many teaching patterns seem to have theoretical saliency, *then* frequency might be taken as the determining factor for selection.

Some patterns derive saliency from their relationships to other patterns. It sometimes occurs that although analysis has unearthed a dozen patterns and although each such pattern may seem significant enough to warrant treatment in supervision, some single pattern or pair of patterns occupies a superordinate relationship to the others. Under such circumstances, Supervisor may select that single pattern that most thoroughly expresses the others' significance and may choose to grade saliency in this manner. Once a super-pattern has been examined in the supervision conference, it is often possible to introduce its subordinate patterns rapidly, as examples, and without elaborate analysis.

Another sense of saliency is represented by an instance in which, although Teacher manifested many inherently strong teaching patterns, B, C, and D, their potential effectiveness was lost because of weaknesses in architectonic pattern, A. For example, Teacher's initial directions were ambiguous (category: direction giving; pattern: ambiguous directions), but once the children had been set to work, his manner of circulating among them, accepting their questions, and rendering individual assistance was exemplary. It might nevertheless be demonstrable that the degree to which they required individual clarifications and the degree of redundancy characterizing Teacher's remarks to individual students betrayed the initial weakness.

Or, similarly, saliency might be attributed to patterns resulting in broken sequences, in missing links that undermined an otherwise successful lesson. For example, if Teacher's directions were perfectly clear, if the children's tasks were clearly defined and seemed acceptable to them, and if the teaching incorporated a hundred other virtues but at certain critical moments the lesson broke down because, when the time came for using laboratory equipment, the children were uncertain of which apparatus to select and discovered that there was not enough material to go around, then Teacher's failure to muster appropriate equipment beforehand, his faulty pattern, "failure to provide appropriate materials," or "failure to identify relevant items of equipment," or "failure to prepare the children to deal with ambiguities and shortages beforehand" might justifiably be considered salient and be isolated for supervision. In short, saliency can sometimes be defined in relationship to weak keystones or to missing pieces in otherwise cogent structures.

Saliency may also be construed in normative terms, that is, in relation to commonalities among teachers. In a departmentalized secondary school, for example, in which children are instructed by many teachers in a normal day, certain teaching patterns that do not seem particularly significant in the context of any single teacher's performance, may nevertheless acquire a collective saliency that (we hypothesize) has important cumulative effects upon the students. Should it become apparent that all teachers, B–Z, employ didactic instructional approaches in which all questions and directions are formulated *for* the pupils, and should it occur that Teacher A manifests this same tendency, then, in view of the children's total experience under such teaching, Supervisor might justifiably elect to address these patterns in A's teaching (or in anyone else's). While a varied diet of instructional methodology might easily provide for such teaching in certain instances, an unvaried regimen of didactic teaching would fail to provide important intellectual opportunities for the learners. Saliency, therefore, may be related to the surrounding scholastic environment and may be situationally determined.

I have tried to save the best for last by closing this inventory with the suggestion that saliency may be defined in relationship to what Teacher feels is important. Specific problems or teaching patterns that have been isolated in earlier supervision and upon which Teacher is deliberately working, or categories of teaching in relation to which

Teacher has expressed special concern during Stage 1, can generally be placed at the top of the list of things to be considered in supervision. Relevant patterns disclosed by analysis automatically achieve a status of saliency. This is one sense of what I mean by references to "Teacher's frame of reference."

This method can be adopted in simple or in complex strategies. In the simplest manner, Supervisor may select patterns for the conference that Teacher has named in advance: "I want you to keep track of my verbal rewards to the children." Supervisor detaches reward patterns from the data and examines them with Teacher in the conference. In a somewhat more complex strategy, Supervisor may decide that certain patterns are salient, not so much because Teacher has named them explicitly beforehand, but rather because he suspects significant relationships between such patterns and special problems in which Teacher is interested. Using the same example, if Teacher's rewards happen to be highly responsive to idiosyncracies among the children's behavior, and if, in other dimensions of his teaching, Teacher also displays great sensitivity to individual differences, for example, in the problems he assigns, in the assignments he makes, and in the questions he asks, Supervisor might reasonably cite patterns of questioning, assignment giving, and the like in order to demonstrate that in addition to mastering "good" reward patterns, Teacher's teaching, overall, constitutes a composite of patterns in which responsive behavior is pervasive. Or, to use a negative example, if Teacher's rewards are stereotyped, and if stereotypy is also evident in other categories of his teaching, then patterns belonging to such categories could be cited along with reward patterns in order to identify the broader phenomenon.

In summary, some methods for selecting patterns on a criterion of saliency are to examine them in connection to:

Their frequency and abundance in the data.
The existence of demonstrable effects upon the students.
Their theoretical significance.
Their structural importance in the lesson.
Their commonality among teachers.
Their known or predictable significance in Teacher's already existing professional frame of reference.

Because *fewness* is a criterion that Supervisor generally employs *after* he has selected on *saliency* and *accessibility*, I will change the order of things at this point, examine some methods for deciding accessibility, and save *fewness* for last.

ACCESSIBILITY OF PATTERNS FOR TREATMENT: The writing in this section will probably make things more difficult and complex, especially if this material is being employed for developing methodological guidelines. Its difficulty stems partly from complexities that inhere in clinical supervisory practice, and in this sense is beyond control. Partly, however, the difficulty reflects my deliberate intention to keep things appropriately complex in this context. I have seen supervision collapse time and again because supervisors exercised poor judgment in selecting issues for treatment, and in many cases it has become apparent, later on, that their faulty judgments arose from simplistic thinking or from an absence of thinking about the motions likely to be associated with examination of certain behavioral patterns for certain teachers.

One of the terrible mistakes in my own early practice of supervision was, consistently, to underestimate—or to fail to estimate—the emotional significance of my supervisory behavior for the teacher. My fascination with technical problems and with substantive issues often tended to make me rush through elaborate analyses of this pattern and that pattern as though I were explaining the derivation of a statistical formula. As you might guess, it wasn't long before my appearance sent teachers scurrying into broom closets. In our early days, the supervision conferences we conducted often consisted of flamboyant displays of analytical virtuosity: within ten minutes three blackboards would be covered with diagrams of patterns that had been unearthed. "You must understand," we would reassure our supervisee, "that you are not personally under attack. This is simply an objective analysis of your teaching. Let's forget that you happen to be the teacher in question and consider these simply as problems in teaching."

On other occasions, my students and I became so excruciatingly aware of emotional variables and so committed to "therapeutic" approaches that we either panicked when supervisees displayed anxiety and ended supervision conferences prematurely, or wasted unnecessary hours pussyfooting around in innocuous chitchat (which, incidentally, generally made teachers more anxious than ever), under the naive assumption that to do so protected the teachers from emotional "damage." At this extreme, too, we were guilty of simplemindedness generated, this time, by our own anxiety.

Before broaching methodological techniques in more detail, I should like to touch on some general questions pertaining to clinical competencies required of clinical supervisors. Such questions are particularly germane because we have reached the point, in this hypothetical sequence, where Supervisor must make predictions about the emotional loading that specific issues are likely to have for Teacher and must employ such predictions in deciding which patterns to select for the conference.

We confront the sticky problem of how much psychological sophistication Supervisor needs, of whether, in fact, he must know what a well-trained clinical psychologist knows in order to deal with emotional variables—even to think about them—in the teacher's existence. Granting that Supervisor's conceptualization of Teacher, his interpretations, his "diagnostic" constructs, and his basic conceptual framework may be substantially different from Psychologist's, what can be said about supervisors generally, that is, about clinical supervisors who have not had concentrated psychological training? What kind of understanding should Supervisor be able to bring to the notion "emotional loading"? Without being made into a beard-and-couch psychoanalyst, what can he be taught in his professional training that will provide a grasp on emotional factors?

It is probably enough for Supervisor to be able to read internal and external signals of anxiety, that is, of his own and of Teacher's, to be able to determine whether experiences anxiety is of immobilizing intensity, and to be able to recognize some common patterns of defensive behavior.

Our work with supervisors suggests that with appropriate training and with some supervised practice, most of them are able to recognize expressions of anxiety, to alter their strategies responsively in the face of such symptoms, and to appreciate reasons for maintaining sensitivity in this context of supervision. Some fewer supervisors, after a time, have also proven capable of monitoring their own feelings in supervision, of reading their own distress signals, and of making appropriate decisions about what and what not to do when such signals flash during supervision conferences.

As one might guess, psychologically untrained supervisors often speak in untechnical language about emotional interference and about emotional factors generally. They speak of being nervous, of feeling upset, of seeming tense, and the like, and it has never seemed particularly important to us for them to use more clinically precise terminology. While Psychologist may conceptualize anxiety in theoretical terms, Supervisor is more apt to regard such phenomena in behavioral terms and to think about them empirically. While Psychologist may have reason to be concerned with the unconscious sources of anxiety, and while his treatment strategies may depend, in some measure, upon diagnosis at that level, Supervisor tends more to deal with manifest anxiety and to "treat" it operationally. An especially sharp distinction between these specialists is generally that while Psychologist may *have* to contend with the antecedent, personal experiences in which the patient's present anxiety may have originated, it may be sufficient in most cases—this is one of clinical supervision's most difficult questions— for Supervisor to focus upon *situational* determinants, namely, upon elements in the immediate scholastic environment that trigger anxiety responses and upon possibilities existing in the immediate situation for managing anxiety, for coping with it, for deintensifying it if that seems necessary, and for converting it into forms of productive energy.

It is most important to note that in certain senses Supervisor's job, in this connection, is not intellectually or technically easier than Psychologist's. His problems of understanding and of treatment are likely to be extremely complex. The point is rather that Supervisor's clinical functioning may not demand the same background of substantive knowledge as Psychologist's.

Some examples of the serious difficulties with which the supervisor is confronted are (1) those difficulties associated with determining the intensity of expressed anxiety and the question of what it should imply: to stop, to go on, to deal with feelings directly, to depersonalize the issues being addressed, that is, of what differences such anxiety should make, if any, for supervision; (2) those difficulties of identifying which of the manifold stimuli operating at any moment in supervision are affecting Teacher's anxiety; (3) those difficulties related to recognizing whether one's own behavior is being governed rationally or by psychological stress at any particular moment; and (4) the difficulties of separating one's own feelings from the supervisee's; of determining, in other words, whether the teacher's apparent tension or its absence is what it appears to be or is a projection of the supervisor's own mental condition instead.

As in the therapist's case, Supervisor must be able to handle the problem of how to translate moment-to-moment "diagnostic" insights into appropriate supervisory behavior. Again, it seems true that while Supervisor's interpretations and techniques are somewhat different from Psychologist's, they are nevertheless technically difficult to master. Although it may be different, it must certainly be as complicated for Supervisor to focus upon how Teacher is responding to him, *qua* Supervisor as it would be for Therapist to deal with how the patient relates to him, *qua* "father."

My reason for taking this moment to compare psychological and supervisory practice in these terms stems primarily from assumptions made by many supervision students in the past, namely, that because supervision is "superficial," for example, in comparison to psychotherapy, it is consequently an easy clinical profession. I don't believe it. If clinical supervision is superficial in any real sense, that is the sense in which it deals chiefly with current experience rather than with archaic childhood experiences, it is more committed to phenomenological models of behavior than to Freudian ones, and, in a majority of cases, supervisees manifest the problems of mentally healthy people (they are no more nor less crazy than the rest of us) rather than problems of pathological intensity. When all is said, however, those problems of existence left to supervision are rarely simple ones, and Supervisor would be mistaken to view his practice, his requirements of knowledge and technical proficiency, or himself as something elementary and uncomplicated. If anything, Supervisor's work may be harder than

Therapist's because of his paucity of theoretical models by which to make human behavior intelligible and because of certain self-imposed professional limits. By and large, Supervisor's clientele stops short at the threshhold of emotional disorder. It behooves the clinical supervisor to concentrate his practice on basically strong, intelligent, and well-functioning teachers, instead of attempting to "save" professionally marginal personnel. His successes will be relatively undramatic compared to those of the hospital psychiatrist.

It was originally conceived that because, after all, clinical supervisors would not ordinarily be trained in psychological counseling, and because clinical supervision has a unique disciplinary identity and is something different from counseling, and because, in any event, supervision cannot ordinarily provide the protections of counseling, it should therefore be employed to treat superficial behaviors and to treat on a superficial level. That is, that supervision should only attempt to modify surface behaviors which, predictably, would be amenable to change and should not attempt to affect Teacher's "underlying identity" despite the certainty that no matter how seemingly superficial, all behaviors are expressions of that identity. The only trouble with these precepts is that the supervision they generate doesn't work in most cases, and the assumptions they incorporate about human behavior and human change are substantially false. It is incidentally interesting to observe that because of their fear and abhorrence of any practice that smacks of "amateur psychologizing," some of clinical supervision's chief proponents persevere in this belief (in superficial supervision of superficial behaviors) despite overwhelming evidence that it is untenable.

Experience has confirmed that supervision cannot live by substance alone, that its success is every bit as contingent upon the manner in which it operates as it is upon the issues it includes. It is just not enough in most cases to tell Teacher what is wrong and what is right in his teaching and what to do about it (as if anyone were really likely to know such things). When all supervision does is to focus upon specific technical elements of the teaching performance, its effects often do not change the overall quality of the teaching. What generally happens is that one "symptom" gets exchanged for another; as one faulty pattern is brought under control, another emerges to take its place, and the general character of the teaching doesn't change significantly. What I have learned, as one of my colleagues aptly put it, is that "it is not enough for the supervisor to be right" and that it is often self-defeating, as I have already noted, to treat the teaching as though it were somehow disembodied and independent of the teacher doing it.

Sometimes Supervisor becomes involved in futile relationships. Most of the time, although he has established useful relationships, the problems of teaching and learning and understanding and modifying behavior with which he must deal are awesomely complex, and, in either case, if Supervisor is likely to constitute any kind of menace, it is when he takes an uncomplicated view of himself and of his practice.

Let's turn now to the question of method, namely, of general techniques for selecting patterns for treatment. How does Supervisor decide which teaching patterns are likely to be treatable and which are likely to be refractory to supervision? One elegantly straightforward method is to ask. Although one can readily imagine many problems in this method, Supervisor may, nevertheless, invite Teacher to choose among issues with which he (Supervisor) is prepared to deal as a result of his analysis and planning. This technique, incidentally, represents one possible strategy for "full analysis," a special variation of the basic model of clinical supervision which we will examine later on.

For the present, let us imagine a sequence of supervision in which, for one reason or another, Supervisor has the primary responsibility for planning what to treat, so that we can glimpse some of the methods available to him. Perhaps his first step should be to estimate whether a given problem (embodied by a specific pattern or set of patterns) is likely to be too hard, intellectually, for Teacher to comprehend.[1] One tends, in time, to develop a feel for the level of conceptual complexity at which Teacher generally treats problems of practice and an after-image of the species of past problems that have been handled productively and those that have not. I do not mean to suggest that one should not deliberately aim to strengthen Teacher's capacity for conceptualizing tough problems or that supervisors should steer clear of issues that seemed intellectually unmanageable in the past. I mean simply to say that of all the predictions that Supervisor must make in order to judge "accessibility," those relating to whether a problem is too hard or not will probably be the most valid. Subjectively, at least, it has seemed that way.

Particularly in the early days of a supervisory relationship, before Supervisor has been able to collect many data or to form strong impressions of this kind, "shotgunning" can simplify selection on this criterion. Supervisor may, in other words, risk introducing a problem because, even though he cannot predict, precisely, the conceptual level at which Teacher will treat it, he determines, nevertheless, that the problem permits conceptualization at various levels, almost any one of which could be useful for supervisory purposes. In this context, "method" *is*, first of all, an active awareness of selection on a criterion of logical complexity and, secondly, the acts of (1) analyzing the pattern

---

[1]It should not sound as though one must assume that supervisors are naturally brighter than teachers. If Teacher were planning the conference in question, he might logically select issues on the same criterion, namely, of whether Supervisor seemed intellectually capable of dealing with them. The whole question of precisely how intelligent a man must be in order to teach or to supervise decently requires extensive study but is not a problem for this book.

(problem, issue) itself in such terms; (2) analyzing one's collected perceptions of Teacher, in these terms; and (3) estimating whether problem and Teacher seem made for each other, with as much precision as possible. Given that high-level precision is unlikely, Supervisor will generally deal in probabilities, namely, the probability that Teacher's range of conceptual behavior and the problem's range of productive conceptualizations will overlap.

The less stereotyped Supervisor's impressions of Teacher's intellectual behavior are and the more versatile he is in understanding the significance of teaching patterns at multiple levels of complexity, the more likely is Supervisor to confront Teacher with issues on which he may get some mileage. Intuition obviously represents a large element of Supervisor's work in this connection, but experience suggests that intuitive processes can be sharpened and educated to some degree by deliberate effort and practice.

Having decided that in the absence of emotional interference, some pattern will probably not be too difficult for Teacher to handle, Supervisor moves on to other considerations. He may try to ascertain the quality and degree of emotional loading that the pattern in question or that the process of examining that pattern may have for Teacher, if any. His assessments of emotional loading will generally be in relationship to anxiety, that is, to his predictions of whether a problem is likely to produce "too much" anxiety for Teacher to be effectively treatable at the moment. From a more positive perspective, he may also select patterns which, he predicts, will provide emotional income for Teacher to treat, patterns whose identification and treatment are likely to be rewarding. Although it is said more easily than done, another process in which Supervisor may engage at this stage is to scan his own feelings and motives for selecting any pattern in particular; his own tendencies to choose or to avoid, to reward or to punish, and to rationalize his decisions.

How can Supervisor make such predictions? What information is there for him to consult? Let's begin with the problem of predicting anxiety, and let us suppose that Supervisor has already developed some repertoire of cues by means of which to detect anxiety, for example, postural cues, defensive patterns, manifest agitation, verbal pitch and tempo, and so on. The following diagram illustrates sources of pertinent information:

INDIVIDUAL DATA — Experiential (Empirical)
  — Theoretical

NORMATIVE DATA — Experiential (Empirical)
  — Theoretical

SELF-EXAMINATION

Most of the time, Supervisor operates from empirical data. He recalls, in effect, past instances of Teacher's apparent anxiety in supervision and tries to discover similarities and differences between the substantive content and supervisory processes that occurred in former incidents and those that would occur if he broached the pattern in question in the forthcoming conference. He tries to recall whether similar problems or processes have forced Teacher into defensive behavior in the past.

He might, for example, remember that the last time he raised questions relating to Teacher's degree of physical contact with certain children (which was also evident in today's lesson), Teacher became very agitated and (seemingly) defensive, and supervision appeared to break down. This recollection might influence Supervisor either to include or to reject that pattern from treatment, depending upon his impressions of changes that may have occurred in Teacher, in himself, or in supervision, during the intervening period, or on deliberate differences in supervisory process that Supervisor might introduce, presently, in relation to the same substantive issue. He might recall that in the past his method of addressing the "petting pattern" was to employ a direct confrontation including both the data and his own hypotheses: "You know, every time Jack raised his hand and you went to his assistance, you crouched beside his desk and put your arm around his shoulder and were very close to him physically. He squirmed and blushed, and I wonder if so much physical contact isn't embarrassing to him?" Rather than automatically rejecting this pattern because of how upsetting it seemed to Teacher the last time around, Supervisor might, this time, attempt to develop the issue inductively by inviting Teacher to examine his observation notes (or a video tape) and by providing an opportunity for him to identify the pattern himself if he felt ready to deal with it.

Or, although he believed it might still be threatening to Teacher to examine this pattern, he might nevertheless address it because he also believed that, by this time, the supervisory relationship had been strengthened sufficiently and enough mutual trust had been established to indicate a calculated risk, namely, that although Teacher will probably become upset again, the generally supporting quality of supervision is strong enough to withstand a period of stress. (All of these decisions, incidentally, presuppose that Supervisor has reevaluated the pattern in question and has decided, again, that it is important enough to treat.)

On the other hand, Supervisor might have reasons to believe that although the "petting pattern" was still evident, it no longer had the emotional significance for the children that it once seemed to. Or, he might decide that since the pattern's effects were speculative to begin with, it would be wise to engage Teacher in formulating some strategy for finding out whether it carried undesirable significance for the children or not. Or, he might suspect that to treat the pattern at all was contraindicated because it seemed, last time, that Supervisor's effect was to reinforce this behavior; that after Supervisor had raised the question in supervision, Teacher displayed this tendency more persistently. Or, he might decide to tell Teacher that he had recorded some new data on "physical contact" and then ask whether Teacher felt it would be useful to examine them.

In connection to any such choices—those described above represent a short list—Supervisor might also examine his own motives: "Do I want to punish this guy for doing something I disapprove of (in which case I will deliberately raise issues that I know will upset him)? Do I want to avoid this issue because I am afraid to be confronted by another display of such intense anxiety? Do I fasten on this issue because, somehow or other, Teacher's physical behavior sets off some strong, personal discomfort in me? Do I want to raise this issue again in order to force some display of contrition from him (last time he told me that I was imagining things, and I haven't forgotten that)? Have I good reasons to believe that Teacher's ability to modify this pattern is greater now than it seemed before? Am I likely to be kidding myself when I rationalize that although this issue will upset Teacher, nevertheless his ultimate reward will be very great indeed if he discovers his ability to overcome his anxiety and to master a difficult change in his teaching behavior?"

To predict emotional loading, Supervisor might also refer to normative data, that is, to his past experiences in supervising many teachers. He might recall, for example, that on almost every occasion when he confronted teachers with evidence of sarcastic behavior toward students, they either registered expressions of surprised hurt; or claimed that they were only joking and meant no harm; or claimed that although such behavior might seem like sarcasm to an outsider, the pupils had become accustomed to it and accepted it; or claimed that among adolescents, sarcasm was an accepted mode of expressing affection and respect; or enunciated some other, equally hopeful, denial. Should past experience of this kind suggest that the issue almost always provoked anxiety and defensive behavior in supervision, Supervisor might reasonably expect the same quality of response (although not *necessarily*) from his present supervisee, even in the absence of relevant data from their particular relationship.

A more familiar example: if teachers generally displayed anxiety when Supervisor questioned their mastery of the substantive content they were teaching, he might logically anticipate similar responses in the future. I might note that, in such an example, Supervisor would not have to be thinking in psychologically elaborate terms in order to have picked up such signals. His empirical data and the generalizations they generated might be relatively innocent of theory. This is not to say, of course, that recourse to theory would be unhelpful.

In a somewhat more complicated manner, Supervisor must often decide among patterns that incorporate strengths and weaknesses simultaneously and toward which Teacher's feelings are likely to be ambivalent. The existence of bivariate patterns sometimes introduces great difficulty and confusion into the task of selecting on a criterion of emotional loading and into the supervisor's attempts to predict which stimuli will be anxiety producing. Supervisor's general approach, in this context, is to employ whatever empirical, normative, or theoretical information is at his disposal to predict how threatening any given confrontation is likely to be to Teacher, what quality and measure of emotional support Teacher might require to deal constructively with the issues involved, and then to decide whether he is competent to provide such support, should it seem urgent to address hot issues.

Prior assessments of this kind should focus upon what Supervisor already knows about Teacher, about their previous supervisory interactions, and about himself, in relevant terms. His predictions may arise from both experiential and theoretical knowledge. Even without extensive experience in supervision, Supervisor can frequently predict what will repel or attract or hurt or scare on the basis of his examined, personal experience of human beings. In this sense, Supervisor's personal history may represent a potential resource rather than simply a set of behavioral patterns that must be overriden.

In similar fashion, his history of experience as a supervisor—we have already noted that past experience can generate blinding stereotypes—may sensitize him to forms of defensive behavior that arise commonly among supervisees who, especially when they are new to clinical supervision, are likely to feel threatened by it. One simply picks up images of defensive "types," that is, of common defensive ploys, that *seem* to be perfectly valid. Of course, one problem with stereotypes generally is that they feel that way. Another problem is that one tends to assume implicitly that similar stimuli require similar responses, and it can easily follow that Supervisor begins to treat metaphors instead of people. Nevertheless, one feature of Supervisor's method for planning what to do (or not to do) with potentially threatening material consists of consulting his past experiences with similar dilemmas. He may consult his "catalog" of defensive behaviors that have emerged in other supervisory relationships:

> 1. Teacher A agrees with everything Supervisor says. In fact, he agrees so readily that it is possible to turn him about through diametrically opposed positions.

SUPERVISOR: . . . so one thing to consider is whether the kids understood your directions—

TEACHER: Yes, I'm sure that my directions were perfectly clear.

SUPERVISOR: But when you asked, "Are there any questions about what to do?" almost all of the children raised their hands.

TEACHER: Yes, they seemed confused; they didn't understand.

SUPERVISOR: But then you said, "Hands down!" and the children apparently were able to get to work without any trouble.

TEACHER: Yes, I'm sure they understood.

2. Teacher B consistently disagrees with almost everything and continually attempts to attribute problems to Supervisor.

SUPERVISOR: . . . and I was worried that so much noise and disorder might be hazardous, you know, if it were a real fire instead of just a drill.

TEACHER: Well, didn't you tell me yesterday that one of the things wrong with my teaching is that I give all the directions and the children don't make enough of their own decisions? I thought that's what you wanted.

SUPERVISOR: Yes, but—

3. Teacher C throws up a verbal barrage. He talks so much about so many things that there is rarely enough time to address specific problems thoroughly.

4. Teacher D, in a similar manner, introduces red herrings; problems that seem urgent but which, because they are always focused away from the Teacher's own behavior, effectively preclude supervision of salient teaching behavior.

SUPERVISOR: . . . so we might try to put ourselves in Margaret's place and ask, well, uh, how would you feel if you had prepared a long report like that and had cut out pictures from magazines and drawn diagrams—and then, when you presented this, the teacher sat at the desk filling out the register and the children were whispering and not paying attention and—

TEACHER: Yes, uh—just before I forget, you know—I just don't know what I'm going to do about the acoustics in that room. It's really terrible! The chairs and desks all squeak, and that metal ceiling makes it like teaching in a barrel. Even when they're quiet, there's a lot of noise going on.

5. Teacher E, a professional old-timer, tries to put Supervisor on the defensive.

TEACHER: Um, yes. Uh, by the way—I'm curious—have you ever done any classroom teaching?

6. Before anything else can happen, Teacher F begins to deprecate himself and his teaching in every possible manner. Supervisor is disarmed. Not only does he abandon the issues he planned to treat, but he finds himself offering reassurances and flatteries in spite of the fact that, in his judgment, the teaching in question was not very successful. Some supervisors are able to resist this approach. With them, Teacher F doesn't waste words, but merely cries silently. Should Supervisor be able to resist even this degree of heartrendingness, he will shortly develop a reputation of being a monster.

In this manner, Supervisor accumulates an ever-expanding bank of manifestations of anxiety and defensiveness in supervision, both generally and in relation to specific teachers with whom he works. He must take care, on the one hand, to resist stereotyping that leads him to have the same expectations of all teachers who display similar behavioral patterns. It might be true, for example, that while Teacher A's rapid, breathless talking reflects pronounced anxiety and represents a means for avoiding supervisory analysis, Teacher B's abundant verbal activity reflects unusual fluency and intellectual energy and, if it expresses anxiety at all, derives from a relatively superficial and easily overriddden anxiety associated with periods of silence during conversation.

On the other hand, however, his catalog of memories, in this context, should serve Supervisor by sensitizing him to the symptomatic meaning that supervisory behavior may carry. In other words, such experience should correct assessments of human behavior that record only at face value and that fail to detect implicit feelings that are being expressed: Supervisor should develop some special capacity for sensing discomfort. By collecting and examining such experiences, Supervisor should become progressively less susceptible to disarmament by defensive novelties in his supervisees' behavior and less likely to be toppled into defensive postures of his own because he is surprised or frightened or confused by what Teacher does. By the same token, his repertoire of supportive and useful responses should be enriched by such experiences. Although I have stressed anxiety, these thoughts are equally applicable to the problem of sensing positive emotions. Supervisor should know what kinds of experiences have spelled success and mastery and pleasure for Teacher previously in order to amplify present and future opportunities for Teacher to collect positive rewards.

He must at least recognize, as he selects patterns for supervision, that when Teacher is hurting enough or is angry enough, Supervisor is not likely to succeed in any constructive purpose if he blithely ignores Teacher's condition and continues to follow his plan at all costs. He must believe that emotional interference can easily obscure substantive technical issues and can obstruct rational thinking, and must, consequently, alert himself to emotional valences at the strategy stage even though he might prefer not to.

He must recognize, pragmatically, that to persevere insensitively in the prosecution of "important" issues may be self-defeating if Teacher learns incidentally, as a result of Supervisor's behavior, that Supervisor is punishing and that supervision is hurtful. Once such a process has begun, it becomes progressively more difficult to reverse it and increasingly unlikely that Teacher will gain the technical proficiency that Supervisor wishes for him. In some cases it has appeared that teachers modified their behavior primarily to get rid of supervisors they hated. To get Supervisor off one's back, however, is an incentive that seems inherently damaging and one that I cannot favor. I should unhesitatingly call "success" of this kind, failure.

Depending on his background of study and training, Supervisor may also make predictions of emotional loading based upon general theories of human behavior.[2] For example, he might generally suspect that because human beings so frequently experience conflict in relation to hostile feelings, examination of teachers' expressions (and repressions) of hostility toward their pupils would probably evoke considerable feeling in supervision. Or, given that "authority relationships" present emotional difficulties so often in our culture, Supervisor might anticipate that to treat Teacher's role *qua* "authority figure" in the classroom, or his own (Supervisor's) role of authority in supervision would probably *not* be emotionally innocuous.

It should not be surprising to discover that feelings of anxiety often accompany explicit attention to such issues as personal coldness or aloofness, tendencies to infantilize pupils, tendencies to mother them, tendencies to insult them, seductive teaching behavior, scapegoating, favoritism, and the like, simply because of how psychologically basic the feelings that underlie such behavior are likely to be. In other words, one might reasonably suppose that when the issue in question incorporates feelings and behaviors which occupy prominent places in Teacher's personality or which carry moral connotations or which seem, somehow, related to taboos of the culture or of the scholastic subculture, Teacher's response, though perfectly normal, may involve substantial emotional labor and may generate palpable anxiety.

At this point, let us recapitulate some of the methods available to Supervisor for selecting patterns on the criterion of emotional loading. In short, he should determine as far as possible whether an issue (or process) is likely to be so threatening that Teacher will become too

---

[2]"Theory" represents a gray area in which it is difficult to determine what might constitute adequate substantive preparation for clinical supervisors. The problem, for now, is to define minimal requirements rather than optimal ones.

anxious to work effectively or will spend himself in defensive behavior instead of in analysis and planning for his next episode of teaching. He should, additionally, recognize teaching patterns whose examination would probably contribute to Teacher's real and experienced success. As a rule, he should also give some attention to his own motives for selecting or rejecting the pattern in question and his readiness to deal with its emotional consequences, in either direction.

To make such predictions, Supervisor will consult his past experiences with Teacher. This past represents his first source of data under most circumstances. He may also refer to his general experiences in supervision, to his general knowledge of human beings, and to whatever relevant theory he knows. He may also review the history of his personal responses to Teacher and may try to identify motives to treat or not to treat anything in particular that arises principally from his own past pleasures and frustrations in that relationship. After having examined teaching patterns in this fashion, Supervisor should consciously formulate rationales for introducing specific patterns and, particularly when such patterns are likely to have a high "anxiety quotient," should scrutinize his rationales as objectively as possible. Such rationales, incidentally, will generally be related to supervisory goals, about which I shall talk in a moment.

Supervisor should, additionally, be sensitive to Teacher's overall psychological condition, that is, irrespective of emotional loadings attached to specific teaching patterns. One tends to have good days and bad days (or months or seasons); periods in which one is strong and periods in which one feels fragile; periods of depression, of heightened energy, of fatigue, of ambitiousness, of dullness, of alertness, of uncertainty; small, but often decisive temperamental shifts, any of which may arise from circumstances of living that have no direct relationship to professional supervision but which can, nonetheless, generate propitious or unfavorable conditions for supervision. Such sensitivity should be primarily for the sake of making better guesses about whether any given issue is likely to get off the ground or not, for deciding problems of pacing, or even for deciding whether supervision should be undertaken at all.

Analogously, a good coach must be able to recognize when his player is in a slump or when he is hungover, in order to regulate his regimen of training appropriately. Over-practice can be dangerous, while under-practice is usually ineffective. Under ordinary circumstances it is neither appropriate nor necessary for Coach to begin an inquiry on the effects of Slugger's childhood deprivations. While Teacher's marital adjustment may be none of Supervisor's business, it is very much his business to sense any degree of hopelessness arising from that context which may be psychologically pervasive and may undermine Teacher's morale generally. Some of us compartmentalize emotions less effectively than others.

Again, it does not necessarily follow that because Teacher's tail is dragging, he ought to be left alone, treated gently, or not supervised at all. *Sometimes*, Tender Loving Care will turn the trick and will recover Teacher for supervisory purposes. At other times and with other individuals, work that is harder than ever seems more therapeutic than soft music. Supervisor must get to know, largely by cautious trial and error, who his customers are and how individual supervisees are likely to be affected by various approaches during troubled periods. He can neither ignore the facts of Teacher's life nor employ categorical, surefire remedies for all spiritual ailments.

Teacher's expressed desires to deal or not to deal with specific patterns or problems should also figure in Supervisor's determination of whether specific issues are accessible for treatment or not. Unless positive reasons exist for employing other strategies, a good rule is to treat what Teacher wants to treat and avoid what Teacher wants to avoid. Should Supervisor elect to treat some problem that Teacher has explicitly rejected, then he must, ordinarily, work on Teacher's feelings about the thing before moving into the problem directly. No matter how strongly Supervisor may feel about it, if Teacher isn't having any, then Supervisor might just as well talk to himself. My point, for the moment, is that when Supervisor feels obliged to select some pattern for treatment that Teacher has formerly vetoed, he must also recognize Teacher's negative feelings, his resistance, as a prior problem and must understand the consequences that follow for strategy, namely, that it must include plans for working through Teacher's feelings.

Finally, in simple terms, Supervisor should be able to predict whether any given pattern is likely to seem essentially technical or essentially personal in Teacher's frame of reference. When Teacher has proven to be the kind of fellow for whom everything seems highly personal, then Supervisor must decide whether he will be able to separate technical issues from their personal concomitants in any substantial measure or, if not, whether he is capable of examining the whole ball of wax in order to achieve technical refinements. In some cases this really becomes the problem of whether clinical supervision is possible at all.

I do not mean to imply that in order to be supervised, Teacher must, somehow, be able to separate himself from his products and to treat his patterns of professional behavior as though they were someone else's. Nor do I mean to suggest that clinical supervision aims simply to modify behaviors as though they were disembodied. On the contrary, it is a supervision of whole and integrated people. It sometimes seems, however, that if Teacher is psychologically incapable of any *momentary* separation, that is, if he cannot muster any functional objectivity worth noting and if, in effect, every question, every criticism, and every expressed doubt *feels* like an attack upon his soul, then there is probably not much hope for supervision, as we generally conceptualize it, to be of much use. Problems of this kind will be illustrated in later sections.

FEWNESS: Once sifting has yielded a residue of salient and supposedly treatable patterns, chances are that too much remains to include in any single supervision conference. How can Supervisor decide what to discard, at least for the time being?

The following principles of selection have given satisfactory service generally. They are presented here in an essentially random order, but it should be noted that, depending upon the specific contingencies in any situation, any number of hierarchical arrangements are possible among them. You will notice that some of these criteria have already been examined in the contexts of saliency and accessibility:

Principle of data
Principle of subsumption
Principle of sameness or difference
Principle of loading
Principle of time
Principle of energy
Principle of sequence

Principle of data: If Supervisor has clearer or more abundant data to document some patterns than others, he may select the most substantiative patterns for treatment, all other things being equal. Especially when specific patterns are very clear in the data, and when the effects of such patterns are clearly demonstrable, and when, consequently, it becomes relatively unnecessary for Supervisor to authenticate their existence or to explain their effect lengthily, it can represent a real economy for such patterns to be selected in favor of more ambiguous ones.

Principle of subsumption: Supervisor may select those patterns (Class I) that subsume other patterns (Class II) either in the sense that Class-II patterns represent behavioral components of Class-I patterns or in the sense that the presumed significance of the latter class is incorporated by the broader significance of the former. On some occasions, this method can be reversed, namely, when Supervisor's strategy is to build from small pieces to large mosaics, that is, from patterns of lesser significance toward a synthesis of relatively greater significance. In concrete terms, if Teacher's style seems massively egocentric, Supervisor may attempt to arrive at that construction by identifying specific patterns of egocentric teaching and by developing the pertinent generalization by his own effort. Or, if Teacher's style is essentially charismatic, Supervisor may focus on short illustrative episodes from the teaching in order to give Teacher similar opportunities.

The basic reasoning for such an approach could be that Teacher is more likely to accept the existence of small, specific elements of his behavior than that of large, pervasive characteristics. Or, Teacher might, predictably, feel less overwhelmed or threatened by examination of small parts than by that of large ones. Or, it might seem more manageable, operationally, for Teacher to work on modifying specific teaching patterns than for him to grapple with pervasive stylistic tendencies.

Subsumptive relationships, in other words, can be used in either direction. Logical considerations might indicate selection of superordinate patterns; psychological considerations might indicate an opposite approach. Generally, unless special reasons exist for beginning with secondary patterns, it is most efficient to employ the principle of subsumption to isolate *incorporative* patterns for treatment. Supervisor must be ready, however, to relinquish his logical model in order to make psychological accommodations that may be necessary for clinical effectiveness.

Principle of sameness or difference: Supervisor may select patterns relating to some common category of teaching, for example, all patterns concerning classroom logistics; or may deliberately select patterns from different categories, for example, logistics, questioning, and rewards, for any given supervision conference. Sameness may be desirable if Supervisor wants to develop a concentrated focus on some single dimension of Teacher's behavior. Difference may be desirable if Supervisor wants, deliberately, to deintensify supervision or to prevent an intensification of supervision in any specific category.

Sometimes it seems best to keep things open. Sometimes it seems best to home in, microscopically, with the sharpest possible degree of resolution. Sometimes Teacher needs relief and gets relief by shifting about from one set of problems to another. Sometimes Teacher feels disoriented or frustrated by such shifting and prefers to deal with one thing at a time, until he feels mastery in its connection. Sometimes Teacher functions best when he has choices to make. At other times he feels best not to be bothered by choices. Sometimes specific patterns achieve special clarity when they are treated together with related patterns. Sometimes problems become individually clearer when they are treated, concurrently, with very different problems.

Decisions of this order must generally be altered from teacher to teacher and in Teacher's supervision from time to time. Even though one cannot prescribe, categorically, either sameness or difference as a better principle of selection, I can testify that the principle itself, used flexibly, is a very handy one.

Principle of loading: Depending on what's what with Teacher, patterns may be selected or rejected either because of their predicted emotional loading or in spite of it. Sometimes—most of the time—I will avoid treating anything that seems likely to make Teacher very anxious. Sometimes, however, I may purposely attempt to jolt him into a quantum leap toward greater involvement or lesser certainty or higher energy. Sometimes—especially when I have strong reasons for predicting successful outcomes—I will deliberately open an emotion-laden issue because Teacher seems right on the verge of resolving it and just ready to reap some reward. If it seems that such loading would interfere with technical progress, I should reject the pattern in question. If the opposite seems likely, I should include it. Supervisor's problem is not so much to eschew strong feelings as it is to recognize when emotionality can serve Teacher's interests in supervision and when it is likely to operate against them. Certainly there must be legitimate opportunities in supervision to rejoice, and joy is something to be felt, not simply analyzed. And certainly there must be room in such a complicated business as teaching, to experience awful frustration, and as we know from personal experience, that can either be good or bad.

In any event, although such generalizations are never completely valid, one intuits a relationship between loading and fewness, namely, that fewness may not accomplish its objective—the purpose is to avoid saturation—if each of the few patterns selected is fraught with stressful feeling for Teacher. After patterns have been screened on saliency and accessibility, good or bad decisions on fewness can tell the story: issues which, although they carried profound emotional significance, might have been treated productively can be irretrievably lost if they are lumped together in the same conference in too great a number or in an unfelicitous sequence.

Principle of time: Supervisor should have some reasonable idea of how long it will take to treat specific patterns in the conference. Whether or not Teacher has expressed positive or negative motives to deal with a particular pattern, how fluent Supervisor feels in his ability to explicate the pattern, how fluently Teacher is likely to address it, how logically or emotionally complex or simple the pattern seems to be, how sharply or distractedly Teacher happens to be functioning at the moment, how rewarding or innocuous or threatening the pattern may prove to be, how many data will be required to illustrate the pattern in question, and so on, are among the factors that can be used to determine the amount of time that should be set aside to deal with it.

Common sense tells us that, being a relative thing, fewness can turn out to be manyness if the few patterns selected are each too time-consuming to be handled together in a single conference. Although supervisory issues tend to carry over from sequence to sequence of supervision, nevertheless it often seems that some points are better than others for terminating a conference. It sometimes appears that even intermediate closure should occur at some special juncture of inquiry, not just any place. One problem, consequently, in selecting on the criterion fewness, is to project times and to make decisions accordingly.

Lest this seem altogether magical, we can think of parallel examples from teaching. It may be that the children are engaged in some social studies unit that spans several weeks. Nevertheless, Teacher is likely to consider timing as he plans each day's activity. He is likely, in other words, to plan his lessons so that the pupils formulate some question by the end of Tuesday's work, and discover some set of generalizations on Thursday, and define some relevant problems during Friday's session for which they will prepare problem-solving strategies to present on Monday. Such planning need not be rigid nor homogeneous and, without these defects, might spell the difference in whether the pupils experience sufficient structure to maintain focus or not.

Principle of energy: Logical complexity, emotional loading, clarity of data, and the like will influence the amount of mental energy required to prosecute specific issues in supervision. Recognizing this variable, Supervisor should avoid the likelihood that either member will become prematurely fatigued, as he selects on fewness. Once again, past experiences supervising Teacher represent the best index for judging outcomes of this kind.

Principle of sequence: Whether or not the purposes of fewness are achieved can depend upon the order in which selected patterns are broached in the conference. The general idea in this regard is that if, for example, patterns are ordered so that clear, logical transitions can be made from one context to the next, then, because such a conference should prove less exhausting and take less time than if such transitions were nonexistent, the goals of fewness might be more readily achieved in one sequence than in another.

Analogously, if you presented wooden blocks to me one at a time, each of which was shaped differently but the collection of which could be arranged in order of absolute size, I should more readily make sense of these things if you handed them to me in their order of size instead of in some random order. Should their presentation be random, I might waste time and energy attempting to discover nonexisting geometric relationships.

Supervisory transitions or the organizing principles behind sequences need not, necessarily, be substantive. They might, for example, be qualitative, progressing from essentially weak patterns to basically strong ones. In any event, we find that in most instances it is helpful to tell Teacher at the outset whether the sequence of issues to be broached in the conference is ordered randomly or according to some deliberate organizational rationale, to free him from the necessity of having to guess about such things. Such a simple statement as "There are a few things I thought we might get into, and it doesn't make any difference in what order we examine them" can save Teacher whatever energy he might otherwise have spent trying to sense the direction in which his conference was moving.

So far in this section, our principal question has been related to *how* Supervisor reduces his complete analysis of the observational data by selecting specific patterns to treat in the conference. Our discussion has proceeded as though Supervisor's strategy were being dictated primarily by the press of data, rather than by general goals. Given an analyzed body of behavioral data, I have suggested that selections should be based upon criteria of saliency, psychological accessibility, and fewness; I have offered some rationales for this model and some indication of how, generally, supervisors can perform the work involved, that is, some description, at least, of what kinds of things they might think about when attempting to make such decisions.

V
Methodological Techniques for Analysis and Strategy

PART 2

SETTING GOALS FOR THE SELECTION OF SUPERVISORY ISSUES

There are still numerous problems of strategy to be examined, some of which have already been touched upon in the previous material. At this point, however, let's shift to the question of goals. Besides employing such criteria as saliency, fewness, and the like, and following such methodological guidelines as we have considered, clinical supervisors operate within a broader framework of objectives. In addition to selecting substantive issues and establishing significant relationships among them, Supervisor also considers a range of supervisory processes as he plans the conference, and works toward ends determined by what Teacher wants, by what Teacher does, by who Teacher is, in certain respects, and by his own system of professional values. As we have noted, clinical supervisors aim for both technical and process goals. Our problem: What are such goals like, and how are they formulated?

If Teacher were simply a memory bank into which information could be fed for later recall and application, and if, like a computer Teacher lacked feelings, capacities for pain and pleasure, and tenden-

cies to distort ideas, then it would be enough, having spotted technical
deficiencies, to program Teacher with new technical information and
trust that as long as he remained plugged in, his technical performance
would show improvement subsequently. It may be just as well, however, that Teacher is not a computer because even while that would make
Supervisor's job a lot easier, in the end Teacher's behavior would be
essentially uncreative.

In any case, supervision will have a substantive technical content—
although not necessarily at every point in a cycle—and it is, consequently, appropriate for the supervisor to frame content goals for the
conference. Ideally, such goals will be stated in three sets of terms,
namely, as the new or sharpened concepts that Teacher should acquire
in supervision (cognitive outcomes), as the new or sharpened behaviors
that Teacher should manifest as a result of supervision (behavioral
outcomes), and as the specific level of mastery ("criterion behavior")
at which Teacher should perform in order for supervision to have
achieved at least minimum success.

Here is an example. In the observed lesson, Teacher exhibited a
pattern of naming specific pupils before asking his question: "Johnny,
how many times was the Liberty Bell cracked? Marlene, why was the
Liberty Bell removed to Allentown, Pennsylvania?" Having noted that
every time Teacher called a name the other children proceeded to do
their arithmetic homework even though the lesson was in social studies,
Supervisor decided that the class's attentiveness could be more certainly
assured if Teacher reversed his sequence and asked the question before
calling on any specific child to respond. Supervisor's reasoning: "If the
kids realize that the ax can fall anywhere, then they'll be more likely to
pay attention to questions than if they know in advance that they're
safe." (Whether or not Supervisor's reasoning was valid in this instance
is irrelevant for our purposes. Even though his thinking may have been
simple, the example it provides is also simple and is useful for that
reason.)

Supervisor's technical goal, in this case, is formulated as follows:

CONCEPTUAL OUTCOME: Teacher will understand why it
might make better sense to state questions before identifying
students to respond than after.

BEHAVIORAL OUTCOME: Teacher will enunciate this reasoning during the conference and, in tomorrow's teaching, will
demonstrate the technical modification in question.

CRITERION BEHAVIOR: The frequency of today's questioning
pattern in tomorrow's lesson (assuming that tomorrow's lesson will
be structured in essentially the same manner) will be sharply
reduced. Since, in today's teaching, "pupil first" occurred eighty

percent of the time, that is, in eighty percent of questions asked, tomorrow that pattern should not exist in more than_____ (some specific proportion) of the questions asked. (In other words, Supervisor decides, in this case, that when a certain degree of quantitative change is observed, this technical issue can be eliminated from further consideration in supervision. He may also decide that Teacher should determine the quantitative criterion to shoot for.) [1]

Recognizing that Teacher is more than a computer and, for that reason, is likely to learn more from the supervision than the specific technical information being considered, Supervisor will formulate other goals relating to nontechnical learning outcomes that should result in the conference. Employing the notion of incidental learnings as he does in analyzing Teacher's teaching, Supervisor should plan his own behavior with an eye toward incidental effects it is likely to have upon Teacher. Rather than simply making sure that his agendum of technical points is covered in the conference, without concerning himself with the specific behaviors in which he will engage to make them, Supervisor should formulate his strategy upon the premise that *how* he gets where he's going is at least as important as *what* substantive learnings are achieved and that, in all likelihood, the quality of substantive learning will itself be partly a function of the supervisory processes he employs. In a word, his strategy arises from the presuppositions (1) that the supervisory processes employed will affect the quality of Teacher's substantive technical learning and (2) that they may also affect Teacher's ideas and feelings about himself, his teaching, supervision, and Supervisor, for better or for worse. Rather than leaving such learning to the chance results of random supervisory processes, Supervisor attempts to bring what otherwise might be incidental learnings under deliberate control and, toward this end, formulates a set of process goals in addition to his content goals.

In either teaching or supervision, process goals can be conceptualized in the same terms as any other goals, namely, as cognitive outcomes, as behavioral outcomes, and in reference to some minimally acceptable criteria of mastery. In one sense, the process goals he formulates during Strategy will pertain to Supervisor's own behavioral processes in the conference. In the more unual sense of the term, his process goals will pertain to intellectual and behavioral processes that ought to be established or refined or extinguished in the teacher's future practice.

---

[1]Although such cutoff points will be arbitrary, nonetheless, they do provide a target and will suffice, at least, to demonstrate Teacher's ability to modify the pattern in question if he wants to. Whether the modification is adequate, either in degree or in conceptualization, requires subsequent observation of the pupils to determine.

Here are some examples of how process goals may be stated. Hypothetically: Having worked through several sequences of supervision with Teacher, I (the supervisor) have begun to develop the impression that although Teacher has been generally alert and receptive, has seemingly understood the technical issues put before him, and has strengthened and extinguished various positive and negative teaching patterns respectively, he has generally moved in directions that I set in supervision rather than in directions of his own (although, in light of his successes, I am ready to believe that at some point he adopted problems I had initiated as his own).

By all rights, perhaps, I should be satisfied, but I am not. I am becoming concerned that even though Teacher has proven to be a good student in certain respects, he is also becoming—or has already become—an essentially dependent student. Instead of aggressively initiating his own issues and questions in supervision, he waits expectantly for me to do so. His passivity, in this connection, is hardly surprising, for along with all of the teachers he has had previously, *I have taught him* to behave the way he is behaving. I have happily raised issues and have happily observed him treat my issues, and all of the evidence suggests that I have either taught him to expect, or to have confirmed his prior expectations, that my job would be to teach and his job would be to learn, that I would be the active agent and he the reactive agent in supervision.

The plot thickens. Although the manner in which I permitted our supervisory relationship to be structured may have been a blunder— the trick is to help teachers to function more autonomously, not to enslave them by increasing their dependencies upon Supervisor—it was a blunder of calculated risk rather than of stupidity. After all, I knew when we began the same things that I know right now about artifactual dependencies arising from the kind of supervisory behavior in which I engaged, and I also knew that the best time, probably, to teach Teacher that supervision would not be follow-the-leader was in the very first moments of our work together.

But even in the face of these risks I decided to supervise didactically early on. For one thing, it soon became clear that having never before thought much about teaching as a collection of technical problems and having never examined his own teaching systematically or developed skills for doing so, Teacher's ideas about what kinds of things to tackle and what lines of inquiry to follow were sparse. Perhaps I should nevertheless have let him set his own pace in supervision, but I did not. Partly because I was in a hurry (I have other supervisees and time is short), partly because Teacher seemed intelligent, responsive, and reasonably relaxed, and partly because I guessed that even though it would require extra work, this teacher could learn new modes of behavior in supervision after the supervision had acquired some substance, I decided to take the lead myself in the early stages and then to undertake the development of new Supervisor-Supervisee roles and relationships later on. Implicitly, I decided, "Let's beef up our collection of working concepts first and then do some worrying about our processes after we have become conceptually rich."

Two ideas parenthetically: the first is that perhaps in a majority of cases it is best to *begin* supervision with process goals, lest points of no return are passed before they are recognized. Second, despite the reasoned sound of my decision to begin didactically and to aim for more inductive and less directive supervision after a time, that decision arose partly from caprice. I suspect it grew partly from the same origins as teachers' "show 'em who's the boss for the first week and then you can ease up on 'em later" disciplinary strategy. Being as vulnerable to self-deception as the next man, Supervisor must be wary. *I am as well rehearsed in games of one-upmanship as anybody. I am as flattered and as capable of being seduced by other people's dependencies upon me as the next man, maybe more so because of the history of the professional role I fill. Power is happiness for me as much as for anybody, and it's rather nice to make certain that Teacher is capable of showing the proper humility and deference that my station commands before I turn "liberal." Once it is perfectly clear that my slaves know I am master, then I can be as magnanimous as I please and as self-righteous as I please in my magnanimity. That is not quite the same as being decent and secure to begin with, but I have few delusions about being either a paragon of health or virtue.* The main point of all this is that even the most studiously calculated approaches in supervision can be tainted by rationalization and, knowing that, Supervisor should keep a constant weather eye on his motives, particularly in connection to decisions of the order that we are presently considering.

In any case, we come to the point where, being satisfied that Teacher has put successes behind him and has developed a large enough account of manageable concepts to go into business for himself, I have decided that it is time to begin letting go, to begin reversing the proportions of initiative that we have exercised. I have elevated the process goal "self-initiated inquiry" to the top of my priorities in the supervision, and have formulated it as follows:

> CONCEPTUAL OUTCOME: Teacher will understand and accept self-initiation as a supervisory goal.

> BEHAVIORAL OUTCOME: Teacher will take the initiative for structuring supervision conferences and for mapping the goals and methods of future sequences of supervision.

> CRITERION BEHAVIOR: Teacher will initiate some issues of his own in supervision. Progressively, he will set more problems and tasks until his command of the course we steer will be clearly established.

Let's try stating another process goal, "analytical tool skills":

CONCEPTUAL OUTCOME: Teacher will learn a prolific assortment of techniques for analyzing teaching behavior, particularly his own.

BEHAVIORAL OUTCOME: Teacher will demonstrate analytical versatility by identifying patterns in his teaching, extrapolating issues from the observational data (kinescope or audio tapes; Supervisor's observation notes), arranging problems in order of importance, urgency, treatability, and the like.

CRITERION BEHAVIOR: Teacher's analyses will have logical consistency, will be based upon tenable hypotheses and interpretations, will consider contradictions in the data, will incorporate reasonable inferences (rather than wild ones), will be susceptible to validation by the consensus of other competent analysts.

You will note an absence of exactitude in the definitions of criterion behaviors above. Had our goal been for Teacher to learn to perform certain mathematical operations under certain, specified conditions, then, in less ambiguous terms, the evaluation criterion could have been expressed precisely as a test score, assuming, of course, that the test simulated those conditions under which the learner (Teacher) was originally supposed to have been able to perform the operations in question. Because the test of Teacher's learning in supervision is how he performs, subsequently, in his teaching, it is difficult to conceptualize standard tests that could measure his learning with mathematical precision. Unlike simple mathematical problems, problems of instructional practice rarely, if ever, have solutions that are clearly right or wrong. Moreover, in light of the discipline's ambiguity, disagreements are apt to arise in connection to whether a stratagem that seems right to one educator will seem equally right or right in any degree to some other educator.

Experience suggests that criterion behavior is a tenable concept in supervision and that even failing mathematical precision, criteria of mastery are enunciable and usable. In our first illustration, "behavioral outcome" names the kind of behavior in which Teacher should engage. The criterion behavior introduces quantitative considerations ("progressively . . . more") which, although lacking precision, at least incorporate a criterion of increasing frequency. In the second illustration, although quantitative increase may be implicit, what distinguishes the statement of criterion behavior from that of behavioral outcomes is that while the latter describes categories of behavior that should appear, the former introduces value judgments (for example, "logical, tenable, reasonable, rich") relating to such behavior and stipulates a *desideratum* of consensual validation by a professional jury (generally a jury of one, namely, Supervisor). If disagreements can arise over quantitative outcomes, then disputes over quality are even more probable. Consensus can be established for the wrong reasons and failure to achieve consensus can exist for good reasons, and so on. While such criteria may lack experimental rigor, their value, nevertheless, is that at least they define evaluative contexts in which productive inquiry and professional incentives may arise.

In either case, that is, when either qualitative or quantitative criteria are employed, Supervisor and Teacher must have some means for judging how much change is enough, what degree of frequency or what level of quality suffices. Sometimes "enough" can be determined by testing. If some teaching pattern is seemingly associated with some mean level of achievement by the pupils (or by the achievement level of some specific pupil) and if that pattern's modification can be correlated with improved pupil scores, then even though it might be impossible to prove a direct cause-effect relationship between the modified teaching and the pupils' performance, the logical or theoretical probability of some such connection might justify an assumption of cause at least for the time being. Should future events appear contradictory, then future opportunities may be exploited for experimentation in which the modified teaching pattern is held constant and other variables are manipulated.

As often as not, teaching patterns are modified for the sake of unmeasurable outcomes for the pupils, for example, for attitudinal outcomes whose behavioral manifestations may be substantially delayed, or whose demonstration may require an as yet undeveloped diagnostic technology, or whose behavioral expressions are likely to be too manifold to record or even to recognize in every instance, or which require forms of specialized testing not generally available to schoolmen. I should not hesitate to work on Teacher's tendencies to devalue his students if I suspect that, as a result of his behavior, their images of themselves are being depreciated, simply because I am unable to demonstrate the quality of their self-concepts presently and will be unable to do so a month from now. While I respect government by objective proof, I should not allow myself to be tyrannized by such a requirement or to await the ultimate supervision in which such government may become more generally feasible.

Sometimes the sufficiency of change can be determined by testing the pupils and sometimes not. When testing is germane, its reliability and degree of relevancy will vary. Criterion behaviors must frequently be defined by other considerations. When he postulated effects of a teaching pattern are evident in the pupils' behavior and are susceptible to recording by an observer, then the criterion behavior may be specified in relationship to changes among the pupils, for example, "Criterion behavior: Teacher will pause *long enough*, when beginning new lessons, *for all of the pupils* to give him their attention."

Once content or process goals have been formulated behaviorally, then criterion behaviors, that is, degrees of change in the teaching, will often be determined by what seems realistically possible for Teacher to achieve in the time available in a cycle of supervision. While large, long-range modifications are sometimes adopted as supervisory goals, it is generally best to work at developing incremental approximations of such outcomes in order for small, momentary gains to be appreciable (and reinforceable) in day-to-day supervision. Sometimes estimations of what is immediately feasible for Teacher must serve as the exclusive determinants of a criterion behavior, especially when no ideal degree of modification can be specified, when any change would seem better than neglecting to modify the pattern at all, and when the pattern and the changes in question are particularly difficult or seem that way to Teacher. In this connection, criterion behaviors must sometimes be set intuitively. In another sense, definitions of minimal sufficiency depend upon the importance, the significance, or the urgencies associated with the pattern to be modified. Should the pattern, although it is salient in some manner, be relatively superficial in terms of its hypothesized effects upon the children, for example, then criterion behaviors might be stipulated more modestly than if the pattern seemed to produce profound effects.

In short, the formulation of criterion behavior will generally involve some combination of the factors: how readily able Teacher is to achieve (certain increments of) the changes in question; how important the pattern's effects are likely to be on the children; possibilities for testing the effects of change; possibilities of observing the effects of change (in the pupils' behavior, in Teacher's supervisory behavior, and the like); by objective, quantitative variables when possible and by examined, intuitive reasoning when simple, quantitative testing is unfeasible.

Despite the ambiguities involved in formulating criterion behaviors for content and process goals in supervision, and sometimes, even, in stating such goals in behavioral terms, I strongly advocate this practice for the reasons: (1) unless desired outcomes can be stated behaviorally, there is some chance that, no matter how precious they may seem, the outcomes in question are merely figmental (in this respect, it may represent good reality testing for Supervisor and Teacher to test their prospective goals against the possibility of formulating them in behavioral terms); (2) unless supervisory goals can be stated behaviorally, there is little chance to observe whether or not they have been achieved (because only behavioral outcomes are visible and inferences can easily run rampant and wishfully in relation to desired but invisible outcomes); (3) opportunities for Supervisor and Teacher to evaluate achievement of desired change, to mark progress, and to define required tasks are most favorable when their "contract" specifies minimally acceptable outcomes as clearly as possible (successes are apt to feel more secure and rewards more certain than if outcomes are defined very generally); and (4) if Supervisor can demonstrate goal-setting that satisfies these conditions, namely, that goals shall be stated behaviorally, that conditions for exhibiting the desired behavior shall be specified, and that criterion behaviors shall be defined in advance, then, by turning Teacher's attention to the existence of these conventions in supervision, Supervisor may provide concrete examples of instructional planning that should serve Teacher well in his own work with the pupils. By the same reasoning, Supervisor may take advantage, didactically, of negative examples, that is, of instances in which supervisory success cannot be evaluated because of inadequately framed goals.[2]

I have spoken about process goals primarily in the sense in which they were originally construed, namely, as goals pertaining to learning processes, irrespective of specific content, that should be promoted as a result of instruction (in this case, of supervision). In certain respects, process outcomes are sometimes desirable in their own right, for example, "self-examination" might contribute to a more gratifying way of life than most men can achieve in its absence. For the educator, process goals are also valued because of how persuasive the idea seems that instructional planning which includes them is more likely to result in successful substantive learning than planning which considers only the content to be presented.

In another sense, as I have noted, Supervisor must also formulate goals, in strategy, relating to the processes he intends to employ or to encourage in supervision. *His* processes, presumably, affect both process and technical outcomes for Teacher. On the one hand, Supervisor frames goals for Teacher. On the other hand, he sets instrumental goals for himself, for his own behavior in supervision. Although it creates some semantic violence, I should consider goals in the latter category also to be distinguishable as content and process goals.

Let's consider some decisions that Supervisor might make concerning supervisory processes. Among other things, Supervisor must generally decide whether his approach in the conference should be essentially didactic. This means, more concretely, that he must decide whether he is going to present data (patterns) in relation to which *Teacher* will construct interpretations, perform an analysis, and develop strategies for future work inductively, or whether, instead, he will present his own

---

[2]Robert F. Mager, *Preparing Instructional Objectives* (Palo Alto, California: Fearon Publishers, 1962) is probably the most wonderful and entertaining book on the subject of educational goals.

interpretations of teaching patterns and then recommend strategies for effecting desirable changes in future teaching. Even in connection to the latter approach, Supervisor may choose between techniques involving deductions from principles of theory, for example, "Since we know that children of this age are more likely to learn visually, kinesthetically, and from tactile experience than from exclusively verbal teaching, it follows that your choice of Stern Blocks as the medium of learning in this unit is a sound one," and methods by which the significance of selected patterns is developed by some meaningful synthesis of empirical observations: "So what might you be ready to conclude, having observed that most of the children arranged the blocks in serial order even though, in the absence of any cues from you, they were unable to say what they had done in words that conveyed abstract understanding of serialization?"

Similarly, Supervisor may decide whether Teacher should initiate the issues to be treated in supervision or whether he should initiate them himself. Once again, his basis for such decision making consists principally of his knowledge of what has worked before with Teacher or, in the absence of sufficient data from that relationship, of what has generally worked before with teachers. If Supervisor favors practice in which inductive inquiry and teacher-initiated issues take precedence, he may proceed by trial and error, that is, by employing essentially inductive modes at first and then turning to more didactic methods, perhaps, if the first approach seems unproductive.

Incidentally, with teachers who are unaccustomed to exercising initiative in supervision and who are essentially unfamiliar with inductive approaches to observational data, I have generally gotten better long-range results by employing the novel approach first, retreating into more conventional techniques when that seemed necessary, and then developing an inductive, self-initiating mode by small progressions over time, than I have by the opposite method. It has generally seemed that when I began as I was expected to begin, namely, with didactic, evaluative, deductive, authoritative supervision, the result was to confirm Teacher's prior expectations of me and to teach him, in effect, to occupy a relatively passive (if not defensive) posture in supervision. When I have done it the other way, and when Teacher's initial experiences have confused him, it has often seemed, later on, that after Teacher developed some talent for new forms of supervisory behavior, he was able to make sense of the early sessions, to integrate them into his present framework of meaning, as if by a process of retroactive learning. I confess that these impressions may be somewhat overdetermined by wishes, but, nonetheless, I feel it is just as well to share them, if only as tentative hypotheses.

By now, we have pieced together a picture of Strategy and, more particularly, of methods of strategy, whose principal elements are that Supervisor will formulate content and process goals on two levels, namely, that pertaining to the structure of Teacher's own teaching and that relating to the conduct of supervision; that content and process goals should be defined as cognitive outcomes and behavioral outcomes, and in reference to criterion behaviors; that Supervisor should select patterns from the observational data on the criteria "saliency," "fewness," and "treatability"; and that a dynamic relationship exists between such methods of selection and the specific goals that motivate any given sequence of supervision.

This last thought is intended to convey the expectation that, on the one hand, for example, saliency may be determined by the specific goals established for some episode of supervision, while on the other hand, the goals for any such episode may be generated by salient teaching patterns found in the current data. An illustration:

CASE 1: Because we have been working on problems of terminological precision, I will select those sequences of instruction in which Teacher manifested terminological inconsistencies. In other words, such sequences are salient, vis-à-vis the dominant issues we have been treating during the present supervisory sequence.

CASE 2: Because salient patterns of terminological inconsistency appear in data, I will adopt the goal "terminological precision" for this cycle of supervision.

ADDITIONAL ELEMENTS OF STRATEGY

Besides selecting specific teaching patterns for treatment and formulating or reformulating supervisor goals, Supervisor has other decisions to make during Strategy relating to management of the conference. Some common questions to decide are:

Should I undertake a full or partial analysis of the data?
In what order should the issues of this conference be examined?
Should I deal primarily with strengths or weaknesses in the teaching; to what degree, if any, should + 's and − 's be "balanced"?
Are there specific junctures at which I should test Teacher's comprehension by engaging him in role-play or by asking him to paraphrase a line of reasoning I have presented?
Under what circumstances should I be ready to abandon my own analysis of this lesson in favor of other approaches?

What balance should exist between considerations of the past (analysis), the present (supervisory processes), and the future (planning future lessons)?

What method of recording, if any, should be employed for this conference?

Should Teacher be given *carte blanche* for structuring this conference; should he be offered specific options; should I hold him to the analysis I have prepared?

How many data should I present to document the patterns I have selected?

Should our "contract" be reviewed at the outset; what changes, if any, should be made in our contract?

At what point should the conference end?

Should Supervisor decide to build certain decision points into the conference, points at which Teacher might select among specific lines of inquiry to follow, then, in most instances, he should prepare multiple, branching strategies in advance. In other words, he should be technically and conceptually ready to move in Teacher's directions, particularly if Supervisor has named the available choices in advance. Under circumstances in which supervision is being undertaken by more than one person at a time, Strategy should also incorporate explicit decisions for regulating each member's participation in the conference. Although very elaborate plans can be made for governing group supervision, pertaining, for example, to questions of what material should be treated by which members, who should lead at what moments, who should collect data for a postmortem, and what kinds of verbal and nonverbal signals should be exchanged for altering the order of events or for asking permission to disagree or for deciding it is time to quit or for shifting leadership, and the like, at least such a strategy should dictate which member has overall responsibility for management and, in everyone's interests, should specify agreements (or no agreements) to disagree, with appropriate qualifications.

Life has taught us that if anything is likely to be more disconcerting to a novice supervisee than being confronted all at once by a gang of supervisors, it is being confronted by a gang of squabbling supervisors: "If they can't even agree among themselves, how in the world can they help me?"

Let's examine the elements of Strategy listed above.

Should I undertake a full or partial analysis of the data?   Ordinarily, this question would be decided before Supervisor selected specific teaching patterns for treatment. If he decided in favor of "full analysis," then it would be gratuitous to labor over selections, except under special circumstances.

Full analysis can be construed several ways. By any definition, however, its chief method is to confront Teacher with a more complete collection of data or with a less abridged analysis of the data than would ordinarily be offered as a result of selection on the criteria "salient," "few," and "treatable." Supervisor might, for example, spend the time available for Strategy transcribing his observation notes into some readable form in order to present the complete data to Teacher. His strategy, under these conditions, might be to begin the conference by saying, "Here are the notes. Let's deal with whatever you find in them that seems significant"; or, "Here are the notes. Shall we see what we can find that may be important?" Another variation of full analysis is for Supervisor to present the complete data along with *all* of the patterns he identified during Stage 3, instead of a selected group of such patterns. According to this strategy, Supervisor might or might not include evaluative comments in his presentation of patterns.

Two general disadvantages of full analysis are (1) it tends to be uneconomical of time and often creates the problem of having spent so much time in analysis of past teaching that Supervisor and Teacher are unable to get on to planning future teaching, and (2) it sometimes overwhelms Teacher to be confronted by so much material, either because there is simply too much to assimilate or because the stuff carries too much emotional baggage to handle.

Notwithstanding these disadvantages, Supervisor should decide during Strategy whether the potential virtues of full analysis are likely to offset its problems for the individual teacher he is about to supervise. In general, this approach seems indicated under two conditions, namely, when Teacher is unusually resilient, unusually energetic, and demonstrates unusual capacities for analyzing copious data efficiently, or when Teacher seems particularly threatened by his fantasies of what goes on in Supervisor's mind as he peruses his notes, of what Supervisor is holding back from his analysis and, in group supervision, of what damning things have been said behind his back during Stage 3. In short, full analysis works best with strong teachers because they are strong and with frightened teachers who worry about damage to their reputations in supervisory analyses from which they are excluded.

One might reasonably employ full analysis for a somewhat different purpose, namely, to teach teachers, whose previous work in supervision has been adequate, new techniques for analyzing classroom data. Such supervision might be intended to heighten Teacher's ability to undertake systematic self-analysis or to prepare Teacher for undertaking the supervision of his team members and colleagues. Perhaps the greatest advantage, for all teachers, of an occasional full analysis is that it tends to demystify supervisory processes that take place in their absence.

In what order should the issues of this conference be examined? Particularly when unrelated teaching patterns are to be treated, the order in which they are broached can make important psychological differences in the conference. One must bear in mind that although such patterns may be unrelated in the sense that they belong to different categories of teaching behavior, nevertheless, *Teacher* is integrated and responds as a complete personality to every stimulus impinging upon him. It is impossible to prescribe categorically in this context because of individual differences among teachers that determine whether any specific method will be effective or not. One can, however, describe methodological rationales which may work, depending upon surrounding circumstances.

One might, for example, begin with conceptually difficult issues in order to direct Teacher's interest toward them before fatigue sets in. Or, one might start off with simple matters, as pump-priming. One might begin with "strengths" in order to establish feelings of success against which Teacher may borrow, emotionally, when his attention is turned subsequently to "weaknesses." Or, one might begin with weaknesses in order to alleviate anticipatory anxiety quickly and to be able to close on a positive note. One might begin by treating issues in which Teacher has expressed special interest in order to satisfy his hungers as early in the conference as possible. Or, one might elect to get other things out of the way first as a means of eliminating distractions from the serious work. If Supervisor has found it useful, in the past, to deal with Teacher's feelings about supervision, then he might at least think about whether such treatment has generally seemed most productive before substantive dialogue commenced or after supervisory issues had been opened.

Any number of examples might be developed for this idea, but I think it is enough, presently, to suggest that "order" is something about which Supervisor should think explicitly as he plans what to do in the conference. One way to begin is by asking oneself, "Even though the patterns to be treated are substantively unrelated, does my experience with Teacher suggest that the order in which they are examined is likely to make any important difference?"

Should I deal primarily with strengths or weaknesses in the teaching; to what degree, if any, should $+$'s and $-$'s be "balanced"?   This is difficult to talk about because the question tends to carry misleading connotations. Let's deal with its connotations first.

First of all, as I have already reported, a great number—perhaps a majority—of teaching patterns are $\pm$ rather than clearly $+$ or $-$. This is to say that after its analysis is complete, it generally appears that almost any teaching pattern embodies both advantages and disadvantages, for all the pupils, or for some pupils, at one time or another. Second, it should not sound as if Teacher does not participate in determining the value (or nonvalue) of his own instructional patterns.

Plusses and minuses are not, as a rule, determined *a priori* by the time a conference begins.

Nevertheless, as he examines his observation notes, Supervisor does not, magically, suspend his values and force himself to assume that nothing is good and nothing is bad until Teacher has joined him in determining so. On the contrary, not only do the patterns he uncovers often feel distinctly positive or negative, but according to this model of supervision, they often seem likely to be *emotionally* plus or minus for Teacher to consider, and Supervisor must recognize such possibilities as he estimates whether individual patterns are accessible for treatment.

What results from this confusion is that Supervisor may consult his intuitions concerning good and bad features of the teaching and may consider his predictions of which patterns, if any, are likely to provoke difficult feelings in supervision and may make decisions on "balance" stopping short, however, of definitive value judgments which are left for the conference to determine. His tentative assignment of $+$'s and $-$'s and $\pm$'s is for the purpose of designing a supervisory strategy, rather than an expression of necessarily foregone evaluative conclusions. A third connotation, or possible misconception, attaches to the word "balance." It is generally mistaken to imagine that if Teacher is confronted by an analysis comprising three strengths and three· weaknesses he will experience three rewards and three punishments and will break even emotionally. Although, in our practice, clinical supervision began with this psychologically naive premise, we were disabused of it before very long. Sometimes Teacher will feel punished no matter what Supervisor says, either because he has not yet worked through the self-fulfilling prophesy that supervision will be punishing or because other things are happening in his life that temporarily immobilize his capacities for pleasure. Sometimes Teacher's defenses are so impenetrable that criticisms simply do not filter through. Although Supervisor may be sending, he is not receiving.

Experience suggests, however, that something like balance does occur, and, moreover, the eventual character it assumes can be influenced by prior planning. If our initial assumptions about quantitative balance were foolish, our subsequent decision to throw the concept on the junkpile was premature. Supervisor's problem is to be rather more sophisticated than one-to-one quantitative matching will permit.

Unsurprisingly, his most valuable single source of information for planning in this context consists of knowledge gained in previous sequences of supervision with Teacher. Depending on the adequacy of his recall and the completeness of his records, Supervisor may be able to predict, with greater or lesser accuracy, the emotional valences that are likely to attach to specific substantive issues or to result from specific supervisory processes, based on past experiences. In general, however, commanding unexceptional powers of memory and being derelict in record keeping, Supervisor may at least conceptualize balance in relation to his surface impressions of Teacher's typical responses to criticism and analysis. In other words, his cumulative impressions of Teacher's tolerances, of his saturation points, and of his ability to accept (or tendencies to reject) analysis should provide Supervisor with at least a rudimentary set of parameters for estimating what will be experienced as giving and what will be experienced as taking, in short, of what combination of support and disputation is likely to result in a global, plus-effect for the conference.

While one aim of clinical supervision is to counteract teachers' and supervisors' tendencies to create halos around teaching by differentiating specific elements of teaching in analysis, it also aims to create positive incentives for supervision by enabling Teacher to achieve relevant rewards. Although Teacher would be mistaken to evaluate his instructional practice in global terms, he should, nonetheless, be able to conclude supervision conferences with basically positive *feelings* about himself, about supervision, and about the future. It behooves Supervisor, consequently, to consider subjective balance realistically beforehand, avoiding simpleminded cause-effect construction as he does so.

Perhaps the most important capacity for Supervisor to develop, given that teaching is so devilishly complex and ambiguous and demanding, is that of being able to treat ambiguities and failures productively, that is, in a manner that permits shrewdly examined failures (weakness, − 's) to generate successful modifications in the teaching. One critical element of Teacher's outlook on clinical supervision must be an expectation of failures, but an optimistic rather than a fearful or shameful one. To be a rational educator, one must expect to encounter inevitable failures: the discipline is simply not mature enough for mistakes to be avoidable. For the salesman, there is little reason to rejoice when he blows a sale. The stakes are high, and only success means success. For the teacher, however, or for any clinical practitioner, some strength must be developed, not only for tolerating mistakes, but for seeking them out ruthlessly and for positively rejoicing in their discovery and successful treatment. I propose that in teaching, the only grievous mistake is the one that remains undetected. As a university supervisor, I should be foolish to flunk student teachers who were unable to demonstrate slick performances. On the contrary, my F's go to those students who, in spite of our best efforts, seem utterly unable to find the *chutspah* required for dealing constructively with patterns that seem wrong.

My point, in this, is that "balance" becomes an important concept, perhaps a key concept, for creating a supervision conference in which, although weaknesses are addressed, their identification and treatment energizes and motivates Teacher instead of sucking the life from him. Whether or not examinations of failures were productive often seems to depend upon the emotional residues that remain after a conference has ended.

Are there specific junctures at which I should test Teacher's comprehension by engaging him in role-play or by asking him to paraphrase a line of reasoning I have presented? It is generally wise, at Stage 3, for Supervisor to adopt strategies for protecting the effectiveness of communication in the conference, that is, to insure that Teacher will understand whatever it is that Supervisor wants him to understand at the moment. In the same fashion, he should plan measures to assure his own comprehension of ideas and feelings that Teacher will be attempting to communicate. Let's deal with the first of these problems first.

One problem that exists for all teachers and supervisors is the seemingly universal tendency to confuse one's own fluency (either real or imagined) with the quality of other people's understanding of one's words. I am more likely than not to assume that because I expressed myself fluently, lucidly, simply, gracefully, and the like, you will have understood my ideas consistently with my intended meanings. If, in fact, your own mind was hopscotching around other things, for example, the fantasy "He must think I'm afraid to hear the truth," then I am certain to deceive myself by such an assumption. My chances for deception are multiplied if you not only were tuned out during my soliloquy, but had your eyes fixed on mine in apparent concentration, nodded vigorously from time to time, and performed an obbligato of umhm's.

Presumably, when either Teacher or Supervisor raises a question or defines a problem or expresses a value or reports a feeling, he does so because of some measure of importance he attaches to it. Rather than its being sufficient for agreeable conversation to take place emptily, as at the cocktail party, under such circumstances it may be crucial for talk to be the carrier of substantive ideas and to exist principally for that purpose. Beyond socializing, there must be pertinent conceptual exchange.

The most useful method I know for testing whether or not you read my meaning is to ask you to play it back. The most adequate way I know to determine whether you can translate my ideas or your own ideas into operational behavior (if, as at the conference, we only have each other) is to contrive a role-play in which you have the opportunity to demonstrate the behavior in question. Similarly, the best way I can think of to be sure that I understand what you are saying to me is to try to say it back, one way or another, in some form that will get your agreement. Such methods are doubly virtuous in that they provide chances to correct misinterpretations as well as opportunities to assure consensus.

Clearly, techniques such as these have little place in ordinary social dialogue and would seem downright peculiar in most informal conversation. It follows that one task, for the clinical supervisor, is to establish this convention early in his supervisory relationships; to teach Teacher to tolerate playbacks and role-plays and to demonstrate his own decision to press for clarity by engaging in such behavior himself. Illustrations of these techniques will be provided in the next section, "Methods of the Conference."

At the strategy stage, it is often useful for Supervisor to plan, in advance, special moments at which playback should be particularly valuable during the conference. When might playback be particularly appropriate? Perhaps in connection to an unusually subtle concept; or a very complex one; or an idea that can be understood in various senses, some of which capture the intended point and others of which miss it; or in relation to an issue about which Teacher is likely to feel ambivalent or resistant. Supervisor's primary reason for noting such moments in advance is simply to insure that he will remember to employ playback, if it becomes appropriate to do so, before the opportunity has slipped by. For his own part, paraphrasing Teachers' verbalized ideas should become an almost automatic reflex at moments when Supervisor finds himself confused by what Teacher is saying.

As we shall see later, "too much of a good thing" represents one peril associated with these techniques. Nevertheless, their advantages have clearly outweighed their disadvantages, in my experience, and I commend them particularly to clinical supervisors. Role-play, especially, seems to reinforce what supervision is really after, namely, behavioral modifications. It generally seems more useful and rewarding in supervision for Teacher to *do* whatever it is that he wants to do in addition to simply verbalizing that he understands and that he knows how to do it. Although some "doing" cannot be simulated without the children's presence, there are a surprising number of techniques that Teacher can rehearse in supervision and which, once they have been mastered, should be performable even in a barrel over Niagara.

Under what circumstances should I be ready to abandon my own analysis of this lesson in favor of other approaches? Once a decision has been made to deal with selected patterns, rather than to perform a full analysis, Supervisor must nevertheless be ready to abandon his strategy in response to contingencies arising in the conference. In this respect it seems important to note the frame of mind in which Supervisor should regard his strategy, even if it is not possible to suggest specific methods to be employed in this connection at Stage 3. Although he values strategy because of the general relationship he sees between planning and systematic work in supervision, the clinical supervisor must also be sufficiently resilient to overcome his feeling of investment in a plan he has formulated, perhaps with great effort, if it should turn out that Teacher experiences a sense of urgency to deal with other matters.

Supervisor should at least consult whatever impressions he may have collected, either before Observation or during the lesson, that might lead him to expect Teacher to open certain issues in the conference. For example, if, having succumbed to that bane of all geometry instructors, Teacher said the wrong word while explaining how to "circumscribe" an angle, and if, as the boys giggled, he realized his error and flushed and stammered and endeavored to disappear altogether, and if, during this agony, he perceived that Supervisor's knuckles had turned white, then, although Supervisor might not regard the incident as being sufficiently important to address in supervision, nonetheless he would be wise to expect Teacher to bring it up and, perhaps, to spend more time reliving the episode as an expression of penance.

If certain issues have assumed emotional primacy for Teacher, it is almost certain that he will be distracted from other issues that Supervisor prefers to examine unless deliberate steps are taken to reduce the tension surrounding them. It particularly behooves Supervisor to treat problems that Teacher identified beforehand (in Stage 1), if only to put them aside temporarily, should no pertinent data have been generated during the lesson.

What balance should exist between considerations of the past, the present, and the future? Decisions on this question often determine the success or failure of a conference, particularly in regard to how Teacher feels about it, more than any other single factor of strategy. Concretely, the question is really of how much time to spend, respectively, in analyzing teaching that is over, in examining processes that are operating at the moment in supervision, and in planning future sequences of teaching.

Here again, the history of our experiences is of interest. In the early days, our conferences often consisted of little more than complex analyses of the teaching we had observed. This was great fun for the supervisors, but it later appeared that teachers were often put out because of having had to endure what seemed to be an essentially time-wasting exercise in which critical dissections of their teaching were performed without apparent purpose. Just as racing is the sport of kings, so analysis seemed to the the sport of supervisors.

As we began to feel the ensuing hostility, our work took a new direction, namely, toward planning for future lessons that would be examined during the existing cycle of supervision. We discovered that teachers felt most helped by supervision when it left them with something concrete in hand; something to symbolize real accomplishments; something that would have functional utility "tomorrow"; namely, a lesson plan for tomorrow. We resolved, consequently, that supervision conferences should culminate in the creation of such a plan; that after having refined it overnight, Teacher might show us his polished version in Preobservation the next morning, for example.

Although this approach puts us back into business, it was not, as they say, problem-free. For one thing, it proved difficult to control teachers' growing dependencies upon supervisors to invent lesson plans for them. For another, plans created by supervisors were sometimes distorted badly in the next day's teaching, partly because of invisible misunderstandings that existed yesterday and partly, it seemed, as a result of some teachers' tendencies to subvert anything Supervisor suggested as a way to punish him. It also became clear that although past-and-future had begun to exist in some reasonably productive balance, there never seemed to be time enough for dealing with problems of the present, for example, with problems like the dependencies, to which I have just referred, that were blooming in some supervisory relationships.

This story, as it seems, has no happy ending nor, for that matter, any ending at all. Although it leaves Supervisor with the realization that there is no simple solution to the problem of time balance, it does not project clear, complex strategies for coping with a wide range of related problems that exist, continuingly. By and large, I believe that our first conclusion about the need for concrete, future-oriented outcomes, still holds. Supervision that stays too much in the past soon begins to feel abrasive, and it is generally not enough to hope that if supervision focuses principally upon completed teaching and performs mainly analytical functions, Teacher will make appropriate applications to his own teaching in his own good time. Analogously, the hopeful and ambiguous injunction "I want you to think about that tonight" is, perhaps, the weakest way to end a lesson.

Although it would be inaccurate to say I had discovered solutions to such problems, I have found that certain methods, involving some degree of compromise, help to create a relatively successful and satisfying cycle of supervision. Indeed, the principal strategy for achieving reasonable balance is to think of supervision distributed over cycles instead of aiming, somehow, to crowd every tense into any given supervisory sequence. The way in which to allocate time should be decided at the beginning of a cycle, during the "contract" stage. Decisions about what to do first should be based upon Supervisor's and Teacher's ideas about what Teacher needs the most and wants the most. Clearly, Teacher will have more to say about such things than Supervisor, whose function in such decision making should generally be that of constructive, examining, argumentation. Here are illustrations of some common sequences:

First Day	Second Day	Third Day
1. Analysis	Planning	Analysis-Planning
2. Planning	Analysis-Planning	Analysis
3. Process	Planning	Analysis
4. Planning	Analysis-Process	Planning

In each of these examples, "day" is used figuratively, although in typical practice days often are the most convenient and realistic units of time for planning cycles of supervision. Also, each entry is intended to represent the principal activity of a supervision conference but not, necessarily, its exclusive activity.

Example 1 illustrates a sequence that might logically fit supervision commencing after some period during which Supervisor and Teacher were not working together regularly. In effect, it expresses the strategy: (First day) Let's just take a look at what's going on generally; (Second day) let's do some planning based upon what showed up in yesterday's analysis; (Third day) let's examine how yesterday's plans worked out in today's teaching and then concentrate our efforts on assembling plans for tomorrow and thereafter. This sequence's most salient feature is the way in which it begins, namely, with a general analysis of observational data.

Example 2 might logically occur at the beginning of some unit of curriculum. Teacher is about to take up "Natural and Manufactured Crystals"; the children have just returned from summer vacation; and there is nothing in particular to analyze in order for supervision to get started. The strategy: Let's plan it; let's see what we've got and then plan some more; let's take a good look at how things are working out. By this time Teacher is likely to be ready to lay out plans for the next sequence of instruction without much participation by Supervisor. If, in fact, he was ready to do so at the beginning, then Example 1 might have been more appropriate to follow.

Example 3 also looks like a good way to begin: Let's decide how we're going to operate together; having built a contract, let's do some planning; now let's see how things have worked out, vis-à-vis the processes upon which we have agreed and the plans we have formulated. Perhaps we ought to modify our processes, our plans, neither, or both.

Example 4 could represent one manner for dealing with an impasse: (First day) We planned; (Second day) analysis revealed that in spite of what seemed to be a good plan, the lesson failed to come off, and, additionally, a major problem seemed to be that Teacher conceptualized the initial plan too literally, too rigidly. Let's try to discover what may be happening in supervision to have caused the difficulty (it turns out that Teacher assumed that Supervisor's suggestions were really mandates; Supervisor does his best to loosen Teacher from that set); (Third day) having (apparently) straightened things out between us, let's plan some more.

If time is short for conferences, and if it appears that no single conference can incorporate a satisfactory balance among the variables in question, then, by formulating an appropriate strategy and by agreeing to appropriate compromises, an overall feeling of productive balance and propitious closure may be achieved for a cycle.

From time to time one encounters problems whose solution requires attenuated cycles of supervision, sometimes spanning weeks and months (although, in most cases, not on a daily basis). I have sometimes, for example, had to spend weeks dealing with process—Teacher did not trust me; he was very anxious about being observed; he felt severely punished by analysis—but eventually was able to join Teacher in planning which he experienced helpfully. Had supervision been stopped prematurely, Teacher might never have learned to take advantage of clinical analysis and might not, consequently, have experienced the rewards attainable by that practice.

What method of recording, if any, should be employed for this conference? For many of us, record keeping is a bother and frequently represents a compulsive, ritual activity rather than a useful process. I sometimes think that the key to successful recording in clinical practice consists of one's ability to erase tapes and to burn notes freely and judiciously, rather than of one's rat-like propensity for storing things.

What should be recorded? What reasons favor recording? The easiest records for clinical supervisors to compile consist of the observation notes they record in any event, which can easily enough be dropped into files after each supervisory sequence. To have such records available enables Teacher or Supervisor to capture a view of changes that have occurred in the teaching, particularly among the salient teaching patterns upon which supervision has focused, at moments when looking backward may be particularly reinforcing or useful in some other manner. The question of whether or not to hold onto such notes is hardly worth troubling with: they are there, in any case, and keeping them hardly represents a problem.

It is more problematical to decide whether additional note taking should be undertaken deliberately. Supervisor might keep his blueprints for strategy. He might also take occasional notes during supervision conferences (so might Teacher), or might write them up quickly afterwards, or might tape-record them and keep a chronological library of such tapes. The best reason I have found for keeping longitudinal records of one kind or another is that, especially when supervision is operating toward long-range developmental goals, it is frequently difficult to remember quite how things have gone in the past. At moments of joy and of depression, particularly, some teachers and some supervisors tend to view their past relationships in positive or negative halos. Memories become distorted and obscured; time telescopes back and forth; and a million factors interfere with estimating progress confidently.

In my own experience, tapes have been most valuable for use in the training of supervisors and as material for research in clinical supervision. In practice, tapes and observation notes have frequently been useful when I felt required to enlist the services of another supervisor: to offer independent interpretations of a problem; to bring some specialized knowledge into supervision that neither Teacher nor I possessed; to take over for me, temporarily or permanently; or to help me plan strategies for Teacher's future supervision. It has generally seemed more effective to brief consultants by presenting actual, recorded data, than by simply describing what has gone on. Indeed, my principal motive for employing a consultant is sometimes to test my own views of what has occurred by comparing them to his unprejudiced impressions of recorded sessions.

Some teachers and supervisors find note taking distracting or inconvenient during conferences and follow the practice of listening to their own tapes after the conference and noting whatever they want to during the playback. Listening to tapes of conferences has been particularly useful during periods of supervision in which the major focus has been aimed at supervisory processes, that is, at the quality of interactions between Supervision and Teacher. There have been many times, for example, when instead of confronting teachers with my impressions of their behavior, we have simply listened to tapes of supervision conferences in which they were struck, spontaneously, by their own patterns of dependency or defensiveness or whatever. It has often seemed that when, for example, technical progress was being slowed by some form of resistance, that obstacle was passed more effectively when Teacher was able to perceive his own defensive maneuvers than when I told him about them. While my telling often, self-defeatingly, makes Teacher even more defensive than before, if I employ a strategy in which Teacher is given the chance to identify his own behavior by listening to himself on tapes, and if he uses the opportunity successfully, his achievement of appropriate insights is likely to occur more efficiently and less hurtfully than if I try to force them upon him. One technique for creating such opportunities is to set Teacher free with the tapes:

> SUPERVISOR: I guess we agree that things seem to have bogged down for us, even though it's hard to put your finger on exactly where the trouble is. Let's try something. Instead of trying to make sense out of everything together, when time is short, supposing we

each take some of this week's tapes home and listen to them leisurely and see if, that way, we can spot "causes" that we haven't seen before?"

Needless to say, it is often just as good for the gander to follow this prescription. Time and again I have found, to my surprise, that my own rigidity or defensiveness, rather than Teacher's, had brought things to a halt—or at least, that a tug-of-war requires two tuggers. Although, mercifully, I have generally been able to find my weaknesses by myself, on numerous occasions teachers' independent listening has resulted in direct confrontations from them:

> TEACHER: You know, as I listened to this thing, it sounded more and more like the trouble started when you said that I should decide where to go next in the unit, but then you kept putting pressure on me to do it your way. I think I was confused by this.

Although I cannot prove it, it seems that an effect of each such turnabout in supervision has almost always been to get things moving again and to relax us, perhaps because, in some sense, the psychological score has been evened.

So much for possible reasons to record. Even with good reasons, Supervisor must consider what effects recording, by any method is likely to have on the conference. Even when a tradition of tape-recording has been established in Teacher's supervision, Supervisor should remain alert to the chance that on any given occasion the presence of a recording machine may create tension. Sometimes extensive note taking is useful in a conference, both for its own sake and for the purpose of creating silent periods for thinking. Sometimes it can create welcome diversions from intense eye-to-eye contact. Sometimes it can positively interfere with an intensity of interaction that the situation requires.

During Strategy, consequently, Supervisor should decide first, whether reasons exist for recording the conference; second, whether past experiences with Teacher indicate that recording is likely to be acceptable; and finally, whether any momentary evidence suggests that on this particular occasion it might be best to let recording go. Decisions of this kind may always be tentative, particularly if recording equipment is present and ready to be activated at any moment during the conference. The balance to decide, in any event, is between persuasive reasons to record and the price that recording may exact.

Should Teacher be given carte blanche *for structuring this conference; should he be offered specific options; should I hold him to the analysis I have prepared?* This is not quite the same question as whether or not to employ full analysis or as that of judging the likelihood that reasons will arise in the conference to abandon Supervisor's *a priori* strategy, although these issues clearly overlap. In certain respects, this question is more inclusive, namely, in that it suggests the possibility that Teacher can elect to do anything he pleases with the conference, for example, to discuss philosophies of education; to talk, exclusively, about the lesson that was observed; to ignore the lesson and to talk only about future directions in teaching; to discuss relatively personal issues that pertain, somehow, to Teacher's professional functioning; to discuss a student; to discuss irrelevancies; or to cancel the conference altogether.

What reasons could justify such complete freedom to manage supervisory time? Once again, as with the full analysis, this strategy (let's call it the "open conference") has seemed most sensible to employ either with unusually strong supervisees or with inordinately anxious ones. For teachers in the middle range, the technique is sometimes well suited to special objectives that I will describe in a moment.

It is not difficult to imagine that after substantial experience with clinical supervision, many teachers become quite as adroit at analyzing behavioral data and at charting strategies for modifying their own teaching patterns as their supervisors are. Neither is it unusual to find teachers who surpass their supervisors' skills after a time, particularly in connection to understanding and transforming their own instructional behavior. Such advancement sometimes occurs because Teacher is simply more intelligent or more perceptive or more highly motivated, in certain respects, than Supervisor. More commonly, I suspect, Teacher's ascendency is attributable to his more intimate knowledge of himself, his pupils, and the flow of his teaching, than Supervisor's. Because Teacher is there all of the time, it often develops that he must guess less frequently than Supervisor to make sense out of what is happening, and that his guesses are more often on target than Supervisor's.

Teacher's personal identification with his work, if you will, his ego-involvement in professional performance, can generate a powerful commitment to technical learning and a positive joy in self-evaluation and self-directed training under favorable conditions, just as it can generate anxiety and defensive resistance under unfavorable ones. In the former case, it is unsurprising to find Teacher providing the motive energy and psychological drive for supervision. For Supervisor to be most useful to such a teacher, he must learn, at least, how to avoid distracting him from self-defined tasks; how, in effect, to keep out of the way. Analogously to the training of a virtuoso pianist or of a great painter, Supervisor's role evolves, after a time, into that of coach. He becomes less a teacher of technique and author of assigned exercises and more a critical dialectician; a mirror; an occasional collaborator in invention; a handmaiden, primarily, to Teacher's own strategies; a traveling companion through whatever directions Teacher pursues his own professional muses. More prominently, perhaps, than in any other phase of supervision, Supervisor's principal commitments, at this final level, are to perform whatever functions can help Teacher most to accomplish what *he* wants to.

It is not difficult to sense the appropriateness of open conferences at this level of supervision. Once Teacher is sufficiently in control of his own teaching and of clinical supervisory techniques to apply to his own work, there is, if anything, generally less risk of wasting supervisory time or of using it badly when he decides what to do than when Supervisor does. Because of the likelihood that supervision should be relaxed, or deintensified from time to time, I have found it reasonable to assume, generally, that Teacher is a better thermostat than I and that by following his clicks we create a supervision that is paced just right. Left to their own devices, I have rarely found teachers experienced in clinical supervision who elected to divest themselves of their supervisors because they seemed, somehow, to have become obsolete. On the contrary, it usually seems that the more skillful and autonomous Teacher has become, the more vigorously and creatively he makes use of supervisory consorts. Having learned not to feel threatened by observation and analysis, Teacher tends to reach out more aggressively for supervision than he did in the beginning.

For such teachers, consequently, some rationales for open conferences are (1) that with the teacher in control, supervision may satisfy the condition of being paced according to Teacher's experienced needs and energies, better than with anyone else in command; (2) the open conference enables Supervisor to provide direction by request rather than by default; and (3) the Teacher may operate most autonomously under such conditions by performing self-initiated supervision. The decision for an open conference should be made as early as possible in a sequence of supervision, in order for Teacher to have the time he needs to prepare strategies if, indeed, he wants to. It is particularly important for Teacher to have enough time to examine Supervisor's observation notes or to listen to a tape of the lesson before the conference if there is any likelihood that he will want to perform a full or limited analysis of his teaching.

Open conferences may also have some utility early in supervision, particularly with very anxious teachers. The major problem connected to using this technique with uninitiated teachers is that if they squander an open conference on superficialties or on peripheral or irrelevant issues, and if, having offered *carte blanche*, Supervisor has no choice except to keep the faith, then they may learn, incidentally, that it is all right for clinical supervision to continue to be whatever game they played. One check on such incidental learnings arising from a poorly employed open conference is for Supervisor to stipulate in advance that although the contract calls for *carte blanche*, he reserves the prerogative of examining the conference's success, retroactively, with Teacher.

SUPERVISOR: [At Stage 1.] I think it might be a good idea, for now, for you to think of me as being available for offering any kind of assistance I can. You know, there aren't really any hard and fast rules about this sort of thing. There may be times when it seems best for me to introduce issues into supervision and other times when it would be better for you to take the initiative. We can work out these decisions as we come to them. In any case, I also think it makes pretty good sense for us to stop, occasionally, to try to evaluate how things are going in supervision, just as one needs to stop every so often to examine whether teaching is producing the payoff it was intended to.

Offered this kind of invitation, Teacher sometimes begins testing Supervisor's mettle immediately by suggesting that he remove himself altogether from his immediate existence:

TEACHER: Yeah, I think it might be best if I just tried to work things out by myself for a while and, maybe, if we just skipped supervision for this week.

Hmm. Despite the great temptation for Supervisor to pull back, at this point, and to introduce the qualification that while Teacher may use the supervision as he pleases, he must, nevertheless, use it some-how, I have generally found it best to honor Teacher's request and, implicitly, to give permission for him to resist supervisory intervention. Lest Teacher be startled by my readiness to quit the scene and inter-pret my flight as an indication that if Teacher rejects me I will reject him right back, I generally offer some kind of reassurance (and try to follow through on it):

SUPERVISOR: Sure. I think sometimes it is best for someone to be able to work things out himself. I tell you what—since this is my day to be in this building in any event, I'll stick around and get some other work done. If you should want to get in touch, I will be here; and you can ring me up any time. If we don't see each other again today, I'll check back with you next week to see what's what, and we can decide what to do from there.

It has seemed true, generally, that this combination of willingness to stay away and reassurances that I would, nevertheless, be available, has resulted, after a short time, in teachers' initiation of requests for some form of direct supervision. It has been almost as if once Supervi-sor had passed the test by leaving Teacher alone when Teacher wanted to be alone, that is, once Supervisor had demonstrated that he would not, necessarily, mount a frontal attack on Teacher's resistance, that test no longer seemed so terribly important. Reassured by the knowl-edge that Supervisor won't impose his interventions upon Teacher,

Teacher may feel safer in running risks of supervision: he knows that there is an escape hatch.

Although I sometimes wonder about the degree to which I may be rationalizing my own lack of stamina, I generally tell myself that if Teacher is really so threatened by the prospect of supervision that he needs to beg off (or if, in reality, my supervision has been so inept that he has good reasons for wanting to be rid of me), it is probably best not to force the issue because my efforts would not amount to much under such conditions. When Teacher continues to procrastinate, it is usually a good idea to arrange for a meeting whose purpose is to make sure he recognizes that supervisory time *can* be used in other activities besides observation and analysis: that Supervisor is willing, for example, just to meet and talk about professional issues, at least for the time being. Should Teacher agree to periodic talk-meetings, it would behoove Supervisor to conceptualize such meetings as opportunities for professional counseling and to contrive, eventually, for the talk to center around Teacher's ambivalent or fearful feelings toward clinical supervision. Not only may such counseling give Teacher a chance to work through his feelings, but it may, additionally, provide Supervisor with cues relating to modified models of clinical supervision which could, simultaneously, incorporate enough technical rigor to be worthwhile and avoid certain strategies for which Teacher feels little tolerance. Another way to express this thought is by saying that while Teacher's initial anxiety about supervision may be fairly global, such talk may help to differentiate specific elements of the process or specific areas of Teacher's work that are particularly sensitive to examination and which can be skirted while other productive business is transacted and while, hopefully, more safety is established as a result of supervisory counseling.

When limited or full analysis has failed and the open conference technique has been adopted, consequently, it becomes particularly important for Supervisor to recognize that many gradations exist along the "open-directed" continuum and that more directed analysis can be developed by small degrees over successive cycles of supervision. I do not mean to suggest that having promised *carte blanche*, Supervisor should sneak up behind Teacher when he isn't looking, slip him a dose of supervision, and then fall back into his camouflage. On the contrary, the more honest and more effective approach, generally, is to be perfectly open and explicit with Teacher in reaching agreements that enable Supervisor to begin to introduce his own issues and interpretations into supervision. In the long run, having been forced by Teacher's anxiety to begin with open conferences, Supervisor should attempt to work, by small steps, into cycles of conventional clinical supervision in order to train Teacher in the analytical and self-directed treatment techniques he will require in order to pass, ultimately, to a level of supervision at which, once again, Teacher may take the major initiative: this time because he is strong and competent to do so rather than because he is afraid.

In addition to cases in which open conference is indicated either because Teacher is already professionally potent or because he cannot tolerate anything else, the technique may have other objectives and advantages. Even for teachers who do not experience unmanageable anxiety, it is sometimes useful to reduce the intensity of concentration and effort which can become quite strong in cycles of clinical supervision. Trying too hard to regulate some pattern of teaching or to master some element of technique often reaches diminishing returns: the very intensity that Teacher brings to his task precludes sufficient relaxation to perform the technique in question. An open conference may serve to untighten Teacher on such occasions.

In much the same manner, it sometimes appears that, once Teacher has gained conceptual control over a technique he is trying to establish but is experiencing a developmental gap between his ability to understand what he wants and his ability to execute the technique in question, a truer economy can be enjoyed when Teacher turns to other issues temporarily than when he concentrates exclusively on what he's after. It is as though by declaring a temporary moratorium on the principal task, he enables himself to consolidate his ideas and corresponding patterns of behavior at an unconscious level while he feels preoccupied with other things. It is not uncommon to discover that teachers can master technical problems with relatively little difficulty after a period of ignoring them or that, having begun to struggle with a technique and then having turned to other problems, Teacher discovers, after a while, that the technique in question has become established in his teaching spontaneously, that is, without any focused conscious effort to get it there.

And again, it is likely to be true of any teacher, that Supervisor cannot judge his developmental pace and cannot provide supervision optimally suited to that pace as accurately as Teacher might himself. An open conference or a cycle of such conferences can enable Teacher to find his own stride and may generate cues to guide Supervisor's regulation of the tempo thereafter. "Pace" and "tempo" may sound too fiction-like to imagine in concrete terms. Let us consider some examples. Once Teacher has learned what clinical supervision is like and has experienced conferences in which data have been analyzed and patterns examined and plans laid for subsequent teaching, and the like, and even when supervision seems to have been achieving its objectives, it can be most instructive to Supervisor to give Teacher full responsibility for conducting supervisory sequences. He may discover that the average number of patterns with which Teacher elects to deal in any given session is greater or smaller than when Supervisor made such choices. He may discover some propensity for working in certain categories of teaching behavior more than in others, or for working in a plurality of categories concurrently which, in either case, may be the same or different from the substantive balance generally initiated by Supervisor. He may, likewise, discover avoidance of specific categories which, in his judgment, should be set aside temporarily in deference to Teacher's feelings or, perhaps, should be specifically identified as areas that Teacher avoids (when given his own choice) in order to explore his feelings about them.

He may find that, left to his own initiative, Teacher tends to define problems of practice more complexly or more superficially than Supervisor does. He may discover that although he assumed that Teacher craved simple remedies to complicated technical dilemmas, he does, in fact, take appropriately complex views of his work. He may find that Teacher tends to polarize his value judgments so that specific patterns generally seem either good or bad, or he may discover that Teacher is more subtle in detecting simultaneous strengths and weaknesses incorporated by such patterns. He may find that Teacher tends to jump the gun on evaluating the goodness or badness of various techniques, or that he defers judgment until reasonable evidence can be collected, or that he positively avoids committing himself to value judgments, no matter what.

Supervisor may, in effect, find confirmation in Teacher's self-initiated behavior for the strategies that he (Supervisor) has been employing; he may find contraindications for such strategies; and he may discover productive lines of inquiry that would not have occurred to him had Teacher not been given freedom to take intellectual control. The open conference can be ideal for "diagnostic" purposes insofar as Teacher can be observed in a natural condition, rather than in one that has somehow been imposed upon him, and can, unless his behavior *qua* supervisee has already become stereotyped, provide strong signals for directing future supervision. Having the chance to observe Teacher's spontaneous choices, their substance, their sequence, and their duration, Supervisor may, subsequently, establish a supervision or help Teacher to develop a supervision whose structure and organization and tempo reflect Teacher's corresponding capacities and needs or which, by deliberate calculation, is designed to produce measured tensions between them.

The open conference may, additionally, provide Teacher time to deal with residual issues, that is, with bits and pieces that have spilled over from past cycles of supervision, and with the chance to initiate ancillary activities which, although they may not represent elements of direct clinical supervision, may nevertheless be consistent with supervisory aims. Teacher might, for example, use such conference time to engage Supervisor in designing a professional research project or in planning some technical experiment or in studying supervisory problems and methods in order to develop specialized competencies for use in supervision to be initiated with teaching colleagues.

As for the rest of this question of strategy, Supervisor should decide how important it might be to hold Teacher to some specific analysis or to offer teacher limited choices among alternative analyses that Supervisor has prepared. Often, unless negative indications emerge spontaneously during the conference, it seems best to stick with the planned analysis in order, for example, to pin down certain issues that have previously been ambiguous but which the present data illustrate clearly, or because it seems necessary to follow through on specific patterns that were introduced during an earlier sequence of supervision. Sometimes it seems best to engage Teacher in making decisions about which course, among certain specified courses, to follow. One purpose for limiting choices rather than providing an open field may be to insure that Supervisor will be adequately prepared and adequately fluent to function efficiently in the conference. In any event, Supervisor should recognize that multiple models of clinical supervision do exist and that the model employed for any given sequence should reflect conscious decisions rather than habituation to some general procedure. Of all the reasons I might cite for avoiding mindless routinization, not the least important is that it is more fun for many people to feel engaged in creative behavior than in rote behaviors, in the context of their professional work.

How many data should I present to document the patterns I have selected? Although our primary interest, in this section, is in methods rather than in problems of clinical supervision, it is easiest to broach this question by stating the problem that motivates it. In a word, the problem is that, generally, when Supervisor summons too few data to document a teaching pattern whose features may be subtle or complex, he risks confusing Teacher who, although he nods cooperatively, may have little idea of what Supervisor is talking about. The opposite danger is that Supervisor produces so many data to document a pattern that Teacher already recognizes, that is, that he produces so many gratuitous and redundant data, that Teacher begins to feel as if he were being deliberately humiliated. You might imagine, for example, that if I showed you several instances in which you asked the class multiple questions and if, very quickly, you appreciated the technical weaknesses of that pattern and if, nevertheless, I then proceeded to plow through my entire record of observation, quoting over and over again multiple questions that you asked, before long you might reasonably feel that my motive was simply to embarrass you, to rub your nose in the data, and that, moreover, I was something of a fool to waste time so badly. "Spare me" cries your inner voice.

Previous experiences with Teacher should provide Supervisor with some notion of how much documentation is enough. Specific patterns may be judged with regard to their logical and behavioral complexity, their likely emotional significance, and the like, for selecting appropriate quantities of supporting material. Some general rules of thumb are for Supervisor to have too many data available rather than too few; to select the clearest examples from the data rather than obscure or ambiguous examples; to select well-defined patterns in favor of subtle ones—unless, of course, special urgency attaches to some subtle teaching pattern—to defer treating nebulous patterns until some later sequence during which, hopefully, they will emerge more clearly; and, when in doubt concerning how much documentation is necessary, to test Teacher's comprehension by playback or role-play techniques.

There is no rule, incidentally, that says Supervisor must present all of the supporting data used in a conference. While it may behoove him to know where such data are located in his notes or on the tape, it does not follow that he must be the one to introduce all evidence. In fact, there are likely to be positive advantages connected to having Teacher peruse the data to find relevant material himself.

1. SUPERVISOR: How would you describe the kinds of questions you tended to ask during the review?

TEACHER: I'd say they were mainly "fill-in" type questions.

SUPERVISOR: Yeah. Can you find some examples on the tape (or, "in these notes")? [Or, "Can you recall any examples, verbatim?" or, "Let's see if we can find some concrete examples in the notes."]

2. SUPERVISOR: As I look over these notes it seems to me that today you were using a very varied collection of rewards; that your rewards were almost as differentiated as the differing quality of the kids' responses—which is exactly what we've been after. Why don't you go through this stuff [in this case, a photocopy of Supervisor's observation notes] and name whatever reward patterns you can find, and I'll do the same thing; and then we can compare notes?

3. SUPERVISOR: It struck me several times today that some confusion may have resulted when you gave directions to individual pupils that were really intended for the whole class and when, sometimes, you made comments out loud to everybody that were really being directed to individual pupils, uh, do you know what I mean?

TEACHER: Um, I think so.

SUPERVISOR: Well, uh, maybe the best way to pin this down would be for you to try to find places in the notes where you did this, and then we can try to estimate [from the data] what the results were.

4. TEACHER: I just had the feeling that the kids didn't really understand what they were supposed to do. It seemed like they understood all right when I was walking around looking at their seatwork, but then when they went up to the board they just didn't seem to understand what to do.

SUPERVISOR: I know what you mean. Have you any ideas why that might have happened?

TEACHER: Maybe my directions weren't clear.

SUPERVISOR: OK, why don't we find those points where you gave directions [on the tape or in Supervisor's observation notes] and see whether they sound clear?

TEACHER: Yeah, that sounds good.

[Teacher and Supervisor locate relevant data and decide, having tried to experience Teacher's directions as the children might have, that, in fact, they seem perfectly clear and simple.]

TEACHER: I don't get it. They did seem confused. I mean, they just stood there at the board and didn't do anything.

SUPERVISOR: Well, how could we possibly account for the fact that the very same kids that were doing the work right in their seats just couldn't seem to explain what they were doing at the board?

TEACHER: Beats me.

SUPERVISOR: Do you think it might be that we shouldn't expect there to be much correlation between what they do, silently, in their seats and their ability to explain how they did the examples, up at the board?

TEACHER: How do you mean?

SUPERVISOR: I mean, while I might be able to figure a square root on paper, silently, I might, nevertheless, not be able to stand up and say, step by step, exactly what I had done, that is, out loud.

TEACHER: I never thought about it that way. Makes sense. Uh, in fact, I think some of them feel kind of uncomfortable standing up in front of the class.

SUPERVISOR: Yeah. [Pause.] If it doesn't necessarily follow that they'll be able to recite at the board what they can do successfully by themselves, what might you do to help them perform better at the board?

TEACHER: I guess—give them practice doing things out loud at the board.

SUPERVISOR: Exactly, yes, I think so. That way they would be practicing precisely the things they would be doing, instead of something else. Of course, there's always the question of whether it's important enough to be able to recite that kind of thing out loud to be worth training them to do it.

TEACHER: Yeah. You know, come to think of it, the only one

who did a good job at the board was Freddy; and he stayed after school for special help yesterday, and the two of us were working at the board.

SUPERVISOR: You've also worked that way with Marilyn. Do you remember how she did today?

TEACHER: Um, not really. Wait a minute. Let me find that part in the notes.

There are certainly times when it is most economical for Supervisor to show Teacher, directly, the evidence upon which a pattern has been identified or from which an interpretation has been formulated. Should Supervisor consistently press for "inductive" searching and seem reluctant, ever, to take a swift, didactic approach, his method would probably damage the supervisee's morale and make Supervisor appear to be supercilious and withholding. On the other hand, one must recognize the false economy in didactic telling, particularly when Teacher is not listening—perhaps he has tuned out for perfectly good reasons—or when, even though such telling may be full of wisdom, its incidental effect is to teach Teacher to depend upon it. The active work that Teacher does in supervisory analysis, according to this thinking, should tend to heighten his sense of productive engagement and, consequently, his professional morale. Despite popular suppositions to the contrary, one is impressed time and again by the fact that incentives to do work and opportunities to work successfully are experienced more rewardingly than successfully executed incentives to avoid work. One question for strategy is whether it seems possible for Teacher to function as an active agent in isolating and analyzing data, in light of the economic encumbrances of that approach.

Should our "contract" be reviewed at the outset; what changes, if any, should be made in our contract? It is always a good idea for Supervisor to keep a weather eye on the agreements by which he and Teacher maintain direction. I have sometimes been criticized for being "compulsive" in my thinking about supervisory contracts, and, I daresay, such charges may be well founded. I prefer, nonetheless, to err on the side of compulsiveness than to risk discovering, late in the game, that agreements I thought existed implicitly did not, in fact, exist at all. Experience has taught us to be skeptical and to assume, as a rule, that unexplicit contractual understandings are likely to be simple figments of the supervisor's imagination or projections of his wishes. I take it that when a man's professional practice is under treatment, the stakes are generally high, and that small pains are not too much to take to insure that roles and functions are developing as they should be. Especially because it costs so little (except that Supervisor may seem eccentric after a time), I urge the minimum practice of concluding Preobservation with a statement that begins, for example:

SUPERVISOR: OK, now let me be sure I have things right. My job during this sequence of supervision will be to ____ .

Beyond such simple summaries, I have also found it useful to spend a session, every so often, reviewing the contract in more general terms. It is good practice to remind Teacher, occasionally, that he should redefine roles whenever he thinks that would be advantageous and not to be misguided, by feelings of "rapport," into supposing that because things seem to be going well and because implicit understandings about who does what seem to exist, it is unnecessary to raise the question anyway.

It is particularly important to keep contract explicitly in mind when Supervisor has assumed the principal responsibility for selecting issues for treatment, that is, when he may appear to be "doing things" to Teacher.

At what point should the conference end? We have already seen that one element of strategy consists of technical and process goals which Supervisor formulates for the conference. One way to envision the ending, consequently, would be as that point at which such goals seem satisfactorily accomplished. Unfortunately, unexpected contingencies and the general condition that only so much time is available for supervision conferences create many situations in which, for one reason or another, a conference must be terminated before its *a priori* goals have been met. It is also frequently true that while Supervisor may hope to achieve certain short-term outcomes during a single conference, he is also working toward complex developmental objectives in relation to which closure, if it occurs at all, results as a cumulative effect of many conferences and of long-range supervisory work.

It is easy to imagine all kinds of unpropitious endings that might result when time runs out for supervision: many data have been unearthed, but the patterns they comprise have not been clearly defined; several patterns have been identified, but their significance has not been established; some weaknesses have been examined, but accompanying strengths have not been discussed, or vice versa; certain technical problems have been defined, but strategies (plans) for their solution have not been formulated; Teacher has raised an issue about which he feels some urgency, but there has not been enough time to develop the reassuring evidence or the methods of attack that are required. Just as the patient sometimes begins to weep and to pour out the conflicts that he has been trying to enunciate for six months at the very moment when Therapist says, "Our time is up for today," Teacher sometimes finds what has really been troubling him or just begins to show signs of crystallizing a concept around which supervision has been struggling when the bell has already begun to ring.

Experience suggests that Supervisor is generally better advised to consider felicitous stopping points in advance than simply to run until the clock indicates that he has crossed the finish line. Although other considerations might generate a model incorporating some other sequence of issues for the conference, when the question is simply about economical distribution of time and about when to quit, certain elementary guidelines may be employed. For example, in the absence of opposing reasons, Supervisor might arrange to broach hard things first and to save easy issues for the end, if there is time left. "Hard" things might be defined as issues that are conceptually complex or emotionally difficult to handle or so ambiguous that, predictably, it will take considerable time to develop relationships among the supporting data.

If Supervisor plans to invite Teacher to raise problems as well as to introduce concerns of his own, he is wise to give Teacher the opening time to allow for the possibility that whatever Teacher brings up may be very time-consuming. Once Supervisor has noted favorable stopping points at the strategy stage, he should also plan to provide time, at the end of the conference, for developing some kind of transition into the next sequence of supervision. He might, for example, point out to Teacher that certain issues have not been covered, and may take time either toward the end of the conference or during Preobservation the next day, to discuss whether or not such residual issues should be brought over into the next sequence of supervision along with, or instead of, new business that is likely to arise in the new sequence.

Indeed, if unfinished material seems important to cover, either for its own sake or in order to gain closure on problems already opened, Supervisor and Teacher may decide to eliminate observation altogether from the next sequence in order to avoid any influx of new issues. If a conference has stopped short of developing plans for the next episode of teaching, and if it can be arranged for Preobservation, the next day, to be scheduled some hours before the lesson in question is to be taught; and if, during the intervening time, it can be arranged for Teacher to be free to work through such plans on his own, then tomorrow's Preobservation can be employed as an extension of today's conference. Because of time pressure and problems of assimilation and rehearsal, same-day planning is not generally a good technique, although in emergencies and given the qualifications I have just stipulated, it can sometimes save things very nicely to restructure a cycle in this manner.

As in other sectors of activity, it is generally best to quit when one is ahead. It represents good practice, consequently, for Supervisor to think, in advance, about the moments at which Teacher is likely to experience success, according to his strategy for the conference; to think about such moments as possible termination points; and to remain sensitive to Teacher's feelings, in this regard, during the conference. No degree of prior calculation can substitute for being alert to Teacher's actual experiences, although such calculation can heighten one's awareness of existing feelings. Despite our wishes, Teacher will not necessarily feel the success that our efforts were designed to produce. It follows that Supervisor's method should include deliberate scanning, once the conference is under way, for logical and psychologically favorable stopping points.

SUMMARY

Methods of strategy have been viewed primarily as decisions for supervisors to make, as principles and guidelines for decision making, and as elements (issues, problems, variables) to be kept in mind throughout the conference-planning stage. Perhaps the first of Supervisor's decisions is whether or not to plan an *a priori* strategy for the forthcoming conference. Should he decide affirmatively, Supervisor must then consider whether to present a full analysis, a selected analysis, an open conference, and the like. In each case, Supervisor should formulate technical and process goals which should be stated in cognitive terms, as behavioral outcomes, and in relation to criterion behaviors. In connection to selected analyses or to strategies that offer *specific* options from which Teacher may choose, Supervisor selects teaching patterns on the criteria "saliency," "fewness," and "accessibility for treatment." Saliency of patterns is determined by reference to such factors as frequency, demonstrable effects, theoretical significance, structural importance in the lesson, commonality, and priorities assigned by Teacher. Accessibility is estimated principally in relation to logical complexity and emotional loading which, in turn, are predicted on the basis of Supervisor's past experience with Teacher, his past experiences with teachers, his relevant theoretical knowledge and, sometimes, his professional intuitions.

Self-examination, particularly in reference to Supervisor's motives for selecting specific patterns and specific supervisory processes, is a major element of strategy. "Fewness" is guided by such factors as clarity (in the data), subsumption, sameness or difference among patterns, affective loading, time, energy, and sequence. Additional decisions must often be made in relation to objective balance among strengths and weaknesses and subjective balances likely to arise in Teacher's frame of reference, in conjunction with selected patterns; the use of playback and role-play techniques for clarificationnand rehearsal; alternative strategies to accommodate contingencies arising unpredictably in the conference; temporal balance, that is, distribution of conference time over past, present, and future issues in the teaching and supervision; recording; quantities of documentary data; examination and possible revision of the supervisory contract; and termination points.

VI
Stage 4: Methods of the Conference

THE PLAN FOR THIS CHAPTER

In my current work, involving the professional training of psychological counselors, I was first surprised, then discouraged, and finally amused by the discovery of a phenomenon that really should not have surprised me at all because of how familiarly it exists, on second thought, among classroom teachers and among other clinical practitioners during their training periods. I think of this wonder as "technical primacy" and liken it, in certain respects, to the conditions of cognitive functioning that Piaget has found to exist before the establishment, developmentally, of logical operations. In a sense, technical primacy is to a developing clinician what visual primacy is to a developing child, and it would not surprise me to discover that besides sharing certain superficial behavioral similarities, these conditions are also functionally equivalent, that is, equivalent ontogenetically, as though, somehow, professional development followed genetic sequences just as early epistemological development appears to.

To illustrate what I mean, I must explain that in their early training, counselors are conventionally taught rationales and methods for beginning treatment relationships and, more specifically, for conducting initial interviews. Some of our counseling students are concentrating on individual interviews, and others are examining techniques for group counseling. Largely because of peculiarities in our referral system, much of our attention has been aimed at managing initial interviews with clients about whom the counselor knows absolutely nothing before they first appear in the counseling center. Role-playing is a technique that I employ extensively in technical training of this kind.

As anyone might guess, the counseling students are exposed to various models of initial interviews and learn certain general procedural conventions: the client is greeted; various kinds of "structuring" are begun; confidentiality is explained; use of the tape recorder is discussed; Counselor's remarks are designed to stimulate the client's spontaneous behavior, for diagnostic purposes; a schedule of future meetings may be arranged; and the like. Depending on their theoretical orientations, the counselors employ various methods for "building rapport, establishing trust, developing 'relationship,' " or, heaven help us, for "provoking a utilizable transference," and, in varying degrees, offer certain kinds of questions, interpretations, and reflections of the client's feelings.

My discovery actually began as a spooky sensation I experienced while observing role-play after role-play, a growing awareness of *déjà vu*—a most disconcerting sensation—a dream-like illusion that despite changing characters, the play was almost always the same. On closer examination, it became manifestly apparent that although they maintained some sensitivity and responsiveness to their individual clients, by and large our counselors were performing the same technical litany, irrespective of idiosyncratic differences among them. Now, while it is perfectly true that no client is likely to see his counselor dealing with other clients and that clichés are likely to seem clever and fresh when one first meets them, nevertheless I have become progressively convinced that what I observed, besides being simple recapitulations of technique, actually reflected a stereotyped learning, a rote application of procedures whose appropriateness or necessity was no longer questioned nor any longer adjusted to fit clients' varying individual requirements. In some cases it seemed that Counselor's automaton-like behavior positively interfered with intelligent and sensitive responses that might have been eminently more useful, and positively obscured individual differences which, in some cases, could have proven critical to recognize and to treat. Ironically, some of the counselors who most resembled wind-up toys in these role-plays—"My name is Chatty Cathy. What's your name? Won't you be seated?"—were the most fluent in enunciating Rogerian concepts having to do with understanding the client's frame of reference, the world of objects and feelings as it exists in his experience.

It is not very difficult to understand the phenomenon of technical primacy, that is, the ascendancy of stereotyped technical behavior over intelligent, responsive, and creative functioning, even among trainees who have demonstrated creative intelligence in other contexts of their work. The sense in which I tentatively suspect that this phenomenon occupies a "genetic" position in professional development is that training typically begins by teaching specialized conventions of behavior (before, during, and after the students' exposure to relevant theory). Premiums are attached to technical mastery; evidence of such mastery is rewarded; the students rejoice in the experience of technical expertise; and almost everything around them reinforces the proficiencies in question. What must occur next in this sequence is that having learned to hold on to the prized technique despite his atavistic impulses, the student must learn, subsequently, how to let go of it. Having learned to be something special, he must relax his death grip sufficiently to become, once again, something natural. Whereas his natural history has been an obstacle to overcome, he must find it again in order to mobilize its resources. This resurrection of one's nature, unfortunately, represents a developmental triumph before which too many counselors stop short. Clinical humor provides abundant testimony:

COUNSELOR: So you feel like jumping from that window—

or,

COUNSELOR: You want to find the men's room. You're *anxious* to find the men's room. Hmm.

or,

COUNSELOR: (to himself): I wonder what he meant by that?

My initial surprise was centered in a semiconscious awareness that although the counselors' behavior exhibited superficial correctness, somehow it just didn't feel right. My discouragement accompanied the realization that these excellent students and their gifted supervisors could be such short-sighted simpletons. My amusement began with a subsequent recognition that such an entire, well-outfitted army just couldn't be so badly out of step and led me to this vision of developmental sequence.

This illustration is relevant in at least two respects. For one, analogously, it expresses my misgivings about the manner in which models of supervision are being developed in this text. On the one hand, it seems desirable to avoid being overly specific in descriptions of supervisory method, lest students of clinical supervision become overly scrupulous in their attempts to apply them in practice. On the other hand, some specificity is required, if only to make these supervisory techniques concrete and realistic enough to carry some meaning for the real world. My second difficulty, which is more immediately germane, pertains to the relationship between Strategy and Conference. I see "strategic primacy" as something to be avoided. Supervisors are not unlike teachers and counselors in their notorious avidity for carrying out the plan, the method, the technique, no matter what. This is not only an abstract problem relating to general relationships that should exist between plans and actions in clinical supervision. On the contrary, it is a real and ubiquitous problem that exists in every instance when supervision conferences have been designed in advance.

It is important to recognize that no conferences are precisely the same, just as no two strategies are ever likely to be identical, and that, consequently, anything we might say methodologically is meant to be suggestive but not formula. One sometimes develops the impression that against almost any method one might recommend, another worker could levy criticisms, and that it does not require a captious temperament to raise questions about almost any supervisory ploy. What works with Teacher today may not work at all tomorrow, or, perhaps, with any other Teacher ever. The situation resembles one of my colleague's recent descriptions of clinical supervision to a group of neophyte counselors. He said, essentially, that what tends to make life so complicated in counseling practicums is that the counselor can almost always find some technical defense for his actions, while his supervisor can almost always find some basis on which to criticize them. Nonetheless, we do find it appropriate to speak and to write about clinical methods even though we recognize the discipline's ambiguity and the tolerances for ambiguity that its practitioners must have. No less can be said for classroom teaching or for supervision of instruction.

An explanation of this section's design and of some of the considerations that led to this design may help pave the way for the reader. I have tried to find an adequate solution to the following problems:

1. Because teachers, supervisors, situations, and conferences tend to be so diverse, it requires a great deal of expository writing to cover a representative sample of methods. Whereas a simple, random inventory of techniques might accomplish broad representation, it would simultaneously fail to create a realistic picture of live supervision; and inventory lacks fabric.

2. If the conference were conceptualized in terms of its sequential parts, that is, its beginning, its middle, and its end, then, dividing this section accordingly, we could examine many samples of beginnings, and so on, and, in this fashion, work in a wide variety of supervisory methods. Once again, however, such a section would fail to provide examples of real, live supervision conferences from start to finish.

3. If we were to analyze the typescript (either real or invented) of a complete supervision conference, after a great deal of effort we should only have one representation of supervision; and no

such single representation can begin to demonstrate the
methodological versatility demanded in actual practice.

4. Examining this possibility further, if we were to analyze a
real case, we would, perforce, not be examining an ideal
representation of supervisory method. I know of no such (ideal)
case. I prefer to avoid dealing lengthily with *problems* of
supervision until the next chapter, because it is difficult enough
just to set out uncomplicated samples of method. On the other
side, it would be pointless to try to invent a make-believe ideal
case because there is no such thing.

I have tried to find some compromise among the objectives and
obstacles and have made the decision to develop three parallel cases,
each of which is partly real (that is, based on actual cases) and partly
fictitious and each of which represents a composite of teachers and
supervisors and supervision intended to represent each of three levels
of supervision. The levels to which I refer are first, supervision of a
teacher who is basically autonomous, professionally sophisticated, experienced in the ways of clinical supervision, and highly motivated to
make use of supervisory consultation; second, supervision of a more
average teacher, who is potentially like Teacher #1 but who has not
had much supervisory experience and who tends to be relatively dependent in his professional relationships; and third, supervision of a teacher who is frightened, technically weak, and highly defensive in relation
not only to supervision but to his professional role and professional
relationships generally.

With only three conferences represented, this text will not even
begin to provide an exhaustive compendium of supervisory methods.
We will still resemble the blind men with the elephant, but in this
instance we will have had three chances to feel the beast instead of
only one. Another sense in which these "complete" cases are not
complete at all is that they each represent single occurrences of supervision rather than long-range supervisory relationships or even relatively shorter cycles of supervision. To provide analyzed long-term cases
would not be economically feasible in this writing.

In order to make these conferences seem as realistic as possible, in
each case I have included (1) Supervisor's observation notes on the
teaching to be examined and (2) Supervisor's working notes for
analysis and strategy, with annotations describing some of Supervisor's
unrecorded thoughts about the teaching and about managing the conference. I have additionally included relevant background material in
each case. Although these examples are all intended to exemplify good
supervision, that is, good analyses, good strategies, and good conferences, it is perfectly possible that other conceptualizations of the observed teaching and other supervisory strategies might also have been
good. The existence of plural alternatives in clinical supervision may be

experienced either joyfully or frustratingly, depending upon one's ability to tolerate conditions of free choice.

CASE 1: A FIRST-GRADE LESSON IN NUMBER

Background Information

THE TEACHER: Marilyn Plummer

EXPERIENCE: Three years of teaching; one year as teaching team leader.

HISTORY OF SUPERVISION: Regular clinical supervision since employment began; some training during her third year of teaching in techniques of supervision for use in team leadership roles.

PRESENT SUPERVISION: Ann Davis supervises and functions as a consultant to one intermediate and two primary teaching teams in Cool Meadow School, where Mrs. Plummer is employed. Cool Meadow participates in the preservice training of students from several regional schools of education, and both Mrs. Davis and Mrs. Plummer are involved in the preparation of student teachers. During the present year, Mrs. Davis has provided several cycles of supervision, each of which was initiated at Mrs. Plummer's request. In recent months, she has regularly supervised Mrs. Plummer's supervision of student teachers, sometimes joining Mrs. Plummer in collaborative supervision and sometimes analyzing tapes of supervision conferences that Mrs. Plummer has recorded.
  On this occasion, Mrs. Plummer's request for supervision stemmed from her desire to have Mrs. Davis observe the lesson in which she was employing some instructional materials for the first time. Mrs. Plummer had prepared herself to begin working with "Structural Arithmetic Blocks" by reading *Children Discover Arithmetic*,[1] by Catherine Stern (who originated the materials), *Productive Thinking*,[2] by Max Wertheimer (partly from whose formulations on learning, Stern developed a mathematics curriculum), and by participating in a short workshop on *Cuisinaire Rods* which are, in certain respects, similar to the Structural Arithmetic materials. In her own college and graduate education, Mrs. Plummer received training in "modern

---

[1]Catherine Stern, *Children Discover Arithmetic* (New York: Harper, 1949).
  [2]Max Wertheimer, *Productive Thinking* (New York: Harper, 1959).

mathematics,'' and at one time both she and Mrs. Davis were classmates in a seminar on teaching the new math.

During Preobservation, Mrs. Plummer requested that Mrs. Davis watch particularly (1) what the children were doing with their materials and (2) the degree to which Teacher succeeded in helping the children to move from physical manipulations of the blocks to conceptualizations of what they had done. She showed Mrs. Davis the following lesson plan:

GENERAL AIMS: To teach the children that the blocks can be thought of as numbers (whole and fractional quantities); and to prepare the way for learning what can be done with the blocks can also be done with numbers and that operations on numbers can be demonstrated concretely by manipulation of the blocks.

Content Goals

1. The blocks represent numbers.
2. Operations on the blocks can express operations on numbers.
3. Physical principles controlling the structural arrangements of such blocks correspond to mathematical principles regulating the behavior of numbers. [In other words, mathematical laws can be extrapolated from physical structures; mathematical properties can be found in physical structures; mathematical descriptions can be applied to physical structures; physical structures must obey mathematical laws; and so on.]

Behaviors

1. The children will call the blocks numbers.
2. The children will begin to move from physical terms to mathematical ones as they pose problems, describe events, and the like.
3. The children will begin to name principles (laws) that they discover through play and discussion.

Process Goals

1. Creativity.
2. Cooperative work [play].
3. Self-initiated learning; spontaneity.
4. Logical reasoning; verbalization of inferences.

Behaviors

1. Children will make things with their blocks.

2. Children will build and talk about their activity.

3. Children will raise questions about what they have done and about what they see; they will discover puzzling aspects of their structures.

4. Children will begin to name possibilities and impossibilities; cause-effect relationships; physical and mathematical properties of what they see; will begin to say *why* certain things are true and other things untrue about numbers [or the blocks].

Procedures

The lesson will begin with a period of free play; I will observe and note what is happening and get prepared to deal with what the children have done. After pupils have had time to make things, we will talk about their products. If they do not call the blocks numbers by themselves, I will lead them to do so. Whatever problems we discuss will arise from the children's work.

Evaluation and Transition

Lesson should not take more than 40 minutes. Sometime near the end, we will summarize what the children have learned [reported] and decide what kinds of things we might try to do with the blocks next time.

Observation Notes

A FIRST-GRADE LESSON IN NUMBER: On each of 3 work tables, the teacher has placed a set of Stern's "Structural Arithmetic Blocks" with which the children have been invited to play. [These are wooden blocks that may, for example, represent the numbers 1 through 10, such that the 1-block is a one-inch cube, the 2-block is a two-inch rectangle grooved at the one-inch mark, the 3-block is a three-inch rectangle grooved at one-inch units, and the like, where each block is painted a different color (that is, all 1-blocks are green, all 2-blocks are purple, all 3-blocks are white, and so on).] The teacher walked around the classroom for about 15 minutes while the children arranged their blocks into various horizontal patterns and vertical structures.

1. TEACHER: Boys and girls—let's stop for a few minutes so that we can talk about the things you've built.
2. TOM: I made a design.
3. BILLY: Me and Jerry built a bridge. [Jerry accidentally kicks a leg of the table causing the structure to sway.] Hey. Watch it . . .
4. JERRY: Oops.
[Both boys giggle.]

5. JUDY: We got steps.

6. ARLENE: A staircase.

7. TEACHER: Well, since you all seem to have had fun doing things with these blocks, supposing we take turns, going around the room, and somebody from each group can tell us about what they did. Mark? What did you and Paul do?

8. MARK: Well, we made a staircase like Judy did.

9. TEACHER: Can you tell us how you did that?

10. MARK: Well, we took the smallest piece and then put the next one next to it. And then we put in the rest of them and we got a staircase.

11. TEACHER: Class—look at the staircase that Mark built with Paul. Does it look like a staircase?

[Affirmative nods.]

12. TEACHER: What makes it look that way?

13. RODNEY: Cause they each go up the same.

14. SHIRLEY: It's even—like steps. You could climb up it.

15. TEACHER: Yes—it looks that way, doesn't it? Supposing I change it this way? [She exchanges the 4 and 6-blocks.] Does it still make a good staircase?

16. CLASS: No.

17. PAUL: It's a bumpy one.

18. JUDY: It looks like buildings.

19. SHIRLEY: It's not even.

20. TEACHER: What does that mean—it's not even?

21. SHIRLEY: Uh—they don't go up the same amount.

22. TEACHER: Uh huh.

23. PAUL: You couldn't climb over it—it's too high.

24. TEACHER: Yes, I see what you mean. Children—do these blocks remind you of anything? Are they like anything?

25. ARLENE: They're like steps.

26. TEACHER: Yes, they do look that way when you put them together a certain way. Supposing we wanted to name these blocks? What might we call each block?

[No response.]

27. TEACHER: Well, supposing I wanted someone to bring me a particular block from across the room? How could I tell him which block I wanted?

28. JON: By the color?

29. MARK: Yeah.

30. TEACHER: Yes, indeed. I could say, Jon—would you bring me a block? . . . Let's make believe that someone painted all the blocks the same color. How could I ask for a block then?

31. BILLY: Well, you could ask for the smallest block or the biggest block.

32. MARK: Or the middle-sized block.
33. TEACHER: Is there one right in the middle?
34. MARK: Umm—I think so.
35. TEACHER: Well, you look at your blocks, and tell me when
you're sure. . . . Now, Billy's suggestion is a good one—but what if
you didn't have every kind of block on your table? If I asked for
the smallest block then you might pick the smallest one you
had—but that might not be the same as the smallest block
someone else had at another table.
36. LOIS: You could say the blue block.
37. TEACHER: Ah—But remember, we're making believe that
they're all the same color now.
38. LOIS: Oh, yeah, I forgot.
39. TOM: Couldn't we say them like numbers?
40. TEACHER: Tell us what you mean, Tom.
41. TOM: Well, we could call the littlest block 1.
42. MARK: And then the next one would be 2.
43. PAUL: The biggest one would be . . . . 9.
44. RODNEY: No it wouldn't—it's a 10.
45. PAUL: Oh, yeah.
46. TEACHER: Are you saying, then, that these blocks remind you
of numbers?
[Affirmative nods, yesses, and the like.]
47. BILLY: Not all the numbers—there's no hundred.
[Class giggles.]
48. LOIS: There's no 12—that's how old my sister Carol is, 12.
49. TEACHER: I guess you're right. The biggest number I can find
is 10.
50. MARK: Couldn't you make a 12 with a 10 and then two more?
51. TEACHER: Two more what?
52. MARK: Two more of the green ones—see? Ten—11, 12.
53. TEACHER: Class—do you understand what Mark is saying?
54. BILLY: It wouldn't have to be two green ones—it could be one
purple one.
55. TEACHER: What could be?
56. BILLY: Uh—I forget—uh—oh, yeah—12.
57. TEACHER: Well, that's certainly very interesting. You've told
me that these blocks remind you of numbers, that the smallest
block is like the number 1, the biggest block is like the number 10,
that you can make numbers bigger than 10 by putting together
different blocks, and that some blocks are the same as other blocks
when you put them together—like the purple 2-block is the same
as two green 1-blocks. You've certainly found out a lot of things
about these.
58. MARK: You can make a 20 with two of the black ones—the
10-blocks. Look how big it is.

59. TEACHER: Yes. Can you make a number even bigger than that?

60. LOIS: Yeah—you could put all the blocks like this [begins to arrange them end-to-end] and it would be a giant number. [Class laughs.]

61. TEACHER: You certainly could, but that would be a hard number to name, wouldn't it?

62. PAUL: Uh uh—you'd just count up.

63. TEACHER: All the blocks? Well, you could do it, I suppose, but, uh—why don't you try it and see what happens?

64. MARK: There is no middle block—there's like a space in the middle.

65. TEACHER: Oh, yes. Mark has found that there is no middle-sized block if we take them all.

66. MARK: But if you leave off the 10-block, then the brown one's the middle block?

67. PAUL: Yes, the 5-block.

68. BILLY: Look what I did—I made it all even.

69. TEACHER: Class—look what Billy did—he made a square. How did you do that, Billy?

70. BILLY: Uh—I put the small—the littlest block on the biggest one, uh, no—wait, uh—I put the little block on the next-to-the-biggest one . . .

71. MARK: That's 9.

72. BILLY: Yeah—on the 9—and then I put the next one and the next one.

73. TEACHER: Yes, I see. The 9 with the 1, the 8 with the 2, the 7 with the 3. . .

74. BILLY: And in the middle it changes.

75. TEACHER: Changes?

76. SHIRLEY: It goes like upside down.

77. TEACHER: Ah, yes.

78. BILLY: Yeah.

79. TEACHER: What about the tower that you and Jerry made?

80. JERRY: It's a bridge.

81. TEACHER: I'm sorry—a bridge. It looks like it was hard to build.

82. JERRY: Yeah—because it kept falling down on one side, and then we put something on the other side, but then it would fall down there.

83. TEACHER: How did you make it work?

84. JERRY: Uh—we had to put the same on.

85. TEACHER: How do you mean?

86. RODNEY: Like—there's a green one here and a green one there and a white one here, on this side—and another white one on the other side—it's the same.

87. TEACHER: They balance?
88. MARK: Yeah.

Analysis

NOTE: Selection of blocks and invitation to play seem motivationally effective. The materials are attractive, and the children handle them eagerly.

T1: "We can talk . . ." and "you've built" puts the focus on the ps' experiences [rather than upon Teacher's ideas].

T7: T accepts "fun" as appropriate; "all" may be overgeneralized; does not make use of ps' [five pupils'] substantive remarks; provides organizational structure; selects p not having remarked spontaneously.

T9: "How" provokes extended response.

T11: T focuses class's attention, still on a pupil's product; tries to establish consensus on Mark's perception; creates opportunity for reinforcement from other p's.

T12: T presses for reason; avoids accepting glib response.

T15: T exemplifies sophisticated intellectual behavior; in effect, provides model of altering one variable while holding others constant in order to examine the consequences [in this case, perceptual differences].

T20: T questions for clarification; picks up p's signal as point of departure for inquiry.

T24: T presses for "number." As it turns out, prematurely.

T26: T accepts [an already accepted] response; tries new question for number.

T27: T tries yet another question; strong sense of first person.

T30: T accepts [a presumably disappointing, but nevertheless valid] response. Once again, alters an independent variable. It works: in P31-P32, T gets "size." Evidences alertness to perceptual mistakes: very good pickup on "middle block" [of which there is none in a complete series through 10].

P39: Success!

T40: T lets p own the concept; asks for *his* amplification.
(Lots of p-p interaction; p's actually responding to one another.)

P48-T49: T's rewards discriminate quality responses; rather than dealing with irrelevancies of p's remark, T uses only pertinent material in it; avoids a digression.

T51: Good avoidance of ambiguity.

P52-P56: Holds back, lets p's develop it.

T57: T summarizes. Why not have the p's summarize at this point?

T59: T loosens hold; takes Mark's lead and develops it.

T61: What is the purpose of this remark? Why teach p's conceptions of what is hard? (Maybe T wants to prepare them for grouping; raise this question with her.)

P64-T65: P has apparently been working on an old question, although participating in subsequent inquiries. T picks it up; implicitly keeps promise to accept Mark's solution.

T69: Takes another lead from p's; focuses class. Another "how" q.

T73: Mathematizes p's explanation.

T79: T shifts focus. Why?

T87: T provides vocabulary to name phenomenon already defined.

General Impressions

INTERACTION: Mostly p-p; some T-C [Teacher-to-class; public communication], some T-p.

QUESTIONS: "How? What did you do? What does that mean?" and the like, generally provoke well-developed responses; questions ask for reasoning, explanation, amplification; description and perceptual information. Q's generally seem to stimulate inquiry.

REWARDS: Provided by other p's as well as by T; sometimes in the form of consensus; mainly consist of T's *use* of p's expressed ideas, discoveries, impressions, questions, and the like. T generally accepting; manages simultaneously to take the p's leads but to differentiate useful responses from trivial ones by what she picks up. P's initiate much of the inquiry, but T maintains general relevancy of the discussion. [Probable incidental learnings: "In this place my ideas count for something; I am valued."]

INTELLECTUAL BEHAVIOR: T's own questions and style of structuring problems represent useful intellectual models, particularly her technique of altering antecedent conditions.

FOCUS: Lesson centered mainly on problems arising from ps' work; some 1st-person teaching (summary); generally loose; good pickup; patiently able to accept valid responses even when they do not satisfy T's specific desire (for example, "number").

Teacher's Questions

[Supervisor at first attempted to sketch pupils' block structures, but they altered them so rapidly that she soon gave up the job. During

the discussion period, so much was said so quickly that Supervisor
had no opportunity to record impressions of the children's block-
work, except in the form of their own verbalizations about it.

"How successful was T in moving the p's from nonverbal, concrete
experience to verbalized conceptualizations about what they had
done?"

ATTEMPTS	OUTCOMES
T9	P10 Still mainly visual; too ambiguous.
T12	P13–P14 Yes (evenness).
T20	P21 Yes (uniform increments).
T24	No.
T26	No.
T30	P31–P32 Yes (size).
T33–T35	Yes (middleness) but delayed (P64).
	P39 NUMBER.
T46	Yes, retroactively.
T57	*She* did it (conceptualized), but most
	of it seems to come from the p's.
T63	No (?).
T69	P70 Yes (complementary #'s).
T75–T77	Weak.
T83–T85	P86 Yes (balance).

Strategy: Open Conference

Supervisor is prepared for a full analysis, for discussion of selected
patterns, for discussion of Teacher's original questions or of questions
raised spontaneously during the conference. Past experience has proven
that Mrs. Plummer uses supervisory time aggressively and appropriately and generally does best when she moves in her own direction.
Although she thinks it might be worthwhile to examine a few minor
technical points, Supervisor does not feel that any urgent problems
existed in the teaching.

The Conference

1. SUPERVISOR: Hello, Marilyn. Come in.
2. TEACHER: Hi, Ann. How was the meeting?
3. SUPERVISOR: Oh, you know. Pretty much the same stuff with
a new cover, although he did have some programed materials in
French that we might look over.
4. TEACHER: I'm sorry you couldn't stay for the end.
—the kids came up with the idea of writing number
stories—number pictures, actually—to describe things they make
with the blocks. Rodney drew an equation on the board. He
showed how you could build a bridge without using blocks: [writes
on board] 4+1+1=3   3. He didn't know about plus and equals

signs, but he made his point that numbers can balance just the way blocks do. What a fantastic kid.

5. SUPERVISOR: I should say.

6. TEACHER: This is an excellent group.

7. SUPERVISOR: Yea. Why do you suppose?

8. TEACHER: Huh?

9. SUPERVISOR: I—do you think it's coincidence that you seem to wind up with so many good groups?

10. TEACHER: I never thought about it.

11. SUPERVISOR: So think about it. I mean, you could imagine a hundred groups where if you gave them these blocks they'd be dropping them and throwing them all over the place and raising hell generally.

12. TEACHER: These are good kids.

13. SUPERVISOR: Good kids. Sure they're good kids. What makes them so good? I mean, you've got some pretty smart cookies in there, but it's hardly a collection of geniuses. I mean, their IQ's are pretty normal. Let's face it, they've got a good teacher.

14. TEACHER: Truer words were never spoken.

15. SUPERVISOR: And a modest one, to boot. You know, I'm not kidding. I mean—a lesson like that just couldn't happen all of a sudden; I mean, it just couldn't be a freak, you know? One of the things that keeps getting to me about your teaching is how much, uh, spirit they have. I mean, it's like they don't have to fuss around. They have a better time doing the work than they would goofing off.

16. TEACHER: I try to make it fun for them.

17. SUPERVISOR: I think it's more than that. I think it's the way you use their ideas; the way you respect their ideas and follow through on their questions.—I mean—I don't know—pretty much they seem to be so rewarded by doing the work that it's unnecessary for them to misbehave or to attract attention to themselves. They get plenty of attention as it is. They certainly don't seem bored.

18. TEACHER: Sometimes I feel tight.

19. SUPERVISOR: Yeah, I wondered if maybe that happened today when you summed up for them. I mean, until then, they had really done most of the work, but at that point you sort of took over.

20. TEACHER: Yeah. Frankly, I was so excited that they'd gotten so much out of this that I just didn't want it to get away, you know? I just wanted to grab it and show them how much they'd learned. Maybe it would have been better if I had them sum up.

21. SUPERVISOR: There'll be other chances. Sometimes summarizing is a very useful technique.

22. TEACHER: Yeah. I'll try for it tomorrow. [Makes note.] You

know, another thing, not that I'm anything less than magnificent, mind you, but another thing is the blocks themselves, you know? I mean who could resist them? They feel good to handle; they're pretty colors; they're big enough so that what you build with them is pretty stable; and they just sort of scream "number." I think at this level they're better than the Cuisinaire Rods. They're easier to work with and you can get just as much thinking started.

23. SUPERVISOR: Yeah, I agree. Still, the blocks didn't sprout on those tables. I mean, it was you who brought them in for the kids. [Pause.] Well, I haven't anything special, unless you want to go over the whole thing. Uh, I did try to watch for whether you succeeded in getting them to conceptualize, and I have some notes on it. I wasn't able to get down too much on what they did with the blocks.

24. TEACHER: Yeah. I realized that would be impossible after things got started. At this point I'm still spinning. Did you write this one up?

25. SUPERVISOR: What else?

26. TEACHER: How about letting me have the notes? I'll look them over tonight, and we can talk about it tomorrow.
[Supervisor gives Teacher all of her notes on observation, analysis, and strategy.]

27. TEACHER: Did you notice Lois at all?

28. SUPERVISOR: "My sister Carol is 12"?

29. TEACHER: [Laughs.] Yeah. I'm optimistic about her, though. She seems to be coming around.

30. SUPERVISOR: I agree. Her answers aren't always the best, but she's entering into things more and more.

31. TEACHER: Yeah. I think she's beginning to feel that she has a place in there. The other kids seem to feel better about her, too. Even today, when she said all of the blocks would make a gigantic number, the kids laughed, but it didn't seem like they were laughing at her. At least she didn't take it that way.

32. SUPERVISOR: I had the same feeling. The kids seemed to be amused by the idea of such a long string of blocks. Is her work improving?

33. TEACHER: It's hard to tell. Sometimes she hands in pretty good stuff. I'm just happy that she seems to be coming out of herself more than she used to. She seems more secure.

34. SUPERVISOR: Yeah. Well . . .

35. TEACHER: Let's talk about where to go from here.

36. SUPERVISOR: With the blocks?

37. TEACHER: With the blocks and in their number work generally. I mean, I can see a lot of things growing out of this

experience with the blocks, but I think we should be ready to put them away and to take them out every so often; especially if they've given the kids some place to go where the kids can use other materials or develop their own materials.

38. SUPERVISOR: You mean like with Rodney today?

39. TEACHER: Yeah.

40. SUPERVISOR: Sounds good. What do you have in mind?

41. TEACHER: Well, uh, nothing in particular. Uh, I guess that's why I want to talk about it now. I haven't really given it much thought because I didn't know how things would work out today. One thing I've got pretty strong feelings about already is that if the kids really begin to take off in math, I'm not going to worry about following the sequence that's in the book. I mean, just so the basic topics are covered by the time they're done, I'd rather give the kids free rein to go where they want to. I'd guess that, especially now that they have the blocks, they'll probably cover most of the stuff in the book anyhow.

42. SUPERVISOR: Sounds OK to me. You know, one of the things that fascinated me today was how much *math* they got out of that experience.

43. TEACHER: Yes, hmm, *that's* something that would be helpful; if we could take the time to find out what mathematical ideas they began to touch, today, you know, so that I could have a more exact idea of what leads exist.

44. SUPERVISOR: All right; let's try it. I didn't analyze the lesson for that, but we could look at what I got down. [Supervisor spreads out observation notes; she and Teacher peruse them.] Well, they've got the idea of unit, hmm, wait a minute.

45. TEACHER: Yeah. There's the idea that to build a staircase, the blocks have to go in a certain order, and that only one order will do if the stairs are to be even.

46. SUPERVISOR: OK, so there's something about ordinal relationships, certainly, and when they look at the blocks vertically, the idea of cardinal numbers.

47. TEACHER: And of unit differences.

48. SUPERVISOR: Yeah, the whole idea of regularity; changes of the same amount.

49. TEACHER: They've got "equality" and "identity."

50. SUPERVISOR: Right. Rodney showed that with his balance thing; and "greater than" and "less than." [Pause.]

51. SUPERVISOR: It's hard to decide whether the mathematical ideas that occur to me are really ones that the kids caught or are just what *I* could find with the blocks.

52. TEACHER: I know what you mean, but I think it's OK for now just to begin naming some of them. It won't be the same for all of them anyway. [Pause.]

53. SUPERVISOR: They got "smallest" and "largest," that is, pieces that define limits.

54. TEACHER: And "middle."

55. SUPERVISOR: Yeah, and "odd" and "even," I think, can be developed more along with what they found out about when there is a middle block and when there isn't.

56. TEACHER: Right. [Makes note.] They also did addition.

57. SUPERVISOR: And subtraction—when Rodney had to reduce the weight on one side so it would balance.

58. TEACHER: Right, and "balance" and "weight" as being things that are related to numbers, yeah.

59. SUPERVISOR: And that the units are different from the blocks; that when you add things up, you're really counting the units.

60. TEACHER: Oh, and what Billy did—what do you call that— "reciprocal numbers"? When he put together each pair of blocks, in order, that added to 10?

61. SUPERVISOR: It was interesting that he discovered the symmetry in that, remember, when he said something like, "It goes upside down in the middle"? Gee, there's a lot of stuff to be found in that. Like "A plus B equals B plus A"—and I imagine pretty soon they'll begin to build squares, uh, addition squares in which they use more than two addends for each sum.

62. TEACHER: And squares for other numbers than ten.

63. SUPERVISOR: [Laughs]

64. TEACHER: What's the matter?

65. SUPERVISOR: I was just thinking, you know, that if I had asked yesterday, "What do you plan to teach them in math tomorrow?" and you'd answered, "Well, I think I'll teach them identity, equality, greater-than, less-than, commutativity, maybe associativity, cardinal numbers, ordinal numbers, complementary numbers, the addition facts for ten, some subtraction, weight and balance, sets—like odd and even sets with middles—and so on," I would have thought you were balmy. Sounds a wee bit ambitious.

66. TEACHER: But they're *first*-graders. [Laughter.] You know, seriously, there is the question of how much they're really learned such things or whether it's just that such ideas *can* be learned from the blocks and that people like us, who know about them, "see" them there, in what the kids are doing, even though the kids, themselves, don't really know what they know.

67. SUPERVISOR: Yeah, it's a good point, except I think the kids *do* know what they know. It's just that they don't have our names for it. I think maybe two senses in which they might not know as

fully as we'd want them to are, first, that not all of them had exactly the same experiences in there, so that some kids may have learned things that other kids didn't; and second, they may not know in the sense that they can't generalize from the experiences they had today to facts about numbers generally.

68. TEACHER: Right, I think that's the point; that we may "recognize" more in what they learned than really is there to be recognized. We sort of read the mathematical generalizations into what they say.

69. SUPERVISOR: Yeah.

70. TEACHER: What this makes me think is that maybe we should move into a unit now on number theory, something like, "How Numbers Behave."

71. SUPERVISOR: Sounds anthropomorphic.

72. TEACHER: Oh, let's not get into that one again.

73. SUPERVISOR: [Laughs.] OK.

74. TEACHER: [Laughs.] How about, "From Blocks to Numbers"?

75. SUPERVISOR: Wild.

76. TEACHER: Yeah, I like that. So "generalizations" could be what we were deliberately working on, uh, working to discover.

77. SUPERVISOR: Rules about numbers.

78. TEACHER: Yes.

79. SUPERVISOR: I can see certain problems.

80. TEACHER: Umm?

81. SUPERVISOR: Well, for one thing, there's the problem of what to do with the blocks. I mean, there are two things about that. One is that when the kids started out today, as far as they were concerned, the blocks were something to play with. And they did. And even though you talked with them later about what they had done, it was still pretty much play, you know, "Tell us about what you built." The other thing is that we don't know, really, whether the kids are ready at this point—either in terms of their mental abilities or in terms of whether they need more training with the blocks—to operate mostly at an abstract, verbal level. [Prolonged silence.]

82. TEACHER: Yeah, yes. And another thing, I should find some way to protect against seeing things that aren't there, you know? And to sort of find ways to involve individual kids in this kind of work who may be less able than others to deal with abstract ideas.

83. SUPERVISOR: Sure. I'm thinking of such extremes as Lois and Rodney, for example.

84. TEACHER: Umm.

[Long pause.]

85. TEACHER: Well, now that that's done, let's plan some social studies.

[Laughter.]

[Pause.]

86. TEACHER: One problem I can see with the blocks is that if the kids don't have them in front of them, they may just lose interest in what we're doing; maybe because it *is* too abstract. So they should have the blocks there to use as concrete examples.

87. SUPERVISOR: Or, at least, you should have a set of them up front where *you* can use them for demonstration.

88. TEACHER: Yeah. At the same time, though, if the kids *do* have the blocks in front of them—especially since I've already taught them that these blocks are to play with—they may get to be distracting as hell. I mean, the fact that they're hard to resist can work both ways.

89. SUPERVISOR: Yeah.

90. TEACHER: I guess the thing to do, as you've said, is to keep one set up front—maybe on an overhead projector—where I can use them to show things, or where kids can come up to demonstrate with them. Another possibility, I guess, would be to establish some rules for when to handle the blocks, although that might take too much of the fun out of it.

91. SUPERVISOR: How about something like, "Kids, you know we've been playing with these blocks, which is a lot of fun, and we've talked some about them, but you know, besides playing with things like blocks and bricks and sand, you can also use them to build things. And when you decide to build something with such materials, you begin to handle them in certain ways . . ."

92. TEACHER: It doesn't turn me on.

93. SUPERVISOR: Me neither.

[Silence.]

94. TEACHER: How about, "Kids, let's try something a bit different. You remember yesterday we started out playing with these blocks and then, after a while, we stopped to talk about what you had done with them. Well, let's make believe that we took movies of what was going on in here yesterday. And for now, let's make believe that we're going to show those movies but this time in slow motion." The kids know what slow motion is because last week they saw a film about porpoises that showed them jumping in slow motion, and when it was over we talked about what slow motion photography is. So I could remind them of that and then explain, somehow, that just as slow motion photography made it possible for us to slow the animals down enough so that we could really understand what they were doing, our purpose presently is to slow things down for exactly the same reason, only so that we can "see" thinking rather than jumping. I'd have to polish this up; probably get the kids to make the analogy after I reminded them about last week's film.

95. SUPERVISOR: I think that's a winner.

96. TEACHER: Yeah, and then we—

97. SUPERVISOR: Excuse me. I just want to say that the reason I think that's a winner is that, first of all, the analogy you're using is something that you know they already have had shared experience with, and, most important, I think that if you *do* get the kids to express a rationale for slowing down their own "movie," then whatever rules they develop for using the blocks will be *their* rules, and under those circumstances I think they'd more likely be committed to them than if they were *your* rules, or anybody else's.

98. TEACHER: Good, good. [Teacher has been busily noting things while Supervisor talked.] Uh, I'm listening. I just wanted to get some of this down. And then, depending on how far it seems necessary to pursue it, we could set some rules about slowing down, like, for example, instead of building things and breaking them up very quickly, we could build things one at a time and let them stand long enough to say everything we might want to say about them, before going on to other things.

99. SUPERVISOR: Yes. Yeah. While we're at it, it's also true that with a movie you can rerun sections of film after you've discussed ideas about it. That is, well, in your class, the ideas might come first, sometimes, and then the kids could turn to the blocks as a means of testing out the ideas.

100. TEACHER: Or illustrating them.

101. SUPERVISOR: Or illustrating them, exactly.

102. TEACHER: OK. So what we wind up with, then, is that I have a set of blocks up front and each group of pupils has a set and that, uh, and we have rules to tell us when to actually use the blocks.

103. SUPERVISOR: Yes. Incidentally, I'd be careful, in developing this analogy, not to liken the children to porpoises, or to any other animals, for that matter.

104. TEACHER: Yes, I'm with you. Another thought that occurs to me is that Mr. Carlson has just introduced them to the microscope, in science, and we might talk about examining our ideas about numbers microscopically.

105. SUPERVISOR: Another thing—if you feel that you don't want to spoil the fun, you know, by taking the play out of this too fast, you could arrange, periodically, to have free-play periods with the blocks, and these could serve two purposes, really. They could give the kids the fun of playing again, and they could produce new ideas to examine afterwards in slow motion.

106. TEACHER: Yes, good. [Makes note.] Yeah. I'm feeling much better about this now. [Pause.] There could also be a lot of individual work in this and also times for sharing.

107. SUPERVISOR: Umhm.

108. TEACHER: In fact, now that I think about it, what might come out of this would be interest groups, uh, so that some kids could concentrate, together on, maybe, addition combinations, and other kids could be exploring equivalent numbers.

109. SUPERVISOR: Sure, or different kinds of symmetry, different ways to balance. One thing you might want to try later on is to ask the kids to try to imagine that the block they've been calling 3, let's say, is really a 1, you know? Or maybe it would be better to start with an even block, the 4 or the 2—or even the 10.

110. TEACHER: To get into fractions.

111. SUPERVISOR: Yes.

112. TEACHER: Umm. [Makes note.]

112a. SUPERVISOR: See, one of the reasons I think you might be able to pull that off is that you've already given them experience in imagining such things.

113. TEACHER: I'm not with you.

114. SUPERVISOR: Well, for example, today when you asked them to make believe that all the blocks were the same color or that the assortment of blocks that the various groups had on their tables were different, so that you couldn't ask them to bring you a block by calling it "biggest" or "smallest."

115. TEACHER: I get it, yes. You mean making believe that something exists to discover what effects that would have, uh—

116. SUPERVISOR: Yeah. They've already had some experience with you in that kind of thinking.

117. TEACHER: Uh huh.

[Silence.]

118.TEACHER: In the back of my mind, I'm still bothered by the problem of keeping track of what content they've covered and learned, you know? I keep seeing the topics in the book, uh, and I'm not sure how I feel about that.

119. SUPERVISOR: "Bible blues," huh?

120. TEACHER: No, it's not that so much. But, you know, when they get tested in June, and then Miss McGrady has to know where to start them in September. Another thing, too, is that I'm not sure of whether these ideas really ought to be taught in some particular order.

121. SUPERVISOR: Spell it out.

122. TEACHER: I mean, you know, like if some things should be learned before other things, then things may get fouled up if the kids just go anywhere they please in this.

123. SUPERVISOR: You've read Piaget?

124. TEACHER: *The Child's Conception of Number*, yeah, I've started it. But it doesn't go far enough, I don't think.

125. SUPERVISOR: That's right, it doesn't cover all of the possibilities you'll be working with. But, you know, I don't think there's any real answer to your problem. I mean, I don't think we know enough yet about mental development or about whether there really are sequences that should be followed in learning math, uh, to come up with any foolproof plan. And even if we did, I'm not so sure you'd want to lock yourself up in any sequence beforehand. I mean, in this case, ignorance may be a blessing. [Laughter.] I do think that one of the things you've got working for you is that if the kids make discoveries on their own, you know, if they find certain ideas and then try to develop them on their own, it's a pretty sure bet that they will be doing things they can do, you know? I mean, by definition. I can do what I can do and I can't do what I can't do, and if the kids are actually doing it, that is, doing something, then at least we can conclude that that's not impossible for them because we can see that they're doing it.

126. TEACHER: So that, instead of worrying too much about some special sequence, if they do take the lead, at least they will be tackling problems they can understand.

127. SUPERVISOR: I'd say it's just about guaranteed. And if they do get into hot water, I mean, if things just get too tough, you can always spot that and try to move them back into more workable problems. I do think that in this kind of teaching you really have to keep careful track of who's doing what.

128. TEACHER: Yeah, that's another rough one. How'd you like to be a secretary?

129. SUPERVISOR: I was just going to suggest it.

130. TEACHER: You wouldn't mind? Really?

131. SUPERVISOR: I'd be delighted. At least for a few days, I can try to keep individual records of what each kid is working on and of what answers he's been able to come up with, and what questions, and then the two of us can keep getting together to pool our information.

132. TEACHER: And, among other things, that would help to keep track of topics.

133. SUPERVISOR: Right.

134. TEACHER: OK. If you're willing. I think what I'd better do now is look over your notes and see exactly what's what so I can know what to stress tomorrow, if anything.

135. SUPERVISOR: Yeah. I think there's already plenty of stuff to start with.

136. TEACHER: [Assembles belongings; prepares to leave.] By the way, poor Mildred is climbing the walls. [Mildred is a student-teacher newly assigned to Mrs. Plummer's room.] She's

very anxious. We got into a long one yesterday about, well, her point was that "my kind of teaching" might be all right with gifted kids but that it couldn't work everywhere, which is true, God knows. But the way she was saying it, uh, her picture of my kind of teaching is that the Teacher takes a very passive role. That is, that the teacher just sort of sits back and lets the kids run things. She also has the feeling—she's picked up the expression "nondirective"—she also feels that in nondirective teaching, the teacher doesn't have to do any lesson planning. You *have* to plan lessons where you teach, you know, where the teacher runs everything; but in my kind of teaching, as she puts it, there's no need to prepare.

137. SUPERVISOR: So what's the matter with that?

138. TEACHER: What?

139. SUPERVISOR: I'm just teasing.

140. TEACHER: Oh. Gee, you scared me for a minute. [Laughs.]

141. SUPERVISOR: I would have guessed that passive, nondirective teachers who never have to worry about planning aren't the sort to get scared.

142. TEACHER: Yeah. Amen!

142a. SUPERVISOR: You think there's hope for her?

143. TEACHER: As a matter of fact, the reason she came to mind just now was—I was thinking to myself how nice it would have been if we had tape-recorded this session and the next few, so that we could play the tapes for her, you know, show her "passivity" up close.

144. SUPERVISOR: Sounds like a great idea. Dirty, but great. [Laughter.] Want to try it tomorrow?

145. TEACHER: I'm game.

CRITIQUE OF CASE 1

Before turning directly to the conference, we may note some salient features of Supervisor's analysis and strategy. Our first impression is that while Supervisor's analysis was guided partly by Teacher's requests, namely, for Supervisor to watch for evidence that pupils were moving from simple tactile-visual experiences with their blocks to mathematical conceptualizations of them (it proved physically impossible for Supervisor to satisfy Teacher's other request to record what the children built), she was additionally guided by her own significant impressions of the lesson. In certain respects, Supervisor's analysis had greater breadth than it would have required simply to serve Teacher's expressed wishes; it did what Teacher asked, and then some.

A second impression is that Supervisor stayed close to the data in developing her analysis. Her hypotheses and interpretations, in other words, were generally related to specific elements of the teaching performance. It is also true, for the most part, that Supervisor's analysis consisted of empirical statements describing what Teacher *did*, rather than inferential statements purporting to describe the *effects* of Teacher's behavior. In this example, Supervisor's perspective on the lesson is basically in three parts. She has noted patterns of teaching whose importance (significance, saliency) may eventually be established (1) in reference to Teacher's stipulated requests, (2) in reference to the organization and structure of Teacher's *intellectual* behavior, and (3) in relation to the pupils' (inferred) psychological frames of reference, for example, those patterns noted under the heading "Rewards."

It is interesting that, in contrast to what our basic model of clinical supervision suggests, Supervisor's analysis, in this case, includes numerous value judgments of the teaching, stated in varying degrees of explicitness. What makes this practice seem exceptional is that Supervisor saw fit to pass her written analysis on to Teacher so that, in effect, her value judgments were expressed directly in the supervision. In more orthodox practice, while Supervisor might record "pluses" and "minuses" in his analysis in order to decide which data to select during strategy, his own process goals for supervision would generally lead him to abstain from offering such judgments directly (for example, to avoid reinforcing Teacher's dependency upon him for evaluation). In this case, if Supervisor's technique can be acquitted, it would be because (1) as the conference reflects, Teacher does operate professionally (and as a supervisee) with considerable autonomy; (2) one might guess, after witnessing both members' behavior in this relationship, that in instances where Supervisor's underlying reasoning for value judgments is unexplicit, she would freely exposit such thinking at Teacher's request (although it would be neater if Supervisor's judgments had been expressed verbally, so that appropriate explanations could have been offered on the spot); and (3) one might reasonably suppose, from the history of this relationship, that Supervisor's and Teacher's professional values are generally congruent and that, being so closely identified, either member's assessment of a teaching performance would probably be comprehensible and basically acceptable to the other.

My intention is not to excuse what may have been an inappropriate supervisory ploy, but is rather to explain what reasons might justify such a technique, both hypothetically and on the basis of our available evidence. It is too bad that the data do not extend further into this cycle of supervision, so that our questions might lead to more certain conclusions. In any event, in the absence of contradictory evidence, we may suppose that between these two no consequential loss was suffered because of Supervisor's behavior. This seems, incidentally, like an appropriate place to suggest that the reader perform exhaustive analyses of these case materials on his own, perhaps to arrive at substantially different interpretations from mine. I should value such an outcome even more than prompt acceptance of the author's critique, and I would count it fortunate if, although sacrificing agreement, your own analysis of these data provided pleasurable exercise and generated sufficient evidence to contradict my formulations.

One additionally noteworthy quality of Supervisor's analysis—and here, I confess, I may be overextending the "art" in this process—is how empathic it seems to Teacher's intent. One senses a powerful community of spirit (and of interest) between Teacher and Observer. Supervisor's note (in the analysis) of excerpt P39 seems to reflect her own joy in Teacher's success at this juncture. Her ability to rejoice in vicarious successes contributes all the more to our own pleasure when we are able to observe, concomitantly, Supervisor's readiness to assume a questioning (critical) stance, for example, in relation to Teacher's control of the summary. To observe both these data reassures us that Supervisor is neither enchanted nor antagonistically biased, that she seems capable of blending personal investment with professional objectivity in her relationship to Teacher's work. The conference provides further evidence that both members are receptive and open to one another's minds and, most significantly, that while Supervisor clearly approves, she does not seem fixed in any necessity to make Teacher into her own image, to relate to Teacher merely as an extension of her own values and tastes.

Supervisor's decision to conduct an open conference seems appropriate, again in the absence of opposing evidence. That Teacher would make productive use of an open conference seemed predictable in light of her having initiated this sequence of supervision on her own; her having freely elected to engage in an instructional "experiment" (thereby having made herself willingly vulnerable); and her already demonstrated level of motivation to engage in such teaching and supervision, namely, as evidenced by the elaborate lesson plans she prepared in advance. In this instance, inasmuch as Teacher did express certain prior requests which Supervisor accepted (as "contract"), Supervisor's commitment compelled her to be prepared, as she was, to address the material included under her heading "Attempts [and] Outcomes." Instead of using "open conference" as a reason for not troubling to prepare anything in particular, Supervisor chose to prepare herself for almost anything, that is, for any predictable course that Teacher might elect to follow. Although this "belt-and-suspenders" approach is relatively costly of time, it may nevertheless spell the difference between a full open conference and an empty one. It is incidentally true that this supervisor was so adept at performing analyses of this kind, that her actual expenditure in preparing the entire analysis was less than forty minutes.

Turning to the conference, if it had begun at T94, this supervision might have incorporated efficiency as well as having been basically productive. As it happened, however, these confreres needed time to get started, to build up a momentum of energy and ideas in order to create the strategies in which their conference culminated. In T4 and then again in T27, Teacher's expressed feelings and attitudes toward her pupils seem consistent with the quality of her behavior in the classroom: they have explicit individual identities which she accepts and respects.

From S7 through S17, Supervisor employs three common methods of clinical supervision, namely, to expand the frame of reference in which a supervisee considers specific questions (in this case her students' quality); to press for differentiation of global perceptions (impressions, value judgments); and to examine strengths—supervisors traditionally focus on faults—for the purpose of stabilizing and consolidating them. In S13, Supervisor attempted to shift Teacher's focus away from the ostensible excellence of her pupils and toward the technical quality of her own teaching behavior. This gambit is more frequently employed to counteract more defensive externalization (as exhibited, for example, in the third sample of teaching below). In this case, however, Supervisor's intention was to confront Teacher with successes that could not be entirely attributed to the children's precocity. In S15 and, particularly, in S17, Supervisor began to identify specific elements of the teaching that contributed to its strength and, rather than stating dogmatically that the teaching was good, began to describe the variables in relation to which she judged its quality. In several respects, this example is imperfect. For one thing, Supervisor did not trouble to cite data which illustrated the specific strengths she was defining; her descriptions went undocumented. For another, her concluding remarks were largely gratuitous: speculative, perhaps fanciful. Her argument might have been more potent if instead of petering into homilies about boredom and attention-getting, Supervisor had developed examples of "using" and "following through on the pupils' ideas" more extensively. In any event, Supervisor did well to proceed from Teacher's statement (T16), "I try to make it fun for them," to more serious considerations: "I think it's more than that. . . ."

S19 illustrates the skill that we call "pick-up." Having tucked away an idea concerning Teacher's control of the summary, Supervisor seized the opportunity created by her reference to "tightness" to raise this question. I should not want to go too far in this style of Monday morning quarterbacking; but whether or not my guesses about Supervisor's behavior are accurate, this excerpt does serve to make the point. The point is that, as a rule, it is presumably more effective to offer one's prior concepts at moments when the supervisee has provided a relevant context for them than at arbitrarily selected moments, for example, to break a silence or in the form of an inventory of impressions about the lesson. Analogously, if Therapist has decided that Patient ought to be confronted with his anger toward his mother (Patient having protested, repeatedly, how much he adores her), the timing of the confrontation would be more opportune at a moment in which Patient was experiencing such feelings and was displaying appropriate affect than it would, for example, at the beginning of a treatment session: "It has occurred to me that you feel considerable anger toward your mother" is much easier to reject than, "You're feeling very angry toward her right now." In our present example, one might reasonably suppose that Supervisor's confrontation had greater authenticity than it might otherwise have had because of the direction Teacher's thinking had already taken. Had Supervisor's guess been mistaken, the tentativeness of her remark ("I wondered if maybe . . .") would have probably created less pressure on Teacher to accept it than a more assertive statement, for example, "You really tightened up at the point where you summarized." The technical principle involved here suggests, simply, that when a supervisor sees fit to introduce an undocumented (or undocumentable) psychological hypothesis at all, its statement should be in appropriately tentative language.

The technique exhibited by Supervisor in S21 illustrates one of clinical supervision's most distinguishing features, namely, the practice of drawing teachers' attention to elements of their teaching that can be conceptualized as "technique" in order for them to become consciously integrable into an explicit repertoire of technical behaviors. Consider an additional example of this practice: while listening to a tape of a counseling session, Counselor's Supervisor commented, after one section, that although the client's remarks included expressions of strong feeling, Counselor's questions were generally aimed at eliciting additional information about the situations, circumstances, people, and relationships to which the client had referred. Supervisor made the point that Counselor had generally responded to the substantive content of Client's remarks rather than to the feelings Client was experiencing. Counselor's first reaction was to signify his understanding of the implicit criticism in Supervisor's confrontation, namely, that on this occasion, he *should* have recognized Client's feelings and should have attempted to help the client to clarify them. Supervisor went on, however, to reflect that rather than being inherently incorrect, the technique Counselor had employed could be used deliberately if his *intention* was to deintensify Client's feelings, perhaps for the purpose of making them more susceptible to examination. He reasoned, in other words, that at times when feeling is so heightened that it consumes virtually all of a client's available psychological energy, the client may be unable to do anything more than to experience the feeling itself, that deintensification of that feeling may be necessary in order for Client to command enough surplus energy to examine his feelings with some degree of objectivity, and that one available technique for achieving this outcome was the very technique that Counselor had unthinkingly employed in this instance.

Counselor subsequently stated two learnings incited by this critique, the first pertaining to his management of the case in question, the second expressing his recognition of a technique which he had not formerly conceptualized. In a parallel fashion, Supervisor [Excerpt S21] intended a double learning and, particularly, wanted Teacher to recognize that there is nothing intrinsically wrong with summarizing, that for a teacher to summarize may have positive advantages, and that even with such advantages it may exact certain costs for the children. In general terms, these examples have been meant to express that with or without associated value judgments, clinical supervisors often examine teaching for the principal purpose of making its technical components more articulate, more deliberately employable, and more enduring in teachers' instructional behavior than they might otherwise be.

Once again in S23 (as in S15 and S17), Supervisor attempted to provide rewards for Teacher, to confront her with her own responsibility for the lesson's apparent success: "Still, the blocks didn't sprout on those tables. . . . It was you who brought them in. . . ." One of clinical supervision's premises is that, among other things, supervision should represent a source of adult rewards for teachers who, except in the context of such supervision, would not have regular opportunities for receiving them. In the second half of S23, Supervisor turned from Teacher's comments about the blocks to issues she (Supervisor) considered to be more relevant, namely, the requests Teacher had initiated during Preobservation, by which Supervisor's analysis had been influenced.

It is difficult to understand Teacher's motives for asking Supervisor whether she had written up an analysis and, then, whether she would let her have it to examine for some future discussion. Her reference to "spinning" suggests that she might simply have not wanted to risk diminishing her present exultation by engaging in detailed analysis; or, more understandably, Teacher may have been communicating a desire to prepare herself for analysis by studying the lesson's transcript first. In any event, what captures our interest is Supervisor's decision to transfer the entire caboodle to Teacher, an apparently split-second decision about which I have already commented above. One senses that its momentary effect was to produce a feeling of closure: Teacher introduces the topic, "Lois," which is not a major item of business; Supervisor stays with it, occasionally offering consensus; finally, *Teacher* overcomes whatever has been diverting her and initiates the question of future planning. Supervisor questions to clarify the new "contract," accepts it shortly, and the two eventually shift into a new task. We may note, incidentally, that in S32, Supervisor expressed certain inferences about the pupils' feelings as though they were perceptions, a tendency not generally approved in clinical supervision. Although her inferences may have been entirely correct, they were, nonetheless, inferences (by contrast, for example, to her statement in S30, ". . . she's entering into things more and more," which sounds more like a statement of directly observable behavior).

By T35, Teacher seems to have found sufficient energy to attempt some purposeful work. In S40, we encounter a lovely example of artful abstinence—maybe. In truth, Supervisor's query, "What do you have in mind?" may have been prompted by nothing more ingenious than an absence of ideas. There is no way for us to establish that fact. With hindsightful wisdom, however, and with the advantage of knowing what followed in this conference, it is possible to argue that it was an appropriate and fortunate gambit for Supervisor to have returned the question, rather than to have proposed solutions. Teacher's initial statement (T37) suggests that she was experiencing a confusion of half-formed ideas about how to proceed with her instruction, and that she was searching for some structure, for some way to sharpen and to organize her ideas into a shapely plan. S38 provided an element of clarity. We surmise that S40 ("Sounds good") provided a quick shot of encouragement, and that the principal virtue of Supervisor's abstinence was to provide time (and encouragement) enough for Teacher to begin to find her priorities, to sort her ideas, and to prepare for decisions—in short, to begin intellectual work that might culminate in her own successful solutions. At certain moments, in T41, it almost seems as if Teacher were talking as much to herself as to Supervisor.

S42 offers encouragement, once again, and signals a beginning of active participation by Supervisor, but a most gentle beginning indeed. "You know, one of the things that fascinated me today . . ." offered casually, as a random thought, simultaneously introduces a possible point of departure for purposeful work (which is, in fact, exactly what it provided) and equal chances to go unaddressed as might befit a casual thought. As it turned out, *Teacher* initiated a plan of action inspired at least partly by Supervisor's comment. Had Supervisor, instead of saying what she said, declared, in S42, "Well, I think we'd better go back over the lesson and find out exactly what the kids did learn about math today," then although Teacher might readily have accepted her suggestion and although their "findings" might have turned out the same, nevertheless the whole process—the motive, the thought, the initiative, the decision to act, and the outcomes of action—would have been Supervisor's product rather than Teacher's.

I should have no difficulty in agreeing that if, in this instance, Supervisor had produced the whole business instead of Teacher, the outcome would probably have been inconsequential. What makes this issue important to note, however, is that if Supervisor's behavior in this sequence were typical, then the cumulative effects of such behavior might produce a dramatically different relationship, and substantially different conditions of professional existence for Teacher—over the long run—than if, by contrast, more didactic and directive intervention characterized Supervisor's behavior. The probability that any element of an individual's behavior is more likely to be typical than atypical provides the major justification for making this point, rather than any assumption that Supervisor's conscious intention was to behave as she did for the reasons we have considered. In connection with that possibility, however, I should assert that if supervisors can become artful, as a result of systematic training and examined experience, then their clever and useful intuitions should take the form illustrated by Supervisor's behavior in this example. It is not beyond imagining, in other words, that Supervisor's abstinence and subtlety in this instance is not casual in any sense, but reflects manifest, technical sophistication. As a personal matter, despite the strain upon one's belief that such a possibility creates, I should be even more incredulous toward the suggestion that such demonstrations of technical adroitness, especially when they occur repeatedly, are merely fortuitous.

In S44, Supervisor sets a new contract according to Teacher's suggestion. The episode from T43 to T62 provides an illustration of the quality of *collaborative* analysis for which clinical supervision aims. In S44 we find an example of a supervisor's readiness to participate in unforeseen tasks—to accommodate the teacher by fulfilling reasonable requests even though the work involved had not been anticipated beforehand. It should be emphasized that while supervisors should be flexible in this fashion, there will be occasions on which it would be inefficient, if not foolish, for Supervisor to begin something for which he is unprepared or, his degree of preparation notwithstanding, to permit himself to be drawn into problems that seem diversionary. In the present case, all circumstances favored Supervisor's decision: there was no reason to suspect that Teacher's request stemmed from any particular urgency to avoid other issues; even if it had, it seemed likely that to satisfy her request would result in producing information useful for future planning) there was no other pressing business to be transacted; and despite Supervisor's unpreparedness, there was little to be lost for either member, save time, by performing the task in question. At least Teacher's question was not aimed at superficial or irrelevant matters. One might guess that Teacher's preferred reason, ". . . so that I could have a more exact idea of what leads exist," (T43) assuaged any doubts that Supervisor might have felt. "Finding leads" is one way to name a major objective of analysis in clinical supervision.

In S44-S50, and then from S53-T62, both members contribute on an equal footing, that is, neither one seems particularly dependent upon the other for providing impetus or for producing ideas. In such an arrangement, it is entirely appropriate for Supervisor to "give," without fearing that undesirable incidental learnings will result. To maintain a "nondirective" stance or to hold out for inductive teaching under such circumstances would surely throw suspicion on Supervisor's understanding of these processes.

In S51 we find a technique that could be described in very ornate and esoteric language to no better effect than if we call it "playing dumb." Let's approach this gambit by imagining some things that Supervisor did *not* do at this juncture. She did *not* accuse Teacher of projecting her own fantasies onto the children's behavior. She did *not*, in fact, refer to Teacher's behavior at all. Neither did she ask a direct question nor issue any direction. She did *not* assert any truths. What *did* she do? Among other things, she confessed a problem, but not one of such majesty nor with such intense personal effect to make it impossible for Teacher to continue in the directions of her own inquiry if she chose. Supervisor set a problem and—this is particularly significant—she owned it, that is, she framed it in the first person, with explicit references to "I" and "me." Interestingly, although Teacher's immediate response was to treat Supervisor's idea perfunctorily, shortly thereafter (T66), when she had more nearly exhausted her own inquiries on "mathematical learnings," she returned directly to Supervisor's question, this time as though it were her own, almost as if Supervisor's idea had required a period of incubation before it could hatch, fully developed, in Teacher's frame of reference. Without having created any serious interruption of Teacher's thinking, Supervisor's statement stimulated a new line of inquiry which came to fruition in the next episode of the conference.

Several advantages seem associated with playing dumb, that is, with the technique by which Supervisor frames a problem as if it were essentially his own (whether or not it is truly his own). As with other such gambits, this technique stands to lose its potency if it is used promiscuously. "Promiscuity" brings to mind the question of whether this technique should be avoided because of what may seem, to some, to be its dishonesty. Let us consider its purported advantages first and then deal with the moral question. One benefit is that, as it often appears, the statement of a problem or, more directly, engagement in a problem is not as likely to be resisted when that problem is freely chosen than when, intrusively, it is assigned or attributed by some other person. The subtlety in this formulation is that, on the one hand, we may suppose, engagement in one's own problems is more likely to materialize than engagement in someone else's, just on general principles.

On the other hand, however, it happens from time to time in supervision, that Supervisor properly feels compelled to define a problem, to introduce a problem of his own invention into the supervisory dialogue. His difficulty becomes to manage, somehow, for that problem to be experienced as Teacher's own in order to provoke the investments of interest and energy required for its development and solution. It behooves the Supervisor, consequently, to do whatever he can to avoid provoking resistance as, for example, one is likely to do by seeming to impose issues of one's own, and to avoid instilling a social incentive to please Supervisor by accepting his problem. Playing dumb, in this connection, may have the double advantage of sowing a problem in the least intrusive manner and of eliciting interest by capitalizing on the other member's empathy, that is, by banking on the likelihood that the other member will rally to one's assistance in response to one's confessed problem and, through empathy and by identification, finally adopt that problem as his own. Stated in other terms, playing dumb—I can't think of how to express this more candidly—represents a device for capitalizing on existing affections in order to elicit involved participation in some supervisory issue.

I suspect that their tendency to justify means by ends would enable many clinical workers to employ such a technique without concern for its moral ramifications or, even more likely, without explicit awareness that moral implications exist. Clinical psychiatry, as well as teaching, has established classical precedents, for example, to shoot patients full of electricity or insulin or to confine them to locked wards, entirely against their wills but ostensibly because such treatment will result in cure and, presumably, because the motive to cure people is humane and consequently justifies radical treatment procedures. Cure by coercion is a time-honored clinical tradition.

More relevantly, in educational practice, each time a teacher pretends ignorance in order to stimulate the pupils' inquiry, or deliberately commits an error in order to enable the pupils to "catch" him, or employs a so-called "trick question," he was utilized a ploy which, like playing dumb, involves falsification, constitutes a lie, and may, consequently, be opened to moral scrutiny. Nonetheless, such techniques are practiced commonly. Playing dumb seems all the more problematical because, as I have suggested, it deliberately manipulates existing positive feelings which are drawn upon when this technique is employed. One might argue that if this gambit becomes transparent, for example, because of overuse, the incidental learnings it creates could seriously undermine the supervisory relationship and be damaging in their own right. I am afraid, however, that although we might find pragmatic grounds for accepting or rejecting the technique, to do so would simply evade the moral question.

I am unable to resolve it. To testify that innumerable methods involving the same kind of dishonesty are practiced all of the time in teaching and counseling and supervision, or to assert that the technique is desirable because it generally works, does not, in either case, provide solutions to this problem. To say that I use the technique in my own work is irrelevant. I do so, but not without hesitation and not without wondering whether I should. On some occasions, both to soothe my conscience and for other, didactic reasons, I have identified this strategy retroactively and shown supervisees my reasons for employing it and reasons why they might wish to do so in their own teaching; but even these amends do not close the issue. While I feel incompetent as an arbiter, in this connection, I am at least partly satisfied by taking the opportunity to expose this problem as I see it. It may be that in the absence of a clear categorical imperative, each man must decide for himself individually, according to whatever principles guide him. I think, at least, that awareness of such issues in supervision is necessary for its development as an ethical practice.

S65, as "summary," brings the members' inventory to a close. As a flattery, it seems to have awakened some need in Teacher to take another, somewhat more sober look at what occurred, possibly in order to certify her apparent success, possibly as an expression of embarrassment which is associated with compliments for many people. In any case, T66 recapitulates Supervisor's question of S51. In S67, again, we find an example of differentiation, that is, of a clinical supervisor's attempt to differentiate a relatively simple, polarized conceptualization, namely, *either* the pupils do know, in which case the members are not projecting, *or* the pupils do not know, in which case the members are projecting, by defining more complex possibilities. Those possibilities, in this case, are that the members' projections notwithstanding, the pupils may indeed "know" on an intuitive level, but not at an abstract-verbal level. Supervisor introduced the notion that while intuitive learning may have taken place, the pupils may nevertheless be incapable, at the moment, of translating their discoveries into logical (mathematical) generalizations. She also added the implicit warning that not all of the children were likely to have had identical learnings, to avoid halo effects. Besides applying developmental information to the problem at hand to make its statement more appropriately complex (that is, more sufficiently complex to represent the relevant realities), Supervisor did not totally reject Teacher's initial interpretation.

What is significant in this technique is that rather than building complexity by a simple substitution of her own ideas for Teacher's, Supervisor built upon Teacher's already existing framework by adding concepts to it. One advantage of this approach is that Supervisor's responsive use of Teacher's ideas is more likely to feel rewarding than their dismissal and replacement by Supervisor's own; Teacher's constructs become enhanced rather than replaced. Rather than to have been discarded, Teacher's idea ". . . the kids, themselves, *don't* really *know . . ."* (T66) has been amplified (T68, as a result of Supervisor's intervention by T68,: ". . . we may "recognize" more in what *they learned* than is really there. . . ."

One of the great advantages, for clinical supervisors, in working with teachers as intelligent and informed as Mrs. Plummer, is that, by and large, their own efforts are aimed toward enabling such teachers to arrange their ideas, to clarify and order them, instead of having to teach them ideas to compensate for deficiencies in their professional knowledge. The former activity is less likely to feel abrasive than the latter, particularly to teachers who think of themselves more as "teacher" than as "learner" and for whom it consequently creates less dissonance to be approached as knowledgeable individuals. It is generally least difficult, in other words, to supervise teachers who have the knowledge and intelligence and personal freedom to function autonomously, providing that Supervisor possesses such qualities of his own.

T70 represents a transitional point that, too frequently, is not achieved in supervision conferences, namely, a point at which the focus of supervision shifts from past to future, from analysis to planning. In this example, another ideal outcome is that Teacher initiates the transition, which reflects not only Teacher's success but success of the supervision in which a teacher initiates direction as well. I call these outcomes successful in relation to the values assigned in process education and in clinical supervision to self-initiated behavior (learning, inquiry, structuring, setting direction, etc.) and to functional autonomy generally. It should be noted, additionally, that the shift to planning, in this conference, occurred naturally and as a logical outcome of the preceding dialogue. I have observed many instances in which, although such a transition was accomplished, it came about artificially or ritually, for example, "Well, half our time is gone. Let's turn to planning," or even, "Let's plan." I suspect that when such transitions do occur naturally, the members are less likely to feel controlled by an external protocol and more likely to feel engaged in rational activities than if it were otherwise. Another way to say this is that we value technique that helps to implement natural movement more than technique used to constrain it. We aim for clinical supervisors to be fully in control of their technical knowledge rather than to be under control by it.

In S71, Supervisor introduces an (apparently) old issue; one which the members had studied previously in relation to Teacher's practice. Such references can serve to give supervision a feeling of continuity, to reinforce certain understandings, and to demonstrate Supervisor's commitment to Teacher's work and the importance he attaches to it (it's important enough to remember). In this instance, Supervisor appeared ready either to develop the point further or to leave it alone, as she did in response to Teacher's request. Perhaps the most worthy element of such behavior is not, so much, Supervisor's attempt to apply a relevant and familiar concept as her readiness to resist prosecuting the issue in response to Teacher's signal of rejection. Teacher's own priorities have been allowed to take precedence as, in most situations, they should.

In S75 and S77, Supervisor offered support, agreement. The problems defined by Supervisor in S81 are important and germane to decisions about future lessons. Besides the possibility of having curbed Teacher's enthusiasm by identifying some real difficulties, one might suspect that the prolonged silence following Supervisor's relatively lengthy and didactic intervention represents an example of the problems associated with imposition of a supervisor's own issues, that I have been discussing. Although there is no way to establish what really happened, it would not be inconsistent with this intervention's apparent effects upon dialectical tempo to hypothesize that problems of assimilation and of "ownership" slowed Teacher's behavior, just as one should expect to happen when one member (Teacher) is expected to become engaged in the other member's ideas. This hypothesis becomes particularly compelling when we notice that of Supervisor's two principal statements, the one to which Teacher reacts, after some moments of hesitation, has a much stronger substantive relationship to her own (previously stated) ideas than the one she ignores. Moreover, before arriving at her terminal response (relating to individual differences), which is quite closely related to Supervisor's statement, Teacher's reasoning proceeded through an intermediary response which, although it was not irrelevant to Supervisor's meaning, involved an appreciable distortion, namely, to conform more closely to Teacher's own mental images than it did as it was originally expressed (by Supervisor).

Although I imagine that most readers would agree that these members seem to enjoy a high degree of mutual empathy and rapport, it is nevertheless striking and, in certain respects, reassuring, to witness that, at least in this instance, Teacher's self-consistency emerges as a more potent behavioral determinant than her accommodativeness; her accommodations to Supervisor's thinking are certainly not precipitous. Somehow, my experience suggests that seemingly instantaneous accommodations precipitate replacements of teachers' own thought processes by their supervisors', are not all that they appear to be, and are often neither as significant nor enduring nor substantial as more gradual shifts accompanied by apparent intellectual labor.

In this example, Teacher adjusts her thinking according to Supervisor's statements, and, in time, demonstrates highly accurate understanding of Supervisor's expressed meanings. In T86, we discover more evidence to suggest "cognitive incubation," namely, that after some time has elapsed, Teacher shows that not only did she pick up a kernel of Supervisor's thinking to which she had not previously responded, but, moreover, that she had "processed" the thought sufficiently to have increased its complexity beyond the level at which Supervisor stated it initially. In this example, overtime, Teacher has assimilated Supervisor's idea, reacted, and put her own mark on it, but not, we should guess, as the Pavlovian dog salivates to the bell—not, that is, as a conditioned reflex to a supervisory assertion.

I must explain my reasons for this short but detailed analysis. I have not wanted to develop a model of cognitive behavior or of communications processes per se. Such models properly belong to branches of psychology that lie beyond my competency and beyond our interest. I have rather, by this description, intended to communicate a fairly concrete picture of the condition to which I have frequently referred as "autonomy." My own difficulties in understanding this concept may force me to be unnecessarily insistent on pinning down possible examples, and suspicious that other people have trouble with it too. In any event, this may be one example of one manifestation that professional autonomy can assume. As I see it, Teacher is neither so defensively fixed in her own ideas that, rigidly, she cannot respond openly to other people's; nor is she so uncertain and disdainful of her own ideas that she is at her supervisor's mercy; she does not spin about each time that Supervisor asserts an idea. She seems simultaneously self-confident, self-consistent, and capable of intellectual openness. If this teacher does represent a valid example of such qualities, then, I propose, it should be useful to study her behavior and to see, in at least one form, what professional autonomy looks like. Perhaps it is even more important to examine *Supervisor's* behavior, on the possibility that although Teacher's autonomy can hardly be attributed to Supervisor's actions, as simple cause-effect, nonetheless the supervision itself may be more or less congenial to Teacher's autonomy and such (favorable) supervision ought to be viewed closely. Saying it another way, it is unlikely that Teacher's productive functioning takes place in spite of the conditions of supervision.

In S87, Supervisor suggests a specific technique, in this example, a logistical solution. Although clinical supervision is not, generally, conceptualized as an advice-giving, suggestion-giving practice, neither do clinical supervisors eschew such behavior when the conditions seem right. We do discourage advice-giving as a principal mode of supervision for numerous reasons: advice-giving generally implies hierarchical differences and is more likely to generate dependencies upon authority than autonomous problem solving; when one offers advice (even if it is good advice), one risks that the receiver will not understand, will not care, will not hear, or will not accept the proffered solution.

At the same time, however, we maintain that the acquittal of supervision depends upon its helpfulness, and we acknowledge that to provide suggestions and answers is sometimes the most helpful thing that one can do. For Supervisor to have offered the suggestion in S87 seems entirely appropriate, given Teacher's obvious self-sufficiency, her apparent freedom from aiming to please, and that the suggestion in question is simple, potentially useful, capable of succinct communication, and in no sense crucial to Teacher's future success. Once again, we witness Teacher's delayed acceptance time: it is only after she has expressed an intervening thought that Teacher owns Supervisor's suggestion, and even then, she has placed her own altering mark upon it.

In S91, Supervisor ran a risk and lost. Having ground to a halt in her attempt to create a solution for Teacher's problem (Supervisor's suggestion represented a direct response to Teacher's stated problem), she concurred in Teacher's rejection of her half-finished proposal. While T92 illustrates a flippancy which, although it may have been appropriate in this instance, does not generally represent an acceptable response in clinical supervision (particularly by a supervisor), S97 provides a fine example of the open reasoning of value judgments that we prize highly as a supervisory technique. Two principal advantages are associated with this practice: (1) it protects against the likelihood that Teacher will learn that whether anything is good or bad depends on how the supervisor feels about it, arbitrarily, and (2) it provides an opportunity to broaden Teacher's understanding of values and concepts pertinent to some decision, that is, it tends to lessen the chance that good decisions are made without reasons or for the wrong reasons or by sheer good luck. It is also pleasing to see that in this example, Supervisor's behavior exemplified one principle of teaching that she was enunciating, namely, to establish explicit rationales.

In S99, Supervisor builds upon Teacher's own suggestions, adding details and defining related possibilities. This entire episode of the conference, from T94 to S111, illustrates a virtual frenzy of creativeness; a wonderful example of productive professional collaboration. In S114, Supervisor finds an opportunity to introduce an outcome of her earlier analysis and attempts to insure that Teacher is fully conscious of her own use of a sophisticated intellectual process, namely, that involving the deliberate manipulation of variables in a problem. Once again, Supervisor's timing seems very wise, for instead of presenting her thought, impulsively, at any moment she pleased, she held it until a relevant context and a natural moment for its presentation had developed in the conference. The hypothesis underlying this technique seems strengthened by Teacher's response, which clearly demonstrates her understanding of the issue. I should call this method (of waiting) an expression of powerful technique. It requires practiced technical control to resist the impulses to display one's own virtuosity and cleverness and to express an idea while it is hot, in deference to the principle of relevancy and to a commitment to the assumption that having already been expressed in teaching behavior, a pattern is more likely than not to arise again in the future.

In S125, Supervisor again runs a risk, this time with more apparent success. Teacher's response in T126 suggests that she had followed and understood Supervisor's reasoning and, once again, although we cannot be certain about such relationships, we can at least note that besides its substantive, didactic character, Supervisor's extensive statement seems basically sympathetic and likely to have felt supportive— not a glib reassurance, but a reasoned one.

T128-S129 represents a double triumph for this supervision: Teacher felt free to ask for technical help and Supervisor saw fit to offer it. The clinical supervisor must know when to say yes and when to say no and, assuming Supervisor's frame of reference for the moment, we do not find reasons for saying no in this instance. What Teacher requested was not only reasonable and necessary, but required specific observational competencies that Supervisor possessed. By contrast, her request carried none of the flavor that appeals for classroom assistance sometimes do: "If you're so smart, you do it" or, "If you were sincere, you'd come into the classroom and do some *real* work." As for Supervisor, unlike many practitioners in her field, she expressed no disdain for "mean" tasks; it does not seem to lie beneath her dignity or professional stature to provide (appropriate) "secretarial" assistance.

The impression may be fanciful, but it seems to me that from T136 until the end, Teacher has initiated a topic that tends to "even the score," that is, to reestablish a nonhierarchical, peer relationship between the two members: in the new frame of reference, Teacher is also "supervisor." We don't know whether Supervisor sensed what occurred in these terms, but the dialogue shows that, in fact, she did nothing to inhibit Teacher's effort. Supervisor's own ability to enjoy a peer relationship with Teacher is to her credit. If my impression is valid, and if Supervisor recognized what was happening, and if, with such recognition, she deliberately decided to play Teacher's game, then, beyond simple credit, I should say that Supervisor was very shrewd indeed.

CASE 2: A KINDERGARTEN LESSON IN COUNTING

Background Information

THE TEACHER: Lois Constance

EXPERIENCE: Two years of kindergarten teaching.

HISTORY OF SUPERVISION: No systematic supervision since graduation from a teachers' college. Three widely spaced supervisory sessions during student teaching, intended primarily for evaluation (grading).

PRESENT SUPERVISION: Carl Foster had recently been appointed Elementary School Supervisor for two buildings, including Mrs. Constance's. Early in October (the second month of the school term), Mr. Foster spoke at faculty meetings in each of his school explaining some of his general views on supervision and inviting teachers to call upon him for supervisory consultation. Mrs. Constance approached Mr. Foster several days after his address, explained that she had never really experienced supervision on a regular basis and asked if he would observe some of her teaching and "criticize" it. In their initial conversation, Mrs. Constance confessed feeling "nervous" about being observed, but claimed that she thought it might be valuable to solicit some "disinterested," objective views of her work.

Mr. Foster asked if Mrs. Constance was interested in dealing with any special aspects of her teaching. She replied that what she wanted most was "an overall view" of her work and "suggestions for improvement." Supervisor arranged a time for the first sequence of supervision. During Preobservation, he explained that he would record verbatim notes during the lesson and told Teacher his reasons for doing so. The two agreed that Supervisor would take a broad view of the lesson and that, in this instance, he would select certain patterns of teaching behavior to examine in the conference. Instead of explaining his selection criteria in advance, Supervisor said that he would do so during the conference. Although Teacher showed some signs of tension during Preobservation (she laughed at feeling "stage-fright"), she seemed nevertheless cheerful and still committed to her request for supervision.

During the Preobservation Conference, Teacher gave Supervisor a copy of the worksheet her pupils had employed the day before and volunteered some description of the classroom activities in which they had engaged previously in relation to "number learning." From her discussion, Supervisor collected the following information and impressions which he recorded somewhat more sketchily than they are presented here. Supervisor noted to himself that Teacher seemed more "dressed up" than usual and had carefully applied cosmetics and perfume.

Notes on Prior Lessons

A KINDERGARTEN LESSON IN COUNTING: The children have been taught to draw the numerals 0–9. One method of teaching has been to use mnemonic devices, for example, "2" looks like a swan, "4" looks like a flag, "0" looks like a face, and the like. The children were given practice in integrating the numeral forms into

fanciful drawings of various familiar objects. Next, they
were required to copy numerals placed on the board by the
teacher in rows on their papers, for example,

$$3 \ 3 \ 3 \ 3 \ 3$$
$$4 \ 4 \ 4 \ 4 \ 4$$
$$7 \ 7 \ 7 \ 7 \ 7$$
$$0 \ 0 \ 0 \ 0 \ 0$$

and, finally, they spent some time filling in "dittoed" worksheets
designed as follows:

$$4 \ 4 \ 4 \ \_ \ 4$$
$$8 \ \_ \ 8 \ 8 \ 8$$
$$6 \ 6 \ \_ \ 6 \ 6$$
$$\_ \ 2 \ 2 \ 2 \ 2$$
$$0 \ 0 \ 0 \ 0 \ \_$$
$$1 \ \_ \ 1 \ 1 \ 1$$

Observation Notes

Supervisor arrived at the appointed time, entered through a rear
door and sat in an adult-sized chair that had been provided for
him behind the children, facing Teacher. Teacher made no remark
about his entrance and although some children turned to see him
initially, they seemed to ignore his presence once the lesson was
under way.

1. TEACHER: Now children, today we are going to learn to
count up to ten.

2. TIMMY: [Raises hand for recognition.]

3. TEACHER: Not now, Timmy. All right, children, now you say
the numbers after me. One, two, three.

4. CLASS: One, two, three.

5. TEACHER: Four, five, six.

6. CLASS: Four, five, six.

7. TEACHER: Seven, eight, nine.

8. CLASS: Seven, eight, nine.

9. TEACHER: Ten.

10. CLASS: Ten.

11. TEACHER: That was good, but I didn't hear everybody's
voice. Let's try it again, and this time say the numbers just as loud
as you can. All right, let's begin:
[The entire exercise is repeated.]

12. TIMMY: [Waves hand.]

13. TEACHER: Yes, Timmy?

14. TIMMY: I can count to a hundred.

15. TEACHER: That's very good. Will you lead the class this
time?

All right, boys and girls, now you follow Timmy.

[Timmy leads the exercise again.]

    16. MARCIA: I know a song with numbers.

    17. TEACHER: I wonder if it's the same song I was going to teach you? You listen to my song, Marcia, and then tell me if it's the the same one. Now, children, let's everybody stretch—try to touch the ceiling—and then bring your chairs in a circle around the piano.[The children congregate around the piano.]

    18. TEACHER: Now, children, I will sing the song once for you. See if you know it already. Then we will all sing it together. Ready?

> One, two, buckle my shoe
> Three, four, shut the door
> Five, six, pick up sticks
> Seven, eight, lay them straight
> Nine, ten, a big fat hen.

    19. TEACHER: All right children now return to your seats; it's story time.

Supervisor's Notes on Analysis[3]

I. PUPIL'S PRIOR WORK

    1. Mnemonic devices may encumber pupils with irrelevant, distractive, and [possibly] emotionally threatening associations; the specific mnemonics selected are nonmathematical.

    2. Sequences in which numbers are arranged for board work and on worksheets are unnatural and different from one another, [that is, "3, 4, 7, 0" and "4, 8, 6, 2, 0, 1" are each different, and neither sequence corresponds to the order of natural numbers, namely, "1, 2, 3, 4 . . ."]. *It would be more efficient to employ natural sequences in order to avoid incidental learning (and then, subsequent relearning) of arbitrary sequences.*

    3. Exercises focus exclusively on numerical configuration [that is, by intention] rather than on mathematical properties, for example, quantity or ordination. Visual-motor [drawing] skills are assigned a higher priority than cognitive reasoning.

    4. Assigned tasks aim at rote learning and are the same for all pupils. *Undifferentiated assignments suggest either no prior assessment of pupils' existing capabilities for performing the tasks in question or failure to translate such prior knowledge into individualized instruction.*

---

[3]In their original form, these notes were written in a shorthand code that would be too cryptic for the reader to interpret. For that reason, they have been expanded in this text and set down in conventional language. Supervisor's unrecorded thoughts are represented in italics.

II. THE LESSON

1. (T1)[4] Beginning lacks "transition" either from immediately preceding activity or from the most recently performed work in arithmetic. *Presupposes pupils will learn what Teacher teaches; teaches implicitly, "In this place Teacher decides what is to be done [learned]", presupposes all pupils commonly share ignorance of the knowledge in question (an unlikely condition).* "We" is an obvious affectation.

2. (P2, T3) Teacher's intent takes precedence over pupil's experienced need. *Press for conformity, that is, for all pupils to behave the same; the pupils may learn, incidentally, that it is better to do what Teacher directs than to raise individual questions or to develop original ideas. Timmy, particularly, may learn to avoid spontaneous behavior (if Teacher's behavior, in this instance, reflects a continuous pattern); if Timmy needs physical relief, his learning of whatever Teacher teaches may be sacrificed under organic stress.*

3. (T3-C10) No rationale for choral repetition has been made explicit. *While some pupils may understand a means-end relationship between "learning to count to ten" and this exercise, others may feel that, in the absence of reasons, their job is to do what they are told (no matter how seemingly irrational).*

Teacher decides on method of learning as well as the object [topic] of learning. [The principal point in this thinking is that instead of learning to be self-initiating, spontaneous, self-directing, and the like, to whatever degree Teacher may be central in such learning, the pupils may learn opposite behaviors if the teaching they experience consistently follows the present model; instead of learning rational autonomy, the pupils are more likely to learn passive dependency. Supervisor should discover, empirically, whether such teaching is fairly general in Mrs. Constance's room. In the absence of such data, it is more logical to think of this sample as typical than as atypical.]

Although numbers are now in natural order (*which represents yet a third sequence*), an arbitrary triplet rhythm has been imposed upon them (that is, the pupils are learning a—', —', —', rhythm in addition to reciting number names). The teaching is still nonmathematical, *that is, the children might almost as well be reciting nonsense syllables in relation to learning about "number." Indeed, despite Teacher's expressed intention to Supervisor, the children are* not *being taught to count).*

4. (T11) "That was good...." *Should such remarks constitute a teaching pattern, the pupils might incidentally be taught, first, that*

---

[4]T: Teacher; P: Pupils; C: Class.

evaluation is something that Teacher does (in contrast to self-initiated evaluation) and, second, either that evaluation is essentially subjective or that Teacher's evaluation criteria are secret: in any event, they may learn to depend upon other peoples' unexplicit evaluations.

What about if the children's performance was good? *Reinforcement is global rather than specific and may, consequently, serve to establish unuseful behaviors that were being manifested during the exercise.* "Goodness" seems to be determined by "loudness," or, at least, by Teacher's ability to hear. No logical rationale is provided either for a repetition of the exercise or for saying things loudly [more absence of reasons].

5. (P12-T15) "That's very good." *Another evaluation by Teacher, suggesting that "good; very good" may reflect a pattern of stereotyped rewards.*

"Will you lead the class . . ." *Instead of being acknowledged in its own right, Timmy's offering is superseded by Teacher's lesson plan, that is, his response is used [subverted] as an occasion to advance Teacher's planned lesson. "Very good, you may empty the waste basket" would, similarly, have been an inappropriate reward, one that ignored the inherent substantive or emotional significance of the child's response. A logically predictable incidental learning for Timmy and for the others would be [once again] "What counts most here is what Teacher wants; Teacher's intentions and desires and preferences count for more than pupils'." Although Teacher may have intended to reward Timmy by assigning him leadership, he may, in fact, have felt more of an implicit rejection than an acceptance of his achievement by Teacher's choice of techniques. In any event, such rewards are external and, as such, do not teach the learner to experience satisfaction from the learning itself.*

The exercise is performed a third time, on this occasion with no stated reason whatsoever.

6. (P16-T17) Teacher's response to Marcia is the same as to Timmy: the pupil's spontaneous offering is subordinated to Teacher's plan *(My song is better than your song)*.

7. (T18) Mnemonics, this time a different set. Another arbitrary rhythm, this time duplets rather than triplets.

8. (T19) No transition either into the next activity or into the next sequence of "mathematics." *Rather than seeming predictable and rationally organized, the classroom environment is likely to seem capricious to the children: they neither know what is to come next at any given moment nor understand reasons for doing whatever does come, except, as for Hillary, "because it is there." Sequences of activities are more ritual than logical.*

SUPERVISOR'S INITIAL NOTES FOR STRATEGY

CATEGORIES	PATTERNS
Locus of initiative	All directions come from T. Topic chosen by T. Method of "learning" chosen by T. All rewards and evaluative comments made by T.
Rewards	External. Stereotyped (?). Global, undifferentiated. No (little) intrinsic relationship to P's responses.
Rationales (reasons)	Absent or arbitrary.
Organization of knowledge	Nonmathematical. Arbitrary sequences. Different sequences.
Methods	Rote repetition. Uniform for all P's. Individual differences do not affect the teaching. Superfluous rhythms and mnemonics.
Evaluation	No prior evaluation (?). No explicit evaluation (by T or by P's) of today's learning.
Transitions	None.
Interaction	T-P or T-C (no P-P).

Likely incidental
  learnings:
To depend on T for
  directions and structure.
To depend on T for
  rewards and evaluation.
To learn that T's ideas,
  and so on, are more
  important than P's own.
To suppress individuality
  and to conform [What I
  already know doesn't matter].
To act in the absence of
  persuasive (rational) reasons.
To recite loudly.
Unpredictability.

Supervisor's Reasoning on Strategy

Supervisor recognized, on the one hand, that he could neither be certain about salient patterns in Mrs. Constance's teaching nor about the effects of her teaching upon the pupils on the basis of this single observation and, on the other hand, that Teacher had already shown signs of anxiety about supervision during their two short previous conversations together. He was aware, in other words, of the paucity of data and of the problems that would confront him if Teacher resisted analysis of her lesson. Foster also realized that as Mrs. Constance's first sequence of supervision, the forthcoming conference should be managed most carefully to avoid inappropriate incidental learnings about supervision. In order to follow through on his promise to provide feedback, Supervisor would have to engage in some form of analysis, yet to do so would involve a high degree of speculation (given the absence of demonstrative data). He did not, however, want Teacher to learn that supervisory analysis was essentially conjectural, abstract, and related to actual events only by filaments of Supervisor's imagination. In effect, Supervisor had to balance a weak analysis, a minimum of pertinent information, and what promised to be an anxious conference for Teacher in some manner that would, simultaneously, enable him to keep his promise, to reduce whatever excessive anxiety Teacher experienced, and to teach her the right things and avoid teaching her the wrong things about clinical supervision and the manner in which it would be likely to operate in their relationship. To make things even more difficult, Foster also had to manage his own feelings about the lesson which, in his estimation, was without virtue.

We have seen the evidence of his first implicit decision, namely, to set out the fullest complement of ideas he could assemble on Mrs. Constance's teaching, in order to be conceptually armed. His next decision was to begin the conference slowly, gently enough to provide time in which he might develop some sense of Teacher's immediate anxiety and learn, from her statements, which of his ideas could be assimilated most readily. He decided, additionally, that he would keep his thinking as open as possible, that is, that he would reveal his assumptions, his inferences, his uncertainties, and his reasons for saying whatever he said so that at least, in the absence of convincing documentary material, he might prevent a mystique from developing around his supervisory processes and might avoid excessively arbitrary behavior. Finally, he decided that if Teacher initiated inquiries about her lesson and seemed capable of performing intellectual labor in analysis, he would go in whatever directions she indicated. Should she fail to manifest such behavior, Foster decided that, employing her lesson as a point of departure, he would attempt to shape Teacher's expectations of supervision, inductively if he could, didactically if he must, so that the conference should not be wasted despite its present handicaps. Having collected his wits and all of his available concepts on the teaching, Supervisor committed himself to pilotage as his principal means of navigation.

The Conference

1. SUPERVISOR: Hi. C'mon in.
2. TEACHER: Uh, hi.
3. SUPERVISOR: Have a seat.
4. TEACHER: Thank you. [Pause.] Well, did that set teaching back a thousand years [forced laugh]?
5. SUPERVISOR: Oh, maybe not a thousand. [Laughter.] Are you serious?
6. TEACHER: Well, that's what I want to find out.
7. SUPERVISOR: How effective the lesson was?
8. TEACHER: Not just that. I mean, I know this sounds silly, but—what's confusing to me is how you *know* whether the kids are learning and even what they *should* be learning. Do you know what I mean?
9. SUPERVISOR: Uh, it's hard to know when, uh, if the kids have learned what you were trying to teach them—
10. TEACHER: Yes.
11. SUPERVISOR: And sometimes it's confusing when you think about what you should really be teaching them?
12. TEACHER: Yeah, that's right.
13. SUPERVISOR: That doesn't sound silly to me. These are very difficult questions. [Pause.]
14. TEACHER: It's like I'm never sure.
15. SUPERVISOR: About?
16. TEACHER: About where they are and what should happen next.
17. SUPERVISOR: Umm. Well, I think a good part of the time we just have to make educated guesses, although there are ways to find out what the kids are learning. I mean, you can always test them.
18. TEACHER: But, yeah I know, but that's not really it. I mean—these kids can draw numbers, and they can say the numbers. I don't have to test them. I just know. But, what I wonder about is how *significant* it is for them to do that, you know?
19. SUPERVISOR: How do you mean?

20. TEACHER: I mean, it's not just a question of whether they can say the numbers, but sometimes I'm not sure whether saying numbers is really so important. I wonder, are there other things they could be doing that would be more worthwhile?

21. SUPERVISOR: You worry about wasting their time?

22. TEACHER: Yes. I know it's only kindergarten, but does this sound silly?

23. SUPERVISOR: No. As I say, there's nothing about this that sounds silly at all. In fact, the questions you raise are very sober. These are important and sensitive questions. I admire your candor.

24. TEACHER: Oh, well. [Blushes.]

25. SUPERVISOR: Don't misunderstand me. I'm not trying to butter you up. I'm impressed because of how often it happens that we don't really ask such questions. You know, I think there's often a greater tendency to assume that things are going pretty much the way they should be. You know—the manual's being covered, and all's right with the world.

26. TEACHER: Oh. That manual. I feel so guilty because it doesn't seem right to me; I mean, it seems so babyish sometimes. But I still follow it a lot. It does make things easier.

27. SUPERVISOR: Sure it does. That's what it's intended for. That's what I'm saying: you don't seem satisfied just to take the easy way out.

28. TEACHER: Maybe I'm neurotic.
[Laughter.]

29. SUPERVISOR: Well, look. Supposing we look over what happened today and try to answer at least one of the questions you're asking, that is, what the kids learned from today's lesson.

30. TEACHER: I'm not sure that I want to look.

31. SUPERVISOR: [Laughs.] Now open wide; this won't hurt one bit.

32. TEACHER: [Laughs.] Oh God! You're not going to fill my teeth too, I hope. Yeah, I suppose so. I mean, this is what I asked for.

33. SUPERVISOR: OK. Let's get into it.

34. TEACHER: I don't know why I'm so nervous.

35. SUPERVISOR: Uh, well—that's really why I think it might help to start looking at the lesson. I think maybe that dealing with it won't be so, uh, nerve-wracking as worrying about dealing with it.

36. TEACHER: Yes sir. Uh, may I have a last cigarette?

37. SUPERVISOR: [Laughs.] I'm sorry, sure. Please help yourself. I'll leave the pack here.

38. TEACHER: Oh! You're almost out.

39. SUPERVISOR: Don't worry. I've got a carton in the desk. Help yourself. OK?

40. TEACHER: Thanks. Yeah.

41. SUPERVISOR: All right. Uh, we might take a look later at some of the work the kids were doing before today, you know, on the worksheet you gave me this morning—

42. TEACHER: Yes.

43. SUPERVISOR: But let's start with the lesson.

44. TEACHER: I'd like to do that.

45. SUPERVISOR: And let's start with *your* question, that is, what might we reasonably guess the children learned today?

46. TEACHER: I don't know.

47. SUPERVISOR: All right. Let's try it this way. Sometimes it's easiest to try to imagine yourself in their place and sort of ask, uh, "If I were a child in that class, what might I have learned from that lesson?"

48. TEACHER: Oh, uh, I guess I would have learned to say the numbers. [Pause.] I don't think I get what you're after.

49. SUPERVISOR: OK, I'm sorry. I don't know that I'm *after* anything in particular except to raise the possibility that besides learning about numbers, that is, besides learning the "content," the kids might have learned other things from what you did and from what they did.

50. TEACHER: Umhm.

51. SUPERVISOR: What I mean is, well, let's try it this way. Um, the very first thing you said was, "Now, children today we are going to learn to count up to ten." What might you have learned from those words if you were a kid in there?

52. TEACHER: Uh, [pause] that we were going to do arithmetic? [Pause.] I'm not following you, I guess.

53. SUPERVISOR: No, that's all right. Supposing I ask it this way. Let's imagine that besides learning what you intended them to learn—in this case I guess you wanted them to understand that they were about to have arithmetic—the kids are also likely to learn things incidentally from the way a situation is set up. I mean, do you think such an opening might have taught them anything about their roles in that lesson? Or about yours?

54. TEACHER: [Seemingly confused; thinking hard.] Uh, you mean, uh—like maybe—you mean maybe it sounded phony when I said "we"?

55. SUPERVISOR: Phony?

56. TEACHER: Yeah, like, I mean, they know that I'm not going to learn how to count.

57. SUPERVISOR: All right, maybe. Now, let's hold onto that for a minute and look at the next thing that happens. Timmy raises his hand; you say "not now"; and then you say, "All right, children, now you say the numbers after me. . . ."

58. TEACHER: Umm.

59. SUPERVISOR: How about that?
60. TEACHER: You mean, like "follow the leader"?
61. SUPERVISOR: "Follow the leader"?
62. TEACHER: That what they learn is that I'm the leader, uh, no, that can't be right. I mean, I *am* the leader.
63. SUPERVISOR: Well, don't be so quick to throw your ideas away. Look, uh, I don't know that I really intended it this way, but what may I have been teaching you during the last five minutes?
64. TEACHER: Teaching me?
65. SUPERVISOR: Yes. What might my *behavior*—what might you have learned from my behavior during the last five minutes or so?
66. TEACHER: Uh, that maybe you weren't going to clobber me.
67. SUPERVISOR: What else?
68. TEACHER: . . . Blank.
69. SUPERVISOR: How about, "I've got a secret"?
70. TEACHER: Pardon?
71. SUPERVISOR: I say, how about the game, "I've got a secret"?
72. TEACHER: [Pause.] [Laughs, blushes.] All right. Now I get it.
73. SUPERVISOR: Tell me.
74. TEACHER: That you've got ideas about what happened and that I should try to find out what they are?
75. SUPERVISOR: Yeah, that *I've* got a secret, and *your* job is to guess what I'm thinking.
76. TEACHER: [Laughs.] I didn't want to say it.
77. SUPERVISOR: Didn't—look—uh, "didn't want to say it" because it seems like a pretty dumb way to operate, doesn't it? I mean, if I've got something in mind it might be a lot better, certainly a lot faster, if I just said what it was outright, no?
78. TEACHER: I guess so.
79. SUPERVISOR: Do you suppose that I may have learned things from your behavior during the last few minutes too? I mean, besides what you were telling me directly?
80. TEACHER: That I want you to give me the answers, to solve my problems.
81. SUPERVISOR: How might I have learned such a thing?
82. TEACHER: Well, because I've asked you.
83. SUPERVISOR: Partly. Maybe also because you speak of feeling nervous. You also used the word "clobber."
84. TEACHER: So you could deduct—deduce?—anyway, you could get from that that I *expect* to be clobbered? Or that I feel guilty about my teaching?
85. SUPERVISOR: That's the idea. Sure. OK, let me make the point now directly, instead of playing the "I've got a secret" game. The point is that besides what I might be trying to teach you

directly, or what you might be trying to teach me, we both tend to "learn" things from each other's behavior, indirectly, incidentally.

86. TEACHER: Like, um, that you're not going to give me the answers?

87. SUPERVISOR: Exactly. Excellent. Yes, that's just the point. So that, really, what I'm asking about the kids is what, if anything, they may have learned incidentally from the way you began the lesson.

88. TEACHER: Uh, maybe that I'm a phony? Or that I use phony words? Or, oh, yes, that I'm going to be the boss.

89. SUPERVISOR: Yes, doesn't that seem reasonable? "Her job is to lead, and my job is to do what she tells me."

90. TEACHER: I see, yes.

91. SUPERVISOR: OK, now look. Before we get too far ahead of the game, there are a couple of things. Like, uh, let's go back to your having learned that I was trying to get you to play, uh no, not that exactly, that I was *playing* "I've got a secret." If that's how it seemed, or if that's how it was—is that good or bad? That is, is that a good thing for, let's say, a "teacher" to teach a "learner"?

92. TEACHER: I guess it's bad.

93. SUPERVISOR: Why?

94. TEACHER: Because, uh, it's dishonest. [Startled.] Uh, can I say that? I mean, I don't want to—

95. SUPERVISOR: Yes, yes, yes. Of course you can say that. I mean, that's just the point. What we're trying to find out is how the pupils are likely to feel, in their frames of reference, as a result of what Teacher does. If you felt that I was being dishonest or that I was holding something back, then that illustrates the point beautifully. I mean, do you think I wanted you to feel that way?

96. TEACHER: Why, no. I mean, why should you?

97. SUPERVISOR: Exactly. Why should I? But can you see that maybe what I *really* wanted was more, uh, "justifiable"?

98. TEACHER: You mean, uh, [pause]—

99. SUPERVISOR: I mean that what I really wanted was sort of for you to find "answers" on your own power and for you to feel, uh, for you to learn, uh, maybe, that I *don't* have simple answers and that we'll *both* have to work pretty hard to get some of the answers you're after.

100. TEACHER: I see, yes. You wanted me to learn not to expect certain things.

101. SUPERVISOR: Expectations, yes. So you can see how my intention didn't really come true, OK? I mean, instead of learning that, or maybe besides learning that, and feeling good about it, the way I tried to teach you that didn't really pay off so well. What I taught you, unintentionally, was "I've got a secret," because, well,

I just wasn't able to follow through on my intention with the best possible kind of behavior, that is, with the most appropriate behavior.

102. TEACHER: So, uh, going back to the lesson, what I wanted to tell the kids, really, was that now we were going to do arithmetic—not games or art or stories—so that they should get ready for arithmetic, but what they might have learned was more about that, as you say, their job is to do what I tell them to do.

103. SUPERVISOR: Does that seem convincing to you?

104. TEACHER: Yes, it sure does.

105. SUPERVISOR: So that—the point is that it's very hard just to come up with a definite, quick value judgment: that was good or that was bad, because, well, if my intention was good but my technique was bad, then I wouldn't want to throw the baby out with the bath water. One should really examine the whole business and sort out the pluses and the minuses, to save the good stuff and start getting rid of the bad stuff.

106. TEACHER: Can I try to say, uh, relate this to my lesson?

107. SUPERVISOR: Please.

108. TEACHER: So maybe it was all right. I mean, I think it's good for the children to get ready for what they're going to do, you know, so that they're not doing other things but the way I said it to them wasn't so good because they learned other things, uh, things I didn't want them to learn.

109. SUPERVISOR: Beautiful. But let's slow down again. I mean, there are still at least two questions, and you've raised one of them.

110. TEACHER: What I'm confused about is whether it is bad for them to learn that I'm the leader. I mean, that's what's confusing me.

111. SUPERVISOR: Ahh! Yes. And that's a tough one, you know? Because, as you've said, you *are* the leader; you *are* the teacher after all, so what's wrong with their learning that, right?

112. TEACHER: Yeah. [Pause.] Uh, I think we're playing the game again.

113. SUPERVISOR: "Follow the leader"?

114. TEACHER: [Laughs.] No, "I've got a secret."

115. SUPERVISOR: [Explosive laughter.] Good lord! I've created a a Frankenstein! [Prolonged laughter.] All right, look, oh boy [laughter]—uh, all right, I plead guilty. But, oh, let me raise just one more question before we get back to the lesson, OK?

116. TEACHER: [Laughing.] Be my guest.

117. SUPERVISOR: OK, we've seen how you may have learned, incidentally, from my behavior, this "I've got a secret" thing. Now let me ask, do you think that if I had only done whatever it was

that taught you that once, that is, if it only happened once in this hour and all the rest of the time I behaved differently, do you think that to have learned that, on just one short occasion, would have made a great deal of difference to you? That is, to us? To our relationship?

118. TEACHER: No, it shouldn't.

119. SUPERVISOR: Under what circumstances, however, might such a learning be very significant, in the sense of damaging what we're trying to do together?

120. TEACHER: I guess if it kept happening over and over again.

121. SUPERVISOR: I think so.

122. TEACHER: May I just say something? Another thing, though, is the fact, uh—how should I say this—another thing is that the fact that we talked about it makes it seem different. I mean, I don't think I would mind it so much now.

123. SUPERVISOR: Why?

124. TEACHER: Uh, because, well, I mean if I understand your *reasons* for asking me questions, then I don't mind so much.

125. SUPERVISOR: Ahh! You're really way ahead of me. Yes. That's very interesting. If I understand you, your thought is that one way to deal with incidental learnings, that is, with what might be *unfortunate* incidental learnings, is to make them explicit, to talk about them openly.

126. TEACHER: Yes.

127. SUPERVISOR: Fine. So that—and you'll notice that now I'm *telling* you—[laughter] that, again, one thing that determines whether a teaching technique is likely to be significant, that is, good or bad, is whether or not it is repeated over and over again in the teaching, whether it is a regular *pattern* in the teaching, in which case it might have very significant cumulative effects on what the kids learn.

128. TEACHER: Yes. If I do the same thing all the time, then there's no room for doubt. I mean, what the kids learn, they'll learn "better."

129. SUPERVISOR: Yes, I agree. Now I can tell you that one of *my* problems in trying to figure out whether, uh, or I should say, what parts of your teaching are good or bad, is that I haven't seen enough of it, really, to know what *your* patterns are. That is, I can't really begin to guess how much of your teaching tends to teach the kids what they might have learned about you and about themselves today.

130. TEACHER: I'm afraid to think about it.

131. SUPERVISOR: Yeah, I know the feeling. You know, another thing to keep in mind is that we don't know, for a fact, what incidental learnings, if any, did result from your teaching today.

This is very important to keep in mind. Our guesses might just be wrong. I think, later on, we might take a look at ways that exist for really finding out, more objectively, what kinds of effects our teaching is having. Uh, look, time is beginning to run out, why don't we get back to the lesson now and this time, just to get used to thinking about teaching this way, why don't we try to imagine what incidental learnings might logically have resulted from what was happening at any given moment in the lesson?

132. TEACHER: OK.

133. SUPERVISOR: All right. So what we've got so far, maybe, is that two incidental learnings that might logically have resulted from your opening were, "Teacher decides what we're going to do in here," and, I guess it's pretty much the same thing, uh, the "follow the leader" idea. I think maybe another related possibility is that when Timmy raised his hand and you said, "Not now," that Timmy might have learned, "What Teacher has to say is more important than what I have to say," and the other kids might, from this kind of thing—if it's really an ongoing pattern—learn, "What Teacher wants or says is more important than what Timmy wants or says," or, by generalization, "than what we want or say." Does this make any sense?

134. TEACHER: Yeah. I—you certainly find a lot of meaning in such a little—I mean, I've never—well, I never heard anybody talk about teaching this way. I mean, I guess I just gloss over so much. How do you find so much?

135. SUPERVISOR: I don't know. I guess just by practice. Just one thing though, I remind you that "guess" might be a better word than "find," because, at this point, we don't really have any evidence to prove that the kids were learning anything specific, one way or the other. I guess the way you find meaning in small details is, again, just to look at the teaching in very small pieces and to ask yourself, "If I were a child in this class, what, if anything, might I be learning at this moment as a logical result of what Teacher is doing or what other people are doing?" [Pause.] See, even if this way of looking at teaching is new for you, it shouldn't seem mysterious. I mean, it doesn't take a magician to do this. Why don't you try it? Here, look over these notes. Take your time. Make some educated guesses about incidental learnings that might have been taking place. [Teacher reads through Supervisor's observation notes (*not* his notes from analysis) for several minutes.]

136. TEACHER: [After a long pause.] I did the same thing with Marcia.

137. SUPERVISOR: How do you mean, "the same thing"?

138. TEACHER: I mean, Marcia might have concluded that I didn't think her song was as good as mine because I didn't let her tell what her song was.

139. SUPERVISOR: Would that be a valid "conclusion"?

140. TEACHER: In a sense, yes. I had my idea of the lesson and I just didn't want to go off in all directions, uh, I guess mostly because you were watching and I felt kind of nervous.

141. SUPERVISOR: Umhm. Let me show you something. Hold on a minute. [Supervisor finds the place in his analysis notes.] Let me read this to you. This is a note I made to myself while I was looking over this stuff, uh, it's hard to read but you can look at it with me. [Supervisor reads from his notes while Teacher looks on.] "Teacher's response to Marcia is the same as to Timmy: the pupil's spontaneous offering is subordinated to Teacher's plan." And what I thought was, Marcia might be learning that what she had to offer was not likely to be as valuable as what you had to offer, at least insofar as you were concerned.

142. TEACHER: That's almost uncanny; that we should both find the same thing.

143. SUPERVISOR: I disagree. On the contrary, it seems to me that if this kind of analysis really required a magician, you know, who used mysterious processes, then, in all likelihood, unless you were a magician too and knew the tricks of the trade, we would *not* have arrived at the same thought.

144. TEACHER: I guess so. There is one thing about this that bothers me.

145. SUPERVISOR: What's that?

146. TEACHER: Do you really think that the kids actually think this way? I mean, like, do you think Marcia thought to herself . . . Uh, I guess what I mean to say is that I can't remember learning such things in so many words when I was a kid in school.

147. SUPERVISOR: Ahh, yes! Not consciously, anyhow. Yeah. You see, you've put your finger on a sticky problem; a part of this guessing business. I mean—it's not only that we often have to guess about such things, that is, about probable incidental learnings, but the hell of it is that even if you asked Marcia directly, what she had learned, she might not be conscious of her "conclusions" at all. Even if she were, she might not say so. And that does get sticky. I don't know, sometimes I worry about whether I'm just making these things up, from my imagination. But then, there are two factors that make me feel better. The first, as you've just seen, is that pretty often *other* people arrive at exactly the same conclusions, or I should say "hypotheses," about incidental learnings as I do, and I can't really believe that we all

share the same prejudices so much, you know? The other thing is that even though Marcia might not have learned what we're guessing from this one instance, and even though she might not be conscious of having learned this after many such experiences, it's still possible to imagine that from this kind of teaching pattern, where what Teacher wants crowds out what the kids may want, the kids learn that value unconsciously, just from repeated experiences of the same kind. I mean, I've become accustomed to having this chair right where it is. When I come in here, I lower my body into the chair. I've never really thought to myself, consciously, "that's where the chair is," but just out of habit, I mean, out of a million experiences in which that chair stayed where it is, I've learned unconsciously that it's there; and I've learned to expect it to be there. Without thinking about it. [Pause.] It's hard to make this point because in order to create an example, I *have* to talk about it explicitly; and when I do that, it *is* conscious.

149. TEACHER: Yes, no, that's all right. I understand what you're saying.

150. SUPERVISOR: Tell me.

151. TEACHER: Well, it's like with this "I've got a secret." Even if I never thought about it like that, that is, uh, consciously, I might, anyhow, come in here just expecting things to go that way.

152. SUPERVISOR: In your guts.

153. TEACHER: Yeah.

154. SUPERVISOR: That's the ticket. [Pause.] Uh, oh, never mind. [Perusing his notes.] Let's see. [Pause.]

155. TEACHER: What is it?

156. SUPERVISOR: Huh?

157. TEACHER: Uh, you decided not to say something?

158. SUPERVISOR: Uh, no, I'm sorry, not really. It's just that there are a number of leads we could follow in this lesson, but there isn't much time left, and I was just trying to figure out . . . [Pause.] Uh, look, instead of trying to race the clock, how would you feel about getting together again tomorrow just to talk some more about what might possibly have been going on here for the kids—that is, without my observing your next lesson in arithmetic?

159. TEACHER: Yes. This is very interesting. As a matter of fact, there won't be any arithmetic tomorrow because of assembly. From nine to ten-thirty, I think it is, the primary grades are going to see a safety film that the police department comes around with every year.

160. SUPERVISOR: Could you break away during the assembly?

161. TEACHER: Yes. Mrs. Lacey could keep an eye on my kids.

162. SUPERVISOR: Well, bless the police department. [Pause.] Uh, actually there is one thing we could start getting into today. Uh, we've been talking about incidental learnings that might result from things that happen in a lesson, especially from things that the teacher does.

164. TEACHER: Yeah.

165. SUPERVISOR: And, well, another possibility we might examine is that incidental *learnings* can also arise from things that don't happen. Or, really, that certain learnings can occur or can fail to result from things that don't happen as well as from things that do.

166. TEACHER: [No response.]

167. SUPERVISOR: What I have in mind, uh, here, look at these notes again with me. And this time let's look at the structure of the dialogue instead of at the content.

168. TEACHER: I don't think I understand what you mean.

169. SUPERVISOR: Uh, yeah. What I mean is, uh, you'll notice, as you run your eye down the page, that the predominant pattern of interaction in this lesson was "Teacher-to-pupil" or "Teacher-to-class," uh, and that there wasn't any "pupil-to-pupil" conversation. [Pause.] I guess what I mean is that this was more like tennis than volleyball. That is, uh, you know, in tennis, one player serves and then the other player returns the ball, and then the first player hits it back, and so forth, while in volleyball, often, the ball is hit from one player to another and then to another, all on the same team, before it's returned to the opposing court. I don't know whether the analogy is worth much, but what I'm wondering about is whether your lessons are generally structured like today's was or whether it sometimes happens that instead of only addressing themselves to you, the pupils have a chance to talk to one another.

170. TEACHER: I see. [Pause.] I don't know what to say, uh—

171. SUPERVISOR: Well, I'm sorry to be so fuzzy. My point is that if "Teacher-to-pupil" is an almost exclusive interactional pattern in your classroom, then, number one, over the long haul, certain incidental learnings might result from that pattern and, number two, the kids might fail to learn certain things that you'd want them to learn, because of an absence of opportunities to discuss things among themselves.

172. TEACHER: Umm. [Pause.] Uh, like communications skills?

173. SUPERVISOR: Uh, well, I guess so, yeah, sure; communications skills. Sure.

174. TEACHER: But I can't think of, uh, any incidental learnings—

175. SUPERVISOR: How about, "Speak when you're spoken to?"
176. TEACHER: Oh!
177. SUPERVISOR: Or, "One should wait to be told what to do by Teacher," or "Learning means to talk to Teacher, not to other children; that is, not to other people like me."
178. TEACHER: Yes. I see. Uh, are, uh, is incidental learning always bad? I mean, couldn't the kids learn something good accidentally?
179. SUPERVISOR: Good question. What do you think?
180. TEACHER: Well, for example, if teachers always treat them politely, uh, and with respect, uh mightn't they learn to feel good about being in school?
181. SUPERVISOR: What do you think?
182. TEACHER: Well, yes.
183. SUPERVISOR: I agree. It certainly seems plausible. Uh, gee, this is frustrating, but I think we're going to have to stop in a minute.
184. TEACHER: May I just say something?
185. SUPERVISOR: Please.
186. TEACHER: Uh, this lesson is one I taught in student teaching, uh, for my supervisor. And she, she gave it an "A." What she said was, uh, you need good discipline to teach, and there were no discipline problems. I mean, the kids behaved pretty much the way they did today. And that she could see I was prepared, because the kids had their worksheets. And that since I used music, uh, a song, in an arithmetic lesson, that that showed "creativity"; and that one sign of good teaching is that most of the kids participate, you know? And in this lesson, *every* child participated, and, so, you know, I got an "A" for the lesson.
187. SUPERVISOR: Oh. [Pause.] I guess this must come as a disap—
188. TEACHER: Oh, no! Don't misunderstand me. I feel very good about it. I mean, it was very upsetting to me because I just didn't feel comfortable with, uh, I mean I just couldn't believe that this was such a great lesson, and I was kind of worried that you would say the same thing; and then I'd be right back where I started. No, I think this is good.
190. SUPERVISOR: Oh, well, fine, great. I thought [laughter]. Uh, it just occurred to me, for tomorrow, supposing I run off a copy of my observation notes and leave them in your box and then if you get a chance, and want to look them over beforehand, uh, you could raise whatever issues or questions you wanted to talk about tomorrow.
191. TEACHER: Thank you. Yes, I'd like to do that. Uh, also, [laughs] uh, it's funny, I mean, even though I sort of know better, I

still feel like I want to ask whether, you know, whether you feel there's any hope.

192. SUPERVISOR: You want me to pass on that in spite of yourself?

193. TEACHER: Yeah, uh, I know it's silly.

194. SUPERVISOR: To want approval?

195. TEACHER: I guess so.

196. SUPERVISOR: Human, maybe, but not especially silly. I mean, I could say, "Yeah, I really think you're one of the world's great teachers." So what would that mean?

197. TEACHER: Nothing. [Pause.] But it would feel nice.

198. SUPERVISOR: Good grief! All right. You are one of the world's great teachers. [Laughter.] See you tomorrow.

199. TEACHER: Yeah. Thank you. [Rises to leave.]

200. SUPERVISOR: By the way, seriously, uh, I think I do know how you feel about that. I mean, hell, everybody would like to be able, uh, to be told—

201. TEACHER: You worry too much.

202. SUPERVISOR: [Laughs.] OK. Take care.

203. TEACHER: See you tomorrow.

CRITIQUE OF CASE 2

Mr. Foster's conceptions of teaching, of process goals, and of incidental learnings come so close to those we have already examined together that it is not necessary to deal lengthily with them again. We may, however, note some features of his analysis and strategy in relation to this supervisor's use and applications of such concepts. My first impression of his thinking, particularly about incidental learnings that may have arisen as a result of Teacher's behavior, is that it tends to be overcertain, sometimes arbitrary, rather too "tight" to represent reality adequately. We find, however, as he deals with Teacher during the conference, that he is not quite as hidebound as one's first impressions might suggest and that, in fact, he is appropriately tentative when he is supervising and the chips are down.

He cautions Teacher, for example, that one can rarely be certain about specific incidental learnings at a glance and truly states that while any teacher may represent a potent source of operant conditioning, the pupils, nonetheless, learn about things—themselves, their subject matter, their classmates, the school—from multiple sources. Even so, in my own estimation, while it may be true at any given moment that Johnny's learning is resulting principally from Sally's behavior, over the long run, Teacher is *almost* always more focal and more significant in a pupil's life than the child in the next seat. To be sure, there is some hint of simplism in Foster's teaching-learning models as, indeed, there is in all such existing models. In any event, his "Notes for Strategy" encompass precisely the values, the hypotheses, and the questions that one would expect to find expressed by any clinical supervisor sharing this general orientation.

Supervisor's summary of "likely incidental learnings" seems basically acceptable, assuming his own, stated, qualification: "To whatever degree Teacher may be central in such learning," and assuming that other, dramatic events were not taking place during the lesson which our available data fail to include. Operating under the double handicap of not knowing the teacher very well—this is their first supervisory sequence—and of having practically no data on the pupils' individual behavior (because of how the lesson was structured), Supervisor could not have gone very far in applying our full model of methods for Strategy. "Accessibility" was an almost impossible criterion to employ, "fewness" is difficult to conceptualize without strong indications of accessibility, and even "saliency" would have been difficult to determine on any concrete basis. Indeed, the question of whether seeming patterns actually constituted real and ongoing patterns of Teacher's behavior could not have been decided adequately from this single observation.

Under these circumstances, Foster did well to avoid decisions to prosecute any specific issue(s) aggressively. Another option he might have considered would have been to tell Teacher, straight out, that although he *had* intended to perform an analysis of her lesson, the lesson was too abridged and his experiences of her teaching too limited to enable him to fulfill his intention. He might then have employed the hour to discuss general issues in teaching and supervision and to have obtained information relating to the question of whether the observed lesson's character was more typical or atypical of Teacher's teaching generally. As it was, however, in light of Teacher's initial request, her presumed anxiety around observation and supervisory feedback, and the commitment Supervisor had already accepted, it was probably best for him to have proceeded as he did, even under the disadvantages that had developed.

In the conference, from S1 through S23, Supervisor does seem to have behaved consistently with his double intention to be supportive and to await signals from Teacher. S5, for all its seeming casualness and simplicity, is an exceedingly well turned response. To begin with, it represents the supervisor's first real statement in relation to the lesson and, particularly in a first conference, our experiences indicate that supervisors' initial reactions are often fraught with significance for teachers; that, perhaps, more hangs in the balance at such a moment than at any other time in supervision.

"Oh, maybe not a thousand," and then, "Are you serious?" seem strangely effective together. It is difficult to say why, because this value judgment is essentially intuitive, and intuitive sensations of rightness and wrongness are difficult to explain: there is no strong evidence to cite, nor any but the most tenuous psychological hypotheses to rationalize my opinion. Once more, I can come closest to explaining my approval by speaking first of what Supervisor's response (S5) presumably did *not* communicate. I think it probably did not communicate rejection of Teacher—either of Teacher as a person or of Teacher's anxious glibness.[5] It did not reject Teacher's use of humor as a means of coping with anxiety and, in fact, may have communicated "permission" for such behavior by replicating it. It was not an angry response, a disapproving response, a nonresponse, a punitive response, nor an evaluative response. If my intuitions are correct, Supervisor's response probably produced some momentary relief or encouragement, if not because of what it communicated directly, then perhaps because of what it did *not* communicate. Had I been Teacher, I would have experienced acceptance, rather than its opposite response. My guess is that the query was intended to illuminate the degree of intensity of Teacher's doubts and as a starting point for finding out something more about Teacher's explicit concerns.

We do see that Teacher was not turned off, that dialogue continued to develop. T6 expresses the most common question of all among teachers inexperienced in clinical supervision, namely, "Tell me, was it good or bad?" Implicitly or explicitly, the question of whether Supervisor approves or disapproves is the most ubiquitous question we encounter—a question to which, almost invariably, the evaluative response counts for considerably more than the reasons behind it. Such is the common dependency among teachers (and among people) to be *told* how good or bad they are, that "good" or "bad" frequently terminates the inquiry. "Why" tends to be dealt with at a fantasy level and in a matrix of feeling; we often do not ask for reasons, particularly from hierarchical superiors. The schools generally tend to finish what Mama has begun: "Do what you're told," and "Because I say so, that's why."

S7 is a question for clarification. S9 is also aimed at clarification and additionally represents a reflection of meaning. Reflected meanings, ending in implicit question marks, are often useful to communicate understanding as well as to produce further information. S13 is also doubly motivated: at face value it reveals something of Supervisor's professional values and concepts; more implicitly, it offers support and encouragement to go on. S15, again for clarification, is a good example of parsimonious questioning that is simultaneously responsive and efficient and which, as a supervisory pattern, may teach, incidentally, that supervision will aim to differentiate and to clarify global and

---

[5] Foster's tone, throughout S5, was kindly. "Are you serious?" was spoken sympathetically, not accusatively. His accent was on the word "serious," not on "you."

ambiguous statements. In the episode T16 through T22, Teacher refines her problem, having moved through the sequence: (1) "Did that set teaching back . . . ?" (2) ". . . how you *know* whether the kids are learning and even what they *should* be learning. . . ." (3) ". . . how *significant* it is . . ." and finally, (4) ". . . are there other things they could be doing that would be more worthwhile?" Throughout this episode, Supervisor's statements have mainly been clarifications (or questions for clarification) and attempts to be supportive; to offer (sincere) reassurances that Teacher's questions were not naive ("silly"); that the problems she defined were real and complex.

S25 illustrates an early attempt to teach, indirectly, that if Supervisor offers value judgments, they will not be simple, social flatteries (nor arbitrary rejections), but will, instead, be reasoned out. In S27, Supervisor weaves skillfully among meanings to be intended and meanings to be avoided. At the same time, he accepts Teacher's reliance upon the manual *and* her ambivalence toward using it: implicitly, *"Yes,* since it is designed for that, it is sensible to use the manual to make things simpler," and *"Yes,* it makes sense to feel troubled about using a simpleminded manual." I value this approach because of its restraint from placing restrictions on Teacher's freedom to make choices. Particularly when supervision is new and when, presumably, much of Teacher's learning is centered on what supervision (and Supervisor) is going to be like, there may be appreciable differences on the one hand, between communicating consensus, namely, that Supervisor sees the dilemma in the same terms as Teacher does (and deliberately leaves the problem unresolved), or, on the other, of asserting partisan opinions. To say, for example, "The manual exists because teachers are supposed to follow it; innovations are only OK after the basic manual has been covered," or, "I think it is foolish to use the thing, especially when its limitations are apparent to you," would tend to eliminate Teacher's options instead of encouraging her to develop eventual choices or reconciliations among them.

S29 is problematical. Supervisor may have acted from some impulse to get his own business transacted, namely, the results of his analysis. In any case, his attempt to sector the inquiry seems reasonable inasmuch as discussion had drifted to general and ambiguous issues, for example, Teacher's (facetious?) question of neurosis. Indeed, Supervisor's abrupt shift into the lesson may have been prompted by anxiety arising from that reference. While Supervisor might have chosen to deal with T28 (at least to find out, more accurately, what the statement was really supposed to communicate), I should probably have let it go too, at this very early stage of supervision. I should, for example, want more extensive opportunities to formulate my own impressions of Teacher's psychological functioning before being drawn into discussions about it. I should also, probably, favor an initial structuring aimed at demonstrating analysis of teaching behavior so that, after having discovered that dimension of clinical supervision, Teacher might more readily choose whether to employ conferences primarily for examinations of self or examinations of teaching, at any specific time. We should not, in any case, overstate the virtue of Supervisor's decision: by moving, so quickly, away from Teacher's puzzling self-reference, Supervisor may have failed an important test. Notwithstanding future opportunities to recoup, Supervisor may have taught something about the place of personal or "emotional" material in supervision and about his own anxieties in that connection.

The possibility that the avoidances of S29 arose, at least partly, from an anxiety response, gains credence in light of S31, a response that would be more appropriate to examine in the following section on problems: I see it as a blunder and offer that if it did not, in fact, have damaging effects, that outcome resulted from dumb luck and does not excuse Supervisor's ploy. The first thing wrong with S31 is that it is not appropriately responsive to T30. Rather than accept Teacher's fears empathically, Supervisor tried to jolly them away, to tease Teacher into a courageous posture. To teach, in this manner, that fears should be hidden or disguised, would be unfortunate and at direct cross-purposes to the priority, in clinical supervision, on raising such feelings to a level of explicit awareness where they can be examined for heightened insight and rational management.

A second mistake is that Supervisor's dental metaphor carries precisely the same kind of unknown effect as Teacher's mnemonics, to which Supervisor objected in his analysis. Had Teacher been phobic about dentistry, his allusion could hardly have been a useful one. At another level, I can see no advantage to a remark whose symbolism can be experienced in quite such intrusive terms (at this level, S33 is equally unfelicitous). A third weakness, in my judgment, was to have kept the dialogue at a level of repartee. In such a new relationship, particularly, it is never possible to predict the personal meanings that joking may carry. While humor is not to be avoided, unnecessarily flaky behavior should be. As it was, both members' sobriety was apparently reasserted in time for the supervision to recover, but we can hardly praise Supervisor's activity through this episode.

In S35, he has regained the track. His response to Teacher's statement of "nervousness" is sober, direct, and well conceived. Admitting Teacher's tension and wanting to be helpful, Supervisor offered a cogent rationale for analysis, namely, to alleviate anticipatory anxiety by moving directly into the work. Although one wonders whether, symbolically, Teacher exacted the price of one cigarette for permission to examine her teaching, at least in this episode Supervisor had returned to sympathetic behavior, this time avoiding the trap created by Teacher's continued "humorous" sparring. Adroitly, Supervisor established an emphasis by refocusing on one of Teacher's own, initial questions. From S45, through the next few queries, Supervisor attempted to involve Teacher in an examination of her own performance. In several different ways, that is, by several questions, Supervisor tried to stimulate a picture of incidental learnings in Teacher's imagination. S47 illustrates a standard gambit, namely, to encourage the supervisee to assume the pupils' frames of reference. In T48, Teacher reveals an unsurprising expectation that Supervisor has some specific response in mind that he is hoping Teacher will discover. Supervisor's disclaimer, in S49, is valid and forthright, although Teacher may not have understood its crucial distinction, namely, that while Supervisor was truly not after any specific response, he was trying to establish an inductive process of inquiry.

Again, in S51, Supervisor attempted to guide Teacher into the pupils' (hypothetical) frame of reference and to stimulate inquiry that might lead to the concept of incidental learning. For the remainder of this episode, until S63, Supervisor continued this approach, becoming progressively more didactic from entry to entry. His sequence of questioning illustrates one example of "hierarchical intervention," a concept we examined earlier. His sequence moves, in effect, from an open question (S45), through increasingly focused questions, to S69, in which, for all practical purposes, Supervisor has stopped asking and has offered a direct answer of his own. The only sense in which S69 remains "question" is in its implicit appeal for consensus.

What are some possibilities to account for Supervisor's lack of immediate success, namely, his failure to provoke a useful response by S45 (the first question in his sequence)? Perhaps Teacher's anxiety interfered with clear-sighted, efficient reasoning. Perhaps Teacher's expectation that Supervisor would offer prompt (negative) value judgments on her teaching retarded her ability to respond to his actual behavior. An expectational set may inhibit the assimilation of data that are dissonant or inconsistent with the prior expectation. For example, if I were to describe a relationship involving John and Mary, or a situation involving a doctor and a lawyer, you would almost certainly *not* assume that, in the first case, I was talking about a cat and a goldfish or that, in the second, I was referring to two women. Your prior expectations, or sets, would probably lead to serious confusion if I did not trouble to correct them early in our discussion.

Perhaps Teacher's slowness to manifest the intellectual behavior that Supervisor was attempting to stimulate reflected her inexperience with such processes. She may, in other words, have not been very well rehearsed in the kind of reasoning and imagining that Supervisor was after. Even if Teacher had had experience in such intellectual processes, she might not, nevertheless, have thought to employ them in a supervisory dialogue, again because of existing expectations from which such a possibility was absent. Whereas I may know many games, for example, the son game, the professor game, the husband game, and the gambler game, it is not likely to occur to me to play such games in any but their "native" situations. I am not likely, in other words, to play professor with my wife or lover with my department chairman. In similar fashion, like many professors, I find that my students often fail to recognize me outside of the department, especially when I am dressed for the bush rather than for the university: the situational gestalt is missing. It is not that they lack experience in recognizing me, but rather, that they lack experience recognizing me in the woods.

In all probability, each of these factors played some part in Teacher's slowness to play Supervisor's game. There may have been many additional factors: lack of trust, fear of authority figures, and the like. In connection with incidental learnings that might result from a *pattern* of hierarchical intervention, supervisors must take a calculated risk. On the one hand, the repetition of such a technique may teach that Supervisor values Teacher's own intellectual activity, his own expenditures of intellectual energy in inquiry. On the other hand, Teacher might learn that if he simply sits still for long enough, Supervisor will stop playing the question game and will tell him what he (Supervisor) has in mind. It behooves the supervisor, consequently, to exhibit many patterns of behavior intended to teach the former expectation. Experience suggests that because, for many individuals, when external pressures are reduced, self-initiated inquiry is more apt to feel rewarding than passive acceptance of other people's answers; once such behavior has begun to be established, it tends to be self-reinforcing.

In any event, Supervisor's technique in this excerpt is not only impressive because of his application of hierarchical intervention, but also because of his successful recovery subsequently. Having run dry in his sequence of questioning, Supervisor retrieved his loss by applying another technique of clinical supervision, namely, a "process confrontation." From T52 through T60, Teacher came closer and closer to the behavior toward which Supervisor was leading her. "Phony," in T54 and, especially, "follow the leader," in T60, are good examples of hypothetical incidental learnings. Nonetheless, Supervisor may have sensed Teacher's tentativeness in these conceptualizations, just as I do as I read through the typescript, and may have decided, consequently, to aim for a higher degree of certainty, of conviction, of existential reality, by shifting Teacher's focus away from the children, momentarily, and onto her own, actual experiences during the supervisory episode that had just been completed. From the activity of trying to imagine what the pupils experienced, Supervisor shifted to the question of what Teacher *actually* experienced in her own frame of reference, as a result of Supervisor's "teaching" behavior. One senses that when Teacher finally owned her feeling of being manipulated, that is, of having been drawn into a game of "I've got a secret," the concept "incidental learning" acquired substantially more vivid meaning than it had for her until that moment.

This gambit is particularly significant because it illustrates (1) the quality of self-awareness, that is, awareness of one's own behavior, one's own processes, and one's own ostensible effects upon the supervisee, and (2) the quality of psychological readiness and willingness to examine one's own behavior analytically, for didactic purposes, that are fundamental in clinical supervision. Besides being conscious of himself, the clinical supervisor should have the ability—courage is a simple way to name it—to engage in reflexive analysis in his practice.

In S63 Supervisor took another chance, namely, that Teacher would (could) hold onto the concept "follow the leader" for future reference. He might have elected to use this construct of Teacher's for the purpose he had in mind and might, indeed, have been better advised to do so. All one can conclude about his choice to follow his own train of thought instead of adopting Teacher's is that, as things turned out, it can be justified retroactively, in relation to how the conference developed. We cannot say, in this connection, whether, again, dumb luck operated benignly. I am inclined to give Supervisor the benefit of the doubt this time by supposing that his choice included the reasoning that whatever status anxiety Teacher might be experiencing in their relationship could be reduced, somewhat, by a process confrontation involving an ostensible weakness of Supervisor's own behavior. If, in other words, a part of his intention was to exemplify self-examination and to teach a value for that process—he may also have intended to demonstrate an attitude favoring productive use of failure—then his choices and actions were all the more consistent with our idealizations of clinical supervision.

S73 illustrates the "playback" technique, that is, the technique of requesting a supervisee to communicate his understanding explicitly, once he has indicated general understanding. Some presumable advantages of this gambit are to be sure that Teacher's understanding is not illusory—it could be unfortunate to proceed as though an understanding had been established when, in fact, it had not—to communicate that for Teacher to understand is important to Supervisor (and, that for Supervisor to understand things correctly is important), and to force articulation of Teacher's ideas by requiring their verbal expression. We may note that this episode brought some of Teacher's discomfort to the surface: witness her failure to catch on immediately (T70); her blushing; her laughter and the statement, "I didn't want to say it" (T76); and finally, her surprise in T94, when she allowed herself to express doubts about Supervisor's honesty.

It is generally consistent with our orientation to attempt to surface feelings about supervision in this manner, in order to work them through consciously to whatever extent that may be possible. While Teacher's anxieties about Supervisor may be essentially parataxic and, to that measure, refractory to supervisory treatment, they may also be based upon real and present supervisory behavior, in which case their "treatment" at the reality level could be appropriate and effective. Such treatment should not be avoided, no matter what hypotheses concerning the etiology of Teacher's anxiety Supervisor might be entertaining. There is little to lose by proceeding, initially, from the assumption that Teacher's responses to Supervisor are largely determined by what Supervisor does rather than being basically predetermined by Teacher's transference to Supervisor, that is, by his tendency to relate to Supervisor as though he were someone else, for example, a father.

In S79 Supervisor attempts a "role reversal," another technique employed frequently in clinical supervision. This time, Supervisor asked Teacher to imagine what *he* might have learned incidentally from *her* behavior. One reasonable motive for turning to this method would have been to even the psychological score by shifting away from an apparently self-deprecating analysis. Events moved very swiftly in this episode, much more swiftly than we can examine them. My thought, here, is that Supervisor did well to interrupt an examination of his own behavior which, because it centered on a weakness, might have increased Teacher's discomfort inordinately (had it continued), and that his timing was very adept for developing the understanding that examination of technical behavior was to be valued in relationship to anyone's technical behavior, irrespective of roles. By this point in the conference, Supervisor had already demonstrated a broad array of role-plays. His questions had included (1) that of what the children might have experienced, (2) that of what Teacher experienced (in supervision), and finally, (3) that of what Supervisor might have experienced (in supervision). Another advantage of this role reversal was to focus Teacher's attention on her own implicit communications, on her own behavior, an objective fully consistent with the supervisory process goal "self-evaluation." If one of Supervisor's objectives was to train Teacher to examine her behavior in relation to incidental learnings it might logically have incited, then this short exercise was directly relevant and particularly well conceived because of opportunities existing in the supervisory relationship to confirm Teacher's guesses about her effects upon Supervisor.

S81 resembles S73 in that it reflects Supervisor's unwillingness to accept what could have been a glib response. S83 is a potentially useful response in several respects. For one thing, it demonstrates that Supervisor has been listening and, implicitly, that he cares enough to listen closely. For another, it exemplifies an attention to words, an example of the highly focused attention to words that clinical analysis of behavior requires. The response also demonstrates the practice of finding meaningful connections among separate elements of behavior. In this manner, Supervisor begins to create examples of technical behavior that may later be applied to Teacher's own work, namely, to her evaluation of the pupils' behavior and to processes of evaluation that she may want to teach the pupils for their own employment. S83 also serves, substantively, to keep Teacher's feelings at a conscious and explicit level, where Supervisor may accept them. Finally, by exposing his reasoning processes so fully, Supervisor is likely to disabuse Teacher of fantasies she may have which attribute mysticism to his inferences, to counteract the common appearance that clinical supervisors' inferences are made mysteriously.

In T84, Teacher revealed understanding of incidental learning by her description of logical inferences that Supervisor might have drawn from her previous behavior. In S85, Supervisor nailed the definition explicitly. In T86, Teacher provided more evidence of her understanding and of her ability to apply the concept, at least in the supervisory relationship. In S87, Supervisor offered more encouragement (he had done so in almost every entry in this episode) and, while all irons were hot, quickly restated his original question, namely, of what the children might predictably have learned from Teacher's behavior during the lesson. Once again, he shifted frames of reference, this time back to the children. One way to picture events from S45 to S87 is as Supervisor's (successful) attempt to teach Teacher skills that she required to respond adequately to her own, initial question concerning what the pupils had learned, a question that Supervisor seized partly because of its specific importance, but even more for the reason that it represented such an opportune starting point for establishing general concepts of teaching patterns (also S117) and of incidental learnings to which they may give rise.

In S89, Supervisor translated Teacher's hypothetical response into the first person, that is, into the personal meaning it might carry and personal language with which the idea might be expressed by children who had learned it. I have often found it useful, in supervision, to make this semantic shift. It generally seems, somehow, to make (hypothesized) incidental learnings more vivid and their appreciation more potent to express them in such language and, especially, when *Teacher* expresses them in the first person, as she tries to imagine events as they existed for the children.

In S91, Supervisor moved into the question of values. Having established an image of processes by which incidental learning may be induced, Supervisor proceeded directly to the question of whether such learnings, especially those specifically cited by Teacher, and the "teaching" that produced them, are good things or bad things. At least two reasons support Supervisor's decision. The first is that when the likelihood of specific incidental learnings is deduced from teaching behavior, only half the job has been done. The question remains of whether what has been learned and the teaching behavior that presumably engendered it are likely to be useful to the learner, either in relationship to his substantive curriculum or to his definitions of self and of role. A second reason is that Teacher demonstrated some tendency to evaluate her incidental effects upon her pupils and Supervisor's incidental effects upon her own outlook, negatively.

From this evidence, two related goals emerged for Supervisor: (1) to teach, very quickly, that incidental learnings can be positive as well as negative, and even concurrently positive and negative in certain respects, and (2) to counteract any tendency Teacher might have to form global rather than subtle and differentiated value judgments of such outcomes. Supervisor may also have been motivated to cushion Teacher's denigrations of her own work (which might simply have left her feeling discouraged) and to define possibilities for avoiding various kinds of incidental learning outcomes, and for compensating for them once they have become established, as, indeed, he did later in S125. This sequence partly reflects the priority, in clinical supervision, on moving efficiently from analyses of past events to strategies for the future.

S93 (like S15) is another example of placing the initiative for inquiry on the supervisee. Although, in my estimation, the supervisor in this case was somewhat more didactic and verbose than he ought to have been—again, this is a subjective judgment—he did manage to compensate for his powerful directiveness by interventions of just this kind, from time to time. His reassuring response in S95 was well taken, both as personal reassurance and as a demonstration of Supervisor's priority on objective, authentic, and unhurtful examination of teaching behavior. In this response, Supervisor manifested a capacity to understand one's technical weaknesses without feeling personally diminished or punished by their exposure.

Supervisor's distinction between intent and technique (S101) seems to have been well timed, for in T102, Teacher applied it exactly to her own condition in the lesson being discussed. This kind of ability, to assimilate constructs and then to apply them spontaneously to one's own behavior, signals positive indications to move forward toward the formulation of additional relevant constructs, as Supervisor did repeatedly in this conference. S97 is a good example of making one's motives, and one's rationales for behavior, explicit in supervision. I have found that to do so, rather than to work, typically, from veiled reasons, generally enables one to avoid creating a feeling of being foxed and manipulated by the supervisor. I advocate this technique for teaching generally because of the opportunity it provides for the learner's engagement in a process or in a relationship to be based upon known and cogent reasons, instead of existing simply because he was

required, somehow, to participate. I advocate, in other words, techniques that enable one's participation in any task to be rational rather
than resigned.

In S105, Supervisor nails another point didactically. T106 and
other entries like it, for example, T94, T122, and T184 raise the
question of whether Supervisor's obvious drive and intellectual aggressiveness represented more of an asset or a liability in this conference.
On the one hand, Teacher shows over and over again that she has been
able to understand Supervisor's ideas and that, even further, she has
discovered applications to her own teaching spontaneously. She additionally demonstrates fiber, a certain toughness that enables her to say
when she does not understand, to criticize Supervisor when that seems
appropriate, and to face her own technical deficiencies, at least partly,
without an apparent sense of shame.

On the other hand, however, even by the time this conference
ended, Teacher still persisted in exhibiting a certain deference, as, for
example, by asking permission to speak and to express ideas. Despite
having come to "know better," Teacher's dependency upon external
evaluation, at an emotional level, seems largely unmitigated at the close
of the conference (T191). Indeed, it would be naive to expect such
basic attitudes and expectations as dependencies upon authority to alter
radically as a result of any single supervisory sequence. Significant
changes often fail to materialize even after numerous cycles of supervision. Our problem is, rather, to decide whether, in its didactic aspect,
Supervisor's behavior was more likely to have strengthened Teacher's
latent autonomy and to have reinforced her sufficient behaviors as they
occurred, or whether, by and large, it operated in the opposite direction, namely, toward strengthening Teacher's reliance upon external
authority and evaluation, by having been so potently authoritative.

The best we can do is to identify this question in relationship to
the case at hand. The material suggests tendencies in both directions,
although whether Supervisor's reinforcements of dependent behavior,
on the one hand, and of autonomous behavior, on the other, were
mutually canceling is a moot issue which would require additional
evidence to resolve. The problem, in any event, should not be missed;
analogously, the same question arises in relation to charismatic
teaching. Whereas one commonly supposes charisma to be a virtue, an
attractive attribute among teachers, one must also reckon with the
possibility that in spite of superficial appearances, students of charismatic teachers do not learn as enduringly and as significantly as they
might if their teachers were flatter and their own active participation in
substantive inquiries more focal in the teaching-learning relationship.
Another way to imagine this problem is as the possibility that Supervisor's expertise, his authoritative virtue, may prove to be a fundamental
weakness in the context of *process* if his very expertise kindles stronger

appetites for approval among his supervisees than they might experience otherwise.

In S103, Supervisor contrived to have Teacher render her own decision and suggested, implicitly, that one's (Teacher's) own logical reasoning should represent a basis for assessing the validity of inferences. In T108, Teacher succeeded in being more differentiating in her evaluations. She stated, in effect, that a part of what she had done seemed worthwhile (for enunciated reasons) at the very same time that another part of it seemed weak. The episode from T112 through T116 provides a wonderful example of how tricky it can be to manage one's technical behavior consistently with one's stated idealizations of technical behavior. Right on the heels of having explicitly devalued "I've got a secret," Supervisor inadvertently repeated the very patterns of behavior that had engendered that impression to begin with.

In S117 and S119, Supervisor returned, full throttle, to inductive inquiry. Once more, it is difficult to assess how much the quality of Teacher's participation in this dialogue reflected Supervisor's skill or existed independently of his behavior. By S121, I feel all ready to attack Supervisor's verbosity—by a simple word count, his talk heavily outweighed Teacher's throughout the conference—but then T122 appears and, in light of such an insightful statement, one cannot easily build the case that Supervisor's approach was erroneous. Perhaps Teacher rose to meet his level of energy and would not have functioned as well herself had Supervisor been less active. S125 is an example of playback. In S127, Supervisor has struck out in his own directions again, although the point he makes had been prepared by earlier discussion. In T128, Teacher stated the principle in question more succinctly than Supervisor had done.

In S129, Supervisor attempted to redefine the original contract, to provide reasons not to formulate general impressions of Teacher's teaching. The moment was propitious for proposing this alteration because the construct "patterns" and an image of their potential cumulative effects had already been formulated. An earlier attempt to renege might well have seemed defensively motivated. Supervisor's response to Teacher's expressed fear, in S131, was appropriate but possibly too modest. He chose to handle Teacher's misgivings by intellectualizing related issues instead of exploring her feelings more directly. If his decision arose from an explicit determination not to move deeply into emotional material until he had firmer impressions of Teacher's functioning, or until their relationship had become more trustworthy, then his choice may, indeed, have been well conceived. If, on the other hand, his own anxiousness turned him away from Teacher's doubt (he was, for example, experiencing some time-pressure), then his course of action could more readily be judged unresponsive and inferior to other alternatives.

In S131, Supervisor attempted, decisively, to restructure their discussion so that Teacher might become more active. He also tried to return to concrete problems of the observed lesson. His summary in S133 may have been gratuitous; certainly he might have asked Teacher for her guesses about Timmy's response to her behavior instead of offering his own. Only later, at the end of S135, did Supervisor assume a less central posture. T134 interrupted Supervisor's process, but brought a common and important problem to the surface, namely, the impression of supervisory legerdemain. Supervisor's general decision to elicit some of Teacher's hypotheses and then his split-second decision to show her the section of his analysis, in which he noted precisely the same inference as that which Teacher had just expressed, were excellent gambits. His use of immediate events to demystify interpretive processes was most appropriate: alert, creative, and well intentioned. My enthusiasm for this section rests upon the premise that examination and interpretation of immediate experience, of shared experiences, and of concrete examples generates a more authentic reality, a more persuasive and credible representation of things than abstract rhetoric. Had Supervisor simply said the right things about the openness and logic of supervisory interpretations, he might have been neither as well understood nor as truly believed as his references to immediate experiences and real objects enabled him to be. His demurrer, in S143, incorporates exactly the point that I should have attempted to make under the same circumstances.

Teacher's query in T146 represents another common and important question in clinical supervision. In relation to Supervisor's verbosity, it must be said that Teacher managed to raise extremely provocative issues. One can sympathize with Supervisor's submission to the impulse to lecture, having been stimulated by such a question. This episode provides examples of how difficult technical abstention from information giving can become, assuming, as we might, that Supervisor would really have preferred to behave less didactically. To avoid playing a senseless numbers game or creating the impression that there is something inherently wrong with extensive statements in supervision, I must acknowledge, however, that when the substance of an idea becomes sufficiently complex, there is often no succinct way to enunciate it. The only important point to be considered in connection to long supervisory soliloquies is one that the supervisor made himself (S147), namely, ". . . it's still possible to imagine that from this kind of teaching pattern, where what Teacher wants [analogously, "what Supervisor says"] crowds out what the kids may want, the kids learn that value unconsciously—just from repeated experiences of the same kind."

S150, a request for playback, is a particularly good example of that technique because of where it falls in the dialectical sequence: immediately after a long expository episode (by Supervisor) and an assertion of understanding by Teacher. Implicitly, "If you know, then tell me" represents a neat device for avoiding glib or superficial "yeses" in supervision.

S154 through T157 is an interesting little interlude because of how clearly it reveals the fairly common tendency among supervisees to be excessively alert to signs that the supervisor is hiding something. The fantasy "He is not saying everything he feels about my teaching" is, perhaps, the most ubiquitous we have encountered in clinical supervision. It is particularly fascinating to perceive its operation in this case because there is so much evidence that demonstrates effective communication and relatively spontaneous and uninhibited behavior by the teacher throughout the conference. Rather than being overwhelmed by such suspicions, Teacher's cognitive machinery operated at a generally high level of efficiency. Nonetheless, in this instance, the common anxiety over "hidden secrets" asserted itself. Empirically, it seems, the role of supervisee heightens one's sensitivity to stimuli in this context just as the role of dental patient heightens one's sensitivity to dental pain: whereas I ordinarily am not braced against bicuspid electrocution, the moment I lower myself into the torturer's chair, my jump reflex is all set to fire.

S158 represents an appropriate variation of the basic sequence of supervision; instead of attempting to complete a relevant analysis and to plan for the next day's teaching, all in this first conference, Supervisor wisely abandoned that goal in favor of extending the issues at hand into an additional conference. It is often difficult to judge, in such situations, when it is time to stop, and difficult to determine afterwards whether a conference was terminated too early. In this case, having already managed to create an apparently successful beginning in supervision, Supervisor might appropriately have ended the conference at S158, with the decision to meet again the next day. As it appears, he chose to develop the concept "incidental learnings" further, for reasons about which we can only speculate.

By and large, supervision conferences tend to be too long rather than too short and, in my experience, failures are more frequently associated with the former problem than with the latter. Despite the fact that things continued to go well (as we can see they did in retrospect), I should say that Supervisor ran greater risks by continuing than I would have in his place: an appropriate relationship had been established; difficult substantive ideas had been communicated; teacher had withstood a critical examination of her teaching and had functioned well, cognitively, throughout; some key issues had been defined and related to the teaching; and although she betrayed certain anxieties and dependencies upon Supervisor, Teacher also displayed gratifying intellectual adroitness and autonomy, and, in all, an auspicious commencement had taken place. To quit while one is ahead is as apt a principle in supervision as in other human endeavors, and we should certainly not have quarreled with Supervisor's decision to do so had he made it at this point in the conference.

The episode from S165 through S177 represents a particularly vivid example of didactic supervision, that is, of the didactic component in clinical supervision, of supervision modeled upon teaching analogues. T178 through S183 is good supervision from several viewpoints: Teacher raised a provocative and important question; Supervisor's response acknowledged its quality and invited Teacher to perform the related inquiry. Rather than providing an immediate and direct answer either to T178 or to the question raised in T180, Supervisor correctly assumed that Teacher was competent to develop satisfactory solutions on her own, and made sure to provide a chance for her to do so. Only after Teacher had finally committed herself to a conclusion, did Supervisor provide appropriate consensus. One positive outcome of this pattern of supervisory behavior could be to teach, implicitly, that Supervisor is a figure who can provide or withhold consensus rather than act simply as an answer-giver. If, on the one hand, this short sequence might have been somewhat more efficient if Supervisor had answered Teacher's initial question immediately, on the other hand, their momentary loss of efficiency resulted, at least, in the outcome that the ideas finally formulated were Teacher's own and had been reached by Teacher's own energy and initiative. I prize this process in supervision and in teaching generally because I am convinced that, under normal circumstances, such an outcome is more inherently rewarding to the supervisee (or student) than being told—even, in many cases, when the supervisee has asked to be told.

T186 through T189 stands by itself as an amusing and significant vignette. I value its lesson to those supervisors (and neophyte counselors) who tend generally and fallaciously to assume that their supervisees (and clients) are too fragile to withstand authentic confrontation of their own behavior, particularly when that behavior incorporates weaknesses or problems of one kind or another. Time and again I have witnessed supervisors backing off, pussyfooting, equivocating, and using any of a million ways to avoid suggesting that something might be the matter, even when whatever was the matter was something superficial and, presumably, tolerable to accept by anyone not on the verge of suicide. It is not difficult to understand how a history of insensitive and punitive supervision may have created an excessively "human" counterpoise among modern clinical supervisors. Whatever the origins of such impotency, however, they must be overcome, not only because the supervision they generate is often too innocuous to accomplish anything useful, but also because the premise from which they arise is as false and, in fact, very much the same as the unfortunate premise that motivated crueler forms of supervision in the past, namely, that the supervisee is somehow inferior.

If, as the supervisor, I operate from an assumption of your inferiority and punish you by my supervision, you are not likely to become very much as a result of my participation in your work. But if, on the other hand, because I operate from an assumption of your inferiority but am a humanist, I do nothing but smile benevolently on your products, I am similarly not likely to be of much worth to you. If, by contrast, I proceed from the assumption that you are strong, resilient, intellectually potent, and the like, if, in other words, I allow myself to behave *honestly* with you and employ reasonable discretion in my manner of expression, then I think it is more likely that we will be in productive business and that our work together may eventually count for something.

In Mrs. Constance's case we do not know whether the supervisor of her student teaching was simply ignorant about teaching or whether she was a smiler or whether, because of her own emotional disabilities, she was incapable of discovering faults, owning her discoveries, and communicating them. We do know, however, by the supervisee's own testimony, that rather than having been pleased or flattered or reassured by her supervisor's "generosity," the discrepancy she sensed between Supervisor's evaluation of her teaching and her own misgivings about it produced a very opposite effect: Supervisor's proffered kindnesses created discomfort rather than pleasure and proved, consequently, to have done Teacher much less of a favor than her supervisor might have supposed. Although it may seem puzzling at first glance, Teacher's relief, this time around, at *not* receiving an "A" is not difficult to understand as a manifestation of healthy behavior. Had this supervisor hesitated to examine problems of her teaching, for fear of hurting her, Teacher's losses would have been enormously greater than her gains.

It is difficult to state the implications of this reasoning for supervisory practice because they obtain on so many levels: psychologically, philosophically, theoretically, technically, and so on. Most simply, I propose that while the clinical supervisor must be able to sense teachers' anxieties and to have some understanding of the effects of anxiety on human functioning, he must also recognize, first of all, that teachers are not a clinical population; that is, they are not normally weakened by serious problems that require very special therapeutic attention; and secondly, the existence of anxiety or of ignorance should not be taken as a "no trespassing" sign, as a danger signal, or as an indication that anything besides Tender Loving Care will provoke psychic disaster. Quite the contrary, my experiences seem to tell me that anxiety among supervisees is often *less* likely to be exacerbated by supervisory behavior which simultaneously recognizes its existence but also postulates an underlying integrity and strength, than by supervision that avoids honest confrontations of reality at all costs and runs away as though the supervisee were about to crumble. I should stress that this image of flight is not a strawman, no less among many counseling psychologists than among the ranks of clinical supervisors. T188 might usefully be inscribed above the portals of all teaching-training institutions.

Supervisor's decision to provide Teacher with a copy of his *observation* notes for study until their next meeting was considerate and potentially constructive. The closing episode of this conference seems to demonstrate two facts worth noting. The first is that autonomy and dependency, aggressiveness and passivity, strength and weakness, and rationality and irrationality are in no case mutually exclusive; the positive condition never necessarily precludes the negative one, or vice versa. On the contrary, such opposites often operate concurrently or in rapid succession in the same personality, in the same individual's unfolding behavior; and it behooves the clinical supervisor to anticipate such concurrences rather than to be confused or surprised by discovering them. The supervisor should eschew stereotyped characterizations of individual teachers that may blind him from elements of their behavior that he does not see because of their inconsistency with his prior sets.

The second point relates to S200–T203 and suggests that when supervisors reveal their own anxieties or doubts or guilts or misgivings in supervision, it is not uncommon for their supervisees to sense them and to rally to support their distressed supervisors. This phenomenon should, at least, be recognized, although the question of what to do about it could lead us in many directions. Perhaps there are times when it is not inappropriate for the teacher to feel some responsibility for helping the supervisor to deal with his own issues. On the other hand, however, one should not want generally to encumber supervisees with their supervisors' problems, assuming that they are apt to require considerable energy just to deal with problems of their own work and development. For the supervisee to have to worry about being supportive toward his supervisor seems somewhat inappropriate although, in the first case above, we should be less troubled by such an outcome than in most other cases.

CASE 3: A SIXTH-GRADE SOCIAL STUDIES LESSON

Background Information

THE TEACHER: Clara Smith

EXPERIENCE: Twelve years of intermediate-grade teaching; nine of them in her present position as sixth-grade teacher.

HISTORY OF SUPERVISION: Miss Smith's work at the Miller School began six months before Miss Lyons assumed its principalship. Although, at the time of her appointment, Miss Lyons had had more professional experience than Miss Smith, Miss Smith was several years older, having only begun her work in teaching after her invalid, widowed father, for whom she had cared for many years, died. From the moment of Miss Lyons' arrival, Miss Smith assumed a maternal, protective role, at first acquainting Miss Lyons with the building, then with its customs, and finally with her own perceptions of the other teachers, children, and parents. Coincidentally, Miss Smith's classroom was only one door from the principal's office, and before long, Miss Smith began to function as head teacher, or assistant principal, whether by explicit agreement or by unspoken ones being generally unclear to other members of the staff.

In their nine years of work together, these two developed an intense friendship, one that provoked resentment and criticism from various other workers in the school. Miss Smith maintained her dominating, maternal role; Miss Lyons, her dependent one. The two spent much time in each other's homes, vacationed together occasionally, and rode back and forth to work together daily (in Miss Smith's automobile). For the most part, both women's social lives were confined to their mutual relationship, although Miss Lyons also spent some time with another woman principal from the same school system, of whom Miss Smith was covertly jealous.

During the first three of four years of their colleagueship, Miss Lyons would visit Miss Smith's classroom twice a year, ostensibly to observe for the purpose of writing a semiannual evaluation, as principals were required to do for all teachers. By and by, however, Miss Lyons took to writing such evaluations without benefit of observation—this fact was bitterly resented by certain other teachers who, nonetheless, felt it to be unwise to say anything—with the consequence that Miss Smith received no supervision at all, not even by outward signs.

In the present school year, Miss Lyons had been transferred from her principalship at Miller School to a central office position, namely, Elementary Curriculum Coordinator. The schools were in flux. A new superintendent had taken office the year before and had begun to establish organizational and curricular innovations in the system. In various buildings, work was going on in programed instruction, nongrading, and team teaching. As the community expanded, its population became progressively more transient; it was not uncommon for young families to occupy a neighborhood for two or three years and then to move elsewhere; the turnover of teaching personnel reached unprecedented levels; many new teachers began to infiltrate the system; certain schools had begun to serve as practicum settings for teaching students from a neighboring college; a new department of pupil personnel services had been formed; teaching salaries had been upgraded, but only for entering teachers (the new salary structure was not retroactive and did not benefit personnel of Miss Smith's generation).

Senior teachers generally experienced a depreciation of morale, but many of them remained in their positions, nevertheless, having decided to stay put until retirement. Some of them adapted well to modern novelties, for example, by becoming teaching team leaders, members of professional study groups, and participants in "sensitivity training" programs being offered by the college; but others did not. Many of the latter group, including Miss Smith, tended to withdraw more and more from professional society and to become lonely, unvalued and isolated figures in the community. These teachers generally agreed that the system had betrayed them, that the innovations being instituted were merely momentary fads, and that the schools and the community had both begun to degenerate, partly because of the (ivory towerish) college's ascending influence on educational practices, partly because of the in-migration of "lower class" families (these were generally working class families from religious and racial minority groups), and partly as a result of their own disorientation in response to the dissolution of old families and old landmarks that had formerly been prominent and stable fixtures in their lives.

The news of Miss Lyons' promotion and transfer broke only several weeks before the fall term was to begin. As senior teacher, Miss Smith was asked to assume certain administrative responsibilities in the building until a new principal could be permanently assigned. For a while, Miss Smith cherished the fantasy that she might be promoted to fill the vacancy, but in early October someone else was hired for the job, a woman new to the school system who had served as an assistant principal for several years in a neighboring community. Early in the same term, Mr. Eugene Prentice, about whom more information will be included below, was appointed supervisor for the Miller School.

Her new job took Miss Lyons to another part of the city. Her hours were extended, and, for such reasons, she and Miss Smith saw little of one another during working hours. Neither were they able to ride back and forth from work together. Miss Lyons seemed to reject Miss Smith's social overtures with increasing frequency, often claiming to be too tired for evening visits and otherwise preoccupied during weekends. The two did dine together occasionally. Not only had the physical and hierarchical

distance between these associates been extended, but Miss Lyons
had seemingly entered into a courtship with a local widower, the
brother of the school district's business manager who was
himself, a businessman. Miss Smith violently opposed the
relationship, and although she generally managed not to refer to it
openly in her conversations with Miss Lyons, her feelings were
transparent and created serious tensions between the two women.

In many senses, one might suppose, Miss Smith felt stranded.
Her professional future in the school system was obscure. She was
dismayed by the changes occurring around her, particularly by the
advent of new educational practices about which she was ignorant
and from which she felt excluded. Her hurtful disappointment
about having not been promoted still smoldered inside her. And
worst of all, perhaps, was the virtual mourning she experienced for
the proximal loss of her dearest and only companion.

While formerly no special disaffection had existed between Miss
Smith and her students, all were aware of her growing irascibility
and unfriendliness. Parents had begun to register complaints about
their children's distaste for school and fear of their teacher.
Frustrated and disliked, Miss Smith appeared to be growing more
distant and more tyrannical in her relationships to the pupils. She
had begun to be annoyed by chronic gastric distress and by an
unending series of head colds, and her colleagues occasionally
remarked among themselves about how obviously Miss Smith had
aged during the current school year. Some wondered whether her
hair had grayed all at once or whether, perhaps, she had formerly
tried to disguise its true color but no longer troubled to do so. The
sudden absence from her life of the social diversions formerly
provided by Miss Lyons not only set her loneliness into sharp
relief but brought Miss Smith to a new and awful awareness of the
humdrum of her own existence. Superficial house cleaning, small
attention to her pet bird and to her plants, occasional shopping for
the few provisions she required, and many hours of inattentive
television viewing were the main activities of her after-school life.
Time had seemingly slowed down; her days and weeks of teaching
felt endless. Her acquaintanceships with neighbors were
insubstantial and unfulfilling. In the evenings, when lights came on
in her neighbors' houses and the streets turned quiet, she
sometimes wondered, "Where did my life go?" but such
preoccupations were only fleeting and she generally retired early
for nights of troubled and unsatisfying sleep.

PRESENT SUPERVISION: A clinical supervisor, Mr. Prentice
teaches some graduate courses for supervisors in the local college.
His chief assignment at the Miller School is to train the teaching

staff in supervision, to prepare the teachers to supervise one another in teaching teams that are to be established in the coming year, to teach them techniques for self-supervision, and to help them develop skills for working with student teachers, a number of whom have already been appointed to apprenticeships at Miller School.

Additionally, Mr. Prentice is supposed to provide supervisory assistance to members of the faculty, either by their own requests or according to his assessments of where such assistance might be indicated. According to the present arrangement, Mr. Prentice has no formal evaluative function. The new principal is still responsible for semiannual staff evaluations, and there is an understanding that Mr. Prentice is employed to train and to supervise and that he will neither participate in the evaluative process nor provide feedback to the principal that might be used for such a purpose. For herself, the new principal has chosen to employ self-evaluation by teachers as the major basis for her formal reports. Although the faculty does not fully understand or trust this new regime, it has uniformly resolved to take a wait-and-see attitude for the first year. Mr. Prentice, incidentally, has not exercised his prerogative to supervise any teacher he cares to. Instead, he has spoken formally and informally to the teachers, individually and in groups, about supervision and other things concerning them, and has only undertaken direct supervision when asked to. As it is, he has more than enough to keep him busy in the school.

His supervisory relationship with Miss Smith, only recently established, came about as the result of peculiar and, in certain respects, unfortunate circumstances. As it occurred, Miss Smith entered the Teachers' Room one day in early November while it was being occupied by a number of relatively new teachers with whom she generally did not associate. Realizing that she had blundered into enemy territory, Miss Smith would dearly have preferred to leave, but she felt awkward and unwilling to satisfy the others by obvious capitulation. Making the best of an unpleasant situation, she busied herself over a cup of tea while the "young Turks," as she thought of them, continued their clearly audible conversation.

One particularly outspoken member, who was known for her aggressiveness, had the insensitivity to remark that just about everyone she could think of had begun to take advantage of Mr. Prentice's supervision. Not incorrectly, Miss Smith assumed that the remark had been intended for her, and while she had no idea of whom Prentice did and did not supervise, she knew full well that she was one of the abstainers. An endless silence arose, and although her back was toward them, Miss Smith fancied, again correctly, that their eyes were upon her. Although it subsequently became a coughing fit, one might have supposed that one teacher's choking began as a suppressed snicker. Mercifully, the remark "Well, back to the coal mines" was followed by the group's prompt evacuation—"mercifully," because Miss Smith could not reasonably have taken very much longer to prepare her beverage.

As she felt her heat of anger and defenselessness rise, Miss Smith knew, all at once, that she must show them, that the lesser of all possible humilities would be to invite Prentice's attentions— *Let him do his worst*—as conspicuously (to her colleagues) as possible. She was amazed to discover her own terror, the terror of having to turn around, lest the room not be completely vacated. Even more, she was doubly amazed by her realization that having not done so for longer than could be remembered, she was crying.

Later on the same day, Miss Smith seized a public opportunity to solicit Prentice's assistance. For several weeks she met intermittently with Prentice to talk about professional irrelevancies which, much to her internal shame, she plucked from nowhere but represented as though they had some urgent and profound importance for her. Sensing her anxiety, but without full appreciation of what was happening, Prentice bided his time and willingly engaged in whatever dialogue Miss Smith generated. Inevitably he began to feel the futility of abstract conversation about exclusively hypothetical problems in teaching, and recognizing Miss Smith's ambivalence but failing to understand her motives, he confronted her with his own misgivings and asked if it might not make better sense for him to observe some of Miss Smith's teaching. The logic of his request was unimpeachable, and much to her dismay Miss Smith recognized that she had sprung her own trap and was helpless to retreat.

When it was no longer possible to procrastinate without attracting suspicion, Miss Smith named a day on which Prentice was to observe her teaching a social studies lesson. During Preobservation, Prentice recognized substantial agitation in Miss Smith's behavior, and although he could not understand precisely what she had in mind for the lesson to be observed, he decided that additional questioning might only lead to further anxiety and that it would be best to desist. Her description of how she wanted Supervisor to assist her was stereotyped and undetailed but, again, Prentice could find no way to provoke greater clarity and was reluctant to pursue the issue further: it seemed that the more he asked, the more incoherent her responses became.

Before the two parted, Prentice naïvely asked whether Miss Smith was certain that she wanted him to observe her on that day;

"naïvely," because Prentice still had no adequate insight into the emotional meaning of the drama that was unfolding. This query, intended to provide Teacher a way out if she needed one, produced the opposite effect: Miss Smith frenziedly protested her desire for supervision and, feeling trapped himself, this time by her vehemence, Supervisor closed the question directly. Doing whatever he could to reassure her, Prentice parted from Miss Smith quickly thereafter, confused and dissatisfied by what was happening, alarmed to find the word "hysterical" in his afterthoughts. By the time the appointed hour arrived, Supervisor was fully aware that to perform a sequence of supervision presently seemed contraindicated by Teacher's apparent duress, but equally aware that the effects of abandoning his commitment to do so might ultimately create worse damage. He felt that in the absence of more real and definite reasons for aborting the sequence, his only acceptable choice was to respect Teacher's expressed preference and to proceed as sensitively as possible thereafter.

Observation Notes

3) *A sixth-grade social studies lesson on the American Revolution.*
1. TEACHER: Two weeks from Thursday is a holiday. Does anybody know what it is? Yes, Mario?
2. MARIO: The 4th of July.
3. TEACHER: The 4th of July. What do we celebrate on that day—Nancy?
4. NANCY: There's a parade, and we stay home.
[Class laughs.]
5. TEACHER: What is the name of the holiday?
[No response.]
6. TEACHER: It's called Independence Day. Why was it called that? What does "independence" mean?
7. CARL: Freedom?
8. TEACHER: Freedom? What do you mean?
9. ARNOLD: Like liberty.
10. TEACHER: Raise your hand when you want to speak, Arnold. What do you mean, "like liberty"?
11. ROSE: [Raises hand.] I know.
12. TEACHER: Rose—don't call out. Just raise your hand. What is it Rose?
13. ROSE: It's the day when we became free from England.
14. TEACHER: When, two weeks from Thursday?
[Class laughs.]

15. MARIO: Oh, I know.
16. TEACHER: Raise your hand, Mario—your hand. And stand up when you talk so everybody—Lucy, are you with us? What is that you've got?
17. LUCY: My arithmetic homework.
18. TEACHER: Put it away Lucy—this isn't arithmetic—or haven't you noticed?—Mario, tell us what you know.
19. MARIO: It was when we signed the Declaration of Independence that made us free from England. After the Revolutionary War.
20. TEACHER: Are you sure it came after the war?
[No response.]
21. TEACHER: All right, boys and girls. That's something for you to look up. Write it down—was the Declaration of Independence signed before or after the Revolutionary War? Where would you go to look that up?
22. CARL: The encyclopedia.
23. TEACHER: Where else?
24. ARNOLD: Our social studies book.
25. TEACHER: Yes—or to the library. How would you find it in your social studies book?
26. CHRISTINE: In the index.
27. TEACHER: How? That tells me where. I asked how.
28. RICHARD: You look it up—
29. TEACHER: Did I call on you? Lucy—what is it now? Can't you pay attention? What are you doing? If you have something that's important enough to say to Anna, maybe you'd like to share it with all of us. Would you?
30. LUCY: No.
31. TEACHER: Then keep your mouth closed and pay attention and maybe you'll learn something. . . . How do you find it in the index, Lucy?
32. LUCY: Alphabetically.
33. TEACHER: What would you look for, Lucy? . . . Class? . . . Anybody?
34. MARIO: [Raises hand.]
35. TEACHER: Yes Mario?
36. MARIO: Under "Revolution" or "Declaration of Independence."
37. TEACHER: Did you hear him class? Say it again, Mario.
38. MARIO: Under Revolutionary War or Declaration of Independence.
39. TEACHER: Yes. Perhaps someday you people will learn to speak in complete sentences.
40. IRENE: [Raises hand.]

41. TEACHER: What is it, Irene?

42. IRENE: Well, I thought that we sent the Declaration of Independence to England, and that the king got mad about it, and that's why they went to war.

43. TEACHER: That question is out of order, Irene—it's homework to look up, remember? Now take out last night's homework, and let's go over it.

[The pupils noisily produce their homework assignments (some of them obviously have not done the work); there seems to be more physical moving about and general confusion than the situation warrants.]

44. TEACHER: All right. Settle down. Lucy. Come on, come on. Who can remind the class what the assignment was?

[Many hands are raised; some pupils are half out of their seats, waving vigorously at Teacher.]

45. TEACHER: Carl?

46. CARL: [Reading from his assignment book.] "In what ways is planning a trip like planning a revolution?"

47. TEACHER: All right. Did everybody hear Carl? "In what ways is planning a revolution like planning a trip?" All right. Close your notebooks and let's see what ideas you have. Anyone?

[Silence.]

48. TEACHER: Many of you will be going on trips with your families after school is over. What, uh, where are you going?

49. NANCY: Canada.

50. TEACHER: What other places?

51. MARIO: Atlantic City.

52. ARNOLD: The Jersey shore.

53. TEACHER: Yes. How do you know that you are going on a trip?

54. MARIO: Because my father called for reservations.

55. IRENE: We talked about where to go.

56. TEACHER: "Called for reservations" and "talked about where to go." What do we call these things?

57. RICHARD: [Inaudible.]

58. TEACHER: Yes, what have you been doing?

59. IRENE: Discussion.

60. TEACHER: Yes, what else?

61. IRENE: Deciding.

62. NANCY: Agreeing.

63. MARIO: [Inaudible.] . . . what clothes to take.

64. TEACHER: Writes the word "thinking" on the board.

65. IRENE: Discussing.

66. TEACHER: [Writes the word "planning."]

67. TEACHER: Yes, we must plan before taking a trip, just the way the colonists had to plan before undertaking a revolution. All right. Why don't you discuss this among yourselves? [At this point, Teacher goes to her desk and begins to sort a number of index cards upon which she has written various questions. After several minutes, she addresses the class.]

68. TEACHER: Who can tell us something about the Committees of Correspondence? [No response.] Anybody? [No response.] How many of you know Adams and Paine and Hancock? [No response.] Are you satisfied with your knowledge on this? [Pause.] Do you feel you know all that you should about these men? [Several negative responses.] Are you happy with how much you know? [Teacher then looks directly at Supervisor and says: "I'm rewording it for them."] All right. I have written down some questions on these cards that you are to answer for tonight's homework. [Teacher reads questions from the cards.]

Now let's see . . . . [Teacher begins to walk among the children, distributing one card to each child. At one point she hands a card to Lucy, takes it back, and hands the same card to Arnold, who sits directly in front of Lucy. As she does so, Teacher says to Lucy: "This one is too easy for you."] All right, boys and girls. You may spend the rest of this period [there are approximately ten minutes remaining] going to the library to do research on these questions.

69. CHRISTINE: Miss Smith, do you want us to hand in last night's assignment?

70. TEACHER: No, that won't be necessary. Just put it in your notebook, and I'll check later to see who didn't do the work.

Analysis: Salient Patterns

REJECTS PUPILS' RESPONSES (sometimes even when they are directly relevant): T5, T10[6], T14, T27, T29, T39[6], T43, T64[7], T66[7], T68[8], T70.

SARCASM; DOUBLE STANDARDS: T14, T18, T29-31 (T indulges herself in behavior that, presumably, she would not tolerate

---

[6]T accepts substance but rejects accompanying behavior.

[7]Rejection may be implicit when what T writes on board is different from what P's are saying.

[8]What is the implication for Arnold when T hands him card that she has just called "too easy" for student beside him? What is implication for everyone, when T says to S, "I'm rewording it for them"?

from P's, for example, "Tell us what you know; Keep your mouth closed . . . ; That tells me where, I asked how; and so on." Such comments also imply rejection.)

BROKEN PROMISES: P's required to do homework, but T ignores it (more rejection); P42 response that P might reasonably have felt would be satisfactory, rejected for extrinsic reasons; No follow through on P-P discussion—what was its purpose?

LOSS OF FOCUS; DIGRESSIONS: Many little lessons, for example, T10-12 (hand raising); T16 (hand raising and standing); T16 (Lucy); T21 (sources of information); T25-39 (uses of index); T29 (Lucy); T31 (Lucy); T39 (complete sentences); T41 (homework; out of order); T48-66 (trips—poor analogy; a seeming distraction); T68 (seemingly random questions; for P's, only sense of continuity may be "What these questions have in common is that we don't know their answers.").

AMBIGUOUS DIRECTIONS; CHANGING RULES: Rules of classroom behavior should be taught separately, or in some manner that avoids interrupting topical inquiry. Rules seem obscure; keep changing after game has begun: P4, Nancy calls out and is *not* reprimanded; T10, rule: raise hand; T12, rule: raise hand, and don't call out; T16, rule: raise hand, don't call out, stand for recitation; T39, rule: respond in complete sentences (which T, herself, does not always do); very *risky* and confusing.

AMBIGUOUS DIRECTIONS (ABSENCE OF REASONS):   What is the purpose of "discussing" among themselves? What are they supposed to discuss? Why do homework? Why take out last night's homework and then not pay any attention to it? What is the purpose of going to the library? What specific "research" are the P's supposed to perform? If going to the library is for the sake of answering q's on cards, must P go if he knows answer without looking it up?

RITUALISM: In the absence of reasons, most of these tasks are performed ritualistically: "I'll check later to see who didn't do the work."

REWARDS: There is seemingly no way to win. Not producing is unacceptable; products are generally rejected.

GENERAL: Lesson is dominated by T, her questions, her sequence of activities, and so on. P's treated all the same, except for receiving different q cards (why does T give cards that she thinks P's *cannot* answer rather than vice versa?) Intellectually weak: planning for a trip and planning a revolution are more unalike than similar; similarities are so superficial as to be totally unconvincing. T's frequent glances at S and one direct comment to him suggest anxiety (self-consciousness); ditto for scattered quality of lesson; frequent assertions of T's authority; heightened sensitivity to "discipline"; it sometimes seemed that T was using the lesson and the pupils as a medium for communicating to S; more as means than as end. T seems more concerned with outwardly "correct" behavior than with quality of learning (or its outcomes). Likely incidental learnings for P's: "Whatever I do is likely to be punished; T doesn't like or respect me; I cannot predict either what is going to happen next or how T is going to react; It is hard to know what is good and what is bad."

STRENGTHS: (?) No salient + 's. Am I prejudiced by my own anxiety? T did prepare some materials in advance, but their quality and their use were poor.

Strategy: Alternatives

1. Use conference mainly to provide emotional support. Instead of detailed analysis, help T to express her anxiety and allow anxiety to stand as reason for lesson's failure: it is not unusual for excessive anxiety to create a loss of focus, a loss of intent. Try to define future strategies that can help to reduce T's anxiety (for example, to exclude observation for a while or to delimit its objectives so that it feels safer—maybe to observe Lucy). Try to identify things S may have done to produce such agitation.

2. If T is feeling better, work on future planning; that is, if she says lesson failed because she was nervous, eliminate analysis and move on to plans for the next lesson.

3. If T is feeling better and *wants* to examine the lesson, it might be safest to deal with relevant but somewhat depersonalized (intellectualized) issues, for example, the use of analogies (trip–revolution), rather than "sarcasm."

4. If T seems too upset to talk, eliminate conference with mini-mal loss of face, for example, "Why don't we postpone this meeting for a little while, perhaps tomorrow morning." (If T *can't* talk, that condition will probably embarrass her. Try not to make it any worse.) Let T end the conference quickly if she needs to, but avoid pushing her out; let her go, if necessary, but do not abandon her. Name another time to meet or ask her to initiate a meeting at her convenience.

5. If it seems likely to work, make this an open conference. Unless it will frighten her even more, get T to raise questions and identify issues that she would like to talk about (that is, from the lesson, pertaining to the future, and the like).

[NOTE: It seems clear, from these descriptions of his thinking, that Supervisor expected (1) that T would regard her own lesson as an essential failure, (2) that she would speak of feeling "nervous," and (3) that she would gladly seize "nervousness" as an excuse for her failure, if given (implicit) permission to do so.]

The Conference

1. TEACHER: Hi, Gene, may I come in? [T arrived 15 minutes early.]

2. SUPERVISOR: Clara. Hello. Yes, come in, please. Have a seat.

3. TEACHER: Um, thank you. [Pause.] Well?

4. SUPERVISOR: Uh [arranging his papers], let me get my notes together, here—uh, how are you feeling?

5. TEACHER: I'm feeling fine.

6. SUPERVISOR: Good. Umm, well, uh, we didn't really make very very definite plans about where to go at this point. Was there anything special about the lesson that you'd—

7. TEACHER: I think that was an excellent lesson. [Pause.] I think I was excellently prepared for that lesson. But the children. Have you ever seen anything like it?

8. SUPERVISOR: How do you mean?

9. TEACHER: [Shouting.] They're unprepared. They're supposed to know things by the time they get to sixth grade—and they don't. They haven't taught them things they should know.

10. SUPERVISOR: "They" being—

11. TEACHER: And the materials I am given. They don't know how to read. Some of them, in there, only read on a third-grade level. They can't read the materials I've been given.

12. SUPERVISOR: Some of them can't read sixth-grade material.

13. TEACHER: That's right. And lazy—these children do not want to learn. They are rude—restless—I'm supposed to teach them things they have not been prepared for properly. They should already know about the Committees of Correspondence. They have not been properly prepared.

14. SUPERVISOR: It must be very frustrating to—

15. TEACHER: No, they just don't care; they're not interested in learning.

16. SUPERVISOR: I meant for you.

17. TEACHER: Oh, right, yes. Very frustrating. [Pause.] Their background is meager; totally inadequate for the kind of

brainwork I would expect. I was told that the children were ready––

18. SUPERVISOR: By whom?

19. TEACHER: Uh, that they were ready for sixth-grade work.

20. SUPERVISOR: You mean the teacher they had last year—

21. TEACHER: And it's not just in social studies. It's in everything, in every subject.

22. SUPERVISOR: Umm.

[Pause.]

23. SUPERVISOR: Do you think you were misinformed delib—

24. TEACHER: I had the impression that there might not be enough cards to go around, or, um, I mean, you know, I could read it faster than they could for themselves. But I didn't have my good reading glasses, so that made it a little clumsy to operate. I enjoy reading orally, and the children usually enjoy listening to me.

25. SUPERVISOR: I'm sorry, Clara. I'm having trouble understanding. I mean, it's almost the end of the year, and I'm not quite clear on where, uh, on when it was that the children did not cover material they were supposed to and on who it was that created false impressions about what they were ready for, ready to move on to.

26. TEACHER: Well, I don't know that I want to name names. But I have only had these children for two weeks in social studies.

27. SUPERVISOR: Two weeks?

28. TEACHER: Yes, didn't you know that? We started out, this term, having the children get their social studies from Miss Kuntz and Mrs. Rooney, and I did arithmetic and science and reading. And then it was decided that there was too much time lost moving the pupils back and forth, so now we each have them for everything.

29. SUPERVISOR: I'm sorry, no. I was not aware of that arrangement. So, if I understand correctly, your children were going to other rooms for social studies up until a couple of weeks ago?

30. TEACHER: That's right.

31. SUPERVISOR: And you're saying that they weren't adequately prepared by the other teachers and also that the other teachers led you to believe that they were ready to go on with certain material—

32. TEACHER: But they are not ready.

33. SUPERVISOR: Umhm. I wonder why communications broke down, or why there seems to be such a difference between—

34. TEACHER: So you see, they're just not prepared. They have no background.

35. SUPERVISOR: In anything.
36. TEACHER: It's very disappointing.
37. SUPERVISOR: Including the subjects they have had with you—since the term began?
38. TEACHER: [Giggles.] Yes, and that's another thing. These children are just not motivated to do schoolwork. They are a different element, very lazy and unconcerned about schoolwork.
39. SUPERVISOR: It must be very difficult to deal with children who seem that way; I imagine there is little pleasure in it for you.
40. TEACHER: Things certainly have changed.
41. SUPERVISOR: Changed?
42. TEACHER: Oh, well. [Pause.]
43. SUPERVISOR: Uh, Clara, I wonder if it might help us to get a handle on these things, that is, to understand these problems better, if I read through my notes out loud, you know, and tried just to recreate the lesson as it took place—so that we could examine it in somewhat more detail.
[No response.]
44. SUPERVISOR: Would that be useful, do you think?
45. TEACHER: Oh, you want me to say whether we should do that?
46. SUPERVISOR: [Laughs.] I don't know that I *want*—sure. How would you feel about doing it that way?
47. TEACHER: Very fine.
48. SUPERVISOR: OK. Let me start from the top. You begin things by asking the question, "Two weeks from Thursday is a holiday. Does anybody know what—"
49. TEACHER: This is not a fair test.
50. SUPERVISOR: Pardon?
51. TEACHER: I say, this is not a fair test of my teaching. I know this content very thoroughly, and I have had much experience in teaching; and, as I've said, I think this lesson was perfectly planned, but the children were just unprepared for it.
52. SUPERVISOR: Clara, I don't know whether "test" is quite—
53. TEACHER: Do you feel there were things wrong in what I did?
54. SUPERVISOR: Wrong?
55. TEACHER: Yes.
56. SUPERVISOR: Yes, I do. [Pause.] So what?
57. TEACHER: I don't know what to say.
58. SUPERVISOR: Look, Clara. I'd be less than honest if I tried to make you believe that I don't have feelings about the teaching I see. I mean, the truth is that I make value judgments all over the place. But my point is, well, I guess there are several points. One is that how I *feel*, personally, about a lesson—at least in certain respects—doesn't make a damn bit of difference. By deliberate

choice, I'm not in a position where I could do anything about it in any case. I don't rate, I don't do formal evaluations—I mean, you know this already. A second—another thing, I just about take it for granted that there will always be problems in a lesson. You could call them "weaknesses" or things that are "wrong" or even "failures," it doesn't matter. I generally expect that such things will exist in almost any lesson because teaching is tough. It's complicated. It's a very complicated business. And where I see the use of this kind of supervision is in examining just what did go on in a lesson, not as an end in itself, but for the purpose of clearly defining whatever problems existed in order to be on top of things when planning the next lesson. I don't feel that there's any sin attached to weaknesses or that they should be embarrassing to examine. On the contrary, I think, if there's any sin at all, it's in one's failure to search for the problems, to bring them to the surface in order to do something about them.

Well, uh, I'm sorry, I didn't want to make a speech. I just do want to say, honestly, yes. I do feel there were things that went wrong in the lesson. I hope we can look at them closely and try to work things out for tomorrow's teaching, and the next day's, and I hope, too, that I can say this to you without your imagining that I'm expressing negative feelings about you. I mean, when I say yes, I think certain things did go wrong in the lesson, I'm not saying any more or less than that. [Pause.] Just one last thing, then I'll shut up. And that is that if ever we try to deal with things that went right or things that went wrong, their rightness or wrongness won't exist just because I say so. What I mean is that if I feel that something's the matter, I also feel responsible for expressing all of the thinking and reasoning behind that value judgment: not just, "It's good or it's bad, because *I* say so" or, for that matter, because *you* say so or anybody else.

[Pause.]

59. TEACHER: No one has ever said that to me before.

60. SUPERVISOR: That—

61. TEACHER: That there was anything wrong with my teaching. [Pause.]

62. SUPERVISOR: This is the first time?

63. TEACHER: Yes.

64. SUPERVISOR: And it makes you feel—

65. TEACHER: [Pause.] Relieved. It seems very surprising to feel that way.

66. SUPERVISOR: You experience a sense of relief in being confronted directly by the suggestion that there were weaknesses in your teaching? And you feel *surprised* to discover that feeling of relief?

67. TEACHER: Yes. I have been afraid of this, but it doesn't seem so terrible right now.

68. SUPERVISOR: Yes. I understand what you're saying. [Pause.]

69. SUPERVISOR: It's not a test, Clara. It's a search.

70. TEACHER: A search, yes, a search. I'm not sure I can, uh, perhaps if we just dealt with some of the things, rather than with everything in it.

71. SUPERVISOR: Sure, if you'd like. [Pause.] Is there anything in particular?

72. TEACHER: Uh, no, uh, I thought perhaps there was something *you* felt was important.

73. SUPERVISOR: All right. I think what matters, in the long run, is what *you* feel is important, but I can raise some questions; and then if any of them seem like something we should examine to you, uh,—

74. TEACHER: Yes, that sounds very good.

75. SUPERVISOR: OK. Let's see [glances through notes]. Yeah. Uh, about this analogy between trips and revolutions, that is, between planning for a trip and planning for a revolution. I wondered—

76. TEACHER: That came from the manual. Such a clever idea. I thought, "Now why couldn't I have thought of that myself?" A lovely idea, what with vacation time coming so soon and the children's experiences of planning for trips and vacations.

77. SUPERVISOR: This idea came from the manual?

78. TEACHER: Yes, I have it right here [Teacher reaches for the manual, which was among the things she brought to the conference]. Here it is, "Ask the pupils whether they can see relationships between planning for a vacation and planning for a revolution."

79. SUPERVISOR: Ah, yes. I think I understand better now. Umm. Clara, let me state two questions that may sound very much the same and ask if you can find any important differences between them. Uh, let's imagine that we're pupils in the class and the teacher asked the question, "Can you see relationships between planning for a trip and planning a revolution?" Now, let's try again to imagine the teacher asking a somewhat different question, "In what way is planning a revolution like planning a trip?" Would these questions have different effects upon your thinking?

80. TEACHER: It sounded the same to me.

81. SUPERVISOR: Um, they are very much the same. I'm sorry. The difference I'm wondering about is between a question that asks whether relationships *actually* exist and another question that asks in what ways two things are alike.

[While Supervisor was expressing this question, Teacher shifted posture so that her face was no longer directly visible to him. Her outward appearance, from Supervisor's vantage point, suggested that she was studying something from the manual while Supervisor was speaking. Supervisor's statement was followed by a substantial silence which Supervisor at first attributed to Teacher's examination of his ideas: thinking time. As the pause lengthened, however, Supervisor became uncertain about what was happening and suddenly imagined (correctly), although he could not see her face, that Teacher was weeping.]

82. SUPERVISOR: Clara?

83. TEACHER: [Sobs audibly.]

[Supervisor reaches into desk for a box of tissues which he passes silently to Teacher and from which Teacher selects liberally. A prolonged period of nose-blowing, and the like follows.]

84. SUPERVISOR: Clara?

85. TEACHER: [Sobbing.] I'm not ready yet. [Begins to weep again.] [Long pause.] I'm sorry.

86. SUPERVISOR: Clara, what is it?

87. TEACHER: I'm very, very sorry.

88. SUPERVISOR: No, no. If anything, I am sorry for not sensing how troubled you feel. [Pause.] Do you want to talk about it?

89. TEACHER: I don't understand what's happening. [Pause.] I feel very bad.

90. SUPERVISOR: Is it your health?

91. TEACHER: I don't know. I have been upset recently. Some putrid apple sauce, I think. No, not my health so much. [Sobs.] I feel confused; so many things are happening. [Pause.] I am fearful.

92. SUPERVISOR: Afraid, fearful.

93. TEACHER: Yes, except, except I am—I don't know of what.

94. SUPERVISOR: You're not sure what it is that frightens you?

95. TEACHER: That's it, yes. And, like just now, I suddenly find I am crying or perspiring; I've never had such feelings before.

96. SUPERVISOR: A great deal of feeling has come to the surface; feelings that seem unfamiliar? New feelings. Yes. And new experiences: having your teaching observed; talking about your work.

97. TEACHER: I suppose that's a part of it. I feel faint.

98. SUPERVISOR: Can I help you?

99. TEACHER: No, not now, I don't mean. I mean I have been feeling faint, very tired, disorganized.

100. SUPERVISOR: Have you seen a doctor? A physician?

101. TEACHER: Not in years. Our family doctor died some years ago, and I'm not sure I know any doctors here any more.

102. SUPERVISOR: You don't—

103. TEACHER: I've been meaning to have a physical examination, but it's like a lot of other things—I just don't seem to get around to it.

104. SUPERVISOR: I am new here myself and don't know of anyone personally. If you're looking for a physician, I think maybe Dr. Gephardt could give you some leads; or perhaps Dr. Flynn.

[Dr. Gephardt, a psychiatrist, had recently begun to spend one half-day each week in the schools as a consultant to teachers and pupil personnel workers. Mr. Flynn, a psychologist, directs the pupil personnel services for the school system, which incorporates the health services.]

105. TEACHER: It would never have occurred to me to approach either gentleman.

106. SUPERVISOR: Not at all. I know that either one of them would be very happy to speak with you, to be helpful in any way possible. Have you met Dr. Gephardt?

107. TEACHER: Very briefly, once, at a luncheon. He seems nice enough.

108. SUPERVISOR: Yes, the people here seem to like him. I like him.

109. TEACHER: Perhaps I *should* see a psychiatrist.

110. SUPERVISOR: In such distress, you know, feeling confused, frightened, I shouldn't hesitate myself to take advantage of such a man; he is available. [Pause.]

111. TEACHER: That's not an easy thing to do.

112. SUPERVISOR: No, it isn't.

113. TEACHER: [Sighs.]

114. SUPERVISOR: Is there anything that I—

115. TEACHER: I feel as though I am not a part, left out of things. I have always enjoyed teaching so much, and now, somehow, I feel left out of everything. Maybe it's my own fault in some way. Things happen so quickly and time goes so slowly, quickly and slowly.

116. SUPERVISOR: Changes occur so rapidly that your own work, your own days seem to slow down by comparison; everything moves faster and you feel that your own days slow down, get longer.

117. TEACHER: Yes, yes. That's how it seems.

118. SUPERVISOR: It is disorienting.

119. TEACHER: Yes, very.

120. SUPERVISOR: A lonely feeling.

121. TEACHER: [Crying briefly.] Perhaps you know that Miss Lyons and I are very close friends.

122. SUPERVISOR: Yes.

123. TEACHER: And her transfer has made this place seem—empty, I guess.

124. SUPERVISOR: I have had similar feelings of loss when very dear friends moved away; yes. [Long pause.] I wonder whether, in this setting, what things I might do to help.

125. TEACHER: You've been very kind to let me talk to you this way.

126. SUPERVISOR: We can talk often.

127. TEACHER: I really believe that helps.

128. SUPERVISOR: Talking?

129. TEACHER: Just talking, yes; letting things come out. I have never really done that.

130. SUPERVISOR: Letting things out, yes. And talking to other people here as well, you know, reaching out.

131. TEACHER: I do believe I will call Dr. Gephardt.

132. SUPERVISOR: He's a good man.

133. TEACHER: Yes.

134. SUPERVISOR: I'm wondering what we might do, right here in this situation, to make you feel less isolated, more a part of things.

135. TEACHER: I don't know; I don't know. I feel very ashamed.

136. SUPERVISOR: Ashamed?

137. TEACHER: Oh, not really that, perhaps, but very saddened by the way things have developed here.

138. SUPERVISOR: Feeling apart from things is a sad feeling.

139. TEACHER: [Sighs.] I have given many years of service here; I have been thought of as a good teacher; a respected teacher. The children have always enjoyed having me as their teacher; I have gotten along well with the parents.

140. SUPERVISOR: You feel that you have professional strengths, the strengths of experience.

141. TEACHER: Definitely, yes I do, although not everyone is ready to acknowledge . . .

142. SUPERVISOR: The younger teachers—

143. TEACHER: They do not respect experience. I suspect they think I am ready for the glue factory. They exclude me. They think of themselves as being "modern," the latest ideas, and all that.

144. SUPERVISOR: You don't think very much of them.

145. TEACHER: No. Oh, they're bright, all right, they're smart enough. But they move too fast; they haven't much experience.

146. SUPERVISOR: I wonder if a part of the "exclusion" you encounter may reflect their, uh, may be in response to the way you feel about them.

147. TEACHER: I don't see what you—

148. SUPERVISOR: I mean, you know, if you don't like them very much they must surely sense that. I'd imagine that they respond to your dislike by the exclusiveness you speak of.

149. TEACHER: You think I am at fault?

150. SUPERVISOR: Certainly not altogether, but almost surely a part of this problem, don't you think?

151. TEACHER: I haven't really thought about it.

152. SUPERVISOR: I wonder if friendlier feelings might not develop all the way around if you had some opportunities to work together with some of the newcomers on some project or other.

153. TEACHER: You really think so?

154. SUPERVISOR: I don't know; who knows? It might be worth a try.

155. TEACHER: I think that's something I should think about.

156. SUPERVISOR: I would agree; I think you should think about such possibilities. And then, whatever you decide, the two of us might talk about it. Perhaps I could help to get something started.

157. TEACHER: You are very kind, Gene.

158. SUPERVISOR: I am very eager for you to feel better about what goes on here; to play a happier part in it; to feel more satisfaction.

159. TEACHER: [Sighs.] Yes, perhaps. Well, thank you.

160. SUPERVISOR: Thank you for coming in.

161. TEACHER: We must keep talking.

162. SUPERVISOR: I am happy to.

163. TEACHER: I'm sorry to have made such a display.

164. SUPERVISOR: I—on the contrary, I am glad you felt able to express your feelings. Such things can't stay all bottled up.

165. TEACHER: No, I suppose they can't.

166. SUPERVISOR: Shall we meet again later this week?

167. TEACHER: Please, yes.

168. SUPERVISOR: [Consulting desk calendar.] How's Friday, same time?

169. TEACHER: That's fine, yes; that's good. [Pause.] Will you want to watch me teach then?

170. SUPERVISOR: I think that's something we can talk about, you know, the meaning, the feelings attached to observation; to talking about one's teaching.

171. TEACHER: Yes.

172. SUPERVISOR: It might be best to talk first and then reach decisions about what to do, you know? I don't think observation just for its own sake or without some prior agreements about it is likely to be very helpful.

173. TEACHER: No, yes. Yes, we can talk about it. [Glances at watch.] I must get back; the children are coming back now.

174. SUPERVISOR: Yes, take care of yourself. I'll see you Friday.
175. TEACHER: Goodbye, Gene. Thank you again.
176. SUPERVISOR: Goodbye, Clara, take care.

CRITIQUE OF CASE 3

Clinical supervision is hardest when the teaching it addresses is bad. And although almost any sample of classroom teaching is likely to incorporate strengths and weaknesses simultaneously, occasionally one does encounter a lesson that is so poorly conceived and so badly executed that there are either few positive elements to detect or the potential utility of its positive features is suppressed by its basic and pervasive weaknesses. Supervision of such teaching is difficult, first of all, because of the psychological stresses that inevitably attach to examinations of inadequate behavior. The emotional affront represented by a critical (and negative) analysis of work in which, more often than not, the teacher's very identity is bound up, can be profound: for the teacher to experience and for the supervisor to witness. No supervisory situation is more likely to arouse guilty torment. No problem in supervision sparks greater self-doubt or more tortured self examination for the supervisor than the anxiety, on such occasions, that his analysis of the teaching has been biased, that, in essence, a negative halo effect has blinded him to virtues of the teacher's performance.

Besides stresses of self-examination, the social tensions involved in administering a conference that seems likely to be hurtful inspire little appetite in most supervisors I have observed, even those with the most highly developed capacities for maintaining clinical distance. While many of us have rational understanding that it is not or should not be inherently punishing to have one's professional deficits examined constructively, when the chips are down, very few of us are immune to the feelings of hurt and rejection and loss of esteem that generally accompany such experiences. Despite our ideals about such things, we have not managed to expurgate pain or shame from failures and probably will never be able to do so completely.

Supervisor's analysis of Miss Smith's teaching was thoroughly bleak; it failed to disclose positive sectors in which he might have concentrated the conference if that seemed necessary. There simply were no comfortable places to which retreat was possible; nothing much in the teaching that might provide relief. I have examined and reexamined this protocol and although, from time to time, my impressions of the lesson have shifted—its various elements have moved back and forth, for me, from "figure" to "ground"—I remain in basic agreement with its initial analysis.

Likewise, Supervisor's strategies for the conference seem well construed, despite the fact that his expectation that Teacher would employ "nervousness" as an excuse was misguided. Whether his invalid assumptions can be attributed to the absence of relevant information or whether they reflect some naïveté relating to "secondary anxiety" is moot. Our present interest centers around a phenomenon that is not uncommon in clinical supervision; namely, that with all due preparation and forethought, the supervisor can miss some critical understanding of the teacher or of the situation and may, consequently, find himself flying by the seat of his pants. This case provides an excellent illustration of just such a predicament and offers various examples of clever salvaging of elements of strategy that may have seemed generally inapplicable in the conference's opening episodes.

The writing may already have begun to appear upon the wall in T3: Teacher's "Well?" already suggests defensive girding. T5, "I'm feeling fine," is even more ominous, vis à vis Supervisor's primary strategy. Despite its social sound, S4 (". . . how are you feeling?") was Supervisor's first attempt to encourage Teacher's confession of anxiety, upon whose existence his plans for the conference largely depended. Having failed to get what he expected, Supervisor shifted, in S6, to his fifth alternative, the "open conference." T7, "I think that was an excellent lesson," was totally unexpected (as far as we can infer from Supervisor's notes for strategy) and marked the commencement of Supervisor's pilotage. Perhaps, on second thought, Supervisor was naïve in failing to anticipate a defensive maneuver of this kind: that Teacher would engage in emphatic denial had simply not occurred to him.

S8, S10, and S12 were aimed partly at clarification, but served the additional advantage of buying time (assuming that Supervisor needed some time to recover from his surprise). By S14, Supervisor had collected his wits sufficiently to employ the objective of his first strategic alternative, namely, to offer sympathetic support, as he attempted to do by reflecting Teacher's frustration. Teacher's level of resistance is illustrated by her misinterpretation in T15, that is, by her apparent unreadiness to experience sympathy in Supervisor's behavior.

One might imagine that besides the disarming effects of Teacher's claim to excellence, Supervisor's efforts to rearrange his thoughts were impeded by the ambiguity and confusion of her remarks: plainly, it was difficult to understand what she was talking about. Her feelings were communicated well enough, but her facts were jumbled and difficult to put together. In S25, Supervisor finally decided that Teacher's seemingly random associations were not helping to clarify his understanding; if anything, the more she went on, the harder it was to interpret her meaning. His attempts to isolate Teacher's issues and to understand them one by one were only momentarily effective. By S34 her agitation had apparently intensified again, and her remarks became more scattered. The disorganizing effects of anxiety, unsurprisingly, became manifested in essentially the same manner in both the lesson and the supervision conference: if the teaching suffered because of Miss Smith's tendencies to jump from this to that very rapidly, her behavior in supervision had the same quality. By S39, Supervisor had abandoned his prosecution, having found, by that time, that his questioning was unlikely to resolve inconsistencies or to reduce other puzzling aspects of Teacher's conversation.

As in S14, Supervisor's intent in S39 was simply to express sympathy, to respond to Teacher's discontent, even though he could not understand her facts or implications fully. Although Supervisor could not have recognized its meaning at the time (being ignorant of the personal crises in Teacher's life), Teacher's response in T40 marked her first expression of the problem, at bottom, that really troubled her. I suspect that Supervisor's failure to pick it up, besides being attributable to his ignorance, was also the result of what had come before: Teacher's remarks had been so generally cryptic that one more cryptic statement would have been difficult to identify as being particularly important. It would reflect a very high level of sensitivity indeed, for a supervisor (or anyone) to recognize the expressive nuances that make one remark in a hundred especially significant.

If it is reasonable to assume some cause-effect relationship between the ideational and emotional content of Supervisor's remarks and the character of Teacher's responses (and vice versa), then we should not find it difficult to understand why Teacher chose the particular moment she did to get down to cases. S39 had been especially empathic—more poignant for Teacher, one might guess, than Supervisor could have known. T40 can be understood, in one sense, as its payoff.

Although S43 may have been psychologically inappropriate, that is, in the context of Teacher's actual feelings and experiences, from Supervisor's frame of reference it was sensible to employ a strategy of structuring. Presumably, Supervisor's reasoning suggested that to counterbalance Teacher's scatteredness and unstructure by recreating her lesson descriptively, he might provide a dialectical structure for their conference. He did not catch the significance of Teacher's failure to respond to S43 nor, apparently, of her unhappy capitulations in T45 and T47. T49, however, was inescapable and probably saved the remainder of the conference from becoming a monumental misunderstanding. T53 and S56 together, are probably the most important exchange of the conference and illustrate what is perhaps the greatest strength of Prentice's supervision. Teacher's own testimony (T65) tells us that Supervisor's direct and honest response, "Yes, I do [feel there were things wrong]" helped to deintensify her defensiveness and to reduce her stress, paradoxically, perhaps, by creating the very catastrophe that she feared the most. By "attacking" her teaching, Supervisor relieved the terror that her teaching would be attacked. It is not insignificant that, at the same time, he had already communicated sympathetic acceptance to Teacher at least twice in this conference.

S58 is difficult to evaluate. On the one hand, its length, its didacticism, and its egocentric qualities are disturbing: even Supervisor sensed these problems (". . . I'm sorry, I didn't want to make a speech") and apologized for his behavior several times. On the other hand, however, the remainder of the conference does not suggest that any damage was done in this episode and, to the contrary, leads us to speculate that Supervisor's behavior in this instance created positive effects. For one thing, it provided extensive time for Teacher to find her feelings and to compose her thoughts. Even if she had not been listening attentively to Supervisor's words, his long monologue provided respite. It is also true, substantively, that Supervisor was attempting to communicate important and appropriate understandings; and if, in fact, Teacher *was* listening to his ideas, she would certainly have made useful discoveries about Supervisor's outlook and about its implications for her own relationship with him.

Besides pointing out that Supervisor's substantive ideas in this section are consistent with our values and concepts of clinical supervision, I am unable to generalize many implications, from his behavior, for the professional activity of other supervisors. Perhaps it is enough to conclude that on certain occasions techniques that one generally avoids are likely to be productive and that, consequently, clinical supervisors should energetically avoid becoming methodologically hidebound. While freedom from technical discipline or, at least, from technical orthodoxy, can easily result in blunders, it may also be necessary in order for clever, spontaneous, and useful supervision to exist in such problematical conferences as this one. As a personal matter, I should prefer to risk technical incorrectness if that risk enables me to be professionally potent at critical moments.

It is probably just as well for me to express my ambivalence toward analyzing the remainder of this case openly. One way or the other, I am affected by it, and its effects will become apparent to the reader. Although I feel some authorly responsibility for examining the bits and pieces of this conference, I am also put off by an opposing feeling, namely, that some objects have such powerful inherent beauty or meaning that their analysis is gratuitous and may only distract from their appreciation. Of the case in question, I feel that there is too much possibly to say, and at the same time, it may be sufficient to say very little. While I can comfortably refer to one or two salient technical features and try to focus the reader's attention upon them, I could not possibly address each emotional subtlety or talk about each manifestation of humane sensitivity that appears in the material. Fortunately, it seems unnecessary to do so. I feel confident that if the reader concentrates upon the remaining episodes of this conference intensely enough, he will find more meaning there—a good deal of it will be inarticulate meaning—than he might as a result of anything anyone else could say about it.

T59 suggests that what Teacher heard more than anything else during Supervisor's long address was an indictment of her teaching. S64 was an attempt to bring Teacher's feelings to the surface, this time in relation to a specific event (namely, S56) instead of in more general terms, for example, as in S4. S66 is a reflection of feeling, intended partly to clarify Teacher's immediate experience and partly to provide time for her to assimilate her discoveries, to discover additionally that Supervisor recognized her feeling, and, partly as a result of observing Supervisor's acceptance, to develop some level of self-acceptance around the feelings that had begun to surface. S68 was also intended to communicate acceptance and to provide emotional support. S69 represented an attempt to shift into the future tense and to do so optimistically: while "tests" may be failed, "searches" connotes hopefulness.

T70 seems to have caught some tentative wish to move ahead, but also seems to express a need to do so gently, as if, in effect, Teacher were saying, "Yes, let's try to go on, but softly, because I feel weakened." S71 and S73 are good responses in two respects: they both embody symbolic votes of confidence, namely, an expectation that Teacher has the wisdom and at least the latent strength to take control of her own examination. At the same time, S73 demonstrates a willingness to help Teacher to get started by providing simple structures within which she might begin to operate. In other words, while S73 demonstrates Supervisor's willingness to help, it does not seem to communicate the implication that attempts at helping sometimes do, namely, that the necessity for helping arises from the supervisee's incapacities to make it on his own. It is the difference between helping because one is *unable* and helping because one *is* able.

Supervisor's choice of issues in S75 reflects his third strategic alternative: to deal with relatively academic issues (the aptness of an analogy) rather than with more volatile personal ones (Teacher's use of sarcasm). In T76, Teacher has apparently regressed toward the same patterns of defensive behavior that she had manifested earlier: externalization, denial, and the like. S79 is logically sound and employs a modified role-play technique. T80 is an expectable response in light of the fact that Teacher had already missed the subtle differences that Supervisor was attempting to distinguish. S81 simultaneously accepts Teacher's inability to appreciate the point in question and tries to make that point more intelligible. What went wrong? One might readily guess that Supervisor had underestimated the intensity of Teacher's emotional distress. It seems equally possible that he misjudged her intellectual power, for even without emotional interference, the concept that Supervisor was addressing had been framed in highly abstract and subtle terms and might simply have not been comprehensible to Teacher, even under more ideal conditions.

In any event, although we may allow that in relation to the knowledge existing in his own frame of reference Supervisor's behavior during this episode was not technically unsound, it is equally true that because of things he did not know, and was unable to sense adequately, his strategy proved to be wrong. At least it is clear that he did not get what he wanted to from this line of inquiry because Teacher broke down before it could be culminated.

From S82 onward, although, as it is always, one is able to perform an analysis of the supervisory techniques employed, my conviction becomes stronger that the effectiveness of what took place resulted primarily because of what Supervisor was as a human being rather than, so much, as a trained supervisor. It is very difficult to imagine that any degree of technical training could have generated his behaviors in the following episode, had they not been underlain by a great compassion, by notable personal courage, and by innate self-confidence. In such demanding moments, it is all but impossible to separate Prentice's qualities as a man from his learned, clinical proficiences. One is unable to explain this supervisor's personal constitution. But the existence of his personal strengths must be postulated in order for any analysis of his technical behavior to be worthwhile.

Technically, his toleration of prolonged silence (T83) and provision of facial tissues were precisely the behaviors required by this situation. Nonverbal communication can be fully as eloquent and as powerful as words and, in this instance, probably was. The supervisor often does not need to provide verbal reassurances that it is all right to take the time to compose oneself, if his behavior communicates such reassurance without talk. Similarly, Supervisor does not need to say that he wants to help when providing a box of tissues demonstrates that fact. Although his timing in S84 was off, the typescript suggests that Supervisor consciously tried to hold his verbal intervention for the proper moment; he did not assert pressure for Teacher to recover or force her into conversation prematurely.

S92, S94, and S96 are reflections of Teacher's feelings, intended to communicate Supervisor's understanding and acceptance, and to provide clarification and time for Teacher. It is interesting to note that whereas, in S104, Supervisor's references to the school psychiatrist and psychologist were made, presumably, because of their knowledge of medical services, Teacher's response in T109 was to the real or imagined implication that she should seek psychiatric consultation. Although one might postulate that Teacher's emotional aberrations had arisen primarily from physiological (possibly menopausal) causes, it might, nonetheless, have been useful for her to have spoken out her problems with Dr. Gephardt. S110, in my judgment, was an extraordinarily fine response. Supervisor might easily have backed off from Teacher's half-facetious remark about seeing a psychiatrist. He might, just as easily, have attempted to reassure her that she was really in good shape and that nothing as extreme as a psychiatric consultancy should be necessary. But rather than to have interpreted Teacher's statement as being facetious, Supervisor dealt with it seriously and approvingly. Moreover, he gave Teacher consensus (S112) that, indeed, such a step would not be an easy one to take. I am impressed by Supervisor's sobriety in this instance and by his maintenance of professional responsibility at a moment when he might, so readily, have succumbed to social awkwardness by offering gratuitous and hollow reassurances.

T115 seems to show that instead of being frightened off by this suggestion, Teacher felt encouraged to ventilate more of her distress. S116 represents another highly competent reflection of Teacher's feelings and ideas. The same is true of S118 and S120. Supervisor's self-reference in S124 was intended to provide an indication of understanding and some reassurance that Teacher's feelings of isolation and loss were not unique. It is difficult to judge whether her failure to produce a verbal response should be interpreted as an indication of this technique's failure or success in this instance.

One is struck by the contrast between Supervisor's expressed commitment to follow through with Teacher (in S126) and the more common pattern of hit-and-run that typifies most educational supervision. S134 provides a good example of the priority, in clinical supervision, on culminating supervisory inquiry in active planning for future activity. Under ordinary circumstances, such planning would generally pertain to future lessons. In this case, although lesson planning would have been inappropriate, if not impossible, Supervisor was nevertheless able to shift tenses and, in this respect, may be credited with an ingenious application of this supervisory principle to an uncommon and only obscurely parallel situation. S128, S130, S136, S138, S140, S142, and S144 are additional examples of reflecting and clarifying responses.

Supervisor took rather large risks in S146, but one suspects that his actual observations of Teacher's behavior in the conference and his own use of nonverbal communication (which is not recorded in our case material) enabled him, somehow, to calculate them adequately. Two features of his remarks are noteworthy. Although he did raise the possibility that Teacher's own actions contributed to the problems of which she was complaining, he did not actually accuse Teacher of anything unworthy. It is also true that Supervisor turned rapidly from this idea to optimistic projections of future activities that might improve Teacher's situation. In T153, Teacher seems to have caught some spark of hope and, if anything, Supervisor's restraint in S154 represents a most useful avoidance of lavish reassurances which might only have damaged their later relationship. S164 might have been deliberately intended to reinforce Teacher's decision to consult with the school psychiatrist.

In S170 and S172, Supervisor renegotiated the contract. In effect, the members agreed to defer specific decisions concerning the use of observation in supervision until reasons and protections had been developed for its support.

This case has been included here primarily to illustrate an example of clinical supervision under stress, and of the artfulness with which the discipline's techniques and the supervisor's human resources can become productively integrated in supervisory action. Although Prentice's behavior is not impossible to fault, I am comfortable in having presented this case as a demonstration of good supervision and would be thoroughly delighted if, in practice, supervision were never less competent than this.

Taken together, the three cases we have examined provide an array of technical behaviors that should, at least, express the flavor of clinical supervisory conferences and illustrate the conceptual domain, the framework of educational values, and a variety of coping mechanisms that clinical supervisors may employ in their work.

VII

Stage 5: Methods for the Post-Conference Analysis (Postmortem)

Perhaps the most telling mark of a practitioner's commitment and fitness to perform his professional work is his readiness to have such work performed for his own benefit, by other competent workers, on appropriate occasions. I should be wary of placing my trust in a counseling psychologist who rejected psychotherapy as an adjunct to his own training and development, or a teacher who abhorred the role of student, or a surgeon who resisted surgical treatment of his own maladies, when the requirement for such treatment was supported by medical opinion. I feel this way particularly about educational and psychological disciplines and, most particularly, about clinical supervision. If what's good for the goose is inadequate for the gander, in this field, then something is the matter, for it is all but impossible to imagine a rational double standard that could free supervisors from the necessity of being supervised themselves.

I have already pointed out that supervisory postmortems originally arose in situations where group supervision was being practiced and where, consequently, it was an easy matter for supervisors' work to be observed and analyzed by other supervisors reciprocally. Under such conditions, the models of supervision that we have been examining in relation to instruction could be applied to supervision, with little need for alteration. In most scholastic settings, supervision is not conducted in groups, although the current expansion of team teaching, especially in the elementary schools, creates possibilities for multiple supervision that should be considered carefully by modern school administrators.

For the present, however, we must conceptualize possibilities for reflexive supervision designed to fit existing situations in which, generally, supervision is conducted by one supervisor and involves only one teacher at a time. Although various arrangements can be imagined in which teachers, and even the pupils, participate in supervising the supervisor—I think that supervision's future urgently requires these innovations—for the time being and for practical purposes our question might be, simply, of how supervisors might supervise themselves on a regular and systematic basis.

Procedurally, the most useful device we have found for self-supervision is to tape-record supervision conferences and, along with whatever notes (for example, on observation, analysis, and strategy) are taken in the process, to use such tapes as the objects of analysis. Once the data have been collected in this fashion, the supervisor's operations upon them are essentially those he employs when considering classroom data. Because there is no necessity to plan a conference, and so on, the postmortem represents a highly abridged process, involving only an analysis of the supervision that has taken place and planning based upon such analyses.

Once again, Supervisor works from the assumption that the repetitive patterns in his professional behavior constitute its most potent features; those components that are most likely to lead him toward successes or failures. But intuitively, it seems clear from the very beginning that Supervisor's analysis of his work will not feel or proceed as though he were examining just work, that is, just anybody's work—for once he begins to employ his skills reflexively, he must face the problem of distance more energetically than he would ever be likely to have to in relation to teachers' work. I should say, in a word, that the principal problem of self-supervision *is* distance; the problem of maintaining sufficient objectivity to perform an analysis that is likely to be worth something. The task is doubly difficult because at the same time that Supervisor must strive to be objective, he is also turning his attention toward his own behavior and looking at *his* products in very fine detail. What could be more difficult than to maintain distance in an activity that requires intense concentration upon one's own behavior?

I don't know of any methods per se, that is, of "methods" in the ordinary sense, that can be described for use in the postmortem. I think our immediate problem is more to capture the sense of Supervisor's difficulties in this stage of the sequence and to find some rules of thumb that might help to keep his efforts productive. Most of the ideas I am about to express have arisen from my own personal experiences in supervision; and although I have frequently discussed such things with other supervisors, it is hard to know, in the end, whether my personal processes are idiosyncratic or not: no matter how conscientiously we try to share our experiences of flavor, who could say, when we were done, that the special way in which my buds register chocolate is anything like the way in which yours do? Nonetheless, we must try for common understandings even while recognizing that the limitations of words may betray us.

Basically, my own efforts to stay straight in self-supervision consist of the following general maneuvers. I try to establish a condition of unselfconsciousness by listening casually to enough tape to become somewhat bored with it. By now, I have listened so much to my own tapes that this problem gives me little difficulty, although every so often I feel trapped, again, by a narcissistic fascination with my own voice, my own words, my own wit and cleverness, or my own abysmal mistakes (self-pity is easily tapped for me); and, at such moments, I find it useful either to abandon listening or to listen so much that the love affair becomes jaded, at which point, disenchantedly, I can commence serious listening.

I try to be aware, particularly, of episodes in the supervision about which I feel very positively or very negatively. Working from the assumption that strong evaluative feelings tend to be global and to incorporate halo effects, I watch my own temper rise and fall and try to pay particular attention to those episodes about which my feelings seem least equivocal. As I listen the second time (or third), I pay special attention to Teacher's words and inflections and try very hard to discipline myself from projecting feelings upon him. I try, in other words, to break free from my own feelings—for example, that at some particular moment I had been particularly supportive or accepting or instructive or punitive—and listen to *Teacher's* responses to see what clues they provide about how Teacher was actually responding to my behavior, or feeling about things generally. Even after this kind of effort, possibilities of self-deception remain, but at least one has tried to see things as realistically as possible. In my own work, I am blessed by the availability of many like-minded colleagues upon whom I frequently call for collaborative analysis of critical episodes: I ask them to listen cold and to tell me what they hear. More generally, however, I go *directly* to the source when I feel that it is important enough to matter and that it will not interfere with what we are after in the supervision, and replay problematic episodes *for the teacher* to learn better about the significance they may have carried for him. Clearly, no such method is foolproof, although, just as clearly, it is sometimes very useful to take such pains, especially when they protect the supervisor from proceeding on false assumptions concerning the teacher's experiences in supervision.

Besides listening with special acuity to hot spots and cold ones, I try to stay alert to long passages of tape that feel flat and featureless. In my work with neophyte counselors, I have found, repeatedly, that when my supervisee tells me that his client is not producing "significant" material, that he is flat, that nothing much is happening in the counseling, it emerges, more often than not, that flatness is in the ear of the listener and that what has actually been flattened by anxiety or defensive blocking of one sort or another is the counselor's perceptual apparatus or his level of intellectual energy available for finding the significant meanings in his client's behavior. Finding no reason to assume that I am uniquely immune to this phenomenon, I try to overcome my sleepiness by forcing attention to gray episodes. When I find my mind wandering, I try to set it straight again by listening and relistening to the episodes it has wandered from until I feel relatively certain that I have heard whatever there is to hear and that I have found whatever I am likely to find in them. For me, this form of self-discipline is the most difficult of all; the problem of sitting still and being alert when all the rest of me wants to go fishing or to sleep.

Just as our analyses of teaching behavior generally require us to search for likely incidental learnings by trying to assume the pupils' frames of reference, as they experienced the lesson, I try, in the postmortem, to use the same techniques for calculating my effects upon the teacher. My constant question is, "What might Teacher have been learning at any given moment in the conference as a result of my supervisory behavior?" And again, the unremitting problem is to keep as distinct as possible a difference between what *I* would have learned, had I been Teacher, and what, indeed, *Teacher* might have actually experienced.

In connection with incidental learnings, I try, especially, to stay alert to certain questions that have proven critical in many post-conference analyses:

> *Where does the locus of initiative for supervisory inquiry tend to be?* When either Teacher or Supervisor consistently initiates supervisory issues while the other member does not, the imbalance of initiative may signify unproductive processes tending, for example, to reinforce resistance to inquiry or excessive dependency upon the supervisor for structure and direction.
>
> *What kinds of rewards tend to be provided?* Supervisory behavior may be modified appropriately if it should appear, for example, that Supervisor's intended rewards are not experienced rewardingly by Teacher; that rewards tend to be more social than

substantive; that an implicit expectation of punishment has become established as a motivational element in Teacher's work; that initially potent rewards have become ineffectual as a result of excessive employment; or that, except in the supervisory interaction, Teacher experiences a paucity of rewards in his professional work and is at some loss to conceptualize activities from which they will be generated.

What is the proportion of questions in each member's dialogue (and what are the questions' formal characteristics)? A preponderance of questions may reflect avoidance of problem-solving activity. Excessive questioning by Supervisor may create a feeling of "interrogation." Excessive questioning by Teacher may reflect an inordinate dependency upon Supervisor for answers. Questions' formal structure may be identified as a source of frustration, inefficiency, or, on the other hand, of positive achievements in supervision.

Whose products are most abundant in the conference (for example, who authors whatever plans are laid for future teaching)? Especially when Supervisor is the actual inventor of teaching plans, evaluation strategies, and disciplinary techniques that Teacher subsequently employs, he may, as it frequently happens, begin to confuse his enthusiasm for his own products with objective appraisal of Teacher's performance and fail to perceive deficits in the sufficiency of Teacher's technical behavior.

Does either member's behavior become stereotyped? In addition to reward patterns, other elements of supervision may become stereotyped. When supervisory procedures become ritualistic, or established as "traditions," their utility is almost bound to decline. We have generally found it useful, in postmortems, to examine the question of whether any activity, in either the teaching or the conference, has seemingly taken place "as a matter of course."

How abundant are explicit rationales and reasons for value judgments and for decisions affecting future work? For either Teacher or Supervisor to proceed, regularly, on the basis of unexamined value judgments and decisions, would oppose the rational analysis that clinical supervision has been invented to establish more securely in the teaching profession. Supervisor should never teach, incidentally, that the goodness or badness of specific techniques is sufficient to determine on wholly subjective bases, for example, in reference to the simple fact that either he or Teacher likes them or dislikes them.

How likely is it that semantic confusion or the ambiguity of language generally has created illusions of agreement or disagreement? Reference to this question has frequently led to the decision to employ playback techniques more extensively in future supervision conferences.

When I have done the job fully and have prepared my supervision (of the teacher) by planning explicit substantive and process goals and have, additionally, specified my goals in behavioral terms as well as in the form of cognitive outcomes, then I am in the best possible shape to undertake a productive postmortem unless, of course, it became necessary to quit my plans during the supervision conference. But even in the latter case, presumably, my goals are likely to have been superseded by other goals rather than to have been forfeited to aimless wandering. In any event, the existence of specified outcomes is very handy for evaluating actual outcomes. At least such prior goals generate a structure within which it is relatively efficient to evaluate what took place; a set of more or less delimiting categories in which to focus examination. Even when it is possible to refer to *a priori* goals for analyzing the supervision, and to employ them, essentially, as evaluation criteria— this can be done most efficiently if *criterion behaviors* have also been stipulated in advance—it behooves the supervisor to follow the question of what outcomes occurred, irrespective of goals. Sometimes unexpected outcomes are more useful and productive than planned ones. It sometimes appears, however, that while planned outcomes have been achieved, other elements of the supervision have produced cancellation effects or interference or, in some manner, have operated at cross purposes to the supervisor's explicit intent. Most commonly, such static takes the form of negative process learnings incited concomitantly with intended substantive learnings.

Although it is possible to perform a postmortem without having tape-recorded the supervision, it is generally clear that to do so is more difficult, less efficient, and less trustworthy than with analysis of tapes. The more memory work required, the more distortion will occur, and the less valid will be the processes and outcomes of Supervisor's self-analysis. Although I do not mean to suggest that in the absence of recorded data the supervisor should give no afterthoughts to what he has done, there is little room to doubt that the more actual data are available, the more decent are Supervisor's chances to achieve something useful from his efforts. Planning for the next sequence of supervision often begins in the postmortem, inescapably so when Supervisor unearths puzzles whose solution requires Teacher's participation.

In actual practice, not even the most committed supervisor is likely to have enough time or psychic endurance to postmortem every sequence of supervision in which he functions; nor, one suspects, would it be necessary or useful for him to do so any more than it would be good to apply our complete model of clinical supervision, in all of its procedural detail, in every instance of supervision. Such scrupulosity would quickly produce diminishing returns. As in most other human and professional endeavors, the question becomes to determine how often and how much and at what moments a potentially useful activity should be undertaken. I have not found any certain answers, but I think there are guidelines that can be followed.

I think, for example, that to build some protection against avoiding self-analysis regularly in just those relationships or at just those moments at which it might be most critical to undertake, the clinical supervisor should discipline himself to perform the postmortem, in full dress, at some arbitrarily decided interval, for example, in conjunction with every fourth or fifth sequence of supervision performed. More rationally, depending upon his purposes, Supervisor may decide to employ a postmortem at the conclusion of a supervisory cycle (if he is interested, generally, in keeping watch over his professional development) or, depending on the difficulty and complexity of the supervision in question, to do so with special rigor during the initial sequences in a cycle. However he decides, it goes without saying that the postmortem is most likely to succeed when it involves the participation of a second supervisor, if only because, under such conditions, Supervisor is relieved of some of the terrible burden of keeping himself honest.

Unless there are important contraindications, I am especially enthusiastic about the idea of having the teacher who is being supervised fill the role of Supervisor's supervisor at propitious moments. First of all, no one is more likely to have pertinent information about Supervisor's effects than the teacher he has affected. Secondly, and I see this as a pregnant proposition for research, I am becoming progressively more convinced that one measure to relieve some of the old status anxieties of supervision, to cut across its real and imaginary hierarchies, to enhance Teacher's feeling of dignity in the supervisory relationship, to enable Teacher to gain higher degrees of objective distance on his own work, and to keep Supervisor fully aware of the taste of his own medicine, is to create precisely such role-reversals on a regular and dependable basis. One bonus I see in this strategy is that, among other things, Teacher stands to gain some supervisory competency by such an arrangement and, consequently, stands to become a more potent and valuable member of his faculty in that respect. It is easy enough to envisage such collaboration in connection with the second case we examined above. Perhaps a more sobering test of this image is to ask what the implications of such an arrangement might be for the teacher in the third case we have studied (Clara Smith).

While there is no clear-cut methodology for self-supervision, neither should the postmortem be understood simply as good intentions and ritualistic motions. It is not a rite or a penance or an absolution or a nicety. It should be a time for professional self-examination and management that exists for the profession's good: for the supervisor's own growth and development no less than for the teacher's protection and advantage. It is probably true that every man must work out the incentives and tools of self-examination for himself and that no man can chart the engagement that should occur for all men as they search to be better. Although these limitations may be inevitable, it is nonetheless frustrating to be unable to do much more than to express these wishes and simple injunctions to clinical supervisors, in this context, presently.

VIII
Problems[1]

PART 1

The proportions of space devoted to the various sections of this book are apt to create a false impression of how our work in clinical supervision has developed historically and of how its current issues are balanced in the minds and in the activities of workers in the field. In my own experience, this discipline began conceptually: as models and rationales for practice and as methodological constructs. It began, in effect, as ideas and images and reasons. From conceptualizations, I moved to practice, in which my basic motive was to explore the applicability of the ideas I had assembled about what supervision should be and how it should work. This phase of activity, which is still in progress, was very much like the shakedown trials of a new rocket. Two things began to happen: I began to develop more concrete under-standings of how the supervision we had dreamed about would actually take shape in practice, and I began, very quickly, to discover that various elements of the existing model were unessential and that other, new elements ought to be incorporated, back at the drawing board.

---

[1]All references in this section to clinical supervisors' behavior arise from our observations of clinical supervisors with whom we have worked directly.

Most important of all, although the bulk of our original thinking seemed to survive these trials, many of our ideas acquired connotations and implications that we had not anticipated in advance.

In its current development, clinical supervision has entered a third phase (even while Phases One and Two are still operating), in which, rather than to explore what the model looks like in real life, my major preoccupation is with problems—difficulties, puzzles, hazards, weaknesses, and the like—that are generated by this approach and which may prove, ultimately, to be unexcisable concomitants of the discipline. The sense in which I suspect that the proportions of this book may be misleading is that the *most* of what exists, presently, in clinical supervision, *is* its problems. And among the manifold problems it embodies, there is a large subset that we might just as well call its mistakes. One cannot really begin to appreciate where clinical supervision has been or where it is going without a vivid sense of the mistakes it makes, the errors it has committed, and the predicaments that confront its practitioners.

This section is intended to bring such elements to life and is motivated by several purposes. Although the point must surely have been demonstrated by my writing thus far, I can think of no better way to drive home the understanding that clinical supervision, while its future may be bright, is presently no panacea for educational reformers, than by showing, candidly, some of the things that go wrong. I hope that one result will be to attract more minds to its development. I also hope to increase other workers' efficiency and to enable them to make better beginnings in this field by proceeding from the assumption that to be forewarned is to be forearmed, even though I am fairly convinced that each individual supervisor must inevitably learn from his own blunders and from the vicissitudes of his own practice.

Instead of using extensive case materials this time, I will proceed from stage to stage of the supervisory sequence and, in turn, will describe the most common problems we have encountered in each of them. Where it seems potentially useful, I will illustrate the problems in question by short excerpts of supervisory dialogue and accompanying explanations of the significance they carry for me. Many of the issues to be addressed in this chapter have already been touched upon from time to time in the writing above.

For the most part, I will try to limit this examination to problems which, if they do not actually "inhere" in clinical supervision, are, at least, commonly experienced by clinical supervisors. It is hard to distinguish among problems of supervision that antedate the models expressed in this writing—problems that arise, culturally, in almost all instances of human interaction, and problems to which our models themselves give rise. Perhaps such distinctions are superfluous, inasmuch as clinical supervisors must cope, somehow, with whatever problems present themselves, irrespective of their sources. Nonetheless, in this chapter, I should like to avoid becoming involved, on the one hand, in inquiries pertaining to fundamental psychological issues in human relationships, and in human development, for example, problems of transference and countertransference, problems of identity, problems of authority, and problems of self-definition, *as theoretical problems in psychology;* and, on the other hand, in problems of school administration and logistics, for example, of rating and formal evaluation, in the economic problems of supervision, in scheduling problems, and so on. Although clinical supervision can be treated academically, I am primarily interested, for the moment, in taking a concrete and pragmatic approach to this topic and in avoiding treatment that is more theoretical than it has to be in order to project vivid images of the professional lives we lead and the difficulties that confront us in daily practice.

We may draw confidence from experiences that have proven that many common problems of clinical supervision may be prevented from arising when they are identified and examined *a priori*. Personal experiences have also strengthened my belief that, in all likelihood, no systematically encountered problems of this discipline will ultimately defy solutions formulated from the collective knowledge of practitioners who are committed to its perfection.

STAGE 1: PROBLEMS OF THE PREOBSERVATION CONFERENCE

The worst mistake that could occur during Preobservation happens, curiously, to be the most common one that clinical supervisors commit in practice, namely, to unnerve Teacher so badly, just before his class, that his adequacy becomes impaired and his lesson is weakened. Of all the things that supervisors might do to undermine teachers' confidence and equanimity before class, the most common I have observed is to introduce new elements into the teaching plan that are unassimilable in the remaining time or to raise questions about the plan, that is, to attack it, when too little time remains for the teacher to take corrective measures.

It is not difficult to understand the impulses that generate such errors. In some cases, supervisors seem unable to avoid exercising their analytical muscles. Their avidity for unearthing ambiguities, plural alternatives, and dubious underlying assumptions is difficult to check. Some supervisors, like some artists, don't know when to stop and persist in adding a final stroke which, rather than enhancing their product, muddies it. Some supervisors are unable to resist the impulse to control or to direct and, even when common sense indicates it would be best to leave well enough alone, seem forced to assert their influence without considering the probable consequences. Psychological problems of this order are manifold and seem unnecessary to delineate in further detail.

Other causes, although they certainly incorporate psychological variables, seem, more characteristically, to arise from the supervision itself. For example, one feature of supervisory collaboration as we conceptualize it is that Supervisor owns some measure of Teacher's successes and failures; he is invested in Teacher's performance, and although he cannot claim responsibility for it, he should be able, nevertheless, to rejoice in Teacher's triumphs and to share Teacher's frustrations. With such involvement, it sometimes occurs that Supervisor wants Teacher's success too badly; he wants it so much that he tries to refine Teacher's plans, right up to the finish line. His mistake, in this behavior, is not to realize that although his last-minute conceptualizations of the lesson may be wonderfully ingenious or creative, despite his powers of expression, he is unlikely to be able to communicate his visions, in complete detail, in very little time, unless unusually great rapport exists. Over and over again, I have observed frustration among supervisors and have experienced the same defeat myself, when a beautiful image became distorted by Teacher's implementation and when the principal cause of the distortion proved to be that Teacher never really possessed the same picture as his supervisor. Such discrepancies are much more likely to arise as a result of hurried communication (such as in the preobservation conference) than of the painstaking, careful planning that should take place, if at all, during supervisory conferences.

A related problem is that when, for one reason or another, such conferences have not culminated in refined plans, supervisors sometimes feel driven to compensate for yesterday's weak planning by a surge of architectural activity in today's Preobservation. A third difficulty, not unrelated to these phenomena, is that supervisors sometimes make the wrong decision in relation to whether it would be more useful to protect Teacher from troubles that seem likely to result from his existing plans (such premonitions often occur near the last moment) by attempting to modify them, on the one hand, or leaving things as they are in order not to disturb Teacher's equilibrium, on the other. The problem of calculating these risks and of deciding between them is rarely simple; and although mistaken choices can be forgiven, they may, nevertheless, be most troublesome.

Another common problem of this stage is that although Teacher has explicit needs that could be satisfied efficiently in Preobservation, for example, to practice a series of questions or to test some sequence of activities, Supervisor's own priorities on business supersede them. In such circumstances, Preobservation may be unsuccessful not, so much, because of what the supervisor does, but as a consequence of what he fails to do:

> SUPERVISOR: All set to go?
>
> TEACHER: Pretty much. Uh, I'm not quite sure, at this point, whether to use the diagramming worksheet or the information sheet first, and I thought—
>
> SUPERVISOR: Umm. You know, it occurred to me while I was driving in this morning that, on this question of actually how to work process goals into the teaching, uh, I have some case materials that show some lessons done by teachers who . . .

In this example, while the issue Supervisor has isolated and the method he has conceived for working with it may be sound, his timing is off. His own intentions have, apparently, dulled his responsiveness to Teacher's expression of a problem that would have been appropriate to treat at that moment.

Sometimes supervisors create unnecessary anxieties by raising last-minute questions which, although they may be valid, generate uncertainty rather than calmness.

> SUPERVISOR: Ugh! I just thought of something. I don't think you should be worried that the kids won't understand how to record their results. I mean, that might happen, but we've been through this enough times that I don't think you should really worry about it.

Until Supervisor had expressed all of this, in fact, Teacher had *not* been anxious.

An occasional error, in Preobservation, is for Supervisor to prolong discussion at this stage unnecessarily. Experience suggests that perfunctory conversation before observation, followed by some free moments in which Teacher can simply be by himself for whatever meditation or activity he requires, is more likely to energize his teaching performance than involvement in unessential dialogue with his supervisor. In my own work, I have sometimes felt compulsively obliged to conduct a preobservation conference—after all, the model prescribes it—only to discover, afterwards, that Teacher really should have been using the time we burnt up to run off mimeographed materials he needed for the lesson and that he felt inhibited from asserting his need for fear of offending his supervisor or, somehow, of breaking the rules.

A more subtle and profound problem of Preobservation is that of separating one's (Supervisor's) own optimism or anxieties for the lesson from those of the teacher who will actually have to perform it. It sometimes happens that my own doubts and fears lead me to assume that Teacher experiences the same feelings with the same intensity as I do, and, consequently, I become involved in offering gratuitous reassurances and protections which, at best, waste time and energy and, at worst, instill doubts in Teacher that would have been better to avoid. More commonly, I observe that supervisors tend to make the opposite mistake, particularly when they feel some special investment in the lesson to be taught—perhaps because of having played an important part in its conceptualization—namely, that their own buoyancy obscures Teacher's doubts; their own optimism becomes projected onto Teacher, with the result that unwitting pressure is put on Teacher to execute a lesson toward which he may have serious misgivings and about whose success he feels basically insecure. To state this problem more directly, it seems more usual for teachers and their supervisors to become committed to lessons prematurely, that is, to lessons that Teacher feels unready to teach, than to err in the opposite direction, namely, by delaying a lesson that might actually have been successful. The general tendency to encourage teaching despite justifiable reservations concerning its success is much more prevalent than the strategy that says, in effect, if you don't feel ready, then don't teach it. There seems, somehow, to be a general reluctance to jettison high-risk lessons and a characteristic impatience, among school people, to move on quickly, to hurry up fast, to get the work done, even though such speed may result in bad instruction while free time for the pupils might, at least, have provided something positive in their own experiences. Supervisors are as likely to be trapped by such false economies as anybody. The lure of closure is difficult to resist.

A problem that one encounters repeatedly, particularly among neophyte supervisors, is that having become enchanted by the methods of inductive inquiry and by the seeming humanism of "nondirective" approaches, they foolishly invoke these spells at the worst possible moments. All things considered, Preobservation is more apt to be the time for straight talk, that is, it is more likely to be the time in which straight talk is the most productive kind of talk, than any other stage of the supervisory sequence. If Preobservation is construed as a time for practical assistance rather than as a time for elaborate inquiry, then cherished methods of inquiry may be best reserved for other stages.

> TEACHER: [With ten minutes left until class time.] Just one thing—do you think it would be better to send the kids to the lab tables by rows, or to tell the whole class to go to their places at the same time?
> SUPERVISOR: In what ways is this a problem for you?
> TEACHER: Well, I want them to be able to get involved with the equipment right at that moment when their interest in the problem

is at its height, and I'm not sure which system would be most efficient. I guess I'll send them row by row, as fast as I can.

SUPERVISOR: Umm. Something to consider, though, is that by the time the kids in the last row get called, they may have cooled off pretty much.

TEACHER: Yeah, maybe you're right. [Pause.] OK, I'll send them all at once.

SUPERVISOR: OK, but then you have to take into consideration that if things get too noisy or out of hand and you have to stop things to discipline them, then that would delay the lab work too.

TEACHER: [Glancing at his watch nervously.] That's true. [Long pause.]

While one should avoid being dogmatic about such things, I can testify from my own experience that, by and large, the efficacy of such analysis is lost while the sand runs out in Preobservation and is much more likely to agitate Teacher in Stage 1 than it would be during the planning time of the regular supervision conference.

If Supervisor is loath to function directively because Teacher appears to be inordinately dependent upon supervision for advice and directions, I would propose, nevertheless, that some relaxation of "tried and true" autonomy-building strategies can be helpful and appropriate during Preobservation. I should make the point clearly that it is not so much a question of abandoning "autonomy" as a supervisory process goal (in Stage 1) as it is of softening one's attachment to the methods commonly employed for working toward this condition. One must reckon that, after all, Socratic processes were originally put to use in slow and sunny places and that whereas their adaptability to more frenzied circumstances may be tenable and even advantageous, it does not betray Plato to remember that in just a few minutes a bell will ring. One must steer, somehow, between opposite dangers. On the one hand, as I have tried to say, there are problems of methodological rigidity. On the other, there are always possibilities that Supervisor's behavior in Preobservation, particularly when expediency assumes a high priority, will operate at cross purposes to his process goals for the supervisee—specifically, for the conference toward which the supervision is moving.

Perhaps the best general solution to this dilemma consists of making supervisory process goals *explicit* and of being open with one's reasons for behaving as one does. I suspect that if Teacher understands, explicitly, that his self-sufficiency represents a principal goal of the supervision, and if he is shown—such "showing" may proceed inductively—that Supervisor will deliberately engage in certain behaviors at certain times, working from the assumption that such behaviors will be more instrumentally effective than others, then behavioral inconsistencies between relatively directive and economical action in Preobservation and more contemplative and analytical behavior in the conference may be less distracting, less dissonant, and more readily reconcilable in the Teacher's experience than if the entire business were undertaken unexplicitly.

One further problem, in Preobservation, occurs when Supervisor does things that would be better for Teacher to do in order for Teacher to benefit from the rehearsal.

> TEACHER: I'm not quite sure how to phrase the question so that it stimulates a lot of discussion, you know?
> SUPERVISOR: Yeah. Well, I think if you ask them how it might be possible for men to build underwater dwellings, you know, and not give them any direct hints and not ask them *whether* such a thing might be possible, uh, I think that should get them going on it. Let me see, uh, "How could we build . . . ?" (and so on).

Supervisors should not mistakenly assume, nor should teachers, that because their own understanding of a technique is articulate and that because they have verbalized their understanding it follows that the supervisee (or the pupil) understands it too. In this example, I suspect that Supervisor's repeated attempts to frame an efficient question for the lesson will be of considerably less utility to Teacher than opportunities for trying to frame his own question would be.

It should be noted, finally, that another common deficiency of preobservation conferences is that supervisors lose sight of "contract" as a central issue of Stage 1. In some instances they simply fail to review the supervisory contract in order to make appropriate changes, for example, to omit observation from the current sequence. Even more commonly, they do not trouble to review a complex contract to insure clarity and mutual understanding. Typically, the first of these errors results in rote practices which, because they are unessential, create unproductive supervisory sequences. The second error, namely, of working from an ambiguous set of agreements, results, at best, in wasted time—supervision grinds to a halt, and the participants must repair to recalling exactly what they had decided to do initially—and, more seriously, may result in disappointment, confusion, and frustration, particularly when functions that should have been performed were not performed.

STAGE 2:   PROBLEMS OF OBSERVATION

Seeing intelligibly is hard. Hearing intelligibly may be even harder. Seeing and hearing straight are hardest of all. Why?

In almost any natural situation, particularly in one as phenomenally complex as a classroom, one perceives selectively: it is impossible to see everything—certainly impossible to have a sense of having seen everything in equal measure, according to its intrinsic magnitude. The problem is not that perceivable *phenomena vary* in their duration and size and volume and other sensible characteristics but is, rather, *to see* things as they are objectively in their natural relationships, in their natural proportionalities, not as they are reflected by our mental fun mirrors. If the purpose of observation is to collect objective, behavioral data, and if the purpose of such data is to provide a basis for reconstructing the realities of a lesson in order to analyze them, and if, according to human nature, perception is always selective, then problems of observation—problems of seeing and hearing straight—are among the most critical problems of clinical supervision.

While one commonly acknowledges the distortions of memory, we tend not to be as consciously aware of perceptual distortions that operate from moment to moment in all of us. Quite to the contrary, seeing is believing; on-the-spot witnesses condemn men; and even though we know about the gross inconsistencies that frequently arise in the testimony of eyewitnesses, we tend, nonetheless, to trust our eyes and to behave as if they informed us truly. Our problem is not, so much, that the hand is quicker than the eye as it is that we see apperceptively: previous experiences have taught us perceptual expectations which screen dissonant, inconsistent, alien, and freakish stimuli from the data we assimilate or which bend our perceptions of novelties toward (more or less) related familiarities and, consequently, obscure their novel aspects.

In varying degrees, men differ according to their perceptual hierarchies: while visual stimuli may be the first and most vivid I record, my co-observer may be relatively more sensitive to auditory stimulation or, heaven knows, to the haptic, kinesthetic, or olefactory press existing at any moment in any situation. I have, in fact, survived one experience that provides a neat illustration of the point. During my first year of graduate study, I visited the wards of a state psychiatric hospital along with several other students at my level of training. It was the first time that any of us had visited such a place. Each of us was thoroughly shaken by the experience. In my own case, I slept badly and sensed unusual degrees of anxiety and depression for some weeks afterward. Even now, my memories of that encounter are disquieting. At the time, I remember being struck by certain differences among us, namely, that while, for me, the sounds of human screeching and verbal violence had virtually blotted out all other impressions, one of my friends was clearly hung up in his horrified visual impressions of seminudity and tangled hair and wild stares and bizarre postures while yet another student seemed to be gasping to rid herself of the place's odors and dampness: the smells of bodies and of excrement and of antiseptic and the palpable humidity of the place had infused her and, seemingly, had dulled her senses of sight and sound. She reported wanting, desperately, to leave that place in order to breathe unfouled air.

Even in the generally less tormenting atmosphere of the classroom—some classrooms have filled me with the same visceral terror—such differences in sensory "preference" will result in differing observations of the events that take place. Some of us register strong impressions of shoving and pushing and throwing and physical movement while others are more distracted by levels of sound: yelling, whispering, mumbling, drumming, stamping, furniture creaking, and so on. The point of these remarks is simply that one's sensory hierarchy will shape one's observations of events and that the same events, consequently, are likely to be perceived and reconstructed differently by different observers, on this basis.

At another level, my perceptions are likely to be affected by my momentary temperamental condition, by my mood, and by mental and organic requirements I may be experiencing unconsciously during the period of observation. Sometimes my mood becomes projected onto my environment: feeling happy myself, I tend to see happy people. Feeling tired and cynical, I tend to see the teacher's fatigue and the pupils' cynicism. Sometimes I see what I want to see—my supervisees demonstrate strong evidence of having learned from me—and sometimes I see what I particularly do not want to see. Sometimes I see more than there really is, and sometimes I see less. It depends on one's frame of reference. A little snow for the skier seems like a lot of snow to the motorist. My perceptions may be clouded by anxiety or confused with wishes. Sometimes I see parts, but cannot perceive wholes. And sometimes I generalize too much from single instances and see halos and other global phenomena that are not actually there. What I see is clearly affected by my values and prejudices and biases. I see bureaucratic waste and inefficiency; I see underdogs; I see dangerous reactionism, where other men might see a tight administrative ship, inferior social classes, and endurance of the good old ways. Sometimes I do not see anything intelligible because so much goes by so fast. At other times, I fail to see enough because I have only looked for things at which I had some prior intention to look. Often, my perceptual distortions arise from my tendencies to understand events as I have understood events previously. I fit new things into old patterns, even when the fits are poor. I frequently fuse inferences with perceptions and believe that I have seen things that are invisible, for example, that people like or don't like me. I even think I see invisible relationships, such as in cause-and-effect, and even more often I see "effects" for which I imagine erroneous causes. Whatever I see as figure, I have made figure. To have shifted my gaze thirty degrees would have generated different figures in different grounds.

If much of what I allow myself to see corresponds with my beliefs about how things actually are, then that is particularly true in relation to my beliefs about myself, my concept and definition of myself. I tend to censor data that are inconsistent with my self-image. Stinging awareness of my unworthiness cancels out impressions of other people's esteem for me. Perceptual constrictions occur most frequently in my observations of human behavior. Especially when stimuli are vague and ink-blottish, I see projections of my own fantasies; for example, I see the disdainfulness and covert hostility of students who remain forever silent in my seminars. Sometimes my perceptions distort reality because they are single-focused: most classroom observers fix on Teacher and record much more of his behavior than of the students'. Often, I operate in perceptual dichotomies and fail to perceive subtle nuances and gradations of behavior. I tend, in other words, to see strengths and weaknesses more often than I see patterns of teaching behavior that simultaneously incorporate both qualities, even though I recognize that the latter class of behaviors is much more abundant than the former. And because it is so difficult to divorce moral issues from technical ones—weaknesses are "bad"—my ability to see Teacher clearly is often influenced by my readiness or unreadiness to sense his goodness or badness, that is, to judge him.

A different way to express such problems is by saying that, as the psychologist terms it, "reality testing" is never quite as easy as one might wish and that projection, denial, and repressions by the ego all tend to affect what we all perceive. Transference also skews perceptions when we "perceive" meaningful behavior that we have learned to see in past relationships but which does not truly exist in present ones.

Of a somewhat different order are problems of observation arising from variations in physical and psychological distance. When the observer sits at the back of the classroom while Teacher teaches from the front, his perceptual frame of reference cannot coincide with Teacher's (nor could it, exactly, under any circumstances). The realities he reconstructs, consequently, can never correspond perfectly with those experienced by Teacher; and whereas that fact provides a great advantage in clinical supervision, it may also create serious difficulties.

Emotional distance is also a troublesome variable. On the one hand, presumably, some sense of investment and involvement in Teacher's work seems necessary if Supervisor's participation in his life is to count for much. On the other hand, however, especially when a result of his participation is that he has helped to create the very products that he must subsequently analyze, Supervisor's closeness to and involvement in his own (shared) products may easily depreciate the objectivity with which he views them. Similarly, when teachers appear to value their supervision, their supervisors seem more apt to observe progress in their development than when they seem to have little or no use for it.

Another problem of observation, long familiar to investigators of human behavior, is that of understanding and compensating for the artifacts produced by the observation itself, by the observer's presence in the classroom. While a great bulk of our experience suggests that teachers' common apprehensions that the presence of observers will inhibit the children are unwarranted, it seems inescapably true that observers have effects that are often difficult to judge but whose existence one intuits strongly. It seems true, incidentally, that although children generally tend to adjust quickly to the presence of observers and, eventually, to tune them out in large measure, when teachers experience severe anxiety during observation, *their* tensions often seem communicated to the children with the result that the pupils freeze up not because of the observers' effects on them but rather because of their teacher's response to the observers' presence.

Some common errors committed by clinical supervisors stem from their impulses to engage in behaviors, during observation, that make them conspicuous in the classroom. I have seen supervisors correct teacher's substantive errors while teaching was in progress. I have seen others engage in conversation with pupils, sometimes intervening directly in their work, and still others engaging in audible conversation with co-observers as they sat at the back of the room, during lulls in instructional activity. One observer, in a training institute in clinical supervision, was noted to laugh audibly and to cluck "tch, tch," in response to behaviors by pupils which she found particularly amusing or distasteful.

On numerous occasions I have seen teachers who were new in the supervisory experience and who, apparently, had not been coached properly for observation, deliberatively focus attention on the observers before, during, and after the moment of their arrival in the classroom:

1. TEACHER: Now, children, there will be someone here visiting today, and I want you to use your best company manners.

2. TEACHER: Boys and girls, my supervisor is coming to watch me teach today, and I want your full cooperation so that I don't [nervous laugh] lose my job.

3. TEACHER: Good morning, Dr. Goldhammer. Girls and boys, this is Dr. Goldhammer. He comes from the university. Shall we put our papers away and sing the song we have prepared for him? Ready? "Where have all the flowers gone . . ."

4. TEACHER: Joel, will you please give your book to Dr. Goldhammer so that he can follow along with us, and then you share Michael's book.

5. TEACHER: [Across the room, to Supervisor.] We found, yesterday, that they really couldn't do the work they were supposed to know and so today we're just reviewing mixed numbers.

6. SUPERVISOR: Good morning, Mrs. Kowalski. Good morning boys and girls. I will be visiting with you for a little while, and I want you just to make believe that I am not here at all.

7. TEACHER: You have disgraced me. I have never seen children behave so rudely when visitors were present. This must never happen again. We will have no recess period today.

8. SUPERVISOR: Zzzz, argh. Zzzz, argh. Zzzz, urmph.

Supervisors sometimes inadvertently distract teachers by behaviors that are appropriate to manifest but whose meaning is misinterpreted, especially during initial observations, because they have overlooked the practice of explaining them beforehand. Note-taking represents one practice that clinical supervisors all tend to take so much for granted, as a basic activity of their work, that they sometimes fail to warn teachers about it and to explain its purposes explicitly in advance. It is easy to imagine how unnerving it could be to an unsuspecting teacher to perceive Supervisor writing frantically throughout his lesson. Some common fantasies, in this connection, are that Supervisor must be writing down all the bad things and that, consequently, the lesson must be terrible, or that Supervisor's writing has nothing to do with the lesson being taught and reflects a total lack of interest in Teacher's work.

Late arrivals and early departures often seem to raise teachers' anxieties unless they have been led to expect them and know the reasons for them before the lesson begins. As a rule, it seems best for supervisors to work out contracts on observation before inaugurating regular sequences of supervision; to describe, sometimes in picayune detail, the behavior in which they will engage during observation; and to avoid behaving, subsequently, in any manner that is likely to seem inconsistent with the expectations they deliberately created for the supervisee.

If the selectiveness of human perception constitutes one problem of observation, then an even more abrasive difficulty, one that compounds the distortions of such selectivity, is that of being generally unable to record one's perceptions as completely and as unbrokenly as one experiences them. Twixt the ear and the page, there's many a slip. No matter how disciplined a recorder, the clinical supervisor will inevitably take short cuts that omit words or actions, or which select a single phenomenon from many simultaneous phenomena to record, or which result in abridgments of spoken dialogue that may incorporate serious distortions of what was said. Notations of nonverbal behavior tend to be substantially more impressionistic and descriptive than those of spoken words because of the absence of any rule as clear-cut as that of taking down spoken material verbatim. By the time Supervisor has performed his second-level selections, that is, selections of what to write down among those events that have already been perceptually filtered, the authenticity of his record may have been diminished exponentially.

Recording comprises mechanical problems. Because one's eyes must be fixed on one's note pad so much of the time, one fails to see much of what occurs in the classroom. Keeping up with events can be especially difficult when many words are spoken, for example, when pupils are clustered in work groups in which they talk to one another.

We have not discovered sure solutions to problems of perceptual distortion, to problems of deliberate selection, to problems of creating artifactual effects by one's own presence, or to the mechanical difficulties of recording behavioral data. Observation by plural observers sometimes compensates for the single observer's perceptual biases, but often at the price of generating even more confusing artifacts than the solo observer would be likely to. And multiple observation never offers any guarantees of authenticity. So many educational values and stereotypes are shared by schoolmen and by members of the culture generally that rather than achieving protective weights and balances by multiple observation, it sometimes happens that distortions are replicated from one observer to the next and by conference time, "majority rule" has, in effect, established tyranny of misperceived "facts."

If one is ready to believe that self-knowledge, particularly knowledge of one's own values and biases, already constitutes some measure of control over such biases, then a commitment to knowing oneself in these terms would be appropriate to demand of clinical supervisors. To know what I like and what I dislike, to know what kinds of experiences tend to threaten me, to know something about my problems of distance, and to know, for example, of my tendencies to focus more on teachers than on pupils and to perceive verbal behavior more consciously than nonverbal behavior is necessary, if not sufficient knowledge, to enable me to compensate deliberately for these factors for the sake of objective recording. To collaborate in observation with another supervisor who knows about himself in analogous terms increases the odds, presumably, that the lesson will be seen fairly and accurately. Especially during one's initial training in clinical supervision, the importance of collaborative observation and rigorous postmortems cannot be overstated. In the absence of opportunities for such arrangements, role-reversals, for example, in which Teacher supervises Supervisor's behavior. or group supervision of some form, by means of which Supervisor may create observational roles for several teachers with whom he works in order to create possibilities for multiple observation and for observation of his own behavior represent potential methods for coming to grips with these problems.

Some form of process or sensitivity training or counseling, that is, some set of experiences that enhance supervisors' self-knowledge, their capacities for self-monitoring, and their abilities to teach teachers these same capacities must accompany their basic training and should be provided for on a continuing basis as they proceed through their careers. Supervisor's own openness to examination and ability to integrate the insights produced by analysis of his professional behavior—his ability to modify his behavior accordingly—must exist in reasonable measure and must progress constantly in his development if he is to engender equivalent capacities among the teachers with whom he works. In this connection, his own, self-supervising behavior should constitute a model of the autonomous self-supervision for which the teacher is ostensibly being prepared and which, incidentally, rather than rendering supervision by other people obsolete should result in capacities for making such supervision progressively more useful and efficient. To the extent that what one observes tends to be a function of how one perceives, the latter question must be focal in the supervisor's attention to himself and to his supervisees, and in the array of teaching skills (including observation) that his supervision aims to establish.

STAGE 3: PROBLEMS OF ANALYSIS

There is often no sharp distinction between problems of observation and those of analysis, the latter frequently arising from the former. If, for the most part, observational problems tend to emanate from unconscious biases and perceptual selectivity, then, by and large, problems of analysis are more likely to be errors of logical reasoning, errors based in cognitive activity consisting of erroneous assumptions, invalidly construed relationships, superficial organization of data, and plain bad guesses, particularly in relation to the children's actual experiences. I have already referred to a number of key problems of analysis in the earlier sections dealing with rationales and methods of Stage 3. Some of these can be amplified presently. There are two principal problem areas in the context that generally overlap in relation to any given teaching pattern: problems of categorization and problems of evaluation.

We have noted that even after rigorous measures have been taken to protect the observer's objectivity, their effectiveness may be lost by the manner in which his data are treated. Reviewing some earlier statements, we recall that most processes of categorization are partly subjective, that categories are human inventions, and that one's tendencies to reify various categories, especially those to which one has become accustomed, often become virtually irresistible. Some descriptive categories seem more amenable to objective application than others. For example, much of the time the classification of an element of teaching by the category "questioning" requires only an observation of grammatical structure. "Rewards" is somewhat more problematical:

definitions of "rewards" may vary and, irrespective of definition, the term itself is likely to carry implicit qualitative connotations that under-lyingly influence one's classificatory process. To employ a categorical definition that allows for the existence, let us say, of "positive" and "negative" rewards may represent a partial solution, but one that is easier to adopt than to implement because of prior sets we tend to have around the term, whose unconscious instrusion may lead us to favor positive examples and to overlook negative ones.

As we have seen, it is sometimes hard to know whether one has unearthed a behavioral pattern or not. One problem is that the supervi-sor may simply fail to recognize significant patterns in the teaching and consequently may wind up centering his supervision on relatively unim-portant issues. Failure to identify critical patterns may stem from their attenuation, from an absence of relevant constructs in the supervisor's professional frame of reference (I cannot arrange red things together and green things together if I am color-blind), from the possibility that supervisor perceives only tangential regularities rather than central ones, and so on. He may find parts without recognizing their relation-ships to more significant wholes. I have watched some supervisors develop analyses of teaching in which they had isolated "I" patterns, that is, patterns of teaching in the first person, but in which they failed to make a fundamental distinction, between "I's" which might inciden-tally have taught unfortunate role definitions and "I's" that were perfectly appropriate because Teacher had been describing a personal experi-ence (in the case of which I am thinking, a trip he had taken to France) that was completely relevant to the lesson.

One's appetite for closure and for answers often interferes with categorization by prompting one to stop thinking about a pattern once it has been classified and, in that manner, results in premature dismis-sal of patterns that might have been understood more significantly in connection to multiple categories. A similar problem consists of one's tendency to discover likenesses and to generalize from such discoveries that what was found existing in certain instances truly exists in all instances. For example, once the supervisor has unearthed a pattern of stereotyped rewards, it sometimes seems that he becomes less alert to the existence of rewards that are uniquely responsive; he tends to avoid conflicting data.

Another issue requiring study is that, seemingly, although we can make the separation for didactic purposes, distinctions between catego-rization and evaluation are frequently blurred in practice. When the supervisor finds that each time a pupil has offered a response the teacher replies, "Yes, thank you; very good," he may call this pattern "stereotyped" and may classify such examples under "stereotyped re-wards" but, almost certainly, that very classification implies a value judgment as well as an application of certain formal criteria. In connection to such an example, the analyst generally does not advance to the next step of analysis by asking himself whether, in the case before him, the existence of such stereotypy was good or bad. Indeed, to do so would probably seem pedantic. Nonetheless, because our imaginations indicate that under special circumstances and for deliberate purposes the calculated use of such stereotypy might be fully appropriate—for example, if Teacher were teaching about inflation and decided to use his own rewards promiscuously in order to demonstrate inflationary depreciation—we should not ignore the possibility that such separations are sometimes not made when they ought to be.

One's appetites for closure, uniformity, and simplicity also create tendencies to evaluate teaching patterns monadically: one typically avoids ambiguous classifications and value judgments, and variables in the teaching performance tend to be regarded as strong or weak, good or bad, but not commonly enough as strong-and-weak, or good-and-bad, that is, as $\pm$ patterns. Many supervisors tend, additionally, to avoid reverse interpretations and to avoid playing devil's advocate to themselves except at special moments when they set out consciously to do so. One effect of this condition, to which I have already referred, is that the supervisor generally hangs with a value judgment once it has been formulated and commonly does not consider contrasting interpretations after his shutter has clicked initially.

And again, recognitory behavior seems more prevalent—perhaps because it requires relatively little mental energy—than creative, synthesizing behavior, and supervisors seem to project known configurations onto ambiguous data more naturally than to discover novelties, that is, unique patterns among them. We generally take normative views of human behavior and employ normative strategies for modifying it. In a recent informal seminar, my friend Burton Blatt pointed out, quite correctly, the clinician's tendency to treat any homosexual as he has treated past homosexuals, generally employing methods that have worked previously. Blatt also noted, relevantly, that the very same person's speech impediment will be treated by one mode at one university clinic and by another mode at another university, depending upon the orthodoxies in vogue at the training center at which the patient presents himself. In analysis of observational data, one tends to find what one has found previously; one tends to recognize patterns one has encountered before; one tends to classify the data by categories with which one is familiar; and being neither good nor bad, such behavior simply reflects laws of the mind without whose existence the mental apparatus could hardly function. But it is nonetheless true that what I call "bat" is not bat at all but is truly an inkblot and that, analogously, what I have categorized under the rubric "discipline" might much more realistically and constructively have been classified under other denominations, if only I had known them.

One often relies on consensus for insuring the validity of interpretations, that is, upon agreement among a jury of analysts; and although consensual validation undoubtedly does provide some measure of safety, it is difficult to escape the misgiving that, agreements notwithstanding, we may, at bottom, have simply arrived at some commonly shared phlogiston-like fiction: very real, very convincing, completely logical, but false. I point this out not to wax philosophical, but to stress that at critical moments in analysis and, subsequently, in the remaining stages of the supervisory sequence, it is almost always more reasonable to concede uncertainties than to assert truths, despite the feeling of conviction by which certainties are generally accompanied.

If it is likely that analyses are affected by projective processes and by prior sets, then it is a certainty that the data are distorted by any process of condensation, irrespective of the analyst's objectivity. When the data are condensed they are changed. Although it is an unhappy metaphor, shrunken skulls come to mind: even the most skillfully deflated noggin bears little resemblance (I suspect) to its original, unsanforized forebear. It is not only smaller, it is different: its physiognomic proportions and relationships have been changed. Even when contraction is perfect, the final product may be unrecognizable because of differences in scale. For example, we think of the earth as a rough-hewn, oblate lump whose complexion is marred by high mountains and deep trenches, rather like an ugly fruit. I am told, however, that if a model of the earth were constructed to correspond to the size of a billiard ball, and if every surface feature were reduced proportionally, the resulting object would be virtually as smooth as a billiard ball. To make matters even more complicated, the reductions of clinical analysis are more like sculpting than like shrinking. Supervisor streamlines his data by eliminating factors from them. I am reminded of the conundrum:

QUESTION: How do you sculpt an elephant?
ANSWER: You take a stone and carve away everything that does not look like an elephant.

The "stone" with which Supervisor begins, namely, his raw data, will certainly be transformed by his analysis. The problem is of how closely it will resemble itself when he is done: will it still be characteristic of the lesson he observed, or will it look more like an elephant? Decisions affecting which data are included in the final analysis and which are not arise partly from judgments that Supervisor makes concerning what is important and partly from his perceptual capacities: he cannot include patterns that he cannot see. One might reasonably ask whether, inasmuch as parts of the teaching will be examined in the conference rather than the whole lesson, it is not sufficient, simply, to preserve parts of the data as perfectly as possible. I think that the answer should be affirmative and that, additionally, it is good practice to keep even the discarded parts near at hand (namely, the full observation notes) during the conference. Although, year by year, this question seems more imponderable to us, we cannot dismiss it on grounds of insolubility. The problem of relationships among parts and wholes, of how each is defined by the other, remains real and constant in clinical supervision. The concrete forms it typically assumes consist, for example, of teachers' protests that supervisors' analyses are invalid because they treat components that have been "taken out of context," even, sometimes, in reference to individual lessons that were originally conceived in a preceding sequence of lessons, not all of which the supervisor has observed. In the opposite direction, teachers and their supervisors often sense, correctly, that although the lesson, as a totality, failed to achieve its intended purposes, it nevertheless included episodes of teaching that were technically potent and momentarily effective, vis à vis those same purposes.

It would be mistaken to suppose that because so many problems of analysis revolve around ontological questions, problems of knowing what truly exists, they lie beyond the pale of manageable issues for clinical supervision. To the contrary, just as it follows from the unconscious trickery that causes perceptual distortions during observation, the implication is, rather, that supervisors must summon all the more energy to examine themselves, to maintain objectivity, and to compensate for whatever cosmic or personal interference operates to undermine the integrity of their work. Although various administrative and logistical strategies exist to fortify professional self-discipline, for example, team teaching in which group supervision may be undertaken, no such device can assure it. Although the profession may be laden with policing devices of one sort or another, it seems inescapable that, ultimately, its success depends on the magnitude of commitment and skill and energy manifested by its individual practitioners, that good clinical supervision represents a way of living, professionally, and a state of mind that one either values or does not value. As much can be said for any other clinical practice of which I know.

Problems of Strategy

In the most sweeping sense, the principal problem of this stage seems to be one of too little or too much. I find, generally, that when supervisory conferences seem unsuccessful, it is often because the supervisor failed to plan adequately beforehand or because his prior plans were executed too rigidly. Our memories are filled with visions of conferences that meandered and floundered and leaked away and seemed to be generated off the cuff because, in fact, they were generated off the cuff. Any full-time observer of teaching is likely to have countless analogous memories of lessons that failed for the same underlying reason. Also, analogously, we are thoroughly familiar with the phenomenon of preplanned lessons—and lectures—that were enacted so doggedly that Teacher's only clear victory was to have finished saying what he set out to say. The problem of strategy is, consequently, twofold: consisting, on the one hand, of formulating cogent and appropriate plans and, on the other hand, of knowing how to use them.

Most difficult of all, perhaps, is to master the art of framing plans whose effect is to make Supervisor more sensitive and understanding and responsive to Teacher instead of insulating him from Teacher's immediate feelings and experiences. While I have asserted, already, that planned strategies are more likely to result, regularly, in productive outcomes than random ones, I should only see half the picture by failing to recognize that in supervision as well as in teaching, frequently, the activity of planning, the existence of plans, and the implementation of plans in professional action, taken together, represent a massive avoidance of empathic human intercourse. When the practitioner's relationship to plans substitutes for what might, otherwise, have been relationships to people, he has lost the game badly. Even while granting the necessity for teachers and supervisors to be trained in skills of strategy, one wonders, disconsolately, about the incidental learnings given rise by numberless hours, in the methods courses, spent in mastering "instructional planning" while training in human communication and interaction went begging. It has been a fairly common experience for me, in varied geographic and economic settings, to hear young teachers claim that lesson planning was either at the top or near the top of their lists of important professional activities while, at the same time, never once referring to children or to themselves as having any special consequence in the educational enterprise.

Although I have made some attempt, in the previous chapter, to provide illustrations of supervision conferences in which *a priori* strategies were used well, I cannot prescribe neat solutions for the question of how to avoid existential constriction by preconceived strategies. I suspect that besides being impeded by limits of imagination and experience, I am also handicapped because, rather than to generate avoidance behaviors and professional aloofness in their own right, it seems, as a rule, that supervisory strategies are put to such service by individual supervisors whose personal needs for psychological distance come first. Their plans, seemingly, serve already existing requirements for aloofness and do not create them. When such defensive requirements exist, there is little we can prescribe technically. Under more psychologically favorable circumstances, it seems generally advantageous to make a practice of developing plural strategies for most supervision conferences, that is, alternative strategies designed to compensate for one's margin of prior uncertainty about individual teachers' needs. An even more useful accommodation, where it is logistically feasible, is to engage teachers' participation in formulating strategies for their own supervision. It seems, by and large, that the more Teacher has had a hand in creating the plans that will guide his own supervision, the more that supervision tends to fit his actual requirements, except in special cases when Teacher uses his prerogatives to flee toward safe and innocuous issues—in effect, to escape supervisory analysis.

If strategies falter because sometimes they are overplanned and sometimes they are underplanned, in a parallel fashion, conferences occasionally fail because, from the teacher's frame of reference, they have either provided too much or too little of one psychological commodity or another: ideas, rewards, punishments, feelings. Excessive or anemic input can often be traced to deficiencies of strategy, and such deficiencies sometimes appear to have been avoidable, had the supervisor only used his available information more judiciously in planning. Sequentially, the basic decisions of strategy pertain, first, to the selection of patterns and issues for treatment from those disclosed by the analysis and, second, to the order in which such issues should be examined and to relationships appropriate to develop among them.

One knotty decision that the supervisor must make frequently is of whether to continue focusing on issues with which Teacher has begun to deal—to do so may already have been stipulated in the day's contract—or to turn to new problems arising from the observed lesson. There are clearly two ways to blunder here, each of which I have observed from time to time and both of which I have committed in my own supervision. On some occasions I have felt so persuaded that some new manifestation in Teacher's performance represented its most salient and important attribute and that, despite prior agreements to deal with other matters, the conference would be most productive if it centered in the new material—let us imagine, returning to our old examples, that although Teacher and I had agreed to examine his questioning patterns, on this occasion, he suddenly (in my experience) began to employ a highly individualized and responsive system of rewards which I believed was important to examine explicitly and to stabilize in his teaching—and have proceeded to develop conference strategies accordingly. It has not been uncommon, under such conditions, to discover that the teacher felt listless and somewhat disoriented, even when such new material was of a "positive" nature, and generally frustrated by being put off the track he had expected to follow in that supervisory sequence. Several teachers with whom I have worked predictably responded in this manner to unexpected changes and reported, quite vividly, having felt too distracted by their disappointed expectations to deal very efficiently with new issues. With others, I have muddled things just the opposite way, by fighting my temptation to seize onto something new because of regard for existing agreements on specific elements of the teaching to be treated that day. Particularly when the teacher himself is aware of the novelty his performance has incorporated and feels some appetite to deal with it, the conference can seem bleak if it doggedly pursues old business simply because of an earlier decision to do so.

The most obvious solution to such dilemmas is to examine both the old stuff and the new stuff in the same conference. Shortages of time, however, often make this ideal impractical. Another sensible tactic is to renegotiate the conference after analysis (or observation) in light of unexpected developments in the teaching. The difficulty here, however, is that quite often, in practice, one is unable to reach the teacher during the period between observation and conference because of how full professional schedules tend to be. The problem with renegotiating an agendum at the beginning of Stage 4 is that no time remains, at that point, to develop new strategies, unless it is borrowed from the conference or unless the conference is postponed, neither of which arrangement seems generally satisfactory. A third sensible solution consists of preparing alternative strategies in order to be conceptually armed to deal either with old business or to proceed to unanticipated topics, and, indeed, to prepare multiple strategies seems worthy on general principles. Once again, however, time becomes a nuisance because no matter how liberally Supervisor has arranged his schedule, it generally turns out that he is lucky to be able to develop one full-dimensional strategy, let alone several.

Although it may seem like trial and error of the most rudimentary kind, in my own practice, having been disenchanted so often by seemingly sensible solutions, I have generally resolved this dilemma on an empirical basis, namely, in reference to my collected impressions of whether or not (or in what degree) sudden shifts to or avoidance of new, provocative issues are likely to disturb the individual teacher with whom I am working. Additionally, several simple guidelines have proven to be useful. One is to begin the conference by explaining to Teacher that in addition to issues already identified for treatment, my observation and analysis have disclosed new patterns (problems, issues, and the like) that also seemed worthy of attention and that, consequently, because it would be too hurried to attempt to deal with everything at once, I think it would be best to plan an extra conference at the earliest opportunity. Such a conference would stand alone instead of being included in a complete, five-stage sequence of supervision. When I am quick enough to sense the existence of something new (that is, previously untreated or existing at a higher level of proficiency than before) during an observation and can think things through quickly enough, I will sometimes raise the question with Teacher on my way from the room:

SUPERVISOR: I have the feeling that there's some interesting stuff here on social interaction in the pupils' work groups. If I can put it together, would it suit you to take a look at it today?

While I should not want to exaggerate the typical consequences of changing directions because of newly observed phenomena and of modifying or violating preexisting contracts by deciding, in strategy, to do so, I do, nonetheless, think it is important to make the point that even though sudden changes are more likely than not to be integrable by the teacher (Teacher rarely becomes so disoriented that he cannot function), it has been true, frequently, in my experience that even subtle stresses created by elements of surprise or change or behavior somehow inconsistent with Teacher's prior expectations can be substantial enough to cut Teacher's efficiency and investment in a conference significantly.

Problems arising from the process of selection, in strategy, are legion. The very fact that Supervisor performs such selections, especially when that represents a constant feature of his work, is likely to increase Teacher's dependency upon him to do so. Because strategies may be conceptualized in various frames of reference, possibilities always exist that Supervisor's chosen framework(s) will be inappropriate. He may, for example, select patterns to examine which, under the right conditions, would capture Teacher's interest and seem important to him but which, because Supervisor paid inadequate attention to the means he would employ for treating them, failed to produce such effects in the conference. More commonly, errors of selection are associated with misjudgments pertaining to the timeliness and possible urgency of beginning, on the one hand, from the data themselves, or, on the other, from issues current in Teacher's supervision, or, alternatively, from some relatively abstract developmental model upon which Supervisor relies for guidance in projecting supervisory frameworks.

When the supervisor's selections are governed by the principles of saliency, treatability, and fewness, although these categories are designed to strengthen supervisory strategies and conferences, he risks mistakes in his assessments of pertinent variables. To begin with, such notions as saliency are subject to a wide latitude of interpretation. As we have seen, whereas frequency is often a correlate of saliency (because, presumably, frequently repeated teaching patterns, being more pervasive than infrequent ones, are more logically apt to influence the pupils' learning), it is sometimes insufficient as the sole criterion for saliency. We feel that besides being abundant, teaching patterns (and the demonstrated or hypothetical effects one attributes to them) must be "significant," somehow, to be worthy of supervisory treatment. Significance, however, depends upon the conceptual framework, the system of values, and the particular perspective in connection to which teaching and learning are construed by the supervisor and teacher who are involved in professional collaboration.

Some educators are predisposed to regard quantitative substantive learning as the principal measure of instructional quality, while others tend to deemphasize such learning in favor of priorities on so-called intellectual "tool-skills," for the sake of whose establishment they envision content as means or medium. Some educators favor behavioristic perspectives on teaching and are principally concerned with the efficacy of reinforcement techniques, while others define educational goals in terms of personality development and favor highly supportive, democratic, student-centered teaching. Some educators look toward curricular revisions and the development of more rational organizations of knowledge as the major source of educational reform and improvement of instructional efficiency; others are more interested in the social parameters of scholastic education and in the influences upon socialization that the organization and structure of instructional groups may have. And besides the existence of relative purists in each such professional camp, the field is populated by a million workers, both unsophisticated and greatly sophisticated, who represent every hue of eclecticism in which such outlooks can merge. The question of significance, consequently, is highly relative and subject to countless contingencies arising from divergent educational viewpoints.

Whereas professional pluralism is not to be deplored, it does, nonetheless, make it extremely difficult to discuss *significance* in general terms although one maintains the conviction that, at least, by terms that are mutually acceptable and cogent to Supervisor and Teacher, by one definition or another, patterns selected on a criterion of saliency must satisfy such a condition. Perhaps one way to cut across this confusion is to stipulate that, irrespective of the specific conceptual framework in which they happen to be operating, Teacher and Supervisor must *feel* that the issues they have isolated are significant ones and if their precepts happen to be naïve and their values reactionary, more the pity: at least they stand to maintain some decent level of professional morale as they set out to work together.

One sadness I experience in the course of my consulting in this field is not, so much, that professional thinking differs abruptly from situation to situation but, rather, that in too many instances there is seemingly no rigorous conceptual framework at all to guide the activities of teachers and supervisors who are trying to create something worthwhile together: I feel distressed by the seemingly random motions of so many hardworking educators. In one setting, we find people energetically at work attempting to institute team teaching (that is, to apply some model of teaming that was probably invented elsewhere and may have little relevancy to their own requirements) while they ignore problems of curriculum and methodology. In another setting, we encounter frantic curricular revision unaccompanied by explicit concern for improving instructional techniques or inventing useful administrative adjuncts. In yet another instance, we find a tremendous investment of money and of professional talent in developing a system of individually prescribed instruction, that is, of a highly individualized format of teaching, based upon obsolete curriculums which everyone agrees are basically educational junk.

One must obviously be content to observe almost any efforts toward educational improvement, and one must, additionally, accept that human beings are generally incapable of doing everything at the same time. Even with infinite forbearance, however, it is hard not to have one's blood curdled by the general absence of unity and coordination and efficiency and communication that characterizes contemporary efforts at constructive change. I am certain that my allergic sensitivity to such phenomena is partly determined by my embarrassed awareness of the absence of tough fiber in my own knowledge of professional education and in my general ability to conceptualize strategies for making it better.

In any event, to make the point, a quality of significance is critical in the isolation of salient teaching patterns. And while educational pluralism precludes any statement of simple solutions to this problem, I suspect that clinical supervision can, at least, provide some minimal safeguards consisting (1) of the practice of deliberately maintaining openness and resiliency in relation to the very framework in which significance is assessed; (2) of maintaining explicit attention to the frame of reference in which specific patterns are isolated instead of accepting, *ex post facto*, that because such patterns have been isolated they must be important; and (3) of devoting considerable time, particularly in the initial phases of a supervisory relationship, and on a regular and appropriate basis thereafter, insuring that both members understand and agree to the basic values, concepts, and perspectives from which the teacher's work is being viewed. When there is disagreement, its existence should be recognized and explicitly understood. While reconciliation may sometimes be impossible, at least to understand such differences may be necessary for productive collaboration to proceed.

As I have suggested, another vantage point from which to decide saliency is that of the pupils' scholastic situation instead, primarily, of the teacher's. In other words, as one effect of the diversity and pluralism of educational practices and because various competing systems seem uniquely valuable, Supervisor's judgments of saliency should sometimes derive from a composite view of the school and of the collective instructional experiences the children have there. Rather than aiming to shape all teachers to the same image, their roles on the faculty may be deliberately differentiated according to stylistic and technical differences and to differing substantive specialties among them. I should not, for example, become as readily devoted to weaning Teacher from his preference for lecturing if I were confident that his pupils experienced a rich assortment of other instructional techniques on a daily basis and that the subject matter he taught was susceptible to didactic development. On the contrary, I might join him in supervisory analyses of his lectures, *qua* lectures, in an effort to approximate the most productive potentialities of that teaching method.

On the one hand, Supervisor's consciousness of the pupils' complete scholastic environment can free him, especially when he has some control over programming the children into various classroom relationships, to follow individual teacher's self-initiated issues in their supervision. It is easiest to commit supervision to outcomes that Teacher wants when one has some reasonable optimism that, taken together with what the other teachers want, the total effect of their individual successes would constitute a strong educational environment for the pupils. On the other hand, however, even with such thorough administrative autonomy, the supervisor is not guaranteed smooth sailing. For one thing, he may not be sufficiently free from professional biases of his own or sufficiently versatile in his ability to understand the strengths and weaknesses of widely divergent instructional styles to succeed in such checkered practice (although a team of supervisors might enjoy a better chance of doing so). It might equally fail to satisfy his own professional standards, and the teachers', to settle for supervision within narrow methodological limits for each individual faculty member, as though he were training insect citizens of a hive to perform their peculiar specialties.

It may, additionally, be invalid to assume that, by and large, the pupil's experience of the school is so well integrated that he can be expected to sense some rational personal unity in the collection of highly differentiated instructional approaches he encounters. He might, instead, merely be disoriented by such diversity and compartmentalize his classroom experiences, being turned on by some teachers and turned off by others. While such an effect may not be inherently damaging, it hardly represents an illustration of scholastic efficiency. In reality, one suspects that children differ in this respect and that their abilities to integrate diverse instructional experiences are as varied as their other capacities and talents. Ideally, by matching individual teachers with individual pupils (in groups), Supervisor could make productive use of stylistic differences among instructors, but the variables that would have to be defined and then measured to do so are essentially mysterious to us at this time. In any case, Supervisor may always take a comprehensive view (that is, of the pupils' larger environment) when to do so enables him to work productively with a teacher who, were that option unavailable, he might otherwise have to write off.

Such a possibility is relevant, presently, because it implies that estimations of saliency may be formulated in both clinical and normative frames of reference. Two basic types of errors are possible to commit in this context: Supervisor may incorrectly assume a principle of constructive experiential integration by the pupils; or he might overinvest his prosecution of some clinically salient teaching pattern whose significance is less consequential than he estimates, vis à vis the pupils' total scholastic encounter.

In a somewhat different sense of the term, Supervisor may attribute saliency to teaching patterns which, although they do not seem strikingly significant in the immediate lesson, have recurred, significantly, among many teachers and in many lessons, in his experience. The principal hazard involved in this kind of normalizing is that, being drawn to familiar issues, Supervisor may fail to recognize unique, offsetting factors that exist in the present situation. For example, although Supervisor may have observed T–P (teacher-to-pupil) interactional patterns a million times and may have correctly concluded that such a pattern predominates in most classrooms and, that the less varied it is, the more impoverished the children's opportunities become for learning what they might through interactions with one another, he might seize, prematurely, the dominant T–P pattern in the present lesson, failing to recognize its appropriateness to the business being transacted. Although this may seem like a remote or, perhaps, an unlikely possibility, I can only assert that I have witnessed such rote supervisory behavior—what, in this instance, I am calling erroneous attributions of normally significant saliency to a teaching pattern—time and again, even among supervisors who were supposedly well enough trained to know better.

If selection on a criterion of saliency implies that a teaching pattern is significant, then, in turn, significance must be understood in terms of the pattern's probable or demonstrable effects upon the pupils. The problem, in other words, is not simply to isolate teaching patterns that stand out somehow, but is rather to examine outstanding patterns whose effects are likely to be particularly strengthening or damaging or problematical for the children. As I have already noted, for a seemingly vast majority of salient teaching patterns, significance must be inferred or hypothesized and cannot be observed directly. I may postulate that Teacher's continual use of the subject matter as an instrument of punishment is likely to alienate the children from their curriculum, although to prove it quickly enough for supervision to provide an airtight case would be impossible in most instances. At precisely the moment when strategy begins to rest upon such assumptions, however, it has become vulnerable because Supervisor's assumptions and inferences may be wrong.

They may, for example, be simplistic in the sense that Supervisor fails to conceptualize the pattern's range of significant effects or that it produces diverse effects or complex ones. He may not understand, even when his vision of effects is essentially valid, that, nonetheless, the pattern in question does not stand in a simple causal relationship to its effects but, in fact, is potentiated by other elements of the teaching which, although they are relatively inconspicuous, are necessary to modify just the same. Supervisor may fail to allow for a pattern's differentiated effects among individual students or may be too unequivocal in his views of how it should be modified. Even more likely, he may fail to recognize that the very pattern that generates unwanted difficulties in one context of teaching may be deliberately employed to produce positive, calculated effects in some other context. Perhaps the greatest problem of all, in this connection, is that Supervisor's psychological formulations (about learning, development, cognitive behavior, emotional functioning, and the like) may be incorrect or only partly correct, first of all because supervisors generally are not schooled in advanced psychology and secondly because theories of learning and development and personality have not, as yet, arrived at final and certifiable solutions to most enigmas of human learning.

When, for one reason or another, Supervisor's and Teacher's conceptual frameworks are basically different, then their identification of salient teaching patterns may differ accordingly. Supervisor consequently runs the risk of finding that patterns which seemed rich in significance to him and, for that reason, were selected in strategy seem meaningless to Teacher subsequently. Or, in the opposite direction, Supervisor may fail to isolate teaching patterns which, because Teacher feels they are significant, should have been incorporated into the supervision conference (if only because, while Supervisor treats other issues, Teacher's mind may be distracted by them). It is relatively difficult to attend to someone else's issues when one's own mind is filled with others that seem more important. In estimating saliency, consequently, Supervisor cannot generally afford to lose sight of the question of whether Teacher might also have selected the same issues or, at least, of whether he can be led, efficiently, to appreciate their significance.

While it might seem more reasonable to ask Teacher, directly, which of the patterns revealed by analysis he prefers to treat, instead of attempting to guess about such things, the very act of such questioning can generate problems too. It sometimes happens, for example, that when Supervisor refers to the existence of a pattern which, had he simply introduced it into the conference without asking, would have proven excessively threatening to Teacher, the very mention of it also heightens Teacher's anxiety (and, in that respect, defeats Supervisor's purpose for asking) and puts him in a bind, namely, that on the one hand he wishes to avoid the issue but, on the other, he is tortured by his fantasies of what Supervisor has to say about it and reluctantly agrees to have the problem examined: not so much because he wants to but, rather, because he is afraid not to. If, additionally, Teacher has some need to please his supervisor, then his choice may be even more overdetermined. If Teacher says yes, in spite of his anxieties, and if he is unable to relax sufficiently to examine the patterns put before him, then the conference is unlikely to be helpful. If, however, he says no, but is subsequently unable to concentrate effectively on other issues because those he rejected for treatment have left a part of his mind wondering and wandering, then, again, the conference may suffer.

That such problems can exist, however, should not imply that questioning is to be avoided because, most often I suspect, it achieves its proper purposes and does not upset things in this fashion. Perhaps, once again, the disquieting implication that should be drawn is that Supervisor must know his clients well enough to be able to predict, fairly reliably, when a specific teacher will be helped by asking and when he will not be. I have worked with some supervisees for whom such problems virtually never arose and others who simply could not tolerate even the most remote possibility that I was not "telling all," that I was withholding something. For such people, ignorance is anything but bliss, and a part of supervision should aim for the general cure of such anxiety as well as for more conventional, technical outcomes.

Some additional problems around saliency are first, as we have already noted, that when a salient pattern also turns out to be a superordinate pattern, that is, a pattern of teaching behavior that subsumes a collection of coordinated patterns, and when, at the same time, positive reasons exist for working from "parts" to "wholes" in the conference, rather than in the opposite direction, then although the superordinate pattern may be salient, its treatment, per se, may nevertheless be contraindicated. In more general terms, there are some occasions on which data that satisfy a selection criterion of saliency should, nonetheless, be withheld temporarily from supervision. The supervisor's dilemma, in this connection, arises from the tendency to incorporate salient patterns into a supervisory strategy because of the importance we generally attribute to them, because "saliency" is usually the first criterion applied to the data, and because of one's natural disinclination to abandon an issue once it has been unearthed. A second, closely related, problem is that the *salient* regularities of a teacher's performance are also most likely to be the patterns most firmly anchored in psychological bedrock of one form or another and, consequently, are often least ready to yield to supervisory efforts to modify them. Here, once more, the supervisor must overcome whatever resistance he experiences to skirting salient issues, in deference to the "accessibility" criterion.

Judging accessibility (treatability) is even more problematical, generally, than determining saliency. In the most general sense, Supervisor's problem in applying this criterion is to avoid confusing his fantasies of what will be manageable for Teacher with pertinent realities, more specifically, to avoid projecting his own anxieties and intellectual limitations onto Teacher. Besides by projection, Supervisor may misjudge Teacher's readiness to deal with difficult or sensitive material as a result of his own general anxiety about "hurting people," born, sometimes, of personal guilt but even more often, I suspect, of supervision's guilty traditions. On the other side, as a result of unconscious denial, he may fail to allow possibilities that the material he chooses to treat or the supervisory processes he plans to employ will be confusing or hurtful to Teacher.

As well as arising from supervisors' own projections, miscalculations tend, also, to result from incorrect generalizations, for example, from stereotypes according to which Teacher is erroneously expected to respond like "other teachers" or in which, because of the fixity of Supervisor's earlier impressions, Teacher is expected to respond presently just as he responded previously to certain issues or processes. While both such forms of generalization constitute basic tools in clinical supervision, bringing order, as they do, to data that might otherwise seem random and disconnected, they also give rise to errors of strategy more frequently and ubiquitously than any other cause that comes to mind. Analogously for teachers and psychotherapists—particularly the latter—it sometimes seems that the more vividly they know who their clients have been, that is, what they have been like, the more opaque they become to their minute developmental gains and behavioral changes. It has not been uncommon in my experience to observe counseling trainees conceptualizing their clients, months after counseling has been initiated, in basically the same variables as they did at the beginning, even when significant changes in their functioning were recognizable to other workers. And once Teacher has decided that William is a shy child, that perception may endure even after he has won the Distinguished Service Cross.

Treatability is difficult to judge both because of the large number of pertinent factors that can be taken into consideration and because of the ambiguity that often surrounds them. For selection on this criterion to be perfect, Supervisor would have to know the character and quality of Teacher's cognitive and emotional behavior as well as of his own. He would have to know, for example, the typical patterns of reasoning, of conceptualizing relationships, and of formulating and solving problems, that were salient in his own and in the teacher's intellectual style. He would need to know each member's capacity for assimilating ideas in various quantities and at various levels of abstraction. He would have to recognize each member's prominent (and subtle) biases and habits of perceptual and logical distortion, their general and special anxieties, the effects of anxiety upon their professional behavior, their predominant defenses, their patterns of coping with data, with intellectual problems, and with requirements for modifying their own behavior. He would have to know such things about Teacher in order to plan successful supervisory strategies at a maximum level of confidence, and he would need to have such self-knowledge in order to be sure that his plans for himself were tenable and that his motives for taking any particular course of action with Teacher were realistically in touch with Teacher's actual intellectual condition.

But it should be obvious that knowledge of such information is never likely to exist in fine detail or with complete certainty. Even when the dimensions along which Supervisor views his own work and Teacher's are abundant enough to provide a fair representation of relevant realities, the degree of accuracy and completeness with which his knowledge of elements on each such dimension exists is likely to be sparse. It is as though he must aim at fine targets but is handicapped by the grossness of his sighting apparatus.

Peculiarly, gross aiming at fine and gross targets has often appeared to result in productive supervisory effects in our experience—of course our evaluation processes are correspondingly gross—and for that reason I should not abandon hope too quickly because of the seeming unlikelihood that judgments of accessibility will have great precision or validity in most instances. Nor should I worry too much about the fact that our tools and lenses in supervision and teaching are like shovels and punchbowls. One trusts that the perfection of our technology and understanding in supervision will come in time and that, meanwhile, work is possible although it must often proceed clumsily and will include many false starts.

Although, as I noted earlier, clinical supervisors seem better at selecting issues in relation to their conceptual difficulty and in making decisions concerning teachers' intellectual capacities than at predicting the emotional correlates that any given issue or process is likely to incorporate (for example, Teacher's general level of motivation to examine it, the anxieties he may experience in its connection, or the intensity of satisfaction he will experience from its treatment), such a distinction cannot often be drawn validly. We presume that how much intellectual energy is available to Teacher at any moment and how potent his conceptual ability is and, for example, how many variables he will be able to hold onto at the same time, and so on, will always be influenced by the range of emotions that Teacher is encountering at the time of his supervision. Over a period of time, Supervisor may estimate Teacher's "general intelligence" with some accuracy, but specific predictions of accessibility must almost always reflect variations from that general level; good days and bad days and vicissitudes of the supervision itself are so certain to affect Teacher's ability to understand and to do intellectual work that supervision will surely flounder if Supervisor relaxes too much in his contented knowledge of Teacher's strengths.

There is probably no limit to the number of ways in which it can be stated that what makes "accessibility" so tough to utilize as a principle of selection for strategy is that it requires Supervisor to know things and to guess at things that sometimes seem unknowable and imponderable. I doubt that it is necessary to make the point repeatedly. My intention, presently, is to offer some additional examples of such difficulties rather than simply to strengthen the assertion that problems exist in this context. These examples are intended to make such problems more vivid and familiar.

If it is difficult to understand people and, in particular, to comprehend how they acquire information and how they transform such information into technical behavior and how they are motivated and how they succeed and fail, then to know such things about oneself is probably most difficult of all, notwithstanding that self-related data are more extensive than those on external objects, for everyone. Inescapably, determinations of accessibility must involve self-examination in some degree, because, besides trying to decide what effects Teacher will experience from certain, planned, events, the problem is, additionally, to recognize that what results in such decisions emanates from the supervisor's peculiar existence as well as from objective, logical "computation" of external factors. In other words, the deciding process does not exist independently of the decision-making person.

One must ask, for example, for what possible causes might a supervisor decide that certain patterns or supervisory processes are too anxiety-provoking (for Teacher) to include in a conference. What conditions might motivate such an outlook, besides valid appraisals of Teacher's strengths and vulnerabilities? I have already suggested that distorted impressions of one's own destructive power are not uncommon, particularly among neophyte supervisors (and teachers and counselors). There is no way to specify what the root of such a problem will be in every case because it will never be quite the same in every case. Nonetheless, I can report how it has seemed in various situations that stick in my memory.

In some cases it has seemed that Supervisor's avoidance of issues that he thought were volatile expressed a general tendency toward avoidance of human encounters and, particularly, of human confrontations, that is, of assertions of feeling or judgment or perception, offered directly to someone else. We are not unfamiliar with persons who are known by their general incapacity to assert anything about almost anything, individuals whose needs require them to equivocate and to qualify and to turn about 180° in their thinking if pressure is put upon them to do so. In some cases, a general disability of this kind seems accentuated by the special tensions of communicating directly with an individual on problems centering in his own work. If some supervisors quaver at the prospect of direct, evaluative confrontations, others seemingly manifest a need to avoid provoking their supervisees' dependencies upon them. While it is fully consistent with our outlook to eschew practice that reinforces excessive dependencies among teachers, I must also assert that sensitive and judicious fulfillment of *specific* dependent needs is a critical element of successful supervision and that if Supervisor elects not to provide certain forms of income, that should be a result of rational decisions not to do so, rather than an effect of his emotional incapability to open himself to such requirements.

I have often mused over the question of whether, somehow, if it is not simply a general human condition, there is something about educators and school people particularly, some psychological aberration among supervisors, that makes them substitute records and forms and a paper existence for encounters involving analysis and affection and dependency and frustration and, sometimes, anger. Perhaps such formalized activities as record keeping and checking and rating and other similar avoidance behaviors are merely the manifestations of any bureaucratic system and should not be laid to psychological origins. As a casual observer, however, I find it hard to avoid such fantasies.

From time to time certain supervisors have seemed, to me, to prosecute issues in supervision with excessive vigor, so excessively that one could not escape the notion that their behavior was being motivated by underlying feelings of competition or hostility or needs for self-aggrandizement or an authoritarian propensity and that, in every such case, these underpinnings were well rationalized, or, in some other manner, disguised from the supervisor himself. Although I should be hard put to prove it, it has seemed abundantly probable in relation to one experienced supervisor whose work I have observed extensively, that his narcissism requires so much of this man's sensitivity to be attuned to his own charisma that he absolutely blocks out perceptions of his supervisees' distress and of their behavior generally, as he canters through elegant and, sometimes, ruthless analyses of their teaching. Still other supervisors apparently have dominating needs to be liked and consequently shy from confrontation, even the most innocuous criticisms, in order not to jeopardize "rapport." As you might guess, being generally blind to their own requirements for approval and esteem, such supervisors almost universally insist that their gentility is motivated by a professionally well-founded desire not to injure their supervisees. And in yet another variety, it has sometimes seemed to me that certain supervisors, generally individuals who have experienced serious emotional deprivations or rejections of their own, manifest an aloofness in their professional relationships which appears, if anything, to spell protection against developing emotional involvements predestined, so it would seem, to repeat past injuries to the heart.

I am willing to expose my diagnostic amateurism in this manner in order to create examples that suggest how delicate the process can be of assessing the accessibility of specific issues for supervisory treatment and to demonstrate that if ever Supervisor's own hangups are likely to put him off the track, that will almost certainly be at the moment of making such judgments in strategy, when his own motives and frailties and ambitions, and the like, subtly and unobtrusively regulate the decisions he must render. I am convinced that a part of the clinical supervisor's training must include self-study, in one form or another, that will deepen his understanding of factors that influence his professional behavior and that heighten his ability to exercise deliberate control and discipline over it. I am equally persuaded that beyond his initial training, the supervisor's practice should include provisions for continued, guided, self-examination on a systematic basis.

Another problem associated with the accessibility criterion is that inquiries in this context sometimes stop short at the diagnostic level and fail to touch upon supervisory techniques, existing in the supervisor's repertoire, whose application might affect the degree of accessibility of specific issues. In other words, the supervisor sometimes tends simply to think about Teacher as he tries to predict the kind of impact that certain events will have for him and does not examine, very closely, the processes available to his own performance for modifying that impact one way or another. Analogously, the counselor cannot simply think to himself, "If I raise the problem about his mother, he will become depressed." Beyond that, he must think about the possible advantages or disadvantages which the existence of such experienced feelings and his own participation in provoking them might have, and about methods he might employ for treating his client's depression, before making his final decisions about what to do. It generally appears, in my work with supervisors, that when such inquiry is terminated prematurely, it is often because Supervisor does not maintain clear conscious awareness that, in fact, he *has* a repertoire of technical behaviors, or because his existing armamentarium is small and incorporates more numerous devices for analysis and conceptualization than for producing a calculated impact upon Teacher or effects upon his praxis.

"Fewness" recapitulates most of the problems we have examined in connection to saliency and accessibility, and there is little need to ponder them again. When Supervisor applies this criterion to selection, the stakes are higher than at any other stage of strategy. Still faced with all of the enigmas accompanying his other decisions about what material to treat, Supervisor undertakes a new risk, namely, of eliminating issues that might better have been included, on the one hand, or including issues that would have been sounder to eliminate, on the other. Some errors occur commonly enough in this context to be worth noting.

All other things being equal, clinical supervisors often err by choosing teaching patterns represented by too few data in preference to other patterns capable of being more fully documented. When the necessity for having extensive data is reduced, perhaps because of the high level of efficiency and quality of communication that have been developed in a supervisory relationship, then it is sometimes sound practice to select patterns for treatment whose significance have been defined intuitively and with few data. When the conditions are right for such a choice, it may be best to select such patterns on purpose. Exercising this option appropriately is one hallmark of artful supervision. But in most instances, perhaps, when inadequately documented patterns are selected, Supervisor's selection process has been faulty.

A related problem exists when, although the supporting data for a pattern are abundant, their meaning is obscure. This problem generally arises in connection to data whose intelligibility depends upon highly complex abstract formulations, for example, upon formulations requiring the assumption of many conditional propositions. If, in relation to such complicated proofs the data themselves are ambiguous additionally, then unless Supervisor and Teacher are in telepathic communication, the whole business would be better to avoid.

As I have noted, subsumption of various patterns and categories by one another represents another process related to selection on this criterion. One mistake we occasionally observe is for Supervisor to isolate several minor patterns while failing to include the superordinate pattern (or category) from which their principal meaning derives. This mistake seems so silly that one wonders how it could ever occur. In most instances, it has appeared that Supervisor's error was to confuse his own sense of connectedness with the relationships that Teacher would perceive among the patterns presented; one's own fluency and familiarity with a specific analysis is sometimes likely to produce a generalized expectation that other people will see things the same way and that, for example, their understanding of relationships among parts will be the same as one's own, even without requiring explicit articulation of the organizing whole. In other instances it has seemed that supervisors simply experienced intellectual lapses, having lost sight of the original conceptualization in connection to which the patterns in question were considered important. More frequently, just the opposite error occurs, namely, to isolate a superordinate pattern without presenting a sufficient array of subordinate patterns to enable Teacher to perceive the critical "gestalt." This error, too, seems to arise from the supervisor's own fluency: no longer requiring many examples, himself, to understand the sense in which certain patterns are associated with others, Supervisor falsely assumes that Teacher will comprehend the analysis as though he were equally familiar with its underlying reasoning.

The basic error, in both cases, stems from misjudgments resulting in too few inclusions, that is, from an overly restrictive use of the criterion "fewness." "Too much" and "too little" are errors of selection that often occur in conjunction both to documentary data and to multipattern categories. While too much of anything may encumber a conference, too little of whatever may be required to establish the facts and reasons in question will also lead to failure. In either case, when subsumption exists, "fewness" poses special difficulties, namely, that in order to provide full enough evidence to demonstrate an incorporation of certain patterns by others, Supervisor may have to exceed the limit suggested by his appraisals of Teacher's abilities to deal with specific quantities of information and analysis. Under such circumstances fewness can become a most difficult criterion to administer.

Occasionally supervisors miscalculate optimal quantitative selection by selecting a few patterns for treatment which, despite their small number, are too many for Teacher to handle effectively all in one conference, either because they are incorporated by separate and unrelated categories or because, for emotional or conceptual reasons, they are too rich in meaning to comprehend and to cope with all at once. Although the criterion might seemingly be satisfied, let us say, by a selection of only three issues and their related patterns for examination in the conference, if one such issue has to do with Teacher's means of structuring questions for discussion (in connection to which a need for extensive analysis of questions and some rehearsal in formulating them might be indicated), and the second relates to the ostensible consequences of his biased selections of historical data for classroom study, and the third has to do with the unevenness of his attention to various students in the class (and the pupils' complaints that he "plays favorites"), then because, in certain respects, these patterns are associated with rather different dimensions of classroom experience and because, consequently, a new frame of reference, a fresh start, and a new mobilization of mental energy will be required to broach each such issue in the conference, the end result may be to have inadvertently saturated the conference. In effect, "few" has become "too many" and the goals set for supervision have become too ambitious.

Whether or not such an outcome will truly occur depends largely upon Teacher's individual capacities for shifting gears, which may depend, in turn, on variations in his general level of energy or on the specific loading he attaches to certain issues, and on Supervisor's ability to sense fatigue and alertness and to time the conference's separate sequences propitiously. It is common, in this connection, for supervisors to exceed teachers' endurance and to continue beyond appropriate quitting times because, having already satisfied themselves in their administration of "fewness" during Strategy, they become fixed in the assumption that timing has already been taken care of and screen out contradictory evidence that emerges subsequently.

If the quality of fewness can be illusory when, in the manner I have just described, the few patterns selected require radical mental adjustments to treat, then the opposite effect may also occur in some cases, namely, that because all of the issues selected for treatment are the same, for example, in that they all pertain to closely related patterns or all derive significance from a common category of teaching behavior, Teacher is put under excessive stress by the lengthy prosecution of whatever their common theme happens to be. If I have tendencies to withdraw my attention from *different* stimuli when they occur in rapid succession, I may also tend to retreat from too much of something when, in my subjective experience, it remains the same for too long; I become bored.

More subtly, Supervisor may misjudge the collective impact of various issues taken together, even after he has performed a valid assessment of each such issue's individual significance for Teacher. Sometimes the simple juxtaposition of certain categories all in the same conference will create special meanings or special tensions for the teacher. If, hypothetically, at some level of consciousness, Teacher experiences serious doubts about his ability to communicate clearly and if, by chance, each of the several patterns selected for a given conference is related, somehow, to problems of communication instead, for example, of pertaining to a variety of professional issues and including some analysis of technical strengths, then Teacher's total response to the conference may be inordinately depressed, notwithstanding Supervisor's valid prior assessment of each specific issue's treatability in Strategy.

A kindred phenomenon may arise in conjunction to the sequence of order in which specific teaching patterns are examined. Consequential cumulative effects of a sequence may arise from any number of variables inhering in that sequence. For example, irrespective of their substantive content, if the issues to be treated are presented in order of ascending complexity, then, by the time the final issue is broached, Teacher may have dissipated his available energy in the examination of relatively simple problems which might better have been saved for last. On the other hand, when the issues are sequenced in order of descending complexity, an anticlimactical sensation may diminish Teacher's sense of accomplishment or significance or gratification as the conference draws to its conclusion. It should be clear, even while we consider such possibilities, that beneficial opposite effects might equally well derive from sequences arranged this way. My point is not that either arrangement is necessarily ineffectual but is, rather, that depending upon the circumstances and upon knowledge obtained from his previous encounters with Teacher, Supervisor should be alert to the possibility that potential problems may materialize from such variables as "sequence," particularly during Strategy when there is some chance to avoid problems by prior planning.

Another common mistake relating to the order in which issues are addressed is for the supervisor to have misjudged the effects of dealing, on the one hand, with the lesson's principal strengths first and then with its weaknesses or, on the other, to reverse that order, or, as a third possibility, of dealing, back and forth, with plusses and minuses throughout the conference. There are many times, in clinical supervision, when "strengths and weaknesses" per se are not focal in analysis and where these terms or substitutes for them are not employed.

There are also innumerable conferences in which, even though the critical objective may be to identify good and bad elements of the teaching, their evaluation arises from both members' examination of the data and is developed inductively, that is, there are many instances in which Supervisor has not made up his mind about such things in advance and does not, simply, tell Teacher what is right and what is wrong.

But when identification of strengths and weaknesses and the formulation of strategies for stabilizing and modifying them, respectively, are focal, even though essentially inductive processes may have been employed in the inquiry, it has not been the least bit uncommon in my experience for many teachers to feel that despite having arrived at value judgments by the power of their own analysis and reasoning, there was some underlying trickery that led them to what they suspected, in the supervisor's mind, had been inevitable conclusions. Perhaps, as often as not, it has been that way, but not generally, I trust, as a result of deliberate deception. Often, when I arrive at my own judgments about a sample of teaching, I decide that the best way to move in supervision is by some method that gives Teacher an opportunity to formulate judgments from the data freshly, as though I had not already done so myself. My rationale for such behavior is generally twofold: first, I am likely to assume that there is more good in it for Teacher to have practice at analyzing observational data than there would be for me to perform that drill all by myself. If I can benefit from such practice, then surely he can benefit too. Second, there is little question in my mind that, as a rule, if there is much need or latitude to doubt the validity of an interpretation, it is better for Teacher to have formulated it than it is for Supervisor to try to persuade him.

My principal point, in this regard, is that whether as a result of Supervisor's prior conclusions or of collaborative analysis of the teaching, a conference distinguishes strengths and weaknesses, the order in which they are considered or in which the data from which they arise are presented can generate favorable or unfavorable effects for the teacher. I have frequently observed all of the following outcomes in actual practice:

1. Supervisor begins the conference by dealing with "strengths." Teacher feels that he is being set up for the punch, that Supervisor is keeping something from him, that there are things so basically wrong about the teaching that Supervisor is afraid to deal with them.

2. Supervisor begins the conference by dealing with "weaknesses." Having little tolerance for "criticism," Teacher becomes so anxious or agitated or depressed that he cannot, subsequently, accept or feel gratified by a disclosure of "strengths," seeming sop-like, he cannot trust their authenticity or Supervisor's motives for presenting them.

3. Having identified significant strengths in his own performance and having received consensus from Supervisor, Teacher becomes euphoric or, for one cause or another, becomes unready to give up his pleasure by turning to less satisfactory elements of the teaching. In effect, he tunes them out and fails to invest sufficient energy to understand them and to discover means for improvement.

4. Having discovered significant faults in his work (perhaps alarming ones), Teacher becomes too depressed or remorseful or stricken to perk up the optimism needed for finding positive elements subsequently.

5. Because he tends to polarize value judgments and to see things starkly as "good" or "bad" and, concomitantly, because of his hunger for simple, fast, and definite conclusions—both these tendencies, incidentally, seem substantially more common than uncommon and, in my opinion, partly reflect the degree to which we have all introjected such values from the scholastic environment—Teacher is unable to withstand a conference that deals predominantly with plus-minus patterns, comfortably: he feels confused; he suspects hedging; his anxiety is provoked by the ambiguities and lack of certain structure in such an analysis. He is left feeling empty.

While it may be that preventive solutions to such problems must be developed idiosyncratically, it seems equally important for supervisors to recognize the existence of such outcomes and to understand that besides the specific loading that may attach to any single value judgment, no matter by what processes it has been formulated, the impact of good-before-bad or bad-before-good or of good-and-bad together in any sequence of supervisory inquiry can be critical in determining psychological effects. Even though it may often seem difficult or impossible to predict such effects in advance, it behooves the supervisor, nonetheless, to tap this dimension of strategy as he prepares approaches to a conference. Despite the seeming ethereality of such appraisals and precautions, I have frequently observed, in my supervision of supervisors, instances in which, on the basis of a teacher's past behavior in supervision, one might have predicted one of the outcomes described above and, presumably, have taken measures to avoid it. I have also seen preventive approaches of this kind employed where the undesirable outcome in question did not occur subsequently. While I cannot prove cause-effect conclusively and have not subjected the hypothesis to systematic testing—we really must produce hard research in this area someday—I am nevertheless confident that on a majority of such occasions, things were, in truth, as they seemed to be.

Another problem associated with sequential order, as we have already seen analogously in connection to other supervisory behaviors, is that sometimes, while the supervisor knows the organizational principles according to which he formulated a specific sequence of questions, the teacher does not. And not knowing where things are headed or why they are headed that way, Teacher may fail to comprehend the sensibility of what is occurring, at least not in time to profit from the initial stages of inquiry.

I recall a particularly vivid example of this error in which the supervisor had developed a shrewd analysis in which it seemed clear that the teacher's behavior had been substantially self-defeating. In Preobservation, Teacher had declared that one of his chief goals was to give his students practice in *verbalizing the reasoning* by which a certain category of algebraic problems could be solved. He subsequently had the pupils solve a number of equations at their desks and then directed each of them to select one such problem for presentation to the class and to put it on the board. When every student had completed his boardwork and returned to his seat, Teacher began to question everyone in turn about the work he had performed. So far, so good. What happened, however, was that Teacher succumbed to two temptations, either of which might be considered useful under the proper circumstances, but both of which operated at direct cross-purposes to his stated intent. His first mistake (which could have been avoided had someone at least told the students the correct solutions to all problems before they were asked to display their work) was to become embroiled in substantive errors that the pupils had made and to press, it seemed frantically, for corrections, lest incorrect information be propagated to the other students. All of the time he spent in this undertaking, as it happened, was wasted in relation to his stated goal. His second mistake, once his anxiety had been reduced by correcting all of the boardwork, was to engage the pupils in discussion where, instead of their being permitted to enunciate their ideas and to describe the reasoning they had followed, Teacher speculated aloud on how each student had performed his solution and then turned to him for a statement of agreement (many of which occurred, I suspect, by default).

The conference on this teaching began on Supervisor's request for Teacher to restate the outcomes he had intended. Once again, Teacher said words about practice in verbalizing mathematical processes. Supervisor asked how Teacher felt the lesson had gone. Teacher replied that he felt it had been successful. In the best traditions of poker-faced noncommitment, Supervisor then proceeded to lead Teacher through a fairly exhaustive examination of his observation notes and, episode by episode, he asked, "And what was happening at this point?" Having no idea what the supervisor was driving at, Teacher repeatedly responded to such questions in terms that were more or less relevant to the central point, but which never hit it squarely. After twenty minutes or more of this activity, during which Teacher exhibited progressively more fidgit-ing, moment by moment, Supervisor finally made the point, namely, that *Teacher* had done what he said he wanted the *pupils* to do, in relation to which all of the preceding examples had been intended. It became perfectly clear, later on, in my supervision conference with *Supervisor*, that his misguided processes had not originated from a deliberate strategy of inductive inquiry but, instead, had arisen from a mistaken assumption that, all along, in some part of his mind, Teacher had understood the common feature of the examples to which Supervi-sor had directed him. Their relatedness was so clear to Supervisor that he simply assumed that it was equally clear to Teacher and—this is fascinating—that assumption withstood the contradictory evidence rep-resented by Teacher's initial statement that the lesson had been suc-cessful and by the subsequent irrelevancy of many of his responses to Supervisor's questions.

In retrospect, we both felt relatively certain that if Supervisor had begun, early in the conference, by telling Teacher that his performance had operated against his intended goals and that he (Supervisor) planned to provide Teacher with relevant illustrations from the data, the conference would have proceeded more efficiently, required less time, and avoided the confusion which, presumably, underlay Teach-er's increasing restlessness. In the next sequence of supervision involv-ing these individuals (on the next day), a similar situation arose. Teacher stated, in Preobservation, that the pupils seemed sloppy in their use of mathematical terminology and that, after stressing the desirability of linguistic precision in that subject and after giving them fair warning, he would interrupt the pupils' recitations whenever a terminological error was spoken and would require the erring pupil to restate his idea correctly. As we might suspect, in light of the previous day's problem, what actually happened was that after beginning the lesson, as he said he would, Teacher stopped each pupil who employed terms incorrectly, restated the response himself (in correct language), and then asked the pupil whether he understood.

This time, having been burnt the day before, Supervisor made special note in Strategy to begin the conference, once again, by asking whether Teacher felt successful in achieving what he had been after. Supervisor then determined that if Teacher's response did not hit the nail on the head, he would begin by offering Teacher his general interpretation and would then provide sufficient data to illustrate the point. As it happened this time around, Supervisor did find that Teacher failed to recognize his error (Teacher readily agreed, once the pattern had been identified for him, that it was in error), from which point he implemented his new strategy just as he had conceptualized it. Teacher not only caught on in something under two minutes, but he then seized Supervisor's observation notes and identified additional examples of the pattern avidly and spontaneously. At least in this regard, as I see it, the story ended happily. I should hazard the guess that for most people, a jigsaw puzzle is easier and, except for a handful of purists, more fun to assemble if one has seen, first, how the final picture is to look.

It becomes clearer and clearer as we study clinical supervision that many of the errors commonly committed by supervisors replicate those we encounter in the teaching that we observe. Even when Supervisor has a highly developed understanding of faulty technical patterns and recognizes their existence in his own work, it does not follow, necessarily, that they will, thereafter, be eliminated from it. As we move further into reflection upon problems of getting ready, it would be well to keep in mind that they are often very much the same for teaching as for supervision and that in order to close the gap between the worker's intellectual comprehension of his mistakes, when "mistakes" are his problem, and the establishment of appropriate behavioral modifications, measures going beyond the simple identification of faulty patterns must be taken in most cases.

Another common weakness one may observe among supervisors is their failure, too often, to conceptualize their own goals for teachers in behavioral terms. I should be rich, at a dollar apiece, for every sequence of supervision I have observed (or performed) in which, at the very same time that Supervisor was instructing Teacher about formulating instructional outcomes behaviorally, he had failed to do precisely that in relation to his work with the supervisee. Even more often, formulation of criterion behaviors is a practice that supervisors neglect. It seems probable that among the various causes of such dereliction, the absence of rigorous and systematic postmortems in most supervisory sequences ranks high. In other words, while clinical supervision incorporates evaluation of the teaching upon which it is focused and, for that reason, is almost compelled to stipulate behavioral outcomes among the pupils against which to appraise instructional effects, reflexive evaluation is not automatically built into the supervisory process, even when attention is focused explicitly upon the impact it is having on Teacher's feelings, ideas, and behavior.

If one chooses to do so, one may avoid postmortems forever. When omissions of this kind occur, that is, when Supervisor fails to conceptualize Teacher's gains behaviorally, the question of whether or not supervision is actually resulting in productive payoff tends to be resolved at an intuitive and subjective level and, for example, although things may seem to be going well—perhaps Supervisor and Teacher like each other very much and enjoy their association—success may be more illusory than real, a condition that inevitably catches up with one at the most embarrassing moments. The time for formulating such evaluation criteria and criterion behaviors is in Strategy. Although the supervisor may always go back, after a conference, and identify behavioral modifications retroactively, this process tends to be haphazard and clearly more subjective than one in which goals are formulated properly beforehand.

Even when Supervisor is careful to plan Teacher's supervision with attention to behavioral objectives, his job is not done, for all sorts of problems arise in connection to such goal setting. One common error is to misjudge the behavioral correlates of conceptual gains, to be inaccurate in visualizing the forms in which ideas will become manifest in technical behavior. Although Supervisor's images of qualitative changes may be valid, his expectations of the degree to which such behaviors will occur may be too subtle or too gross, that is, he may set inappropriate criterion behaviors. He may, additionally, over or underestimate the amount of time required for Teacher to demonstrate the new behaviors in question. He may mistakenly assume that because certain technical behaviors have begun to appear, they are underlain by adequate understanding of relevant concepts or, in the other direction, he may mistake verbalizations of conceptual understanding for achievement of corresponding technical strengths. Experience suggests that stereotyped (rote) statements of proposed technical modifications— particularly when such modifications have been formulated by the supervisor—are more rule than exception, not because teachers are devious, but, rather, because of the inevitable developmental gap between verbalization and complex action and because of the peculiarity of language and thought that enables men to sense underlying meanings from words even when they do not truly exist in the speaker's mind.

An example we have already considered occurs when Teacher expurgates the pronoun "I" inappropriately from his verbal behavior, as a result of conferences dealing with the egocentric qualities of his teaching. To literalize or to overgeneralize proposed modifications represents essentially the same phenomenon, for example, when Teacher employs inductive processes at moments when didactic telling would be more appropriate or when, instead of participating in the students' inquiry authentically, Teacher contrives an illusory participation. Only yesterday, I witnessed such an event when my graduate assistant, whose teaching I supervise regularly, riveted me to the spot by exclaiming to our students, at one point in a tortured line of reasoning, "But I don't want to say it because then you'll know what I'm thinking of." With good reason, the students glared back sullenly for the remainder of the session and kept mumbling things about being "manipulated." Far from being any kind of dullard, my assistant is as intellectually talented as anyone. This episode simply illustrated that in spite of her intelligence and the fact that the two of us had talked lengthily about inductive approaches in the seminar, our dialogue had not overcome the effects of her own past scholastic experience which had taught her, in effect, that Teacher is supposed to know all outcomes (answers) in advance and that questioning students is just a technical trick for leading them to foregone conclusions in a flattering manner.

In other instances, the following examples of inappropriate behavior occurred *after* the supervisor had prosecuted related issues in conferences and had falsely assumed that Teacher had "improved" on the basis of what he said, that is, on the basis of his verbalized understanding of pertinent concepts (but in the absence of behaviorally defined objectives). After examining an analysis of his teaching that disclosed a general failure to reward pupils' responses—Teacher often neither remarked on what the pupils said nor made use of their responses, even without explicit comments—and eliciting an avowal from Teacher that he would be more conscious of "rewards" subsequently, Supervisor observed a lesson in which, to an absurd degree, Teacher fussed over almost every utterance his pupils made and acknowledged even their most puerile offerings.

In another case, Supervisor had gotten Teacher to "see" that it might be more useful, under appropriate circumstances, for him to record his pupils' statements verbatim, on the board, instead of in his own, "teacherly" words. Although a technical modification was conceptualized in behavioral terms in this instance, no rehearsal was undertaken and too much was left to chance and to the assumption that Teacher understood the issue thoroughly, because of his verbalized agreements in the conference. What occurred, subsequently, was that during the next sequence of instruction, Teacher recorded pupils' statements so scrupulously that huge amounts of time were lost, the board was filled with a confusing and extensive array of superfluous verbiage, and the pupils became uncontrollably restless during the long interludes when Teacher had his back to them as he chalked their primitive wisdom for posterity. At one point, during this lesson, I experienced a most compelling fantasy that the children had caught on to an ingenious trick and were deliberately saying outlandish and endless things just to see Teacher sweat. In yet another case, after having discussed reasons for enabling the children to formulate their own value judgments about their intellectual products—Teacher's yesses and no's had represented the exclusive source of evaluation—but having failed to think the issue through in operational detail, Teacher became absolutely relentless in his noncommittal posture, to such a degree that one child actually cried in his frustration to discover whether an answer he had found was acceptable (to the Teacher) or not.

On many occasions, I have had to check my own initial disappointment that arose from misguided criterion behaviors that I had conceptualized in relation to some intended modification. On one memorable occasion, after having spoken with Teacher about her tendency to remain physically aloof from the students, even when they were engaged in deskwork in which she might have helped them if she had been in closer proximity, and even after having learned, in conference, that Teacher experienced a veritable phobia toward physical closeness to her students (most of whom were physically larger than the teacher), I observed what seemed to be the same, aloof behavior during the next lesson. In my impatience, I raised the issue again, somewhat more punitively than I should have. To my amazement, Teacher pointed out—and my own observation notes confirmed it—that, in fact, she had moved into the pupils' ranks several times, briefly. Selectively, I had seen what she had *not* done rather than what she had; having observed that she did not dive into the sea, I failed to perceive that at least she had tested it with her toes.

It has begun to seem fairly clear to me that, rather than as an afterthought, the preparation of supervisory objectives in behavioral terms and in relation to criterion behaviors really represents, or can represent, a basic outlook on supervision and instruction which, unlike a reluctant addition to an otherwise complete process, generates special methodologies and special systematic practices of its own. A basic deficiency or traditional supervision (along with others to which we have referred) was that sometimes supervisors were content to deal in principles, in rationales, and in educational ideologies almost exclusively in their work with teachers. Such supervisory grist enabled supervision to remain relatively impersonal, relatively safe, but nominally addressed to "vital issues," at least enough to salve professional consciences. In the other direction, supervision has often aimed at modifying teaching behavior, but its weaknesses in this connection have been first, that the behaviors it sought to influence were often superficial or educationally irrelevant, and second, and this is more important to us for the moment, in his zeal to "correct" some faulty pattern, the supervisor failed to comprehend that the pattern in question was symptomatic of some well-rooted, underlying emotional or conceptual structure. Time and again, I have watched supervisors engaging in random and seemingly endless exercises in symptom-reduction, without ever recognizing the symptomatic character of patterns upon which they were operating or understanding why it seemed to be that no sooner was one technical problem brought under control than another emerged to take its place. Considering this distinction in terms of value systems, we have, on the one hand, supervision whose principal deficiency is to deal almost exclusively with values and to leave behavioral changes to fate and, on the other hand, supervision that is so operational that it neglects to reach beyond manifest behaviors to affect the values and ideas and feelings that motivate and regulate them. The first form is grossly inefficient for changing *teaching* while the second tends to be potshot and, in its peculiar way, equally inefficient.

Many problems of strategy may be obviated if the supervisor, assuming that he already is knee-deep in the psychological quagmires of supervision, has developed a "set" on behavioral objectives and criteria, a characteristic leaning in this direction. For example, it follows almost automatically, from such a predisposition, that Supervisor will foresee opportunities for role-playing and playback techniques, and other forms of rehearsal as he engages in planning for a conference—in time to think through the details and timing of such devices during strategy. One is more apt to be satisfied by superficial yesses and other stereotyped expressions of understanding or agreement when such an orientation is absent from one's general outlook, than when one's fix on *behavior* dictates the very imagery one brings to preparing for a conference.

Of all the reasons that exist to incorporate behavioral outcomes and criteria in the plans laid during strategy, one of the most compelling is that to do so helps to avoid creating the sense of dogmatism and mystery by which, so often, supervision is impeded. Feelings of confusion seem, more frequently, to accompany supervision in which value judgments, suggestions, and dialogue are held at a very high level of generality than supervision in which the basic work deals concretely with specific technical behaviors. An appropriate balance, one that varies between technical detail and *related* theoretical issues on an individual basis, seems most likely to sustain positive morale. "Behavior" provides structure and articulation for objectives and judgments that might otherwise be vague and excessively open to misinterpretation. Two common problems of strategy that omits behavioral formulations are first, that its transformation into real supervisory processes sometimes fails to materialize for that reason, and second, even when the conference has apparently succeeded, subsequent teaching sometimes reveals that shared conceptualizations of desirable changes did not acutally exist although, in discussion, they seemed to.

Another problem arising from Supervisor's failure to picture the forthcoming conference in terms of the actual behavior to be enacted there, for example, its rehearsals, examination of data, invention of teaching plans, and contractual revisions, is that his sense of timing generally and of quitting time particularly, may prove to have been highly unrealistic. Accurate predictions of how much is too much and how much is too little and of when the best time would be to stop, besides requiring great sensitivity during the conference, to be fulfilled, depend, in large measure, upon Supervisor's ability to foresee the manifest behaviors that will occur when he meets with Teacher.

In fairly rapid order, some additional problems of Strategy, common enough to note, are Supervisor's failure to consider the questions of contract and of whether his existing agreements with Teacher require revision. Such an omission may become particularly troublesome when the supervisor assumes certain contractual changes implicitly but neglects to broach them directly with the teacher. Although the game goes on, if the rules have changed secretly, Teacher should be expected to lose sorely. Another problem: Supervisor's natural impatience to generate a plan of action sometimes rushes him through Strategy without adequately considering the incidental learnings likely to arise from his supervisory behavior. Problems arising from this omission generally emanate from dialectical processes rather than from selected substantive content inasmuch as the latter tends to be screened more scrupulously than the former, at least in much of the supervision I have witnessed, while the former is often permitted to take shape randomly.

Three relatively important problems that commonly occur are first, that Supervisor makes the wrong choice among the alternatives of full, open, or directed conference during strategy; second, that Supervisor's decisions on content and procedure are motivated by emotional requirements of his own, of which he has no explicit awareness; and third, that the very fluency which Supervisor has developed as a result of his analysis and strategy places Teacher at an irrevocable disadvantage.

I suspect that the most common error in selecting a conference style is to choose a directed conference, that is, one in which Supervisor takes the major initiative in presenting an analysis of the teaching, when, indeed, this degree of control is unwarranted. For this to be so is unsurprising in light of the strong and familiar traditions of didactic teaching in which all of us are so thoroughly versed, or, even when the supervisory processes employed are fairly loose, as a result of the popular assumption, in our culture, that to teach (in this context, to supervise) implies control over and initiation and guidance of events that occur in the course of instruction. The chief penalty of this error is to have deprived Teacher of engagement in processes of self-initiated evaluation, and so forth, at a time when, presumably, there was no good reason to do so. Such conferences are unlikely to foster the establishment of professional self-sufficiency as a supervisory process goal.

When Supervisor misjudges Teacher's readiness for a full analysis, that is, for a conference in which all of the data and Supervisor's complete analysis of them are presented unabridged, the clearest danger is that Teacher will be overwhelmed by the sheer quantity of material put before him. Although full analyses are occasionally undertaken in order to allay teachers' anxieties about "withheld" material, more generally they are employed with teachers who are judged to be strong, who function well in supervision, and who do not seem to require the protection of carefully selected supervisory issues. Even among highly anxious teachers, the ostensibly reassuring effects of full analysis depend upon the specific patterns that existed in the observed teaching. If the teaching in question seemed generally abominable, then full analysis would be less likely to ease Teacher's distress than if the picture generated by such analysis included positive patterns of technical behavior.

Truistically, the decision to employ an open conference is a poor one when such an approach is unlikely to work. Open conferences are more likely to succeed when Teacher has had some time to examine the data before meeting with his supervisor than when he has not. Chronically, unless Teacher has had extensive practice participating in this form of supervision, open conferences produce meandering, inefficiency, and treatment of uncritical issues, which seemingly result from a feeling of ritual commitment to treat *something*. It is not uncommon for such conferences, especially among beginners, to lapse into social processes, having veered from technical ones.

Irrespective of the specific approach that Supervisor decides to employ for the conference, one of clinical supervision's most troublesome problems is that his selections of data, of patterns, of processes, or of the general supervisory format will be unconsciously motivated by personal needs of which he is unaware, and then justified in terms of Teacher's welfare, rationalistically. Although we have touched upon this problem several times already, it should be duly recorded in this section. By one means or another, practically every problem of supervision can be understood in reference to origins such as perceptual distortion, biased selections of data, misjudgments of specific issues' treatability, misguided selections of format, and the like, and may, at any moment, arise from irrational nuclei of the supervisor's mentality. While preventions and remedies for such emotional interference may be readily conceptualized—although, perhaps, not so readily implemented—in the context of postmortems, the problem also carries an implication for Strategy, namely, that disciplined self-examination should be undertaken concurrently with Supervisor's other preparations for the conference. If the existence of intruding emotional variables is so deeply repressed that even deliberate self-examination will fail to reveal them, then, of course, Supervisor's introspection may not produce useful results. Nevertheless, we advocate the process of examining one's own motives as exhaustively and as objectively as possible during this stage of the supervisory sequence because we believe, and experience tends to confirm, that, repression notwithstanding, one is often likely to discover the operations of one's underlying impulses and defenses if only one troubles to look for them intentionally. Discovery of such variables represents the first step in bringing them under deliberate control. This enjoinder may be expressed in plain terms as well as in fancy ones. Plainly, we advocate that from decision to decision, in strategy, Supervisor should ask himself, "Why am I doing this?"

Finally, in this review of problems, is another upon which we have already touched and which may be stated presently in its most general terms. The essential strength of strategy can also be its most irrevocable weakness, namely, the fluency it creates (that is, the fluency it is *supposed* to create) for the supervisor may provoke feelings of relative incompetency for the teacher instead of resulting in useful benefits to him. As long as it is typically true in practice that supervisors have opportunities to prepare for supervision while teachers do not, special compensatory measures will have to be incorporated to heighten teachers' fluency in supervisory dialogue. Their schedules *should* provide time to prepare for supervision. Cycles of supervision should be arranged to enable supervisees to participate in the invention of strategies for their own supervision. Some combination of devices should be established to heighten teachers' abilities to analyze the work they have done and to decide what changes to make, out loud. Whereas, for the supervisor, to hear such statements as, "How do you manage to find so many things in my teaching?" and, "You've said it so much better than I could have," may, gratifyingly, fill his sails, such attributions signal a persistence of supervision whose effects are more likely to glorify Supervisor than to result in instructional practices that make better sense for Teacher. Constant reaffirmations of one's own potency, like crackers with caviar, are difficult to resist and particularly difficult to avoid deliberately by taking complicated measures to enhance the other member's potency. It may be sobering to bear in mind, however, that caviar is fattening.

IX
Problems

PART 2

STAGE 4: PROBLEMS OF THE CONFERENCE

Problems of the conference are innumerable. The best that can be done is to identify types of problems that have occurred frequently in our practice, other problems which, although they do not occur so frequently are, nevertheless, of special consequence and, particularly, problems for which we have no certain preventions or solutions. Essentially, this section will be an inventory and will include illustrative examples of supervision whenever possible.

Perhaps the greatest difficulty of all, for the clinical supervisor, one from which many categories of problems derive, is to experience professional existence generally and supervision particularly as Teacher does in his own phenomenological frame of reference. In the first chapter of this book, I attempted to portray some of the craziness that can result when teachers fail to understand how children sense the school, how it impinges on their experience from moment to moment. I have tried to make the case that when too little congruence exists between Teacher's perspective on the classroom and the pupils' visions and feelings of what goes on there, the discrepancy may generate a comi-tragic misunderstanding of long-term and monumental proportions. It can lose and waste a lot of "educational" time and can produce, among other outcomes, a lasting intellectual rigor mortis among the learners.

By the same imagining, I come to the conviction that when Supervisor occupies an experiential domain whose boundaries fail to overlap Teacher's in large measure, the same kind of frightened, silly, and wasteful, helter-skelter scurrying can result and, as history suggests, most probably will. If supervision in the schools has been or has become something dumb, then one cause of that failure must be that, to a sorrowful extent, Teacher and Supervisor have viewed the world from different peaks and their communications have become obscured, following this metaphor, by the echoes resounding between them.

Traditionally, and in our own time, teachers and supervisors have been separated by hierarchical distance, by frequently conflicting objectives, and by differences in professional focus that have tended to keep supervisors aloof from classroom teaching while the teachers have been constantly up to their ears in it. Not infrequently, their differences have been tantamount to class struggle, as exists, classically, between labor and management, despite each group's tendencies to define itself as a professional discipline. Besides losing sight of teachers' lives because of their increasing distance from them, I suspect that supervisors have tended, progressively, to meet with distrust when they attempted to redefine their professional relationships more constructively, empathically, and intimately. One of the most common problems we encounter among teachers experiencing clinical supervision for the first time— sometimes this persists indefinitely—is that they seemingly cannot believe or trust their supervisors' apparent attempts to comprehend their professional experiences in essentially the same terms as they do themselves.

In any case, one discovers that supervision conferences abound in problems of this genre:

Supervisor flatly asserts his own view of things without attempting to envisage Teacher's.

1. SUPERVISOR: I have noted several specific reward patterns that I think we should look at today.

TEACHER: I've been terribly concerned about whether the children should be prepared in some special way for the achievement tests that are coming up.

SUPERVISOR: Well, I think we really have plenty of time to talk about that, but this question of rewards pertains to the teaching you're doing right now, and I think it should come first.

2. TEACHER: I find Anthony's behavior very distressing. I want to be kind to him, but I'm afraid that if I give in, he will just continue to take advantage of me.

SUPERVISOR: Oh, I don't know. I think maybe you just aggravate yourself too much. He's not such a bad kid. In fact, I admire his boyishness.

3. SUPERVISOR: So, really, we want the children to take much more initiative themselves for deciding what to do and for getting their jobs done.

TEACHER: But they need to be disciplined, or else they just get wild and disorganized; and nothing gets done.

SUPERVISOR: Yes, that's what I mean. They must exercise more initiative in disciplining themselves.

Supervisor "plays it from rank."

1. SUPERVISOR: I've decided that instead of my filling out this evaluation form for the county, this time, it would be better if the two of us went over it together and then countersigned it.

2. SUPERVISOR: I thought you'd be pleased to hear that I've recommended you for a merit increase.

3. SUPERVISOR: Well, you certainly have my permission to try it if you'd like to.

Supervisor is overly committed to uniformity among various teaching processes and classroom procedures.

1. SUPERVISOR: I can see why you feel that way; but, nevertheless, since all the other sixth-grade teachers assign homework on a regular basis, I think it's important that you do too; otherwise it will seem unfair to children in other classes.

2. SUPERVISOR: Yes, that would be nice for the children, very appropriate, except they're only supposed to take two field trips per year, and then, all the fourth-grade classes are supposed to arrange something together.

There are other important senses in which the supervisor's own frame of reference may obscure his supervisees'. He may, for example, be too distracted by his own anxieties to be able to sense the quality or intensity of Teacher's. He may react defensively to Teacher's behavior, instead of taking some psychological distance on whatever Teacher happens to be doing in order to understand his meaning and, perhaps, the urgency it has for him. He may be distracted by his own feelings of gratification, the flatteries that Teacher pays, the pleasures of being an object of Teacher's dependencies. He may, simply, be distracted by problems of his own that have nothing to do with the supervisory relationship but which, nevertheless, cause his mind to wander away from supervisory issues. In both teaching and supervision, it is very common for the worker to misperceive his trainee's experiences because of strong tendencies to generalize from his own and to assume, implicitly, that things seem to others as they do to himself. If, for example, I have always felt that whispering among the pupils constituted a personal affront (that is, when I was a teacher), I might invalidly assume that my supervisee's feelings about such behavior were essentially the same.

Especially when he is a beginner, Supervisor's conscious preoccupation with his own professional technique may eclipse the ideas and feelings that Teacher is trying to communicate. Transference-like processes may, additionally, cloud each member's views of the other. Supervisor's *idealized* image(s) of teachers may partially blind him to Teacher's *actual* condition. And, perhaps, most commonly of all, when clinical supervisors fail to comprehend their supervisees' frames of reference, that is partly because they do not understand strong reasons for doing so or because, even having reasons, they don't know how, that is, they lack practice in quieting their own internal speakers sufficiently to hear other drummers and to assimilate others' experiences.

One common manifestation of incongruency between Supervisor's and Teacher's frameworks occurs when Teacher is principally concerned with the problem of what to do next, that is, in tomorrow's teaching, while Supervisor is caught up in the mysteries of analysis. Sometimes this discrepancy works in reverse: Teacher is anxious to know, fully, what Supervisor thought of the lesson he observed while Supervisor, sometimes for good reasons, thinks it is better to get on to planning for the future and only to pay cursory attention to the completed lesson. Closely related is the frequent discrepancy between Supervisor's concern with relatively abstract issues while Teacher hungers for concrete solutions. The opposite condition occurs occasionally, but not nearly so often, in my experience, unless intellectualization is operating in the service of avoidance.

Depersonalization—at least to the extent that dialogue hinges on technical issues and disregards such things as what Teacher hopes for or what makes him afraid, his feelings generally, and his feelings of the moment—is another common phenomenon in supervision conferences. In this connection, besides simply failing to share the teacher's perceptions of and feelings toward the performance of his work, the supervisor also avoids sufficiently intensive human encounters with his supervisees to produce "therapeutic" and developmental benefits that require a high degree of emotional rapport. Unempathic supervision, that is, supervision that lacks sensitivity to the teacher's emotional vectors, frequently is coupled with technical primacy: an analytical virtuosity which, for the supervisor, assumes dominance over other forms of intellectual behavior. Instead of functioning as a facilitator of Teacher's professional development and of his fulfillment in terms that he himself formulates, Supervisor sometimes sets out to make Teacher into his own images—to create, in him, a protégé.

Judging from complaints that teachers have generously and candidly shared with us in various supervision practicums, some of their most common grievances relating to conferences are, as they are typically expressed:

1. It's just a lot of talk; we never seem to get anything done.

2. I'd be much better off to have that time for planning and for reading papers (that is, pupils' papers).

3. No matter what I come up with, he (the supervisor) always finds some way to make things more complicated by raising all sorts of questions.

4. If I didn't have so much teaching and preparing to do, then this kind of thing might be OK; but as it is, it just burns up time that I don't have, then, for doing other things that have to get done.

5. He always seems to feel I have problems in my teaching; he doesn't seem satisfied unless he can find problems to discuss.

6. I wish he'd come up with more answers; it's like we never come to definite conclusions about anything.

7. Sometimes I can't really see what he's after.

8. We keep going over the same basic things, time after time.

9. I know why he wants me to take the lead in analyzing my own teaching; but he's better at it than I am, and it wastes an awful lot of time to do it this way.

10. When he tells me what effects some of my teaching patterns are having on the pupils, I think he's just guessing about that most of the time. I don't know where he gets these ideas from. It's like a contest of wills.

11. I'd feel a lot better if he'd just come right out and say when things are good or bad.

12. He seems fixed on the things he wants to talk about but not very interested in things *I* feel are important sometimes.

13. He seems to be afraid that if he says anything, he'll hurt my feelings, or something.

14. I never feel that there's time to fully understand what he's trying to show me. And so, often, I don't have anything to say, and then I feel kind of stupid.

15. This kind of supervision makes me feel like a rat in a maze, like a guinea pig.

16. It's as if there's no connection between the analysis and the plans we make for the next lesson.

17. I don't think he's had much teaching experience. I mean, I don't think he really knows what it's like to be in there with the kids. Also, there are times when he does the very same things he's telling me not to do, like saying *"I"* a lot when you teach.

18. He tries to make believe that we're equals, you know? But that's foolish; there's nothing democratic about this. I mean, he's the supervisor, so why doesn't he just say what's on his mind and get it over with?

19. He seems to ask a lot of questions to find out whether I think he's doing a good job as a supervisor.

20. I get suspicious when he makes such a point of analyzing *his* technique. I don't know what he's trying to prove.

21. This business about "it's OK to fail," you know, "to make mistakes"—that's all right for *him* to say.

22. No matter what I say, he finds some way to attack it.

23. He seems to spend a great deal of time just talking about what we're doing, you know? That is, besides just doing things, he keeps talking about doing things: why we should do them, and how we're doing them, and things like that.

24. Sometimes I get the feeling that he really feels that it [the teaching] stinks, but that he has to find something good to say about it anyhow.

25. He seems much too worried about me—like I'm about to fall apart any minute.

26. Sometimes I worry about him because he seems to worry so much.

27. I'm sure he really has ideas about how to do these things, I mean, after all, he is a supervisor; but he just won't tell me the ways he's used, and I can't understand why he's so resistant. I know it's better to do things for yourself, that you learn better that way, but, well, there must be some reasonable limits to that sort of thing. Is this how he would really want us to teach the kids [that is, by "never" telling them how to do things]?

28. Sometimes I get the feeling that he's treating me as if I were a mental patient.

29. I often get the feeling, and sometimes it makes me very uncomfortable, that he's putting me on—that he knows the answers he's after, but he's just going through a lot of phony motions in this "inductive" business.

Such complaints seem to fall into a relatively few prominent categories. Partly because of conditions that often surround supervision and partly as a result of mistakes that supervisors make, teachers often seem to feel thwarted by the pressures of time; by absences of closure; by the unavailability of simple solutions to professional problems; by apparent "manipulations" to which they are subjected, but whose reasons and intentions they do not understand; by intellectualizations and analysis at a level of abstraction to which many teachers are unaccustomed in their work; by an absence of authoritarianism, whose motives are difficult to understand and to trust; by an equally unfamiliar, unstigmatized conceptualization of "problems" and, even, of "failures"; by the practice of unearthing implicit assumptions and playing devil's advocate, which sometimes seems more like personal attack than professional inquiry; by inquiries whose outcomes are not foregone; by a novel absence of value judgments, particularly of unreasoned ones; by a seemingly unremitting insistence upon examining ideas, behaviors, and practices; by interpretive hypotheses concerning the effects of teaching upon pupils which seem, often, to be figmental; by "gentleness" that sometimes seems implicitly condescending and which occasionally gives rise to fantasies that Supervisor views Teacher as being psychologically fragile (this effect seems to result, simply, from an absence of punitive supervision which many teachers tend to expect and against which they sometimes seem perpetually girded); by a feeling of unproductive repetition, of redundancies, very much like those of patients in psychotherapy who often protest returning, over and again, to issues that seem to be exhausted; by a seeming unconnectedness between abstract inquiries and activities aimed at developing concrete products, for example, teaching (sometimes) and planning; by a feeling that, from a safe vantage point, Supervisor criticizes but is, himself, invulnerable to criticism; by inconsistencies between Supervisor's own technical behavior and his technical prescriptions; by reflexive examination, that is, of Supervisor's own processes, that seems unauthentic or whose reasons are not clearly understood; and by tempos of supervision that are too rapid for effective assimilation to occur or too slow for interest to be sustained.

When supervision generates perceptions and frustrations of this kind and, especially, when Supervisor is not aware of their existence and cannot, consequently, rectify them, the professional relationship is in trouble; and its constructive potentialities may diminish rapidly. It seems, developmentally, that various problems of trusting and of understanding—problems, more generally, of operating by new conventions and, often, within essentially new conceptual frameworks and value systems—are inevitable. It is not as much their existence as it is the possibility of failing to recognize them that constitutes a hazard in clinical supervision. In this connection, one deficiency that commonly exists in our practice is that supervisors often become so absorbed in issues of the moment that they neglect to take longitudinal and developmental views on teachers' professional behavior and maturation.

Two errors tend to result from this omission: the first is that supervisors sometimes become unduly alarmed by the manifestation of certain problems which they fail to recognize as being basic; and the second is that because it may require a developmental perspective to articulate existing difficulties, such difficulties remain undetected for want of appropriate sighting.

The following short compendium is of developmental and acute problems, most of which arise from conditions inhering in the supervisor's behavior, rather than from external factors.

1. Either Supervisor has squandered too much time on analyzing the observed teaching to enable planning to take place in the conference, or he naïvely assumes that the positive modification of faulty teaching patterns requires only an identification of those patterns rather than development of new teaching strategies and their rehearsal.

SUPERVISOR: So you see that to make use of the students' substantive responses, using their own terminology, is likely to provide much stronger rewards for them than to merely say "very good" or to paraphrase everything in your own terms, as you've tended to do. OK?

TEACHER: Yes, I understand what you're saying.

SUPERVISOR: Fine. Keep these things in mind then; this is something for you to work on.

At least, in this example, Supervisor's injunction is relatively specific and might, therefore, be taken up by Teacher constructively—more likely than if Supervisor had said, more baldly, "Your rewards seem pretty ineffectual; that's something I would urge you to work on." In any event, Supervisor did not trouble, for example, to role-play a series of responses in order to give Teacher some opportunity to try using the technique himself.

2. Supervisor reverts to "social conventions" where professional ones are indicated.

TEACHER: I don't know. Sometimes I just feel like giving the whole thing up, quitting this work altogether. I get very depressed.

SUPERVISOR: Oh, things aren't really so bad, although I know they seem that way sometimes. Cheer up. Tomorrow's another day, and things are bound to get better. They always do, you know.

In this example, Supervisor's glib reassurance resembles the kind of social response one might typically expect from a friend or neighbor, unless one lives in a neighborhood of friendly psychoanalysts. He might have had a supportive effect by merely reflecting Teacher's feelings in a manner that conveyed his own understanding of them. He might have attempted to encourage Teacher to explicate his feelings and to make them more articulate, especially in their connection to factors capable of being influenced by supervision. He might have provided some kind of concrete assistance to Teacher, for example, by helping him to formulate plans for the next lesson or, possibly, by providing materials that would increase Teacher's chances of success. And, indeed, Supervisor might have done any of a number of things that one would generally recognize as professional acts in favor of his silly offering. Had I been Teacher in this case, I should certainly have thought to myself, perhaps without giving words to the idea, that, in fact, things do *not* always get better and that, if he really believed such a thing, my supervisor was a ninny. At least, if I thought of him as a nice guy who really wished to be helpful, I should also be troubled by his obvious impotency to help.

3. Supervisor has begun to operate according to a new "contract" but has failed to define it explicitly.

SUPERVISOR: . . . And so those are the categories in which I think, particularly, the patterns in today's teaching were significant.

TEACHER: Umm. [Pause.] Uh, did you get much about Paul?

SUPERVISOR: Pardon?

TEACHER: Uh, I had asked if you'd keep an eye on Paul to get some idea of where it is that he begins to lose touch with things.

SUPERVISOR: Oh! Yes, uh, yes. Truthfully, I became interested in this whole business around problem solving, and, I guess, I lost touch, myself, with Paul. I don't really have any observations of him that I think you'd find useful. I'm sorry.

Two additional problems occurring, occasionally, in relationship to contract setting are first, that Supervisor permits himself to accept a contract, stipulated by Teacher, that centers around issues or processes of whose value he is skeptical and, second, that Supervisor stipulates a contract that is either unacceptable or, in some measure, incomprehensible to Teacher who accepts it nevertheless, often out of deference to Supervisor's "elevated" status. More baldly, teachers are not unknown to accept odious supervisory contracts simply because they are afraid to resist. Supervisors err when they are unalert to such possibilities and fail to detect differences among agreements arising from genuine interest and optimism and those resulting from feelings of coercion.

4. In his zealousness to engage Teacher in objective, systematic, self-evaluation, Supervisor fails to function as a source of adult rewards whose effects upon Teacher could be highly reinforcing and gratifying.

TEACHER: . . . And so it suddenly seemed that after having struggled with it for so long, the questions were coming out just right today. I could just feel it, as my words were coming out, that the questions were being formulated in just the right terms—and their response! I've never seen them so active in a discussion before. And I could tell, uh, that is, I was aware, even while I was saying them, that the kinds of words I was using in the questions would have to stimulate discussion, you know? Instead of the short, flat, answers that they usually give.

SUPERVISOR: You really felt more success in "questioning" today than you had before.

TEACHER: Yes.

SUPERVISOR: Umhm.

5. Although Supervisor espouses a priority on "self-supervision," that is, on self-initiated inquiry and self-examination among teachers, his own avidity to analyze teaching behavior compels him to perform supervisory acts that, were he more restrained, Teacher might have performed for himself.

TEACHER: So it began to seem to me that it was mainly when the kids had nothing in particular to do—not just to keep busy with; I mean something to do in which they were really interested—that their behavior began to get disorderly. And from your notes, it seems that way too. When they were really doing things they cared about, there wasn't any discipline problem at all.

SUPERVISOR: Yes, that's how I feel about it too. Let me show you, here, exactly at which points they began to act up and then to make some suggestions about how you could time tomorrow's lesson, uh, the sequence of activities in it, so that they don't run out of things to do.

In this example, Supervisor assumed a degree of responsibility for planning which, at face value, seems gratuitous. One might infer from his remarks that Teacher already possessed both the insights and the incentives to exercise his own control and the ingenuity to create appropriate modifications.

6. Sometimes discrepancies among professional values undermine successful collaboration in supervision, often because Supervisor underestimates their importance; sometimes because he aims directly at modifying values when, more efficaciously, he might deal with the technical behaviors they generate, that is, at the behavioral level; or, in reverse, he deals with behaviors that are unlikely to change as long as their underlying values are not examined explicitly. In the following example, Teacher's vehemence might be taken as an indication that

rather than to attack the value in question directly, and to provoke sharp resistance by doing so, Supervisor might be better advised to work toward less central and conspicuous *technical* modifications which, even if they did not have influential effects, initially, on Teacher's professional outlook, might at least result in immediate benefits for the pupils.

> SUPERVISOR: . . . So, it seems inescapable to me, that the kind of instruction that aims, simply, to teach the kids a lot of specific information is largely a waste of time. They have to be given enough freedom—to make decisions and to follow through on them—to really learn, from experience, to be intellectually sharp and creative.
>
> TEACHER: I get what you're saying, but—I just know that, I mean, anyone who's constantly in the classroom with these children will tell you—you just have to show them who is boss in the beginning. You have to start tough and then, gradually, ease up and give them controlled freedom. If you don't, they'll figure you for a pushover and learn that they can get away with murder, right from the beginning. These things you're talking about might be OK for very bright, gifted, suburban children, maybe, but they won't work here. You know, I sort of see this as frosting. And what these kids need is more basic. They need, most of all, to find out who's in charge, in no uncertain terms.
>
> SUPERVISOR: Well, I don't see it that way. I think it's mistaken to assume that the way these kids learn is especially different from the ways in which any kids learn. And I think, to the contrary, that if what they learn from the beginning is that you're the boss, it will be exceedingly difficult later on for them to learn to behave more independently.
>
> TEACHER: Well, I don't want to disagree with you, but all I can say is that if *you* spent some time teaching these kids I'm positive you'd find out that I'm right. I mean, if you want to try this approach with them—I'd love to see it. If I could see it, then maybe I could believe it.

7. Supervisor permits global perceptions and interpretations to go unchallenged and, consequently, to remain undifferentiated.

> TEACHER: These children are just lazy and negative. I've never had a group like this before. They're all impossible.
>
> SUPERVISOR: You can't find any way to get them in line?
>
> TEACHER: No. They are all totally uncooperative.
>
> SUPERVISOR: Well, maybe, then, it's time to get tough with them and also to find special ways to motivate them better.

In this example, Supervisor has apparently accepted Teacher's characterization of the pupils which, first of all, incorporates ambiguous images, namely, "lazy," "negative," and "uncooperative," and, second, implies that, in relation to these characteristics, all of the children are the same.

8. Supervisors are sometimes trapped by some teachers' tendencies to externalize problems, mainly by attributing them to outside sources, and, relatedly, by their use of external issues as substitutes (evasions) for genuine problems in their teaching, by whose confrontation they feel threatened.

> SUPERVISOR: . . . So I wonder about what price you pay for the efficiency you enjoy when all of the children make exactly the same kind of Christmas wreathes at the same time. I also wonder, more generally, how useful an experience it is, for them, to work on decorations for a teachers' dinner that they won't even attend.
>
> TEACHER: Yes, perhaps. But the other fourth grade prepared the Thanksgiving decorations and I guess, the way they feel about it, it's our turn now. Mrs. Johnson just told me that she thought it would be best for our group to do it; and since she's more experienced here than I am, I thought it best to follow her suggestion. The children seem to enjoy doing this very much. Yesterday we spent all afternoon on it, and you could have heard a pin drop. By the way, we're running very short on red and green construction paper, and I'm not sure we'll be able to get the entire bulletin board covered. They have been very slow in filling requisitions for materials this month.
>
> SUPERVISOR: You need more art supplies immediately?
>
> TEACHER: Yes, if they want us to finish this job.
>
> SUPERVISOR: Have you tried to borrow. . .

9. Supervisors are sometimes too assertive in their references to incidental learnings. What ought to be hypothesis too often becomes reified and is proffered as an element of reality.

> SUPERVISOR: So, when you constantly repeat what the children say, they'll learn, from that, that they never have to listen to anybody except you and they won't listen to each other.
>
> TEACHER: You think they actually think of it that way, I mean, "We don't have to listen to anyone except Mrs. Hardesty"?
>
> SUPERVISOR: Yes, of course.

10. Supervisors sometimes seem compelled to include some reference to both strengths and weaknesses of the observed teaching in supervision conferences. In most such cases, it has seemed to me, even

more basically, that the supervisor's principal error was to lose sight of the possibility that, in fact, he is never forced to render value judgments on any specific occasion, that conferences may proceed without including specific value judgments at all, and that when evaluation is appropriate, many processes can be employed that may enable Teacher to initiate his own examination and evaluation of the issues in question. Indeed, such errors generally reflect immaturity in the clinical supervisor's conceptualizations of his role.

> *a.* SUPERVISOR: I must say, though, that your personal warmth toward the children is most impressive to me.
> *b.* SUPERVISOR: By the way, I know it's not terribly important, but, at one point, you did say, "preventative" rather than "preventive." That's the only thing I can find. Except for that, the lesson was very successful.

11. Too often, supervisors (as well as teachers) provide too little time for their supervisees to assimilate important questions or to engage in reflective thought pertaining to the salient issues with which the two are dealing. When time for assimilating questions is insufficient, such questions are likely to take on a ritualistic and rhetorical character. Certainly, any question to which one is unable to begin formulating a response is a gratuitous question.

> *a.* SUPERVISOR: You don't mind, do you, if I tape-record these sessions for the seminar in supervision that I'm attending? [No pause.] The first thing we ought to do, I think, is begin talking about the "cycle of supervision" and how it generally operates.
> *b.* SUPERVISOR: Do you think it would be better for the children to evaluate their own work in this unit? I think they could use some practice in objective self-evaluation and that in social studies you have an ideal opportunity to give them that. I think the way to handle this is to . . .

12. Supervisors' errors may be most disastrous when they parallel the very errors being addressed in the conference.

> SUPERVISOR: What I'd really like you to do for me is to try not to teach the lesson in the first person. I mean, I think that when you use "I" so often, the kids are likely to learn that whatever they do in school is for your sake, this is, for Teacher's sake. I really wish you'd try to work on this pattern.

13. A closely related phenomenon consists of the tendency to operate by double standards so that, for example, values espoused in the supervision are not fulfilled in the supervision.

SUPERVISOR: I can tell you, from a great deal of professional experience, that it's bad to expect the pupils to take information mostly on faith. It just teaches them a slavish dependency upon authority and dulls their critical thinking. A fact should never be accepted just because you say so and because you use your authority to impose it on the students.

TEACHER: I think that a teacher *should* represent authority and authoritative information to the students. After all, I'm an adult, and I've been around; and they're still children.

SUPERVISOR: Well, studies show that that's poor teaching, in the long run, and I'm afraid I must insist that you try to improve in this respect.

14. Perhaps the most rapid and efficient way to alienate one's supervisees is by hedging and by pussyfooting.

TEACHER: So you think I was really sarcastic with them?

SUPERVISOR: Uh, no, I didn't really say that. You are generally sympathetic and friendly with the youngsters, but some of your remarks today, were, uh, less kindly than I've know them to be in the past.

TEACHER: Some of my behavior today was unkindly?

SUPERVISOR: Well, uh, no, not really, but, uh . . .

Many additional problems of the conference, a good number of which have already been cited at various points in this writing, are difficult to illustrate by short excerpts, but are nonetheless vivid and common in clinical supervision. Primarily for the simple purpose of simultaneous viewing, I have brought them together in the following short inventory. Collectively, they project an image of conferences at their most troublesome complexity; conferences in which problems are generated sometimes because of supervisors' errors but, ironically, sometimes as a direct outcome of well-executed clinical supervision. Any professional discipline may be badly performed because of inadequate understanding or poor technique. But every such discipline also creates or embodies problems that result not so much from its practitioners' technical weaknesses, as from the premises, values, and theoretical formulations that constitute its very fiber, and which generate certain difficulties even while they prevent or remedy others.

1. Supervisors' zeal to take active leads in analyzing teaching and in developing strategies for its modification may, self-defeatingly, repeatedly reinforce teachers' dependencies upon them for such activity.

2. Supervisors sometimes misjudge the most productive process to employ at any given moment in supervision—whether, for

example, to use the conference primarily for diagnosing professional problems, for dealing with emotional ramifications of the teacher's professional work, for addressing technical issues didactically, or for developing concrete aids such as teaching plans or instructional materials for Teacher's use. When timing is off, not only may the potential efficacy of any specific approach be lost, but the gains that might otherwise have been achieved by an alternative approach are lost as well.

3. Supervisors sometimes use their data ineffectually, either because their meaning is inherently obscure, or because too few of them have been collected to document the issues in question, or because they are examined excessively and redundantly after their purpose, namely, of demonstration, has been satisfied.

4. Supervisors occasionally err by confusing literal patterns of teaching behavior with the effects upon the students that they are supposed to produce. If anything, besides the misdiagnosis, which may result from this process, the tendency to identify effects with causes generally creates intellectual closure; that is, it stops inquiry from commencing at precisely the moments when its continuation might be most critical.

5. Supervisors sometimes confuse the goal of avoiding *unexamined* value judgments with a practice of withholding value judgments generally. In some instances we have even observed clinical supervisors enjoining teachers to defer their own *reasoned* evaluations as a result of this misconception. Such supervisors get the idea that it is bad to say good or bad, but seem to miss the point that what is wrong with such judgments generally is that they are glib, global, dogmatic, and uninstructive. That they are indeed value judgments does not make them inherently undesirable. To the contrary, the principal purpose of analysis is to formulate such judgments in order to modify the teaching performance rationally and constructively on the basis of objective evaluations of the teacher's work.

6. Psychological defensiveness represents a category of behavior with which clinical supervisors are often least competent to deal. On the one hand, being untrained in such issues, they sometimes fail to recognize the defensive underpinnings of various behaviors in which teachers engage in conferences. On the other hand, they sometimes become angered by teachers' defensiveness by which they, in turn, feel threatened, and toward which they react subjectively rather than with appropriate clinical distance. Additionally, supervisors are often unaware of their own defensive responses and deceive themselves by not recognizing the sources of their ideas and strategies and professional behaviors generally, that is, by not understanding the defensive origins of motives for

the actions they take in supervision. Too often, it appears, supervisors feel required to attack teachers' defenses, to strip them away as quickly as they can. Unfortunately, their impatience to do so generally results in wasted motions, largely because it prevents them from dealing sympathetically and supportively with the teacher in order to alleviate the anxieties that give rise to such behavior in the first place.

7. Not only in relationship to anxiety and defenses, but in connection to feelings generally, to frustrations, disappointments, confusions, and needs for acceptance and support, supervisors often lack sensitive "pick-up." The same deficiency pertains to their ability to interpret the meanings of interactional processes that occur during supervision conferences—the implicit meanings attached to explicit communications in which Teacher engages, meanings that frequently communicate affection or hostility or fatigue or distraction but which require considerable clinical acuity to recognize.

8. Suggestion making and advice giving are problematical techniques for various reasons. Besides being generally inconsistent with process goals aimed at establishing self-supervision at progressively more autonomous levels, the two most common difficulties arising in this connection are, first, that supervisors withhold suggestions at moments when, still being relatively dependent on such things, teachers have little tolerance for anything but suggestions; and, second, even after teachers have demonstrated that they will subvert the supervisor's suggestions by following them literally and rigidly to outcomes in which failure is practically inevitable and can be blamed on Supervisor's poor advice, some supervisors persist in suggesting things, self-defeatingly.

9. A general problem, whose specific forms are countless, occurs when supervisors fail to be innovative and flexible during conferences, when they hold on tight to prior strategies, largely as a result of their own anxieties, and fail to respond creatively and spontaneously to unpredicted events. The opposite problem, namely, to be unprepared with supervisory strategies, is considerably less common among clinical supervisors.

10. Supervisors sometimes underestimate their supervisees' personal and professional resources and falsely assume their own indispensability in Teacher's development. More accurately, they misconstrue the sense in which supervision may be *truly* indispensable, namely, as a dialectical medium and, instead, think of themselves as having power to change, to cure, to reform: in effect, to *create* better teachers. The implicitly condescending assumptions of such a posture seem, from what teachers tell us, to

be communicated so potently that nothing positive is likely to result from the supervision to which it gives rise. When the teacher senses that, somehow, his supervisor thinks of him as a needy patient or that Supervisor's responses are censored instead of being authentic, his self-confidence and his confidence in supervision generally falter.

11. Until he has reached the stage in his own professional development where the various functions he performs and the processes he employs are integrated into a cohesive supervisory style, Supervisor's shifts from didactic to diagnostic to "therapeutic" roles are likely to seem awkward and inconsistent and to disorient his supervisees. By and large, it seems that such images of apparent instability operate against the establishment of relaxation and trust in supervisory relationships.

12. Because they sometimes rely upon rote formulas of "accepting" and "supportive" supervisory behavior, some supervisors invalidly assume that when they have "been supportive" with a particular teacher, that teacher has felt supported; that is, they confuse their intentions with their effects.

13. Some supervisors err by refusing, out of hand, to deal explicitly with personal material that teachers sometimes introduce into supervision conferences. Others would like to respond to such material but feel very shaky about how to do so. Still others seem so set on ferreting out such issues that, in effect, they trespass unwarrantedly on teachers' privacy. Although teachers generally seem ready to forgive lack of technical sophistication in treating personal issues, they also seem, often, to feel rejected both by refusals to look at such things and by excessive interest in them. Even well-intentioned and relatively sophisticated clinical supervisors frequently find it difficult to sift spontaneously presented personal issues in order to maintain a *supervisory* relationship (rather than a treatment relationship) by enforcing a criterion of relevancy (namely, to Teacher's professional activity).

14. Particularly during their early period of work with teachers inexperienced in clinical supervision, various factors tend to produce a mystique around the supervisors' professional activity. For one thing, supervision in the schools has always been a fairly mysterious process, even to those who practiced it. Additionally, the clinical supervisor's unprecedentedly detailed analysis of Teacher's work, coupled with his tendency to play devil's advocate, creates novelties in the teacher's experience that, not infrequently, he reverts to "magic" to explain. "He can make things come out any way he pleases, good or bad" is not an uncommon allegation for teachers to level against their clinical supervisors early in the game. Once, I was actually asked whether

I could read minds by a teacher who, in other respects, did not
appear more paranoiac than anybody. Partly because they have
become so accustomed, one might suspect, to dichotomous criteria
in professional evaluation (most things are either good or bad,
right or wrong), such teachers often mistake their supervisors'
complex evaluations of teaching patterns, especially of patterns
that seem concurrently useful and hazardous, for cowardly
equivocation.

15. Supervisors sometimes revert, themselves, to evaluational
polarities, either for want of the energy required for complex
analysis or because they have followed their supervisees' thinking
in that direction and have become subtly trapped by it.

16. Supervisors' own anxieties generate a multitude of
problems in supervision conferences. Most commonly, I suspect,
anxious supervisors hold on too tightly to their prior strategies and
lose spontaneity and flexibility when in a state of heightened
anxiety. By contrast, other supervisors—my experience suggests a
smaller proportion—lose sight of their strategies and become
scattered and unfocused in their conferences. Often, his own
anxiety sparks defensive behaviors and diminishes the supervisor's
objectivity. Under such conditions it sometimes appears to the
outside observer as though Supervisor's perceptions of and
responses to Teacher arise principally from a transference-like
relationship instead of from the objective realities constituted by
the teacher's actual behavior. Clearly, when the
supervisor-supervisee relationship assumes the character of a
parent-child or sibling relationship, particularly when Supervisor is
unaware of its parataxic character and is, consequently unable to
do anything deliberate about it, the supervision ceases to produce
the outcomes for which it is generally intended.

17. I have already pointed out in connection to "the
supervisory mystique" and other issues, that supervisors
occasionally lose by neglecting to say what they are doing in
addition to executing the act in question. Especially when the act
represents a novelty in the teacher's supervisory experience, its
rationales and purposes must sometimes be stated explicitly in
order for its intended outcomes to be realized. For example, if
Supervisor truly believes in making productive use of failure and
conceptualizes failure in a dispassionate and constructive manner,
his ability to educate Teacher's values in order for him to confront
his own failures without shame—an objective that sometimes
seems impossible to achieve—may be enhanced if he takes the
time to explain his conceptual framework around failure or to lead
Teacher through inductive inquiry on that issue. When Supervisor
simply proceeds, without warning or explanation, to name failures

and to deal with them, Teacher is likely to feel beaten up by the process—if, while Supervisor moves blithely along, Teacher remains encumbered by all of the old painful connotations of failure that he has accumulated in the past—simply for want of appropriate preparation. The same difficulty attaches to process confrontations which, if they are suddenly made without warning, may simply seem argumentative or unduly aggressive to Teacher who, one might ordinarily predict, is unaccustomed to facing such questions as, "What, exactly, have you been doing in this conference for the last ten minutes?" And again this same problem arises in connection to Supervisor's technique of employing examinations of his own technical behavior for didactic purposes in the conference. Having probably never witnessed such behavior by a supervisor before, Teacher is often dismayed and distrustful and unable, without some prior explanation, to make very good use of Supervisor's gambit. Without understanding the purpose of such public, self-examination, it may easily seem overly righteous or defensive.

18. Process confrontations are sometimes made so frequently that they distract supervision from the substantive issues being addressed. More often, supervisors err by neglecting to make such confrontations at moments when the dialectical process has bogged down, for one reason or another, and might be freed again by refocusing inquiry in its direction.

19. Depending on the stage of his own training, the supervisor may commit one of two general errors related to the technique, "hierarchical intervention." Early in his training, if he errs at all, he is most likely to move, precipitously to the terminal, highly directive steps in that process (sometimes because he is impatient; more often, because he has not fully recognized the technique's applicability to the issue in question). More highly trained clinical supervisors are more likely to be overly scrupulous and to overextend the duration of early stages in this process, even after Teacher's manifest confusion and the ambiguity of Supervisor's own behavior should have been taken as indications to move on through the sequence.

20. Supervisors frequently misjudge the timing of conferences, more often by extending them too lengthily than by quitting prematurely.

21. In connection to special, clinical techniques, we find innumerable errors, some of them relating to the question of when a technique should be applied, others relating to the technique's actual use, that is, "how to do it." Role-plays, playbacks, role reversals, and reflections are sometimes employed gratuitously, lost by missed opportunities, or implemented awkwardly. One

must be able to judge, for example, at what moment a reflection of feeling or of meaning is likely to lead toward heightened insight and to provide a point of departure for more efficient inquiry. One must, moreover, reflect accurately or, second best, reflect tentatively enough to permit corrections toward accuracy, lest the technique fail altogether. One must be able to distinguish between reflections rightfully rejected on the basis of inaccuracy and those rejected for precisely the opposite reason, namely, because they are *too* accurate, too anxiety provoking, and, in short, too generally threatening to be accepted all at once. Such determinations require considerable clinical finesse and, unsurprisingly, are performed erroneously in many instances in clinical supervision.

As one might expect in relation to any professional relationship, we find, abundantly, in our observations of clinical supervision, that faulty techniques, weak conceptualizations of the supervisory model, or intellectual or emotional deficits that interfere with the supervisor's performance, all tend to leave the teacher somewhat resentful or frustrated or angry or vaguely dissatisfied and, almost always, with a feeling of having been manipulated by the professional worker. While one's reactions to such a feeling may vary broadly from person to person, among the teachers with whom we have worked they seem, inevitably, to be negative in one form or another. Indeed, it is easy to feel empathically toward clients whose discomfort and anger are provoked by faulty professional processes. I, for one, do not enjoy the feeling that my barber, my attorney, my psychiatrist, my surgeon, or my embalmer are *learning* on me, or that in some manner that I do not understand, I am serving as an experimental subject for them. While I might readily donate my body to medical research or place my ego at the temporary disposal of psychiatric alchemists, when I commit myself to that sort of thing, *I* want to be the one who made the deliberate, if silly, decision to do so. What troubles me is the uneasy feeling one sometimes develops that without one's explicit knowledge or consent, one is being employed in services other than for oneself. Commonly, in new clinical supervisory relationships, teachers are inclined to ask, "What does he [Supervisor] get out of all this? Why does he bother?"

Summing up, problems of the conference are essentially problems of operating at many levels and performing many functions concurrently. Supervisor must hear what Teacher is saying and must, additionally, understand Teacher's intended meaning and other meanings, the implicit communications, that may underly his spoken words. At the same time, he must hear his own inner voices, his motives, his impulses, his anxieties, and so on, and, especially, his values and professional biases as they rise up to influence his mental responses and his outward behavior. He must maintain an awareness of his prior strategies and engage in behavior that is consistent with his intended outcomes and, simultaneously, must be sufficiently sensitive and flexible to move in Teacher's directions, often when such movement follows unanticipated itineraries. He must be able to transform ideas and intentions into action and must, thereupon, engage in technically adroit actions. All at once, he must draw upon his technical repertoire, instantaneously and without labored effort; he must function by the specialized conventions of his discipline and must, with equal authenticity, draw upon the mental resources he possesses as a human being: his "human" resources.

He must generally be directed toward both long-term and immediate goals and should sense the developmental outcomes and developmental unfolding that constitute the overall framework in which his supervision of a specific teacher is occurring and must understand how to treat issues of the moment in a manner that facilitates those outcomes as well as meeting Teacher's immediate requirements. His professional behavior should exemplify many of the same processes and values and technical standards that have been set as goals for Teacher's performance. He must be self-reflective and insightful and controlling, and must devote equivalent energies to self-examination as to the examination and analysis of Teacher's work. He must perform counseling and didactic functions and know which compromises between diagnostic and "treatment" goals are optimal at any given juncture in the supervision. He must be committed to process goals as well as to substantive technical outcomes and must possess such theoretical information concerning professional development, human actualization, and learning as his clinical accomplishments require. He must want, very badly, to be a successful supervisor.

In the existence of these conditions and in their establishment, we have problems in a positive sense: disciplinary problems, as problems of theoretical physics are problems of the parent discipline. When these conditions do not become established or maintained, or when they are imperfectly established, then we have problems in the negative sense; namely, we have supervision in which something is the matter. Problems of the conference are, in effect, a composite of all the problems of clinical supervision. Inadequate Preobservation, faulty observation, erroneous analysis, mistaken strategies, and a failure to have examined one's own professional behavior objectively, all become manifested in the conference, in the central and critical transaction that exists between the supervisor and the teacher. No matter how eloquently Supervisor has performed the surrounding functions, he may, nonetheless, blow the whole business in this moment of encounter if, despite his most elaborate precautions and preparations, he is generally or momentarily unfit for productive interpersonal transactions. In short, he must be both well trained in the ideas and methods of his work and potent, stable, and well assembled as a person. Godlike, no; but with strong capacities for learning and for changing. I suspect that Supervisor's own continuing enhancement and development are necessary concomitants of successful clinical supervision and that when he is unable to engage in relationships that are mutually facilitating for the teachers and for himself, then, as they say, "We've really got problems!"

STAGE 5:   PROBLEMS OF THE POST-CONFERENCE ANALYSIS (POSTMORTEM)

Two tendencies—(1) to feel as though one knows, generally, what one is doing and (2) when the opposite feeling exists, to shrug one's shoulders and to avoid looking closely at one's own behavior in order to understand more clearly what the trouble is—lie at the source of problems in this context of clinical supervision. There are various ways to express the basic difficulties of this stage. At bottom, there is the problem of taking objective distance on one's own work and on one's own behavior. In this connection, many specific problems may be pinned to the various defenses that operate in human personalities to obscure or to deny or to rationalize or to avoid reality, often in the same manner for all of us but always, in some detail, differing from one individual to another.

In my own experience and in those of colleagues with whom I have been closely associated, we often find that supervisors feel consciously afraid to look inward. When a scared feeling does not exist explicitly, the underlying anxiety is variously experienced as fatigue— "I really believe in the postmortem but, generally, by the time I've finished going through a whole sequence of supervision, I'm just too pooped to get involved in one." —or as an absence of motivation: "There really didn't seem to be any need for self-analysis. I mean, it wasn't as if it had been a particularly complex sequence up until then." Occasionally, it seems, the supervisor's mechanism for protecting himself from the threatening potentialities of self-examination, is, instead of consciously feeling tired or afraid, to actually *perform* postmortems, but in a superficial and ritualistic manner. Going through the motions tends to satisfy both purposes: Supervisor has done what he ought to do, and he has done the job painlessly, albeit self-deceptively. In my work with supervisors it has frequently seemed that although their performance of supervision sometimes became jaded and automatic and rote, these characteristics became manifest much earlier in connection to self-supervisory activity. The postmortem is generally the first stage of the cycle to atrophy in practice.

Problems of the postmortem, especially among beginning supervisors, are occasionally associated with inadequacy of analytical skills across the board. When the supervisor is not competent to interpret behavioral data generally, there is no reason to expect him to be particularly competent in analyzing his own behavior. From time to time, incidentally, I have observed an interesting related phenomenon, namely, that Supervisor was, in fact, highly capable of performing insightful analyses of his own work but less capable of analyzing Teacher's work and of conducting conferences based upon such analyses. In such cases it has usually appeared that the supervisor's problem, even in Stage 3, derived from his anxieties around confrontation; that is, besides lacking the fortitude for confrontations in the conference, the supervisor could not even prepare himself adequately for prospective confrontations during strategy. In one case that left me with particularly vivid impressions, the supervisor was so inhibited in this respect that although his self-analyses were quite sophisticated, his analyses of other people's teaching, *even when performed upon case materials,* were generally puerile.

In yet another sense, failure to achieve successful postmortems frequently seems associated with a simple lack of self-discipline that is expressed in other manifestations of sloppiness throughout the supervisor's work. The very same supervisor whose observation notes are slipshod is likely to be the fellow who forgets to employ a tape recorder during the conference or, even more typically, activates his machine with such a low volume setting that nothing is recorded. Less neurotically, inadequate self-discipline is more likely to be expressed by the habit of promising oneself that although there really isn't time or energy enough to perform a postmortem today, one will definitely do so tomorrow—and tomorrow, and tomorrow. Lazily, some supervisors also do not bother to specify behavioral outcomes and behavioral criteria for successful conferences beforehand and, consequently, reduce the certainty and efficiency with which they might otherwise evaluate conferences retroactively.

Sometimes the supervisor represses data pertaining to his own performance. Sometimes, although the data are admitted to consciousness, they are processed through defensive filters. Sometimes the supervisor's findings are influenced by temperamental factors, for example, when a self-deprecatory analysis emanates from a spell of gloominess. Even when the supervisor is able to perform an adequate evaluation of his work, unless he is blessed by the existence of colleagues whom he may employ as professional foils, he is often frustrated, if not hamstrung, by the difficulties involved in progressing from psychic realizations to behavioral modifications. As a rule, his opportunities for rehearsal are not nearly as abundant as those he may provide for his supervisees. While self-supervision represents a highly valued practice to us, ironically, perhaps, once such activity has been established on a systematic basis, it generally seems that the requirement for other people to participate in the process becomes more pressing. This is the principal sense in which I believe that supervisors never become obsolete: the more autonomously Teacher engages in self-supervision, the more productively he can employ his supervisor's services, and the same holds true for supervision of supervision.

Although such phenomena have not appeared with great frequency in our work—perhaps this says, simply, that we did not sense their existence as often as we might have—certain other peculiarities arise from time to time in relation to postmortems. Some supervisors employ the idea that, ultimately, postmortems are performed for the supervisees' sake and manage, by that rationale, to escape genuinely productive involvement in a process also intended to be for their own benefit. One thinks, analogously, of parents, in child guidance clinics, who agree to enter psychotherapeutic treatment of their own but who do so primarily because such treatment represents a condition set by the clinic for accepting their children. If I enter treatment grudgingly in order for my children or my spouse to be offered treatment I believe *them* to need, then the therapeutic effects of my own treatment experience are likely not to materialize very substantially.

We have also observed some supervisors who become so hooked by the postmortem, that is, their self-directed inquiries and fascination with their own behavior become so ascendant that their interests in the supervisees and the energies they develop in supervision are depleted. In such cases it has generally seemed to us—and, truly, these have occurred so infrequently that generalizations drawn from them must be highly tentative—that the supervisors in question made early use of their own supervision and, particularly of the postmortem, as a surrogate for more personally oriented counseling which, in fact, was the service they required. Even under the most favorable conditions, it is not always easy to maintain a productive balance between the teacher's interests and one's own, in the activities of this stage. Being neither simply for the supervisor's own technical development nor for his individual supervisees' welfare, the post-conference analysis must serve both purposes adequately to be consistent with our conceptualizations of its ideal effects.

Just as it is with many analogous processes, the postmortem may come to symbolize many of the wrong things and, even for an individual supervisor, its purposes may fluctuate among appropriate and inappropriate rationales and objectives. It may, as I have noted, become a penance. It may become a source of invidious comparisons between Teacher's willingness and competency to have his work analyzed and the supervisor's own readiness for such activity. It may become a time-waster: one supervisor in training insisted that his repeated failure to prepare certain materials for a teacher, which he had voluntarily promised her, resulted from engaging in lengthy postmortems that consumed all of the time in which he might otherwise have followed through. Implicitly, he assumed that Postmortem was a more noble and more-likely-to-be-rewarded activity than assembling the instructional materials in question.

One cannot escape the conviction that postmortems are most likely to succeed in a context of group supervision or in a training program in which other supervisory personnel are available to participate, on a regular basis, in supervising Supervisor. For individual supervisors working alone, the problem of engaging in systematic self-examination will never be an easy one to resolve. Nonetheless, I cannot overstate the urgency of such activity if clinical supervision is truly to emerge as a potent and useful professional practice.

X

Glances and Glimpses
Forward and Backward

It remains for us to consider what positive potentialities are embodied in the models of clinical supervision we have examined, vis à vis the scholastic aberrations reviewed in the first chapter. Very quickly, let us recall some of the phenomena we considered there.

Notwithstanding the existence of superior schools and superior teachers and the immeasurable virtues of intelligence, dedication, and sobriety that exist among educators generally, one may, almost at random, observe a thousand practices in the common schoolroom whose intent and conceptualization and probable effects are inconsistent with the youngsters' educational and personal welfare. I have reasoned that, bound up as they are in content curriculums and prizing as they do the priorities on answers that are inevitably associated with such curriculums, the schools generally do not facilitate development of psychological autonomy and do not, consequently, turn out pupils having adequate intellectual viability in an age when knowledge and information are prolific. They do not, in my judgment, go nearly far enough in preparing human beings for coping with life and with knowledge, on their own initiative and, successfully, by their own powers.

I grant that for every negative condition I identify, corresponding

positive features are likely to exist in one setting or another. My
intention is not to condemn the schools or to project a balanced picture
of their strengths and weaknesses. I have attempted, simply, to draw
attention to certain of their deficits, and I have proposed that, to begin
with, much of the substantive information taught there is unauthentic
and puerile. Many characteristics of the common curriculum stand to
alienate children from it by making it seem either remote from reality
or starkly falsified. I have offered a manifold of inadequacies by which
curriculums are commonly plagued, pertaining, by and large, to the
selections and omissions of the material they include, the sequences of
presentation into which such content is generally organized, and the
intellectual processes generally associated with their typical methods of
presentation.

I have argued that rather than to enhance learners' understanding
and acceptance of themselves, the school experience often seems to
engender ambiguous and negative self-definitions. Besides a glaring
absence of "self" as an object of study, I have asserted that an absence
of reasons and rationales and purposes that are cogent in the pupils'
frames of reference is more typical than atypical in the school—that, in
effect, the learner's dependencies upon authority, his latent docility, his
aversions to academic inquiry, and the myriad factors in his mental
behavior that militate against intellectual autonomy are often reinforced by the scholastic milieu to an unwholesome degree. In connection both to problems of self-concept formation and to problems of
establishing developmentally valid sequences of instruction, I have
proposed that what occurs, as a rule, under the rubric "evaluation," is
unsound, unsavory, and unlikely to succeed in anything more productive than to generate false and irrelevant information about the pupil's
functioning instead of valid, objective data in that context. Tests, as
they commonly exist, both create lies and propagate them.

Those of us, involved in the development of clinical supervision,
who have sensed these problems and have encountered their manifestations in our daily work over long periods of time, hold the strong
opinion that such curricular deficiencies and faulty evaluation strategies
cannot be remedied, satisfactorily, from a distance. I do not have
confidence, in other words, in the utility of mounting an assault on bad
curriculums by attempting to create better curriculums at some remote
drawing board. Similarly, I have little faith that educational evaluation
will be significantly strengthened at least presently, by the invention of
better standardized tests. Whereas this is not meant to suggest that
better curriculums and better tests cannot be formulated, nor, even,
that professional activity should not proceed in such directions, it does
express my examined conviction that regular, intense clinical supervision of teaching incorporates more abundant possibilities for establishing pertinent reforms in curriculum and in evaluation in today's class-

rooms. It additionally implies an assertion that such supervision, in many instances, represents an ideal mode of improvement rather than, simply, an alternative one.

Educational offerings, unlike mass-produced consumer goods, cannot, effectively, be distributed in wholesale quantities. In the first place, when teaching properly incorporates process goals, the "goods," as such, assume secondary importance. In connection to process goals, teaching aims to create, to strengthen, and to proliferate useful patterns of mental functioning—to expand the learner's cognitive capabilities. In effect, such teaching is aimed at the education of intelligence: at shaping, focusing, integrating, and broadening the human mind. It is, essentially, a form of psychological training.

Because the systematic training of intelligence is such a complex undertaking, simple teaching devices such as textbooks are methodologically insufficient. To affect the learner's use of his mental apparatus requires intensely personal and idiosyncratic processes. If, as Rogers has maintained, learning cannot be taught directly, but can, at best, only be facilitated by another's efforts, then deliberate education should occur in a context of regular and intimate encounters, in close relationships among people.

Clinical supervision is intended to provide such relationships for the sake of teachers' learning and to facilitate the teachers' establishment of such relationships with their pupils and among their pupils. Its observational and dialectical priorities reflect an underlying value on closeness: between supervisors and teachers, and between teachers and students. Our commitment to this value is essentially pragmatic.

We know, for example, that although teachers may operate from canned curriculum, their own values and expressive styles and selective biases will generate broad variations in the subject matter and, particularly, in the connotations it is likely to carry. How the teacher *feels* about the content, for example, will influence the character it assumes as it is mediated to the students. Its character will also be affected by how the teacher feels about his students, about his employment, and, in some measure, about things generally. The assumptions Teacher makes regarding the pupils' capacities for comprehension and their motivation to learn the material in question also represent dynamic variables which affect the learning experience.

I recall, vividly, that while I was in college, a philosophy course based on a syllabus containing primary sources was required for all undergraduate students and was offered in multiple sections, taught by different instructors. There was no reason to suppose that students' selections of specific sections were systematically governed by any consideration other than the times available in their schedules and, in that connection, by their advisors' whims. After a short time, it became publicly known that majorities of students in some sections loved attending O.M.P. ("Organization, Methods, and Principles of the Sciences"), while other majorities detested the experience. Although some instructors seemed more personally popular than others, it was much more frequently in connection to the substantive material that students expressed their positive and negative feelings. For some groups, for example, Descartes was a joy to study while others dreaded having to read his essays. The specific readings were the same in all sections.

Statements such as, "He's a nice guy but I can't stand reading that stuff" and "I can't stand that guy, but the stuff is great," were not only common but, additionally, seemed modally varied from group to group. By the time the year had closed, it seemed to most of us that in many instances the critical determinants of how we felt about the course consisted of the instructor's methods of presentation. Some instructors would go over the textual materials with us, explaining one by one their nuances and esoteric meaning, or would leave the reading to us and then meet their classes, expecting the students to be ready for discussion based upon prior conceptual control of the material. The instructors also varied in their apparent regard or disregard for the students' responses to the material: some instructors showed great patience and sympathy toward the students' frustrations, whereas others scoffed at their struggles and seemed intolerant toward the "slow learners."

There were also differences in the instructors' apparent relationships to the material: some instructors seemed electrified by the content while others seemed, simply, to be moving through another round of routine teaching. In some instances, instructors' charismas heightened the students' excitement in the material. In others, charismatic behavior seemed to distract us from the substantive content. One seemingly-bored and affectively-flat instructor lost all but a few diehards from his class early in the year. Another humble, quiet, inconspicuous professor attracted students by droves, seemingly because they felt a kinship in his scholarly humility and identified with the role of "student" he assumed as we searched for philosophical issues.

In the hypothetical classrooms I depicted in Chapter I, as well as in the college example we have just examined, it is clear that what takes place in the students' experience is partly determined by the specific teaching events occurring in their immediate environments. It seems just as clear that the existential environment is a personal thing. Although the content curriculum may be standard, one's experience of that curriculum is partly subjective and largely idiosyncratic. In any moment, a primacy of subjective self-experience may be operating. No two people formulate exactly the same responses to standardized projective stimuli such as Rorschach blots or TAT pictures, and all stimuli incorporate projective (and subjective) potentialities.

These facts suggest that whether the curriculum of the moment consists of Dick and Jane, or simultaneous equations, or the sexual anatomy of a flower, the experience each child has of that curriculum is, inevitably, his own and is, in some way, different from the others'. His learning is *his* learning, and no strategy for the homogenization of groups can override that fact. No effort at curricular standardization can compensate it. If the teacher is seriously committed to Johnny's learning, then Teacher must find his way into the labyrinths of Johnny's experience to know what goes on there and to affect what goes on there cognizantly and efficiently.

Whereas it is possible to speculate about the incidental learning outcomes likely to be associated with various patterns of teaching behavior, and whereas it is additionally possible to guess right much of the time, the actual existence of such learnings represents an empirical question whose solution requires direct investigation. If the teacher really wants to regulate his own behavior technically in order to produce certain effects and to avoid others, then he must know something about how things seem and feel to that child. His relationship to the pupils must be clinical and direct rather than administrative, detached, and personal.

By the same reasoning, if Teacher's commitment to testing and evaluating Johnny is to count for anything worthwhile, such evaluation must occur in a context of intimate communication and understanding between the two. Intelligence and achievement tests, by themselves, tell virtually nothing. Certainly, by themselves, they don't tell the Teacher what to do next.

I can see no reason to suppose that in their relationships to teachers, supervisors should be guided by understandings and values and professional principles that are any different from those pertaining to the instruction of pupils. As human beings, teachers and pupils are both involved in personal developments. Their developmental requirements for interpersonal *aliment* and interactional stimulation are the same (although, as in regard to all such specific elements, they are *individually* unique).

Supervision from a distance is not likely to be any more useful, developmentally, to teachers, than canned teaching is likely to be for the pupils. In this context, too, clinical intimacy is more helpful and constructive than nonintimacy. While bureaucratic supervision (by directive, by fiat, by form, and by rote) may satisfy administrative priorities on efficiency, it simply does not speak to the critical questions of professional existence that determine each teacher's functioning individually.

Clinical supervision is intended to be both method and model. By exemplifying the very conditions of intimacy and encounter that it aims to establish in teaching behavior, it should both do and show. By its own intimacy, it should establish a mutual trust and openness in which Supervisor and Teacher may build, together, toward satisfying outcomes. Perhaps its most important and distinguishing characteristic is that Supervisor's own behavior and the supervisory relationship itself are as vulnerable and as open to examination as Teacher's behavior, both in the classroom and in the supervision. Only in a clinical supervisory relationship is it possible for a supervisor to get close enough to sense the frame of reference in which Teacher exists: his values, his ideals, his concepts, his feelings, and his anxieties. By providing opportunities for constructive intimacy, such supervision not only can facilitate a teacher's individual actualization, but may demonstrate processes for creating intimacy in Teacher's relationships to pupils as well.

While intimacy, alone, may be a necessary condition for effective clinical supervision (and for teaching and for psychotherapy), it is not sufficient. That is why I refer to "constructive" intimacy. Although I am unable to specify, completely, the characteristics of such relationships— partly because, to be constructive, intimacy should assume different qualities in different partnerships—I can, nevertheless, describe certain elements that must generally be present, in this connection, in clinical supervision.

Experience suggests that positive supervision will not develop unless both the supervisor and the supervisee experience spontaneous and authentic affection for each other. Sometimes, in my supervision, I have found that instead of being present from the outset, some sense of affection arose only after a number of collaborative encounters had occurred. Sometimes inauspicious beginnings developed into emotionally strong relationships. More often, however, the counseling, teaching, and supervision in which I have engaged, when it seemed to produce useful results, generally began with an initial, intuitive liking, and with a common, implicit expectation that affection would continue and deepen. In the other direction, it has been invariably true that neither in my own judgment nor in my supervisee's has supervision ever been productive in relationships in which such feeling was absent. In short, spontaneous emotional attraction appears to be one necessary ingredient in all recipes for good clinical supervision.

Another element of constructive intimacy is its dyadic vector: that is, its thrust in each participant's direction at compatible rates and intensities. I conceptualize this balance as something opposite to one-sidedness, that is, opposite to a condition in which one member's degree of openness or psychological investment or self-exposure is of a significantly greater or lesser magnitude than the other's. When such an imbalance develops, intimacy tends to become unconstructive and to feel, subjectively, like an encroachment upon the overinvested member's privacy; it tends to result in feelings of psychological disadvantage. I have failed most frequently in supervisory relationships in which, as the supervisor, I remained substantially aloof and anonymous while my supervisee allowed his own identity to become highly visible.

Finally, for maintaining constructive intimacy, the focus of the member's inquiries should be primarily oriented toward Teacher's issues, and supervisory goal setting should occur primarily within the supervisee's frame of reference. Although, on the one hand, Supervisor must humanize himself by exposing his own values and biases and strengths and handicaps, on the other hand, the relationship should not become *predominantly* for the sake of Supervisor's enhancement. Concomitantly, Supervisor must derive some benefit from the relationship, and Teacher must be able to sense his own usefulness within the supervisory relationship. I think, analogously, of the necessity to feel needed by one's partner in other intimate relationships, for their endurance. While I may become enriched by what another person gives to me, beyond certain limits my enhancement, my feelings of worth and importance, depend upon his ability to take from me as well—to depend upon me, in some measure, for emotional supplies of one kind or another. Should my partner be only a giver, our relationship would probably not survive my own developing sense of dispensibility. Certainly, the supervisor can at least take stimulation from his supervisees. At least, he can manifest developmental learning in which their participation has been central.

One set of serious questions raised by our professional critics is of whether supervision *should* deal, so much, with "personal material"; whether at certain times it *should* become embroiled in teachers' emotional lives; whether we tend to overemphasize personality characteristics of teachers as variables in instructional effectiveness; and whether, particularly in light of the absence of psychological training in most supervisors' background, it makes very much sense to rely so heavily upon counseling models for supervisory practice. I have been urged, in effect, to back off from the "clinical psychological bent" which, I am beginning to learn, alarms some educators as they view my work initially.

Another fundamentally important question, which arises from essentially the same impression of clinical supervision, is whether "teacher development" is treated too much as an end and whether, indeed, it should be regarded more as an intervening variable, that is, as a collection of means directed toward the establishment of valued pupil behaviors. One critic of this volume, for example, has suggested ". . . in devoting so much of his attention to teachers (one gets the feeling that) Goldhammer believes that we can improve teacher performance without validating our supervisory methods in terms of pupil change. He never shows the need for checking out the effects upon pupils of changed teacher behavior. He seems to assume that analysis of the

teaching act and subsequent acceptance of the instructional implications of that analysis by the teacher will result in improved instruction.
I would not wish to see clinical supervision substitute new stupidities
for old ones: which would likely occur if supervisors and teachers
altered conditions of learning for children on the basis of theory and
logic alone. Validation of practice requires evidence showing that children indeed acquire more independent habits and intellectual behavior
than would be the case without the introduction of changed supervision
and teaching."

I acknowledge the importance of confronting the issues my critic
has raised. At different levels, my responses call for agreement, disagreement, and explanation. The position that innovations in supervision and instruction must ultimately be expressed as beneficial changes
in the pupils' experiences and behavior is unassailable. My own references, especially in Chapter I, to the negative effects of common
teaching practices, and to the damaged psychological functioning they
foster, demonstrate my conviction that the good of all people requires
radical scholastic reforms. Conversely, the efficacy of reform strategies
must be demonstrated in an enrichment of human pleasure, of mental
efficiency, and of living, generally.

I disagree, however, with the implied view that teachers are
consequential only as intervening variables, that they are simply
"means." One of the primary causes of supervision's past failures to
improve educational practices appreciably is that, for all practical
purposes, teachers were regarded as teaching machines: they were to
the pupils, essentially, what wires are to the transmission of telephone
messages. Once telephone wires become frayed, they are either patched
up or replaced; but no one values their existence per se. Just as
teachers have often looked right past the students in their own zeal to
establish knowledge, so have supervisors tended to gaze past teachers
at "learning outcomes." I have observed innumerable supervisors who
became increasingly distressed as their supervisees' ectoplasm began to
coalesce into fleshy identities. It was almost as though the supervisors'
visions of the pupils' achievements became obscured by the interposi-
tion of teachers having complex, opaque existences of their own! While
the teachers' principal focus was upon content, their supervisors' interests centered on curriculums and methods, but at neither level was
either practitioner especially trained or eager to encounter other lives
and to become involved in them. That the schools often graduated and
employed psychological misfits was regrettable, but seen as beyond the
pale of professional objectives.

Even educational shibboleths pertaining to the "whole child" tend
to produce curriculums that circumvent children: the "whole child"
becomes a collection of conceptual oddities that the school establishes

as its curriculum—expanded, now, to include "social" outcomes—and generally does not emanate from real, whole children, from the inside out.

Supervision founded and focused exclusively upon substantive and technical elements of instruction, like therapy that aims only to reduce manifest symptoms, cannot generate stable and significant behavioral changes. If good teaching requires intimacy, empathy, sensitivity, and psychological investment, and if, indeed, it is the relationship that teaches, rather than the text, then supervisees must be experienced as people, not as "intervening variables." Their emotional capacities, their cognitive styling, their views of life and of the world, their values, the terms in which they have learned to meet anxiety, and, altogether, their relationships to themselves represent their teaching essence and must be focal in significant supervisory activity.

The teacher is no less valuable than the pupil, no less "end" than he is, no less alive and, in many respects, no less needy. If my imagery of a supervision that pauses longer with the teacher than repairmen linger over computers seems exaggerated, then perhaps such exaggeration is necessary to compensate for the oppressive abundance of supervisory systems which, if they do not devalue teachers, do not especially value them either. It is no more acceptable to me to think of teachers programing children. Although it has only recently begun to be made systematic, "programed" instruction (and supervision) is really what we have had all along. Clinical supervision is not committed to the development of surer programs. On the contrary, it seeks to replace such things with human beings in human relationships.

Although I have pondered, myself, over questions of psychological training and clinical prerequisites for supervisors, I should not fail to assert, in the end, that to live richly and beneficially, and at least sometimes intelligently, is something different from the practice of "clinical psychology." I am struck by how so many educators respond to questions of human effectiveness and of "personality variables" by imagining psychiatric interventions and clinical solutions. Almost as quickly as we begin to sense a person's (a teacher's) depression or anxiety or rigidity or withdrawal or anger, we think of "therapy." We are much more strongly inclined to *cure* lonely people than we are to *love* them. Tranquilizers are ever so much more efficient than patient sharing. This decade's prominence of "mental health" has left us referral-happy. If the child's error is anything more than a mechanical slip, he is referred to some specialist. If the teacher's dilemma cannot be solved by simple technical assistance, he has "problems"—personal problems, untreatable problems, and is no longer defined as an apt target for supervision.

In connection to measuring supervisory and instructional effectiveness, we have the same impatience and reluctance to be soiled by personal stuff that we experience in the instructional context. We eulogize the whole child, but express the quality of his existence in terms of achievement test scores. And the tributes we pay to teachers as "good people" are mocked by our supervisory fervor to quantify and to compute the effects of our efforts at a level, namely, of pupil performance, that no longer requires even that they should exist any more.

I am at once uneasy with the term "validation" and defensive in response to the suggestion that I am insufficiently concerned with examining pupil behavior vis à vis experimental supervision. Validation of the effectiveness of sensitivity, patience, concentration, and honesty in working with people may be impossible and may be unnecessary. It must, in any event, accept subjective evidence, for example, one's feeling of well being. Even in connection to orthodox psychotherapies, validation studies have been forced to focus, superficially, on reduction or remission of symptoms as indications of effective treatment. Psychological researchers are generally still at a loss to demonstrate, unequivocally, that therapeutic outcomes have resulted directly from deliberate treatment strategies. This problem of validation stems from the fluid complexity and subtlety of psychotherapeutic behavior and of clinical outcomes.

All of the q-sorts and projective tests in the world are inadequate to express a human personality, let alone its minute and invisible changes. In gross terms, we may observe that a catatonic patient is no longer employing schizophrenic solutions. But no such demonstration even begins to represent that patient's identity, certainly not in terms that he would find complete or completely congruent with his own phenomenological experience. In supervision, the problem is compounded by the general absence of such dramatic symptoms. Demonstrations of cause-effect relationships between Supervisor's behavior and Teacher's are often impossible, particularly when effects assume a form of shifting values or lessened anxiety or heightened trust or increased self-acceptance.

The problem of validation becomes doubly magnified when evaluation criteria are framed in a context of pupil behavior, one plane removed from the supervisor's direct actions. If a principal aim of clinical supervision is to open teachers' personalities to feeling, to empathic sensitivity, and to a heightened readiness for human sharing; and if we hope, through such outcomes, to richen their supervisory experiences and to personalize their relationships with children, then to speak of "validation," and, particularly, to conceptualize such validation in terms of measured pupil behavior, is to speak of a difficult and perilous task indeed.

IN FINAL DEFENSE OF CLINICAL SUPERVISION

Probably more must eventually be said about evaluation generally, and about the end-means argument into which I allowed myself to be drawn. However, I have already made extraordinary demands on the time and the emotions of my readers and perhaps the moment has arrived for wrap-up.

In the Preface I acknowledged my unhappiness with the past but asserted my excitement for the future. In it I promised to describe in this work the prototype of a sequence of clinical supervision, to formulate the rationales and purposes of its five stages and to describe the methods that can be employed at each stage. I promised to examine some of the hazards of clinical supervision, and at least by implication I promised to share the reasons for my own devotion to, and confidence in, the powerful model that has been generated.

In summary of much that has motivated this writing, teachers in America have an almost desperate need to understand better the unintended as well as the intended effects of their behavior. In many categories of his work, for example in "disciplining" children or in "motivating" a class, a teacher's actions are often naïvely self-defeating. We tend, it would seem, to reify various psychological constructs when, in fact, they are invalid, and to employ them, often, as fundamental truths in our professional work. I have attempted to demonstrate that teachers tend to lack awareness of incidental learnings likely to result from their teaching behavior; that, most often, they do not plan explicitly for measurable process outcomes; and that, as a typical result, it can easily arise that besides teaching Johnny chemistry, Teacher may also be teaching him to loathe learning, to distrust the teacher, and to think poorly of himself.

Most significantly of all, I have been struck time and again by one particular form of perceptual and intellectual distortion that seems more salient than any other among educators, namely, their tendencies to see and to conceptualize phenomena in global and undifferentiated terms. I am perfectly aware that the human tendency to form such "gestalts" is tremendously compelling and that, even as I discuss this issue in writing, I succumb, in my own thinking, to precisely the tendency in question. All that proves, however, is that my own development as a teacher still has a considerable future before it. In any event, I see this condition, outstanding among the others, as constituting the principal need for clinical supervision to exist, in essentially the forms we have examined above. We require teacher-training methods that help to facilitate strong capacities for differentiated thinking and observing, and my experiences suggest that the ideal arena for such training is in the school, and that the most advantageous medium for such training is supervision of this type.

We require a supervision that is basically analytical and whose principal mode of analysis comprises highly detailed examination of teaching behavior. We require a supervision whose precepts and methods are basically rational and unmysterious and in which teachers may participate with all of their intellectual faculties intact and without intellectual offense to their minds. We need a supervision whose effect is to enhance and to actualize and to fulfill, in degrees that are appreciable and sensible in the teacher's own experiential frameworks. Teachers (like anyone) must be able to understand what they are doing and the goals and processes that govern their behavior, and supervision must provide adequate illumination for such understanding. We require a supervision that is basically teacher-initiated and consistent with independent, self-sufficient action. Our supervision must result, regularly and systematically, in palpable technical advancement; it must have methodological and conceptual rigor and it must produce real and measurable accomplishments.

Because of the ambiguity surrounding most educational issues, such a supervision must be open instead of closed; it must result in discoveries and must name its own directions, rather than to be committed to false, archaic, or otherwise invalid, *a priori* goals. Both the supervision itself and the teaching behaviors in which it culminates, must, in other words, be basically creative and should not strive, as supervision has striven historically, to achieve greater degrees of conformity and uniformity in instructional practices. Of crucial importance, is to have a supervision that is fundamentally humane, one that is emancipated from the dogma and authoritarianism and vested interests of administration and just plain trouble-making that have typified much of the supervision we have known before.

I suspect that no one is more certain of clinical supervision's failure to represent an educational panacea than those of us who have practiced it and studied it during the last several years. We are greatly optimistic, however, in relation to the scholastic deficiencies we have considered, that its general approach and specific habits of method are appropriate, consistent with an orientation that should characterize positive contemporary educational reform, and realistically feasible to establish and to disseminate among schoolmen. Truly, there is nothing spectacularly new in this model. We do not offer it as a wonder drug. We do believe firmly that its design and related issues should be aired extensively, as I have attempted to do in this writing. While its component parts may have existed in many places for many years, it has seemed eminently worthwhile to have drawn them all together in a single presentation and to have attempted to capture their collective potency (and problems) by that effort.

All in one piece, we have found more strength than weakness in a supervision that incorporates explicit contract-building and opportunities for rehearsal (Preobservation); conscientious, objective, highly detailed observation and recording of human data; analyses of such data employing *a posteriori* categories and "patterning" as organizational principles; deliberate and regular planning for supervision which, in turn, incorporates such selection criteria as saliency, accessibility, and fewness of data and in which objectives are formulated behaviorally and in connection to tenable criterion behaviors; regular opportunities for feedback and discussion of the teacher's actual classroom performances, in which Teacher may set the dimensions of inquiry; conferences in which concrete and conceptual preparation for future teaching occurs on a regular basis and in which Teacher strives to define constructive technical modifications for the long-range future and for immediate trial; and a stage in which the entire management and detail of everything that has come before is subjected to critical analysis, the primary effect of which should be to proceed more constructively in the work to follow. I am personally convinced that a supervision capable of fulfilling such conditions can't be beaten, and, in spite of the blunders we have committed, the blindspots we maintain, and the inevitability that we will make more mistakes before it is all over, I have strong reasons to trust what we have been doing and to hunger for continued experimentation in these directions.

It seems, at the same time, that our practices are ripe for evaluative research *and* that such research, analogously to most of the research performed in counseling and psychotherapy, will have to be basically clinical and idiographic, at least for the immediate future. Our idealizations of teaching and of supervision must be modified constantly, as more is learned about human behavior and professional development. Even presently, there are serious questions before us, such as, how to train people to be clinical supervisors of the most ideal sort and how to administer such supervision and training in the typical school setting. Solid curriculums in teacher education and supervisor education have yet to be developed. We have intuitions, in this context, but have not yet done very much about implementing them. We tend to believe, for example, that extensive work in counseling psychology, such as that offered by superior counselor education programs, is directly germane and, indeed, may be of basic importance in the preparation of clinical supervisors. We are largely convinced that work in group process and experience in sensitivity training are very important for ourselves and for our students. We believe that "process education," as it is conceptualized, by and large, by such educators as Glen Heathers and Jerome Bruner and Joseph Schwab, should constitute the framework of values in which our people are prepared. We value personal counseling or psychotherapy as useful adjuncts to professional preparation in supervision, especially in individual cases where as a source of personal learning, such experiences represent efficient approaches.

If our ideas about clinical supervision are still generally tentative—despite the sound of certainty this writing may have had from time to time—our notions of how to train and to administer in the field are even more undecided. It has seemed important to begin by presenting the model. I cherish the hope that it will be sufficiently provocative, in one manner or another, to stimulate a broader participation by workers in the educational field, both in its own refinement and in the invention of training and administrative models for the future.